考研英语成功路线图

U0063173

逆风破浪，
让未来更加可期。

——屈浩民

考研英语全优系列

❶ 考研英语高频词汇2618

❷ 考研英语5500词汇分频记忆

❸ 考研英语语法长难句妙解

❹ 考研英语阅读也轻松

❺ 考研英语高分写作100篇（第2版）

❻ 考研英语二一本通

❼ 考研英语一真题解析

❽ 考研英语二真题解析

❾ 考研英语一全真模拟5套卷

❿ 考研英语二全真模拟5套卷

⓫ 考研英语作文考点20篇

项目	基础段 6月前	强化段 7—8月	冲刺段 10—12月
学习内容 及要求	1. 掌握5500考纲词汇 2. 学习必备的语法知识和长难句破解方法 3. 通过精细分析1993—2009年考研真题阅读理解部分，巩固词汇，具备句子分析能力，进而掌握阅读的解题逻辑 4. 学习写作的词汇提升和句型优化方法	1. 学习阅读理解的解题方法 2. 破解完形填空、翻译和阅读理解Part B的应试逻辑 3. 掌握大小作文的写作手法/高分策略 4. 第一轮刷真题	1. 第二轮刷真题，将方法融入做题中 2. 针对作文进行分析朗读、背诵、默写、套题演练 3. 模拟演练热门写作话题，总结模板
配套教材	《考研英语高频词汇2618》 《考研英语5500词汇分频记忆》 《考研英语阅读也轻松》 《考研英语高分写作100篇》 《考研英语二一本通》 《考研英语语法长难句妙解》	《考研英语一真题解析》 《考研英语二真题解析》 《考研英语二一本通》 《考研英语高分写作100篇》	《考研英语一真题解析》 《考研英语二真题解析》 《考研英语二一本通》 《考研英语一全真模拟5套卷》 《考研英语二全真模拟5套卷》 《考研英语作文考点20篇》

· 考研英语全优系列 ·

考研英语
高频词汇
2618

屠皓民 主编

清华大学出版社
北京

内 容 简 介

本书是全国硕士研究生招生考试备考用书，全书共包含四个单元。第一单元是高频词汇，编者根据对真题和词汇考查重点的研究，精选2 618个高频词汇，帮助考生在短期内高效记忆考研英语词汇。词汇讲解包含单词、音标、词性、中文释义、搭配、巧记、拓展和诵读等内容，内容重点突出。第二单元是词根词缀，编者以考研大纲英语词缀为出发点，揭示词根词缀的逻辑，使考生懂得基本的构词法，突破单词记忆的难关。第三单元是旧词新说，编者依据历年真题对单词熟词僻义的考查重点，通过真题例句讲解单词的基本意思以及常考僻义，帮助考生掌握高频"旧词"的考点。第四单元是必备词组，编者甄选历年真题常考词组，帮助考生在短时间内高效记忆学习常考词组。

本书适用于参加全国硕士研究生招生考试的考生。考生可以扫描书中二维码，随时随地获取作者团队提供的考研英语精品课程。

图书在版编目（CIP）数据

考研英语高频词汇2618 / 屠皓民主编. — 北京：清华大学出版社，2024.3
（考研英语全优系列）
ISBN 978-7-302-65768-2

Ⅰ. ①考… Ⅱ. ①屠… Ⅲ. ①英语－研究生－入学考试－自学参考资料 Ⅳ. ①H310.421

中国国家版本馆 CIP 数据核字（2024）第 056222 号

责任编辑：雷　桢
封面设计：傅瑞学
责任校对：袁　芳
责任印制：沈　露

出版发行：清华大学出版社
　　　　　网　　　址：https://www.tup.com.cn，https://www.wqxuetang.com
　　　　　地　　　址：北京清华大学学研大厦 A 座　　　　邮　　编：100084
　　　　　社 总 机：010-83470000　　　　　　　　　　邮　　购：010-62786544
　　　　　投稿与读者服务：010-62776969，c-service@tup. tsinghua. edu. cn
　　　　　质量反馈：010-62772015，zhiliang@tup. tsinghua. edu. cn
印 装 者：河北鹏润印刷有限公司
经　　销：全国新华书店
开　　本：185mm×260mm　　印　张：15　　插　页：1　　字　数：482 千字
版　　次：2024 年 3 月第 1 版　　　　　　　印　次：2024 年 3 月第 1 次印刷
定　　价：39.90 元

产品编号：105337-01

前 言

对于考研词汇学习，以下是多数考研同学会遇到的六个疑问。

一　为什么单词反复记反复忘？

你是否有过这样的经历？你早上背了单词，下午在看美剧时，突然发现屏幕上出现了你早上记过的单词，瞬间就记住了；你课上睡着了，老师把你叫醒问你某个单词的意思，可能你不认识这个单词，但自此终生难忘。你在生活中，经常说的英语单词可能是 good，bad，very 吧，不用到那些单词怎么会记得住？是的，记忆单词需要结合语境。单词的用法需要在语境中体现。在语境中记单词，才能把单词记住、记牢。

二　可不可以只背高频词汇？

什么是高频词汇？高频词汇是历年真题中出现频率比较高的单词。不过，出题组成员会有变化，文章选材会有不同，作者使用词汇会有差异，在备考初期只背高频词汇是不能覆盖考纲需要的词汇的。在词汇书已经背过几遍、真题已经完成的情况下，回顾高频词汇是很好的复习方法。

三　记词根词缀有用吗？

英语单词的词根词缀类似于汉字的偏旁部首，是一些英语单词的组成部分。有时，借助于词根词缀能提高记忆的效率。但要记住两点。一是有些词根词缀构成过于复杂，不如直接记忆单词；二是词根词缀有助于记单词，但解题中不要用于猜测词义。

四　学习真题的句子对记忆单词有帮助吗？

单词记忆的过程从一开始孤立背诵，到借助语境加深印象，是一个值得推荐的方法。前期将考纲词汇记忆后，通过学习真题例句记单词词汇，不仅能提高单词记忆效率，还有助于学习单词的用法，为后面句子的学习奠定基础，一举多得。

五　背完词汇书需要多长时间?

常见的背词汇书的方法是将一本词汇书划分成若干个部分,规定多少天完成,但是每个考生的学习时间和习惯不同,天数也因人而异。通常完成一轮记忆 40 ～ 60 天为宜。结束一轮再从头开始复习,这样循环三遍左右,效果最佳。

六　哪种方式背单词高效?

能够记住单词的方法都是好方法,有人喜欢一边背一边写,有人喜欢大声朗读……编者根据 20 年的教学经验和学生的反馈,给出的建议是:不要试图寻找一本词汇书帮你记住所有单词。要想实现过目不忘,集合记忆效果最明显。集合记忆即"1+1+1"记忆方法。"1"词汇书:词根词缀、谐音记忆、经典例句(但不完全是真题例句)等统统结合在一起;"1"长难句分析:学会分析,掌握翻译技巧,记忆句中词汇;"1"基础阅读练习:学会做题,了解解题思路,熟记文中出现的单词。如此结合,才能事半功倍。

让我们开始单词记忆的旅程吧。

本书配有由屠皓民老师主讲的考研英语核心知识导学视频。请扫描书中二维码,获取更多备考支持。

欢迎广大读者与屠皓民老师互动交流。

新浪微博:@考研英语屠皓民

微信公众号:考研英语屠皓民

编　者

2024年1月

目 录

Unit 1

高频词汇

《考研英语大纲》囊括了约5 500个单词,但是词汇在真题中的使用频率有所不同。因此,本单元根据词汇在历年真题中出现的频率,甄选2 618个超高频词和高频词。超高频词汇需要会写会用,高频词汇需要会写。帮助考生提高单词记忆效率。

扫码获取免费课程

abandon [ə'bændən] *vt.* 丢弃;放弃

搭配 abandon sb. to sth. 放纵于;使沉溺于

诵读 The market might abandon the stock, and knock down its price. 市场可能会抛售该股票,令其股价下跌。

abnormal [æb'nɔːməl] *a.* 反常的,不正常的

巧记 否定前缀 ab- +词根 normal 正常=反常的

诵读 His abnormal behavior shows that something is wrong. 他的异常举止显示有点不对劲儿。

above [ə'bʌv] *prep.* 在……上面

搭配 above all 首要的是,尤其

僻义 *prep.* 超过,超出

诵读 It is above comprehension. 那是难以理解的。

aboard [ə'bɔːd] *ad.&prep.* 在船(飞机、车)上;上船(飞机、车)

辨析 abroad *ad.* 到国外,在国外

诵读 He has never been abroad in his life aboard a plane. 他有生以来没有坐飞机出过国。

abound [ə'baʊnd] *vi.* 大量存在

巧记 前缀 a- 加强语气+词根 bound 范围=范围里都是→满,溢,富足

拓展 abundant *a.* 大量的,充满的(be abundant in 充满,富于)

abstract ['æbstrækt] *vt.* 提取 *a.* 抽象的 *n.* 摘要

巧记 前缀 ab-加强语气+s 无意义+词根 tract 拉=拉出来→提取

诵读 Some authors in that area are not popular because their writings are too abstract. 那个地区的一些作家因文章过于抽象而不受欢迎。

access ['ækses] *n.* 进入;到达;入口

巧记 前缀 ac-加强语气+词根 cess 走=走过去→接近

搭配 (have) access to 有权使用;去往某地的通道

诵读 My grandfather is a man of difficult access. 我的外祖父是一个很难接近的人。

accident ['æksɪdənt] *n.* 意外遭遇,事故

拓展 accidental *a.* 偶然的;意外的

诵读 My best friend was killed in a car accident. 我最好的朋友死于一场车祸。

acclaim [ə'kleɪm] *vt.* 向……欢呼 *n.* 欢呼,称赞

巧记 前缀 ac-加强语气+词根 claim 陈述=当面陈述一般是好的。

诵读 He was acclaimed (as) the winner. 他被誉为胜利者。

accompany [əˈkʌmpənɪ] *vt.* 陪伴，陪同

巧记 前缀 ac-加强语气+词根 company 伙伴=陪同

诵读 They came to the Grand Canyon accompanied by their daughters. 他们在女儿们的陪同下来到了科罗拉多大峡谷。

accomplish [əˈkɒmplɪʃ] *vt.* 实现；达到；完成

巧记 前缀 ac-加强语气+词根 complish 与 complete 同义=完成

诵读 This mission was accomplished by great efforts. 完成这项使命花了很大力气。

accumulate [əˈkjuːmjʊleɪt] *vi.* 堆积，积累

巧记 前缀 ac-加强语气+词根 cumul 堆积+后缀-ate=积累，堆积

诵读 As evidence began to accumulate, experts felt obliged to investigate. 随着证据开始积累，专家们感到必须进行调查。

accurate [ˈækjʊrɪt] *a.* 正确的；准确的，精确的

拓展 accuracy *n.* 准确；精确（=precision）

搭配 be accurate in... 在……方面是精确的

诵读 The machine can be quick and accurate at figures. 这台机器能快速准确地计算。

acid [ˈæsɪd] *n.&a.* 酸；酸的，酸味的

僻义 *a.* 尖刻的

诵读 Some acids burn holes in wood and cloth. 有些酸类物质能在木料及布料上烧出洞。

acute [əˈkjuːt] *a.* 剧烈的；敏锐的

拓展 chronic *a.* 慢性的，长期的

诵读 Dogs have an acute sense of smell. 狗有敏锐的嗅觉。

admit [ədˈmɪt] *vt.* 让……进入，接纳，容纳

搭配 admit to 承认，通向

拓展 admission *n.* 允许进入（to）

诵读 He has lived the dream of obtaining admission to the bar. 他一直梦想获准当律师。

adventure [ədˈventʃə] *n.* 冒险

巧记 前缀 ad-加强语气+词根 vent 走=走出去冒险

拓展 the advent of... ……的到来，降临

诵读 Age hadn't blunted his passion for adventure. 岁月没有冲淡他的冒险激情。

adapt [əˈdæpt] *vi.* 使适应，使适合；改编

巧记 adapt to sth. 适应某物

诵读 When you go to a new country, you must adapt yourself to new manners and customs. 当你到一个新国家时，你必须使自己适应新的风俗习惯。

adopt [əˈdɒpt] *vt.* 采用，采取；收养

诵读 European dress has been adopted by people in many parts of the world. 欧洲服饰被世界许多地方的人所采用。

addition [əˈdɪʃən] *n.* 附加部分，增加（物）

搭配 in addition 此外，in addition to... 除……之外

拓展 additional *a.* 额外的，附加的

诵读 An additional charge is made for heavy things. 超重的东西要多收钱。

administer [ədˈmɪnɪstə] *vt.&vi.* 施行，实施；掌管

拓展 administration *n.* 经营，管理；行政，行政机关，管理部门

诵读 The physician may prescribe but not administer the drugs. 内科医师可以开处方但不可发药。

adolescent [ˌædəˈlesnt] *n.* 青少年 *a.* 青春期的，青少年的

诵读 The adolescent period is one's best time. 青少年时期是一个人最美好的一段时光。

adverse [ˈædvɜːs] *a.* 相反的；敌对的；不利的

巧记 前缀 ad-加强语气+词根 vers 转=转向相反的方向→逆的

拓展 adversity *n.* 逆境

诵读 Dirt and disease are adverse to the best growth of children. 肮脏与疾病对儿童健康成长不利。

advisable [ədˈvaɪzəbl] *a.* 可取的；明智的

诵读 Is it advisable for me to write to him? 我给他写信合适吗？

advocate [ˈædvəkət] *n.* 拥护者 [ˈædvəkeɪt] *vt.* 拥护，提倡

巧记 前缀 ad-加强语气+词根 voc 喊叫+后缀-ate = 大声喊叫→主张

诵读 Many scientists who support the production of atomic bombs are advocates of peace. 许多支持制造原子弹的科学家是和平的提倡者。

against [əˈgenst] *prep.* 对着，逆；反对

搭配 against the background of... 以……为背景

诵读 We were rowing against the current. 我们逆水划船。

aggravate [ˈægrəveɪt] *vt.* 加重（剧），使恶化

巧记 前缀 ag-加强语气+词根 grav 来自 grave 严重

的+后缀 -ate =使……更严重→加剧

诵读 The new healthcare law does not aggravate the deficit, nor does it do much to reduce it. 新的医保法并没有加重赤字, 但也没有对于减少赤字有多大作用。

aggressive [ə'gresɪv] *a.* 侵略的; 好斗的; 富于攻击性的

辨义 aggressive treatment 积极治疗

诵读 When one animal attacks another, it engages in the most obvious example of aggressive behavior. 当动物相互攻击时, 会表现出非常明显的侵略性行为。

aid [eɪd] *v.&n.* 帮助, 援助, 救助

搭配 in aid of 支持; first aid 急救

辨义 *n.* 助手, 辅助物

诵读 He was a professor's aid for a time. 他曾经是一位教授的助理。

alarm [ə'lɑːm] *n.* 惊恐; 警报 (器) *vt.* 惊动, 惊吓; 向……报警

搭配 sound the alarm 发出警报

诵读 He expressed alarm about the government's increasingly bellicose statements. 他对政府越来越具挑衅性的声明表示担忧。

alike [ə'laɪk] *a.* 同样的, 相像的 *ad.* 一样地

巧记 Great minds think alike. 英雄所见略同。

搭配 look alike 看起来很像

诵读 People who are alike often become friends or are together. 相像的人通常能成为朋友或者待在一起。

allege [ə'ledʒ] *vt.* 断言, 宣称; 指控

巧记 前缀 al-加强语气+词根 leg 说=断言, 宣称

辨析 allege 多指无真凭实据、不提供证据的断言或宣称; assert 多指自认为某事就是如此; affirm 侧重在作出断言时表现出的坚定与不可动摇的态度。

诵读 The police alleged that the man was murdered but they have given no proof. 警方声称这名男子是被谋杀的, 但未提供任何证据。

alliance [ə'laɪəns] *n.* 同盟, 同盟国; 结盟

搭配 in alliance with... 与……联盟

拓展 ally *n.* 同盟者, 同盟国 *vi.* 使结盟 (ally with... 与……结成同盟)

诵读 The two companies have formed an alliance to market the product. 两家公司已结盟来推销这种产品。

allocate ['æləkeɪt] *vt.* 分配, 分派; 拨给; 划归

搭配 allocate... for... 分配……给……

诵读 In order to achieve a goal, we will be required to make choices about how we allocate our time, energy and resources. 为了达到目标, 我们需要对于如何分配我们的时间、精力和资源做出选择。

alphabet ['ælfəbɪt] *n.* 字母表; 初步, 入门

诵读 This is the first time meteorologists have run out of names and have to resort to the Greek alphabet. 气象学家第一次用遍了所有用来表示此类气象的名称, 而不得不借用希腊字母表来表示。

amateur ['æmətə] *a.* 业余的 *n.* 业余者

拓展 professional *a.* 专业的

诵读 We will offer a full range of amateur and professional camera equipment. 我们将提供全系列的业余和专业的摄像器材。

amaze [ə'meɪz] *vt.* 使惊奇, 使惊愕

辨析 surprise 多指因意外的事而引起的惊奇; amaze 指因认为不可能或极少可能发生情况出现而感到惊讶或迷惑不解; astonish 指出乎预料, 意外发生, 但又无法解释而感到惊奇。

诵读 It amazed us to hear that he failed in the exam. 听到他考试没过, 我们都很吃惊。

ambition [æm'bɪʃən] *n.* 野心; 雄心

巧记 谐音: 有野心和雄心的人坚定地认为“俺必胜”。

拓展 ambitious *a.* 有抱负的, 雄心勃勃的

诵读 He wants to expand his business with the ambition of competing with the industry leader. 他希望带着与行业领头羊竞争的野心来扩张自己的企业。

amend [ə'mend] *vt.* 修改, 修订, 改进

辨析 amend 指修改文件, 法律, 规范等; rectify 多指纠正错误等。

搭配 amend one's ways 改过自新; amend the laws 修改法律

诵读 You must amend your way of thinking. 你必须改变你的思维方式。

ample ['æmpl] *a.* 充分的, 富裕的

辨析 abundant 指人、鸟、雨水等量大; ample 常置于名词前, 表示“富足的, 充足的”; plentiful 为 plenty 的形容词形式, 特指食物等事物的“丰富”, 不能用来修饰思想、语言、时间或空间等。

拓展 amplify *vt.* 放大，增强；amplifier *n.* 放大器

诵读 There is ample evidence that climate patterns are changing. 有充分的证据表明，气候正在发生变化。

amuse [əˈmjuːz] *vt.* 向……提供娱乐，使……消遣；引人发笑

辨析 amuse 指以有趣或好玩的事物娱乐他人；entertain 指以事先准备或设计的方式来娱乐他人；delight 使感到愉快或满意。

诵读 I amuse myself by reading detective stories. 我读侦探小说打发时间。

anxious [ˈæŋkʃəs] *a.* 焦急的，忧虑的，担心的

搭配 be anxious about 忧虑，担心

诵读 We had a very anxious time until we knew that they were safe. 我们一直忧虑，直到得知他们平安。

anybody [ˈenɪˌbɒdi] *pron.* 任何人，无论谁

僻义 *n.* 重要人物

诵读 You must work harder if you wish to be anybody. 如果你想要成为重要人物（出人头地），你必须更加努力。

anything [ˈenɪθɪŋ] *pron.* 任何东西 *ad.* 任何方面

搭配 anything but 一点也不，就不是

辨析 nothing but 仅仅

诵读 He is anything but a teacher. 他就不是个老师。
He is nothing but a teacher. 他仅仅是一名老师。

analyse [ˈænəlaɪz] *vt.*（analyze）分析

拓展 analysis *n.* 分析；analytic *a.* 分析的；分解的

诵读 Quant trading uses mathematical models and programs to replace human beings to analyse securities prices and make investment decisions. 量化交易使用数学模型和程序来代替人类分析证券价格并做出投资决策。

ancestor [ˈænsɪstə] *n.* 祖宗，祖先

巧记 同义词 predecessor（前缀 pre-在前面），forefather（前缀 fore-在前面）

诵读 Scream at the top of your voice, and you won't be weaker than your ancestor in the tree. 敞开你的喉咙，作一次长啸吧，你不会亚于你树上的祖先。

ancient [ˈeɪnʃənt] *a.* 古代的，古老的

搭配 ancient Chinese civilization 中国古代文明

诵读 The crafts of many daily items in ancient time even surpass the modern technologies. 古代很多日用品的工艺甚至超越了现代的技术。

angel [ˈeɪndʒəl] *n.* 天使

辨析 形近词 angle *n.* 角度

诵读 All I am, or can be, I owe to my angel mother. 我之所有，我之所能，都归功于我天使般的母亲。

anniversary [ˌænɪˈvɜːsəri] *n.* 周年，周年纪念日

巧记 前缀 anni- 一年+词根 vers 转+后缀-ary= 一年转一次就是周年纪念

拓展 annual *a.* 每年的

诵读 The year of 2024 marks the 75th anniversary of the founding of the People's Republic of China. 2024年是中华人民共和国成立75周年。

announce [əˈnaʊns] *vt.* 正式宣布；发表；通告

巧记 同义词 declare, advertise, broadcast

诵读 The captain announced that the plane was going to land. 机长宣布飞机就要着陆了。

anticipate [ænˈtɪsɪpeɪt] *vt.* 预料；期望

搭配 anticipate doing sth. 预料要做某事

辨析 expect 指确信某事必然会发生；anticipate 是怀着喜悦或疾苦之心来预想。

诵读 We can anticipate what's going to happen next. 我们可以预见下一步会发生什么。

antique [ænˈtiːk] *a.* 古式的 *n.* 古物，古董

巧记 同义词 ancient

诵读 The palace is full of priceless antiques. 王宫里全是价值连城的古董。

anxiety [æŋˈzaɪəti] *n.* 焦虑，焦急，忧虑

拓展 anxious *a.* 焦虑的，渴望的

诵读 Anxiety may be relieved by talking to family members. 和家人谈心能缓解忧虑。

apology [əˈpɒlədʒi] *n.* 道歉，认错

拓展 apologize *v.* 道歉，认错

搭配 in apology for… 为……辩解；make an apology 道歉；apologize to sb. for…/make an apology to sb. for… 因……而向某人道歉

诵读 Write him a letter to make an apology, and suggest a solution. 给他写一封道歉信，并提出解决方案。

apparent [əˈpærənt] *a.* 显然的

巧记 同义词 obvious, evident

诵读 It became apparent that smell can evoke emotional response. 很明显，气味可以引起强烈的情绪反应。

appetite ['æpɪtaɪt] *n.* 食欲, 胃口; 欲望

搭配 appetite for... 对……的欲望, 爱好等

巧记 同义词 craving, desire

诵读 They are worried, though, that their employers —Ford and General Motors—have failed to catch a new appetite for cars that consume less. 但是他们担心的是他们的雇主——福特和通用汽车公司——还没有意识到人们已经开始越来越喜欢耗油量低的汽车了。

apply [ə'plaɪ] *vi.* 申请; 请求 *vt.* 应用; 实施

搭配 apply for 申请; apply sth. to sth. 将……应用到……上

拓展 application *n.* 申请, 请求; applicable *a.* 可应用(实施)的; 适当的; appliance *n.* 电器; 器械; 应用

诵读 When they apply for their first job, they are tested for intelligence. 他们申请第一份工作的时候, 接受了智商测试。

appoint [ə'pɔɪnt] *vt.* 任命; 指定; 约定

巧记 同义词 assign, designate

拓展 appointment *n.* 约会, 约定; 任命

诵读 This insurance company hopes to appoint a new Chief Executive. 这家保险公司希望任命一位新的执行总监。

appreciate [ə'priːʃieɪt] *vt.* 感激; 欣赏

搭配 appreciate sb. doing sth. 感谢某人做某事

诵读 Only the deaf appreciate hearing, and only the blind realize the manifold blessings that lie in sight. 只有聋人才理解听力的重要, 只有盲人才明白视觉的可贵。

appropriate [ə'prəʊprɪeɪt] *a.* 适当的, 恰当的

僻义 *vt.* 挪用, 盗用

诵读 Some view strict discipline as nothing more than a form of abuse, while others argue it is an essential factor for instilling appropriate social behavior. 有些人把严厉的管教看成一种虐待, 而另一些人认为这是逐渐灌输得体的社会行为的关键因素。

approve [ə'pruːv] *vi.* 赞成; 批准

巧记 前缀ap-加强语气+词根 prove 证明=证明正确之后→赞成, 批准

拓展 approval *n.* 批准, 通过; 赞成, 同意

诵读 A majority of Americans approve of how the President is tackling the issue of taxes. 绝大多数美国人都认可总统处理税收问题的方式。

approximate [ə'prɒksɪmət] *a.* 近似的 *vi.* 接近

搭配 approximate to... 与……接近

诵读 Step 2 is to establish the approximate size and location of your planned trading area. 第二个步骤就是要确定你所规划的商业的大致规模和选址。

apt [æpt] *a.* 易于……的, 有……倾向的

搭配 be apt to do 易于, 容易

辨析 apt 指事物/人本身具有某种倾向; likely 则指说话人主观认为某物 "可能会" 怎样。

诵读 You're apt to like people in general. 你总是容易对人产生好感。

arm [ɑːm] *n.* 臂; (*pl.*) 武器 *vt.* 武装起来

搭配 arm in arm 臂挽臂地

诵读 He was armed with many facts and figures to prove his case. 他以事实和数字为依据来证明自己有理。

architect ['ɑːkɪtekt] *n.* 建筑师; 设计师

拓展 architecture *n.* 建筑; 建筑学

诵读 Julius Caesar was the architect of the Roman Empire. 朱利叶斯·恺撒是罗马帝国的缔造者。

arise [ə'raɪz] *vi.* 出现; 发生

搭配 arise from/out of... 由……引起

诵读 Serious obligations may arise from the proposed clause. 由这项提议的条款可能产生一些重大的责任。

army ['ɑːmi] *n.* 军队; 陆军

搭配 an army of 一大群

诵读 An army of ants are moving across the street. 一群蚂蚁在过街。

arouse [ə'raʊz] *vt.* 唤醒, 叫醒; 唤起, 激起

诵读 We aroused him from his deep sleep. 我们把他从熟睡中叫醒。

arrange [ə'reɪndʒ] *vt.* 安排; 整理; 排列, 布置

巧记 前缀 ar- 加强语气+词根 range 排列=安排

搭配 arrange ...for... 为……安排……

诵读 Before going away, he arranged his business affairs. 他在离开前把业务都安排好了。

array [ə'reɪ] *n.* 大量; 排列

搭配 an array of 大量的

诵读 The crowd was met by an array of policemen. 那群人碰上了一队警察。

arrest [əˈrest] *n.&vt.* 逮捕，扣留

辨义 *v.* 阻止；吸引

诵读 The sufferer may have to make major changes in his or her life to arrest the disease. 患者可能不得不对生活习惯作出重大调整以控制病情。

The work of an architect of genius always arrests the attention no matter how little remains. 天才建筑师的作品无论留存有多么少，总能吸引眼球。

arrow [ˈærəʊ] *n.* 箭，矢，箭状物；箭头符号

诵读 Follow the arrows on the wall, please. 请顺着墙上箭头指示的方向走。

artistic [ɑːˈtɪstɪk] *a.* 艺术（家）的；唯美的

诵读 He is known for his artistic taste. 他以艺术品位高闻名。

assistant [əˈsɪstənt] *n.* 助手，助理

辨义 *a.* 辅助的，副的（assistant professor 副教授）

诵读 He is an assistant cook. 他是厨师助理。

ascend [əˈsend] *vi.* 上升；攀登

巧记 前缀 a-加强语气+词根 scend 爬=向上爬→攀登

诵读 We watched the mist ascending from the valley. 我们看着雾从山谷升起。

ash [æʃ] *n.* 灰，灰烬

辨义 *n.*（*pl.*）废墟

诵读 Do not drop cigarette ash on the carpet. 不要让香烟灰落在地毯上。

ashamed [əˈʃeɪmd] *a.* 惭愧的，羞耻的，害臊的

巧记 前缀 a-加强语气+词根 shamed 羞愧=羞愧的

诵读 He felt ashamed that he had done so little. 他因为做的事情太少而感到惭愧。

ashore [əˈʃɔː] *ad.* 上岸；在岸上

诵读 We came ashore from the boat. 我们从小船上岸。

aside [əˈsaɪd] *ad.* 在旁边

诵读 Aside from good exercise, turning summersault is a very useful skill. 翻筋斗除了是很好的锻炼之外，还是非常有用的技巧。

assemble [əˈsembl] *vi.* 集合，召集；装配；收集

拓展 assembly *n.* 集合；会议

诵读 The pupils assembled in the school hall. 学生们在学校礼堂中集合。

assess [əˈses] *vt.* 评估；评价

辨析 形近词 access *n.* 入口

拓展 assessable *a.* 可评估的

诵读 She suggests you first assess your income and outgoings. 她建议你先估算一下自己的收入和开销。

assist [əˈsɪst] *vt.* 协助，帮助

拓展 assistance *n.* 协作，援助；assistant *n.* 助手

诵读 Good glasses will assist you to read. 好的眼镜有助于你阅读。

assure [əˈʃʊə] *vt.* 使确信，使放心

搭配 assure sb. of/that… 担保，使确信

拓展 assurance *n.* 保证；确信；信心

诵读 We tried to assure the nervous old lady that flying was safe. 我们尽力说服那位紧张的年迈妇女，使她相信乘飞机是安全的。

astronaut [ˈæstrənɔːt] *n.* 太空人，太空旅行者

巧记 astro 星+naut 船→驾驶宇宙飞船的人→宇航员

拓展 astronomy *n.* 天文学

诵读 Astronauts need to have strong body. 宇航员需要身体强壮。

attack [əˈtæk] *vt.&n.* 攻击，袭击

搭配 make an attack on… 向……进攻；attack against… 对……攻击

诵读 An attack is said to be the best form of defense. 常言道，攻击是最好的防御。

athlete [ˈæθliːt] *n.* 运动员

诵读 Athletes have to work hard before becoming sucessful. 运动员成功前需要付出艰辛的努力。

atmosphere [ˈætməsfɪə] *n.* 大气（层）；空气

辨义 *n.* 气氛；环境

诵读 Here is an atmosphere of peace and calm in the country quite different from that of a big city. 在乡间有一种和平宁静之气氛，与大城市的气氛截然不同。

attach [əˈtætʃ] *vt.* 系，贴，装

搭配 be attached to 依附；attach importance to 重视

诵读 The meeting sends a clear signal that the government attaches importance to rapidly growing AI technology. 本次会议释放出一个明确的信号，即政府重视快速发展的人工智能技术。

attain [əˈteɪn] *vt.* 达到；完成；获得

巧记 前缀 at-加强语气+词根 tain 拿住=稳稳拿住→获得

诵读 She attained the position of director. 她得到了主任的职位。

attempt [əˈtempt] *vt.&n.* 努力，尝试，企图

诵读 The prisoners attempted to escape but failed. 囚犯们企图逃狱但失败了。

attend [əˈtend] *vt.* 出席，参加

搭配 attend to 照顾

拓展 attendance *n.* 出席；attendant *n.* 随从 *a.* 伴随的

诵读 Please let me know if you cannot attend the meeting. 你若不能参加会议，请通知我们。

attribute [əˈtrɪbjuːt] *vt.* 把……归因于

搭配 attribute…to… = owe…to… 把……归于……

僻义 *n.* 属性，品质，特征

诵读 He attributes his success to hard work. 他认为他的成功由努力而来。

audience [ˈɔːdiəns] *n.* 听众，观众

诵读 He has addressed large audiences all over England. 他曾在英国各地向大群的听众演说。

audio [ˈɔːdiəʊ] *n.&a.* 声音（的），听觉（的）

辨析 形近词 aural *a.* 听觉的，听力的

诵读 The school's audio apparatus includes films and recorders. 学校的视听设备包括放映机和录音机。

auto [ˈɔːtəʊ] *n.* 汽车

巧记 前缀 auto- 表示"自动的"，auto 是 automobile 的缩略形式"汽车"。

诵读 Don't park your auto here. 别把你的汽车停在这儿。

automatic [ˌɔːtəˈmætɪk] *a.* 自动（装置）的；无意识的 *n.* 自动机械

拓展 automation *n.* 自动化

诵读 The goal of the program is to effectively realize the commer cialization and large-scale implementation of automatic driving technologies. 该项目的目标是有效实现自动驾驶技术的商业化和大规模实施。

avenue [ˈævɪnjuː] *n.* 林荫路，大街

僻义 *n.* 途径，渠道，方法

诵读 They explored every avenue but could not answer the question. 他们探索各种途径，但都不能回答这个问题。

avert [əˈvɜːt] *vt.* 防止，避免；转移（目光、注意力等）

巧记 前缀 a-加强语气+词根 vert 转移=转移开

搭配 avert…from… 把……从……移开

诵读 Accidents can be averted by careful driving. 开车小心就能避免事故。

awake [əˈweɪk] *a.* 醒着的，洞察的 *v.* 醒，唤醒

巧记 前缀 a-加强语气+词根 wake 醒（同类词：amid 在中间，await 等待）

诵读 You must be awake to the fact that failure will mean disgrace. 你必须认识到失败即是耻辱这一事实。

aware [əˈweə] *a.* 知道的，意识到的

搭配 be aware of 意识到

诵读 I was not aware of how deeply sad he had felt the death of his mother. 我不知道他对他母亲的去世那么伤感。

awe [ɔː] *n.* 敬畏，惊惧 *vt.* 使敬畏，使惊惧

诵读 The sight filled us with awe. 这景色使我们大为惊叹。

awful [ˈɔːfəl] *a.* 极度的，极坏的；威严的，可怕的

诵读 His sufferings were awful to behold. 他的痛苦看起来令人可怕。

abide [əˈbaɪd] *vi.* 遵守；坚持

搭配 abide by 遵守，信守

同义 comply with 遵守，遵照；conform to 遵守

诵读 If you join the club, you must abide by its rules. 如果你加入这个俱乐部，你就必须遵守规则。

abolish [əˈbɒlɪʃ] *vt.* 废除（法律、习惯等）；取消

诵读 Abraham Lincoln abolished slavery in the United States. 亚伯拉罕·林肯在美国废除了奴隶制度。

abrupt [əˈbrʌpt] *a.* 突然的，意外的；粗鲁的

巧记 前缀 ab-加强语气+词根 rupt 破=破裂很突然→突然的；鲁莽的

诵读 He made an abrupt turn to avoid hitting another car. 他突然转弯以避免撞到别的车子。

absurd [əb'sɜːd] *a.* 荒谬的，荒诞的

同义 ridiculous *a.* 荒谬可笑的

诵读 Bob's belief that he was too clever to be caught in his wrongdoing was absurd. 鲍勃认为自己聪明，做坏事不会被抓到。这个想法是荒谬的。

abuse [ə'bjuːs] *vt.* 滥用；辱骂 *n.* 滥用；恶习

巧记 否定前缀 ab-+词根 use 用=没有用好→滥用

诵读 Her abuse of power has turned her friends against her. 她滥用权力，这使她的朋友转而反对她。

accelerate [æk'seləreɪt] *v.* 使加速，使增速，促进

巧记 前缀 ac-加强语气 +词根 celer 速度+后缀-ate 表动词=使加速

诵读 Sometimes both fertilizer and manure will accelerate the growth of plants, but sometimes they won't. 化肥和有机肥料有时能加速植物的生长，有时却不能。

accent ['æksənt] *n.* 口音

诵读 He had a strong northern accent. 他带有浓厚的北方口音。

accommodate [ə'kɒmədeɪt] *vt.* 向……提供住处

拓展 accommodation *n.* 住宿，留宿

诵读 He could accommodate no more than five people in his large apartment. 他最多能留五个人在他的大套房里住宿。

accuse [ə'kjuːz] *vt.* 控告，指责 *vi.* 指控，指责

巧记 前缀 ac-加强语气+词根 cuse=curse 诅咒

搭配 accuse sb. of (doing) sth. 控告某人（做）某事

诵读 The naughty boy is always accused of making too much noise. 那个淘气的男孩总是由于太吵而受指责。

acknowledge [ək'nɒlɪdʒ] *vt.* 承认；接受

巧记 前缀 ac-加强语气+词根 knowledge=知道→承认

僻义 *vt.* 答谢

诵读 Stephen acknowledged Henry as his heir. 斯蒂芬承认亨利为他的继承人。

acquaint [ə'kweɪnt] *vt.* 使了解，使熟悉

搭配 acquaint oneself with 熟悉，通晓；be/get/become acquainted with 相识，了解

拓展 acquaintance *n.* 熟人

诵读 He is not a friend, only an acquaintance. （我和）他不是朋友，只是相识。

addict ['ædɪkt] *v.* 使沉溺；使上瘾 *n.* 入迷的人

搭配 be addicted to 沉溺于

诵读 You're not much of a TV addict, as I remember. 我记得你并不太沉迷看电视。

adequate ['ædɪkwɪt] *a.* 足够的；适当的，胜任的

巧记 前缀 ad-加强语气+词根 equ 平等 +后缀 -ate（……的）=对等→充足的

诵读 His £10 a week is not adequate to support his wife and children. 他每星期 10 英镑的收入不足以抚养妻儿。

adhere [əd'hɪə] *vi.* 粘着；依附，追随

巧记 前缀 ad-加强语气+词根 her 粘贴→依附；坚持

搭配 adhere to 附着，坚持

诵读 Glue and paste are used to make one surface adhere to another. 胶水和糨糊是用以黏合一个表面与另一个表面的。

adjoin [ə'dʒɔɪn] *v.* 靠近；贴近，毗连

巧记 前缀 ad-加强语气+词根 join 加入→靠近

诵读 Canada and Mexico adjoin the United States of America. 美国与加拿大和墨西哥接壤。

adore [ə'dɔː] *vt.* 反复说；崇拜，敬慕

巧记 前缀 ad-加强语气+词根 or 讲话=反复说→很崇拜

诵读 You will adore this film. 你会喜欢上这部电影。

affection [ə'fekʃən] *n.* 喜爱；爱慕之情

诵读 The dog transferred its affections to its new master. 那只狗把感情转移到新主人身上了。

affiliate [ə'fɪlɪeɪt] *vt.* 加入，隶属于 *n.* 分支机构

巧记 前缀 af-加强语气+词根 fil 加入+i 无意义+后缀-ate=加入→成为……的一部分

诵读 The college is affiliated to the university. 该学院隶属于这所大学。

affluent ['æfluənt] *a.* 富裕的，丰富的，富饶的

巧记 前缀 af-加强语气+词根 flu 流入 +后缀-ent =大量流入→丰富的

诵读 He is an affluent man. 他是一个富有的人。

agenda [ə'dʒendə] *n.* 议事日程，记事册

诵读 Let's talk about the next item on the agenda. 让我们来讨论议程上的下一项目。

agitate ['ædʒɪteɪt] *vt.* 摇动；搅动；使激动

僻义 *vi.* 抗议（agitate for... 抗议要求……）

诵读 She was agitated because her train was an hour late. 她十分焦虑，因为她乘坐的火车晚点一小时。

agony [ˈægəni] *n.* 极大痛苦，创伤

辨析 agony 侧重指精神或身体痛苦的剧烈程度；grief 指由某种特殊处境或原因造成的强烈的感情上的苦恼与悲痛；misery 多含不幸、可怜或悲哀的意味；distress 多指精神上的痛苦，也可指各种灾难带来的痛苦。

诵读 They went through the agonies of war and famine. 他们经历了战争和饥荒的痛苦。

aisle [aɪl] *n.* 过道，通道

辨析 aisle 多指教堂或超市里货架间的纵道；corridor 多指（建筑物或火车内的）走廊，过道，通道

诵读 A quick movement across the aisle caught his eye. 有个人影在走道里一闪而过，引起了他的注意。

album [ˈælbəm] *n.* 集邮册；相册；专辑

诵读 Her first album is scheduled for release in September. 她的首张专辑计划今年九月发行。

alien [ˈeɪlɪən] *n.* 外国人；外星人 *a.* 外国的

搭配 be alien to… 和……不同

诵读 They take more readily than do most Americans to its cosmopolitan complexities, its surviving, aloof, European standards, and its alien mixtures. 他们比大多数美国人更欣赏纽约这个国际大都市的五彩缤纷的生活，它那残存的，独此一家的欧洲社会准则以及它那众多外来民族混杂而居的社会。

alleviate [əˈliːvɪeɪt] *vt.* 减轻，缓和，缓解（痛苦等）

巧记 同义词 diminish，reduce，decrease，decline

辨析 alleviate 多指在痛苦方面的减轻，缓和，同义词有 relieve，ease；diminish 多指数量方面缓慢减少，同义词有 reduce，decline 等。

诵读 We will be able to alleviate the difficulties in teaching ethics and promoting transparency and integrity. 我们将能够减少道德教育中的困难，并且促进透明性和道德感。

ambiguous [æmˈbɪɡjʊəs] *a.* 模棱两可的，有歧义的

巧记 同义词有 obscure，vague；近义词 dim 多指光线暗淡的，看不清的。

诵读 There should not be any ambiguous expressions in a business letter. 在商务信函中不应该出现任何模棱两可的表达。

ambulance [ˈæmbjʊləns] *n.* 救护车，救护船

巧记 谐音记忆：俺不能死——快叫救护车！

搭配 emergency ambulance 急救车

诵读 Many ambulances now come equipped with sophisticated monitoring equipment. 很多救护车现在都配备精密的监控仪器。

amiable [ˈeɪmɪəbl] *a.* 和蔼可亲的，友善的，亲切的

辨析 amiable 用于指人，意为"友好的，和蔼的"（friendly，good-natured）；amicable 则用于指事物，意为"和平友好的"。

诵读 She is bright, and what is better, amiable. 她很聪明，而且很友善。

analogue [ˈænəlɔːɡ] *n.* 类似物；相似体

巧记 前缀 ana-表示平行+词根 logue 表示说话=平行地说话→相似（同根词 dialogue）

拓展 analogy *n.* 类似，相似

诵读 A vegetarian gets protein not from meat but from its analogues. 素食者所摄取的蛋白质不是来自肉类而是来自近似肉类的食物。

anchor [ˈæŋkə] *n.* 锚；主持人 *v.* 使固定

僻义 *n.* 支柱，靠山

诵读 Make sure the table is securely anchored. 务必固定好桌子。

anecdote [ˈænɪkdəʊt] *n.* 轶事，趣闻

巧记 前缀 anec-（相当于 an-尚未）+ec-(= ex)向外+词根 dote 给予=说出尚未（出版）的事情→尚未告知（出去的）奇闻，轶事

诵读 He has a talent for recollection and anecdote. 他在记忆力和讲述奇闻轶事方面颇具天赋。

anguish [ˈæŋɡwɪʃ] *n.* 极度痛苦，烦恼

辨析 anguish 多指"精神上令人难以忍受的痛苦"；suffering 指"身体或精神上的痛苦"。

诵读 No one suspected the anguish he carried on his shoulders. 没有人怀疑他所承受的痛苦。

anonymous [əˈnɒnɪməs] *a.* 匿名的

巧记 前缀 a-加强语气+词根 no 没有+词根 nym 名字=没有名字→匿名的

拓展 anonymity *n.* 匿名

诵读 A small business is much different from a big business, where everybody is more anonymous. 小企业和大企业是有区别的，在大企业里人们相互之间都不熟悉。

appal [əˈpɔːl] *vt.* 使惊骇，使恐怖

巧记 谐音：appal 我怕→恐惧；同义词 dismay，shock

诵读 His eyes flashed up to mine. "I was appalled. I couldn't believe I had put us in danger after all, put myself in your power…" 他的目光射向我。"我很吃惊。我不敢相信我竟然还是让我们面临了风险，不能相信我竟屈服在你的力量之下……"

apparatus [ˌæpəˈreɪtəs] *n.* 器械，器具

巧记 同义词：equipment *n.* 设备，器材；furnishings *n.* 设备，家具；appliance *n.* 用具，器具

诵读 In South China, most houses are not equipped with heating apparatus. 在中国南方，大多数房子里都不配供暖设备。

applaud [əˈplɔːd] *vt.&vi.* 鼓掌欢迎；赞同

辨析 applaud 指因精湛表演或某种行为表示赞许；commend 用于对具体功绩或成就表示嘉奖，通常指上级对下级、长辈对晚辈的赞赏；praise 用于对某人的优秀品质表示钦佩赞美。

拓展 applause *n.* 鼓掌；喝彩

诵读 The audience applauded his performance for a long time. 观众为他的表演长时间鼓掌。

arrogant [ˈærəgənt] *a.* 傲慢的，自大的

巧记 前缀 ar- 加强语气+词根 rog 狗叫+后缀-ant = 狗认为自己是主人，见到生人"傲慢地"嚷叫

诵读 He is spoiled, arrogant and has a tendency towards snobbery. 他被宠坏了，傲慢无礼，而且经常自命不凡。

ascertain [ˌæsəˈteɪn] *vt.* 确定，查明，弄清

巧记 前缀 as-加强语气+词根 certain 确定=确定

诵读 The police determined to ascertain the truth of the matter. 警察下定决心查明事实的真相。

aspire [əsˈpaɪə] *vi.* (to, after) 渴望，追求

巧记 前缀 a-加强语气+词根 spir 呼吸+后缀-e=用力喘息→极力想得到

诵读 Aspiring after truth is his life-long career. 追求真理是他一生的事业。

assault [əˈsɔːlt] *vt.&n.* 突然而猛烈(的)攻击

巧记 前缀 as-加强语气+词根 sault 跳=朝着某人跳去→攻击某人

诵读 The sonic boom was an assault on our nerves. 飞机的声爆损伤了我们神经。

assert [əˈsɜːt] *vt.* 断言，坚称；坚持

巧记 前缀 as-加强语气+词根 sert 插入=强行插入→"断"言

诵读 She asserted that he was not guilty. 她断言他是无辜的。

assimilate [əˈsɪmɪleɪt] *vt.* 使相似；同化

巧记 前缀 as-加强语气+词根 simil 相似的=使相似

僻义 *v.* 吸收

诵读 We assimilate some kind of food more easily than others. 我们对某些种类的食物比别的食物更容易吸收。

augment [ɔːgˈment] *vt.* (使)增大，增加

辨析 形近词 argument *n.* 争论，观点

诵读 He augments his income by writing short stories. 他通过写短篇小说来增加收入。

authentic [ɔːˈθentɪk] *a.* 真实的；可靠的，可信的

诵读 This is an authentic news report.We can depend on it. 这是一篇可靠的新闻报道，我们相信它。

autonomy [ɔːˈtɒnəmi] *n.* 自治，自治权

巧记 前缀 auto-自动的+词根 nom 名字=自己可以决定自己的名字→自治

诵读 Branch managers have full autonomy in their own areas. 分支机构的经理在其管辖范围内有充分的自主权。

award [əˈwɔːd] *vt.* 授予，给予 *n.* 奖金

诵读 His horse was given the highest award at the show. 他的马在展览会中获得最高奖。

awkward [ˈɔːkwəd] *a.* 笨拙的；尴尬的

诵读 This is an awkward corner; there have been several road accidents here. 这是一个不好转弯的拐角，这里曾发生过几次车祸。

abdomen [ˈæbdəmən] *n.* 腹，下腹

accessory [ækˈsesəri] *n.* 附件，附属品

诵读 She also has a good range of accessories, including sunglasses, handbags and belts. 她还有很多种配饰，包括墨镜、手包和皮带。

ailment [ˈeɪlmənt] *n.* 疾病(尤指慢性病)，不适

诵读 His ailments include a mild heart attack and arthritis. 他患有轻度心脏病和关节炎。

allay [əˈleɪ] *vt.* 减轻，缓和

诵读 The police tried to allay her fears but failed. 警

察力图减轻她的恐惧,却以失败告终。

allot [əˈlɒt] *vt.* 分配

诵读 Each passenger slept on the berth allotted to him. 每个旅客都睡在所分配的铺位上。

anesthetic [ˌænɪsˈθetɪk] *n.* 麻醉剂, 麻醉药

诵读 He was given a general anesthetic. 他被全身

麻醉。

averse [əˈvɜːs] *a.* 不愿意的, 反对的

搭配 be averse to (doing) sth. 不喜欢(做)某事

诵读 She was so self-conceited that she was averse to all advice from others. 她是如此自命不凡,听不得别人的任何忠告。

bathe [beɪð] *vt.&vi.* 给……洗澡;游泳

搭配 be bathed in 沉浸在, 沐浴在

诵读 The top of Mount. Tai was bathed in brilliant sunshine. 泰山山顶沐浴在灿烂的阳光下。

bald [bɔːld] *a.* 秃的, 秃头的

辨析 与bald 一个字母之差的bold表示"勇敢的"。

诵读 Hills and mountains in the county used to be bald and lifeless due to decades of intensive and improper human activities. 几十年来,人类活动不当导致全县的丘陵地区一直寸草不生,毫无生机。

band [bænd] *n.* 条, 带;乐队;一伙 *v.* 缚, 绑扎

搭配 a band of 一群, 一伙, 一帮

诵读 Many jobs present noise hazards, such as working in music halls where rock bands are playing. 很多工作存在噪声危害,比如在有摇滚乐队演奏的音乐厅里工作。

bankrupt [ˈbæŋkrʌpt] *a.* 破产的;彻底缺乏的

巧记 bank 银行+rupt 破裂→破产

联想 同根词: interrupt *v.* 打断; bankrupt *v.* 破产; corrupt *v.* 腐蚀; abrupt *a.* 突然的

诵读 The implication of the statement is that the firm is bankrupt. 该项声明的言下之意是该商行已经破产。

bar [bɑː] *n.* 条, 杆;酒吧;障碍

僻义 ①American Bar Association 美国律师协会; Bar Exam 司法考试 ②*v.* 禁止

诵读 After the bombing, the whole area was barred to the public. 轰炸后,整个地区禁止公众通行。

bare [beə] *a.* 赤裸的;稀少的 *vt.* 露出, 暴露

辨析 bare 指缺少必要的遮盖物,用于人时指身体的部分裸露; naked 指全身一丝不挂; bald 指头上无发, 山坡无树无草, 树顶无叶; barren 指缺少肥力或生活能力,多指土地荒瘠不毛。

拓展 barely *ad.* 几乎没有

诵读 He says it would only take him a few minutes to teach a person how to steal a car, using a bare minimum of tools. 他说只需要他花费几分钟的时间就可以教会一个人用最少的工具窃取汽车。

barrier [ˈbærɪə] *n.* 障碍(物)

巧记 同义词 obstacle

诵读 The crowd linked arms to form a barrier. 群众臂挽着臂组成人墙。

basement [ˈbeɪsmənt] *n.* 建筑物的底部, 地下室, 地窖

巧记 词根 base 基础, 底部 +后缀-ment→建筑物的底部, 地下室

诵读 Thrift is the basement of richness. 节约是富裕的基础。

basis [ˈbeɪsɪs] *n.* 基础, 根据

搭配 on the basis of… 根据……, 在……基础上

诵读 The investigation failed to provide enough evidence to form the basis of a case, however. 然而这项调查没有提供足够的证据,以构成这一案例的根据。

battery [ˈbætəri] *n.* 电池(组)

搭配 charge the battery 给电池充电

诵读 Now some researchers in America have developed a battery that generates electricity in a similar way. 如今美国的一些研究人员发明了一种用同样方法产生电能的电池。

bay [beɪ] *n.* 海湾,(港)湾

搭配 keep sb. at bay 截住某人的去路

诵读 The Guangdong-Hong Kong-Macao Greater Bay Area is expected to be built into a world-class cluster. 粤港澳大湾区有望建成世界级产业集群。

beach [biːtʃ] *n.* 海滩,海滨 *vt.* 使(船)靠岸

搭配 hit the beach 登陆;上岸

诵读 We spent the whole day lying on the beach. 我们在沙滩上躺了一整天。

bear [beə] *vt.* 承担;忍受;结(果实),生育 *n.* 熊

搭配 bear with… 对……有耐心;容忍……

拓展 childbearing ages 生育年龄

诵读 All the costs of the repairs will be born by our company. 所有的修理费将由我们公司负担。

bearing [ˈbeərɪŋ] *n.* 忍受;关系,影响;举止

搭配 have some bearing on… 和……有关

诵读 Sometimes the student may be asked to write some articles that have some bearing on the subject being studied. 有时候学生需要写一些和所学习的科目相关的文章。

beat [biːt] *v.* 跳动;击打 *n.* 敲打;拍子

搭配 beat down 镇压,挫败

诵读 I will beat you to the top of that hill. 我将比你先到达山顶。

belong [bɪˈlɒŋ] *vi.* 属于

搭配 belong to… 属于……

诵读 Does this item of expenditure belong under the head of office expenses? 此项开支是否该列在办公费项下?

belt [belt] *n.* 腰带,带子

僻义 *n.* 区域,地带

诵读 He has ten-year civil service under his belt. 他拥有十年的公务员经历。

bench [bentʃ] *n.* 长凳,长椅

诵读 We sat on a park bench for two hours talking about our life. 我们坐在公园的长椅上谈论各自的生活,足足谈了两个小时。

bend [bend] *vt.* 弯曲;屈身;屈从 *n.* 弯曲

搭配 be bent on 专心于;bend oneself to 致力于

诵读 I cannot bend her into changing her mind. 我不能使她屈从改变她的主意。

bean [biːn] *n.* 菜豆,蚕豆

巧记 kidney bean 形状像肾脏的豆子→四季豆

诵读 Every bean has its black. 凡人各有其短处。

beard [bɪəd] *n.* 胡须

巧记 可想象为在 ear(耳朵)两边下的胡须,即将其左右的 b 和 d 看作两边的耳朵

辨析 beard 指下巴上的胡子,moustache 指嘴唇上的胡子,whiskers 指颊须、络腮胡。

诵读 He has decided to shave off his beard. 他决定剃掉胡子。

beast [biːst] *n.* 野兽;凶残的人

巧记 *Beauty and the Beast* 电影《美女与野兽》

诵读 We shall defend ourselves to the last breath of man and beast. (William Ⅱ, King of England) 只要一息尚存,我们就要为保卫自己而战。(英国国王威廉二世)

beforehand [bɪˈfɔːhænd] *ad.* 预先,事先

巧记 before 在……之前+hand 手→先下手的,事先的,预先的

诵读 It's better to buy the tickets beforehand. 最好还是提前买好票。

behalf [bɪˈhɑːf] *n.* 代表

搭配 on behalf of… 作为……的代表

诵读 If ambition is to be well regarded, the rewards of ambition—wealth, distinction, control over one's destiny—must be deemed worthy of the sacrifices made on ambition's behalf. 个人的雄心如果能被正确看待,那么它的回报——财富、声誉、对命运的掌握——则应该被认为值得为之付出牺牲。

behave [bɪˈheɪv] *v.* 举止,举动,表现;运转,开动

搭配 behave oneself 注意某人的举止

拓展 behavior *n.* 行为,举止

诵读 But in theory, matter must behave very differently inside the hole. 但在理论上,在黑洞里物质的运动肯定与洞外有很大区别。

beloved [bɪˈlʌvɪd] *a.* 钟爱的 *n.* 心爱的人

诵读 It wasn't until fifth grade that she met her beloved teacher. 直到五年级她才遇到了她喜爱的老师。

beware [bɪˈweə] *v.* 当心,谨防

巧记 be+ware 注意→当心,谨防

搭配 beware of… 当心……

诵读 Beware of outrageous credit limits, which may lead to uncontrollable spending. 要小心信用额度别定得太高，这可能会导致花费无度。

bite [baɪt] *vt.&n.* 咬，叮

诵读 Do you want a bite of my sandwich? 你想来一口我的三明治吗？

bid [bɪd] *v.* 祝愿；吩咐；报价，投标 *n.* 投标

搭配 bid for... 对……的报价或投标

新义 bid farewell to... 向……道别

诵读 The mayor admitted defeat in his bid for reelection. 市长承认了谋求再次当选的失败。

bind [baɪnd] *vt.* 捆，绑，束缚

巧记 b 和 d 想象成两只手，被捆在一起（in）→捆，绑

诵读 Marriage is an arrangement that binds two people together in a family unit. 婚姻是将两个人约束在一个家庭单位里的安排。

biology [baɪˈɒlədʒi] *n.* 生物学

巧记 bio-生命，生物+ology→生命学科，生物

诵读 The major could be a subject like biology, math or a foreign language. 专业可以是一门学科，例如生物、数学或者一门外语。

bitter [ˈbɪtə] *a.*（有）苦（味）的；痛苦的，厉害的

搭配 bittersweet *a.* 苦乐参半的

诵读 Inflation is yet another new and bitter truth we must learn to face. 通货膨胀又是一个我们不得不面对的新的残酷事实。

blood [blʌd] *n.* 血液；家族；生命

搭配 in one's blood 天生就有的；new blood 新成员

拓展 bloody *a.* 流血的，血腥的；bleed *v.* 出血，流血

僻义 *n.* 人员；血气，气质

诵读 Tom is out of blood. 汤姆意志消沉。

bleak [bliːk] *a.* 荒凉的；冷酷的；没有希望的

搭配 a bleak winter 暗淡的冬天

诵读 Against that bleak scenario, some leaders still hope that the government will tighten regulation of the labor market. 面对这个没有希望的情况，有些领导仍然希望政府可以收紧对劳动力市场的管制。

blend [blend] *n.* 混合（物）*vt.* 混合，混杂

联想 同义词 combine, fuse, mingle, mix

诵读 A melting pot is a pot in which metals are melted in order to blend them. 熔炉是一种可以把不同的金属熔化然后混合的炉子。

blind [blaɪnd] *a.* 盲的；盲目的 *vt.* 使失明 *n.* 百叶窗

搭配 be blind to 视而不见；blind as a bat 完全看不见东西的；turn a blind eye to 视而不见

诵读 Thousands of other blind people find it difficult to learn that system. 很多盲人感觉学习这种系统非常困难。

block [blɒk] *n.* 大块木料；街区

僻义 *vt.* 阻塞，拦阻 *n.* 障碍物

诵读 A book that remains shut is but a block. 有书闭卷不阅读，无疑是一块木头。

bloom [bluːm] *n.* 花（朵）；开花（期）*v.* 开花

巧记 同义词 blossom

诵读 It is like a gardener who was looking at plants: something to be encouraged to bloom in some places and pruned in others. 这种做法就像是一个园丁看着植物，在某些地方应该被鼓励开花，而在其他地方则应该进行修剪。

blueprint [ˈbluːprɪnt] *n.* 蓝图，设计图 *vt.* 计划

巧记 blue 蓝色+print 印刷的图=蓝图

诵读 All the machine parts on a blueprint must answer each other. 设计图上所有的机器部件都应互相配合。

blush [blʌʃ] *vi.&n.* 脸红

诵读 She blushed at their praises. 她因受到他们的赞扬而脸红。

body [ˈbɒdi] *n.* 身体，躯体

搭配 a body of 一群

僻义 *n.* 机构，部门

诵读 Large bodies of unemployed men marched through the streets demanding work. 一群群的失业者在街上游行要求工作。

bottom [ˈbɒtəm] *n.* 底部，基部

搭配 at bottom 基本上，本质上

僻义 *a.* 最差的 *vt.* 使建立在……的基础上

诵读 We wanted to bottom our plan on a solid basis. 我们想把我们的计划建立在牢固的基础上。

boast [bəʊst] *vi.* 自夸，夸耀 *n.* 自夸，大话

搭配 boast of/about 夸耀；make a boast of 夸耀

诵读 He often boasts to his neighbours about the success of his children. 他常常向邻人夸耀孩子们的

成就。

boil [bɔɪl] *vi.* (使) 沸腾, 煮(沸)

诵读 Don't let the pot boil dry. 不要把水壶烧干了。

bomb [bɒm] *n.* 炸弹 *v.* 轰炸

诵读 They were bombed out families. 由于轰炸, 他们被迫离开家园。

bond [bɒnd] *n.* 结合, 联结; 债券; 契约

搭配 national bond 国债

诵读 This new paste makes a firmer bond. 这种新的糨糊黏性较强。

bonus [ˈbəʊnəs] *n.* 奖金, 红利

诵读 The workers got an annual bonus. 工人们领到了年终奖金。

boom [buːm] *vi.* 迅速发展, 兴旺 *n.* 潮流, 兴旺

辨析 doom *n.* 厄运; dome *n.* 圆顶, 穹顶

搭配 baby boom 婴儿潮; economic boom 经济繁荣

诵读 Jones is booming as a novelist. 琼斯作为一个小说家, 声名鹊起。

border [ˈbɔːdə] *n.* 边界; 国界

诵读 The criminal escaped over the border. 罪犯逃过了边界。

bother [ˈbɒðə] *n.&vt.* 打扰, 麻烦

诵读 I am sorry to bother you, but can you tell me the time? 对不起, 打扰您了, 请问现在几点了?

bound [baʊnd] *vi.* 跳跃 *n.* 界限; 跳跃

拓展 boundary *n.* 分界线, 边界

诵读 In a single bound, he was over the wall. 他轻轻一跳就越过了墙。

bow [bəʊ] *vi.&n.* 鞠躬, 点头

巧记 rainbow 彩虹是天上彩色的"弓形物"(bow)。

诵读 I raised my hat to her and she bowed in return. 我向她举帽示礼, 她鞠躬答礼。

bowl [bəʊl] *n.* 碗

拓展 bowling 保龄球

诵读 He finished off two bowls of noodles in no time. 他很快就吃完了两碗面。

breath [breθ] *n.* 气息; 呼吸

搭配 hold one's breath 屏气; out of breath 喘不过气来

拓展 breathe *vt.&vi.* 呼吸

诵读 We had to pause frequently for breath. 我们不得不经常停下来喘口气。

brake [breɪk] *vi.&n.* 制动; 刹车

诵读 The government put the brakes on all our plans by giving us less money. 政府通过减少经费让我们的计划暂停了。

branch [brɑːntʃ] *n.* (树)条, 分支; 分店; (学科)分科, 部门; 支流

诵读 He climbed up the tree and hid among the branches. 他爬上树, 藏到树枝中。

brave [breɪv] *a.* 勇敢的

诵读 It was brave of you to speak in front of all those people. 你在那么多人面前讲话, 真勇敢。

breadth [bredθ] *n.* 宽度, 幅

诵读 His book showed the great breadth of his learning. 从他的书可以看出他知识渊博。

breakdown [ˈbreɪkdaʊn] *n.* 崩溃; 中断

巧记 来自词组 break down

诵读 Peter has had a nervous breakdown for three years. 彼得患神经衰弱已经 3 年了。

breed [briːd] *vt.&vi.* (使)繁殖, 生殖

僻义 *vt.* 引起, 导致

诵读 Some animals will not breed when kept in cages. 有些动物关在笼子里就不会繁殖。

breeze [briːz] *n.* 微风; 轻而易举的事

巧记 微风(breeze)吹化了冰冻的(freeze)河流。

诵读 I enjoy the cool breeze that comes from the river. 我喜欢来自河面的清凉的微风。

bribe [braɪb] *n.* 贿赂 *vt.* 向……行贿, 买通

搭配 bribe sb. to do sth. 贿赂某人去做某事

诵读 The child was bribed with a piece of cake to go to bed quietly. (比喻)给孩子一块蛋糕, 孩子就安静地上床睡觉了。

brick [brɪk] *n.* 砖块, 砖

诵读 The house is brick not wood. 这房子是用砖盖的, 不是木头。

brief [briːf] *a.* 简短的, 简洁的 *vt.* 简短介绍, 简要汇报

诵读 It is a long letter, but in brief he says "No". 那是一封长信, 但是简言之, 他说"不行"。

briefcase [ˈbriːfkeɪs] *n.* 手提箱, 公事包

巧记 合成词: brief 摘要+case 容器→存摘要的容器→公文包

诵读 He requested the old man to look after the briefcase. 他请求那位老人照看这个公事包。

brilliant ['brɪlɪənt] *a.* 光辉的, 灿烂的; 卓越的, 有才华的

辨析 bright 口语常用词, 尤指小孩思路敏捷, 理解力强, 机灵等; clever 强调头脑灵活, 接受新事物快, 有智有谋; wise 一般指有远见, 能明智地处理问题; intelligent 正式用词, 指在理解新的、抽象东西或处理解决问题时, 智力超过一般常人; ingenious 暗示有创造与发明的才能和技巧; smart 与 bright 和 clever 的意思很相近, 但更强调机灵; shrewd 指精明老练, 善于判断, 把握有利机会。

诵读 He is a brilliant scientist. 他是一位有才华的科学家。

broadcast ['brɔːdkɑːst] *v.* 传播 *n.* 广播节目

诵读 Everyone paid careful attention to the radio broadcasts from the war area. 每人都十分注意收听战区的无线电广播。

brush [brʌʃ] *n.* 刷; 画笔 *vt.* 刷, 擦

诵读 She brushed the crumbs off the tablecloth. 她刷掉台布上的食品屑。

brutal ['bruːtl] *a.* 残忍的; 严峻的; 严酷的

诵读 The murder was so brutal that the jury was not allowed to see the police photographs. 这起凶案如此残忍, 以至于陪审团不被允许看警方的照片。

burst [bɜːst] *v.* 爆炸; 突然发生 *n.* 爆发

搭配 burst into laughter 突然大笑; burst out 突然开始

诵读 Everyone suddenly burst out laughing. 大家突然哄堂大笑。

budget ['bʌdʒɪt] *n.* 预算 *v.* 做预算

诵读 They planned a monthly budget for their family. 他们家每月都有预算。

bug [bʌg] *n.* 臭虫; 小毛病

诵读 I am not feeling well; I must have picked up a bug somewhere. 我觉得不舒服, 我一定是在什么地方染上了小毛病。

bulb [bʌlb] *n.* 灯泡

诵读 The bulb of the eye is important for us. 眼球对于我们来说非常重要。

bulk [bʌlk] *n.* 体积, 容积; 主体, 大批

诵读 He left the bulk of his property to his brother. 他将大量财产遗留给他的弟弟。

bull [bʊl] *n.* 公牛

搭配 bull market 牛市 (股票价格上升期)

拓展 bully *n.* 恃强欺弱者, 小流氓 *vt.* 威胁, 欺侮

诵读 The longest bull run in a century of art-market history ended on a dramatic note with a sale of 56 works by Damien Hirst. 艺术品市场一个世纪里最长的牛市以一场拍卖达米安·赫斯特 56 件作品的盛会而告终。

bullet ['bʊlɪt] *n.* 子弹, 枪弹

诵读 Two American presidents was felled by an assassin's bullet. 有两任美国总统被暗杀者开枪打死了。

bulletin ['bʊlɪtɪn] *n.* 公报, 公告, 告示

巧记 BBS 是英文 Bulletin Board System 的缩写。

诵读 They post questions from standardized tests on Internet bulletin boards. 他们把标准化测试的题目发布在网上公告板上。

bureau ['bjʊərəʊ] *n.* 署, 局, 司, 处

巧记 FBI 是 Federal Bureau of Investigation 的缩写。

拓展 bureaucracy *n.* 官僚主义, 官僚机构

诵读 They are trying to set up a credit bureau which would allow them to track clients' overall indebtedness and credit histories. 他们正在试图建立一个信用局, 可以追踪客户的总负债和信用记录。

butterfly ['bʌtəflaɪ] *n.* 蝴蝶

搭配 Butterfly Effect 蝴蝶效应

诵读 It is intermediate between the egg and the adult butterfly. 它正处于卵和成年蝴蝶的中间阶段。

bypass ['baɪpɑːs] *n.* 旁道 *vt.* 绕过

巧记 合成词 by+pass 通过→从旁边通过→旁道

诵读 He recently performed heart bypass surgery on a 30-year-old man. 他最近给一个 30 岁的人进行了心脏搭桥手术。

bargain ['bɑːgən] *v.* 讨价还价

僻义 *n.* 特价商品; 廉价品

诵读 We bargained with the farmer for a supply of milk and butter. 我们和农民讲价, 想购买一批牛奶和黄油。

bait [beɪt] *n.* 饵，引诱物 *vt.* 用饵引诱；激怒

诵读 I decided to flatter him and he rose to the bait. 我决定奉承他，结果他上钩了。

ballot [ˈbælət] *n.* （无记名）投票；投票总数 *vi.* 投票

搭配 ballot for sth./sb. 为某物/某人投票

诵读 I was asked to count the ballots and announce the winner. 我被要求统计投票并且宣布结果。

banquet [ˈbæŋkwɪt] *n.* 宴会 *v.* 参加宴会；宴请

搭配 state banquet 国宴；reception banquet 接待晚宴

诵读 The premier will give a banquet in honour of the distinguished visitors. 总理将要举行宴会招待贵宾。

bark [bɑːk] *vi.* （狗等）吠，叫 *n.* 吠声

巧记 Barking dogs never bite. 会叫的狗不咬人。

诵读 He barked questions at her. 他厉声质问她。

barn [bɑːn] *n.* 谷仓，仓库

诵读 There is a heavy note of hypocrisy in this, a case of closing the barn door after the horses have escaped—with the educated themselves riding on them. 这其中有着浓厚的虚伪色彩，恰如马跑后再关上马厩的门那样，而受过良好教育的人自己正骑在那些马的背上。

barren [ˈbærən] *a.* 贫瘠的；不育的；不结果的

辨析 形近词 barrel *n.* 枪管，炮管；桶

诵读 Many people think of deserts as barren regions, but many species of plants and animals have adapted to life there. 许多人都认为沙漠是很贫瘠的地区，但有很多种类的植物和动物已经适应了那里的生活。

batch [bætʃ] *n.* 一批，一组，一群

巧记 同义词 collection, pile

诵读 The regulator said that the first batch of start-up companies were expected to be listed on GEM in late October or early November. 证监会表示首批在创业板上市的新兴企业预计将于 10 月末或 11 月初挂牌。

beam [biːm] *n.* （横）梁；（光线的）束，柱

僻义 *vi.* 微笑（beam with joy 眉飞色舞）

诵读 Our magazines feature beaming celebrities and happy families in perfect homes. 我们的杂志刊登满面春风的名人和美满幸福的家庭。

benign [bɪˈnaɪn] *a.* （病）良性的；仁慈的，和蔼的

巧记 ben- 表示"好"，例如 benefit 好处

搭配 benign tumors 良性肿瘤

诵读 Dramatic social change seldom takes such a benign form. 巨大的社会变革很少能有这么温和的形式。

betray [bɪˈtreɪ] *vt.* 背叛，出卖；暴露，泄露

诵读 I can't betray her, for it would hurt her feelings. 我不能背叛她，那样做会伤害她的感情。

bewilder [bɪˈwɪldə] *vt.* 使迷惑，难住

巧记 be+wilder 迷惑→使迷惑，难住

辨析 confuse：使混乱，混淆，尤指心中纷乱的思绪使头脑变得混乱；puzzle：使迷惑，困惑，多指复杂的事件或难题使人难以理解、迷惑失措；bewilder：迷惑、困惑，语气最重，指糊涂到了无法清醒思考的地步。

诵读 Some hard problems in reading comprehension bewilder me. 阅读理解中一些难题让我很迷惑。

bizarre [bɪˈzɑː] *a.* 异乎寻常的，稀奇古怪的

巧记 同义词 odd, queer

诵读 It is bizarre that *The Clash of Civilizations* has been misunderstood by so many people. 奇怪的是，《文明的冲突》这本书被这么多人误解。

blackmail [ˈblækmeɪl] *n.* 敲诈，勒索；胁迫，恫吓

巧记 收到之后让人感到恐惧的是黑色（black）的邮件（mail）→恫吓，敲诈，勒索

诵读 The letter she received turned out not to be a blackmail. 她收到的那封信最终发现并不是勒索钱财的。

blade [bleɪd] *n.* 刀刃，刀片

诵读 Mishaps are like knives that either serve us or cut us as we grasp them by the handle or blade. 灾难就像刀子，握住刀柄就可以为我们服务，拿住刀刃则会割破手。

blast [blɑːst] *n.* 一阵（风）；爆炸声 *vi.* 爆炸

搭配 at full blast 全速地；大规模地

诵读 31 people were working in the mine when Monday's blast happened. 当周一的爆炸发生时，有 31 个人正在矿井作业。

blaze [bleɪz] *n.* 火焰；闪光 *vi.* 燃烧

搭配 blaze a way in 开辟道路；blaze abroad 传播出去

诵读 Several shops selling chemicals made the blaze worse. 几个出售化学品的商店导致火势加剧。

blunder ['blʌndə] *vi.* 犯大错；跌跌撞撞地走 *n.* 大错

诵读 Our leader have blundered again. 我们的队长又犯了大错。

blunt [blʌnt] *a.* 率直的；钝的 *v.* 减弱；使变钝

诵读 Too much alcohol makes your senses blunt. 喝太多酒会使你感觉迟钝。

blur [blɜ:] *n.* 模糊不清的事物；污点 *vt.* 使模糊

诵读 The houses appeared as a blur in the mist. 房子在薄雾中显得模糊不清。

bolt [bəult] *n.&vt.* 门闩

诵读 I bolted the two parts together. 我把这两部分拴在一起。

bosom ['buzəm] *n.* 胸，胸部；胸怀；内心

辨义 *a.* 亲密的（bosom friend 知己）

诵读 She held the child to her bosom. 她把孩子抱在怀里。

bounce [bauns] *n.&vi.*（球）弹起 *n.* 弹力

巧记 又跳（bound）又弹（bounce）

诵读 She bounced the baby on her knee. 她让那孩子在她的膝盖上跳来跳去。

boycott ['bɔɪkɒt] *n.&vt.*（联合）抵制，拒绝参与

巧记 该词源自"联合抵制运动"的针对者 Charles C. Boycott（1832—1897）。

诵读 They are boycotting the store because the people who work there are not to join a union. 他们联合抵制那家商店，因为那家商店的店员不加入工会。

breach [bri:tʃ] *n.* 违反，不履行 *vt.* 冲破，攻破

诵读 We won't have any breach of discipline. 我们不会有任何违纪行为。

brochure ['brəʊʃə] *n.* 小册子

诵读 They brought home heaps of travel brochures. 他们将成堆的旅行手册带回家。

brook [brʊk] *n.* 小溪

诵读 I could hear the sound of a babbling brook. 我能听见潺潺的溪流声。

browse [brauz] *vi.* 随意翻阅，浏览；吃草

诵读 Cattle is browsing in the field. 牛正在田里吃草。

bruise [bru:z] *n.* 青肿，挫伤 *vt.* 打青，挫伤

诵读 Pack the pears carefully so that they won't get bruised. 把梨包好，这样它们就不会被压坏。

bubble ['bʌbl] *n.* 气泡 *v.* 冒泡，沸腾

诵读 We could hear the pot bubbling (away) quietly on the fire. 我们能听到火上的水壶轻轻地冒泡。

bucket ['bʌkɪt] *n.* 水桶，吊桶

巧记 a drop in the bucket 杯水车薪

诵读 He poured a bucket of water over the floor. 他往地上倒了一桶水。

bud [bʌd] *n.* 芽，花苞

巧记 同义词 sprout= spring+out

诵读 When spring is approaching, the trees are budding. 当春天即将来临时，树木都在发芽。

bump [bʌmp] *vi.* 碰；颠簸着前进 *n.* 碰撞

搭配 bump into 偶然碰上

诵读 If you bump into something and get a bruise, it generally turns blue-purple over a day or two. 如果你撞上什么东西并受伤，一般一两天后就会变成蓝紫色。

bundle ['bʌndl] *n.* 捆，包

巧记 谐音记忆：绑稻→把稻绑成一捆或一束

辨析 bunch 指有规则地把同类东西固定在一起；bundle 指多件东西被捆扎在一起。

诵读 A peasant boy, carrying a heavy bundle of rice straw, is out of breath under the great pressure. 一个农村男孩背负着沉重的稻草，在重压下气喘吁吁。

burglar ['bɜ:glə] *n.*（入室行窃的）盗贼

辨析 robber 指以暴力或威胁等手段强行夺取他人财物的人；thief 一般专指盗窃者；bandit 指有组织或单独进行抢劫的盗匪；gangster 指结伙进行各种非法活动的武装歹徒；pirate 指海盗。

诵读 She happened to see the burglar leaving the building. 她碰巧看见盗贼离开这幢大楼。

bet [bet] *v.* 赌，打赌 *n.* 打赌，赌注

bite [baɪt] *vt.&n.* 咬，叮 *n.* 一口

诵读 We shouldn't bite more than we can chew. 我们不要贪多嚼不烂。

blood [blʌd] *n.* 血液，血

拓展 bloody *a.* 流血的；血腥的

blurry [ˈblɜːri] *a.* 模糊的；模糊不清的

诵读 My blurry vision makes it hard to drive. 我的视力有点模糊，使得开起车来相当吃力。

bombard [bɒmˈbɑːd] *vt.* 炮击，轰炸，攻击

诵读 Cannons bombarded enemy lines. 大炮轰击了敌军阵地。

brisk [brɪsk] *a.* 轻快的；生气勃勃的

诵读 Eve walked briskly down the corridor to her son's room. 伊芙轻快地沿着走廊走到她儿子的房间。

brittle [ˈbrɪtl] *a.* 易碎的；脆弱的

诵读 Pine is brittle and breaks. 松木硬脆易折。

broker [ˈbrəʊkə] *n.* 经纪人；中间人，代理商

诵读 It was improper of the broker to withhold the information from the stock exchange. 股票经纪人向交易所隐瞒信息的行为是不正当的。

bustle [ˈbʌsl] *vi.* 闹哄哄地忙乱，奔忙

诵读 She is always bustling about the house. 她总是为家务忙个没完。

calculate [ˈkælkjʊleɪt] *vt.* 计算，推算；计划

拓展 calculator *n.* 计算器

诵读 You must calculate all the advantages and disadvantages before coming to a discussion. 在你参与讨论之前，你必须权衡一下利弊。

calorie [ˈkæləri] *n.* 卡（热量单位）

巧记 谐音：卡路里

诵读 The increasing consumption of high-calorie foods is worrying. 高热量食物的消费逐渐增长，这是令人担忧的。

campaign [kæmˈpeɪn] *n.* 战役；运动

搭配 begin/launch/start a campaign 发起运动；carry on/conduct/make a campaign 开展运动；map out a campaign 制订作战计划

诵读 A new campaign of wildlife protection is being undertaken through the Association of South East Asian Nations. 东盟正在实施新一轮的保护野生动物的运动。

campus [ˈkæmpəs] *n.*（大学）校园

搭配 on campus 在校园里

诵读 David visited his university campus for old time's sake. 大卫为了重温往昔，参观了他的大学校园。

cancel [ˈkænsəl] *v.* 取消；删去，划掉

巧记 同义词 abolish, eliminate, dispose, erase, exclude, extinguish

诵读 What happens if I want to cancel my card? 如果我想停卡该怎么办？

cancer [ˈkænsə] *n.* 癌

搭配 lung cancer 肺癌；cancer cells 癌细胞

诵读 British people have been recommended to eat at least "five-a-day"—that is five items of fruit or vegetables every day in order to improve their health and reduce the likelihood of illness, in particular cancer. 英国人被建议每天吃"五餐"——每天吃五种水果蔬菜，以改善健康，降低患病的风险，尤其是癌症。

candidate [ˈkændɪdət] *n.* 候选人，申请者

诵读 The party of the Social Democrat candidate in Croatia's presidential election has claimed victory on national television. 参加克罗地亚总统选举的社会民主党候选人已经在国家电视台宣布获胜。

capital [ˈkæpɪtl] *n.* 首都；大写字母；资本

僻义 *a.* 主要的

拓展 capitalism *n.* 资本主义

诵读 Companies are having difficulty in raising capital. 各公司融资困难。

cash [kæʃ] *n.* 现金，现款

搭配 cash subsidy 现金补贴

拓展 cashier *n.* 收银员，出纳员

诵读 The Secretariat extracted 17,000 euros in cash. 秘书处提取了 1.7 万欧元现金。

cast [kɑːst] *vt.* 投掷 *n.* 演员表

搭配 cast aside 消除，抛弃；cast a cloud on... 给……留下阴影；cast light on 阐明；cast doubt on

引起怀疑

诵读 The holiday tourist boom has shed light on the resilience and strength of the world's second-largest economy. 假日旅游热潮彰显了世界第二大经济体的韧性和实力。

casual ['kæʒjʊəl] *a.* 偶然的；临时的，非正式的

拓展 casualty *n.* 伤亡人员；受害人

诵读 We have a casual dress code. 我们对上班着装规定很宽松。

cater ['keɪtə] *vi.* 满足，迎合

搭配 cater to 满足，迎合；cater for 提供饮食及服务

诵读 Domestic carriers have been ramping up efforts to launch or resume more international flights to cater to growing summer air travel demand. 国内航空公司一直在加紧努力，推出或恢复更多的国际航班，以满足日益增长的夏季航空旅行需求。

caution ['kɔːʃən] *n.* 谨慎 *vt.* 劝……小心

拓展 cautious *a.* 小心的，谨慎的

搭配 be cautious about 谨防

诵读 I'm cautious about jumping into relationships, reliable, old-fashioned, social, and like good manners and well-arranged schedules. 我在步入一段恋情时会十分谨慎，我为人可靠，守旧，善交际，喜欢良好的举止和精心安排的日程。

cease [siːs] *vt.* 停止，中止 *n.* 停止

搭配 cease doing sth. 停止做某事

诵读 The United States had avoided calling for an immediate cease-fire. 美国一直避免呼吁立即停火。

cell [sel] *n.* 细胞；小房间；电池

巧记 cell phone 手机

诵读 Cell phones should be banned in classrooms and schools should limit the time of digital teaching in an effort to curb children's myopia rate. 教室里应该禁止使用手机，学校应该限制数字教学的时间，以遏制儿童的近视率。

cemetery ['semɪtri] *n.* 坟墓，墓地，坟场

巧记 同义词 grave, tomb

诵读 The site had fallen into neglect, until it was used again as a cemetery 2,600 years later. 这个地区一直被疏忽，直到2 600年后才被作为墓地重新使用。

center ['sentə] *n.* 中心 *v.* 以……为中心

搭配 center on... 以……为中心；聚焦

诵读 The Chinese center aims to turn out 5,000 students over the next five years. 这个汉语中心的目标是在今后的五年里培养5 000名学生。

ceremony ['serɪməni] *n.* 典礼，仪式；礼节

搭配 oath-taking ceremony 宣誓仪式

诵读 The appointed hour of the ceremony was drawing nearer. 典礼的约定时间就快到了。

certify ['sɜːtɪfaɪ] *vt.* 证明，证实

拓展 certificate *n.* 证书，执照

诵读 Each year they audit our accounts and certify them as being true and fair. 他们每年对我们进行账务审核，以确保真实无误。

challenge ['tʃælɪndʒ] *n.* 挑战；难题 *vt.* 向……挑战

搭配 take up challenge 应对挑战；intellectual and emotional challenges 智力和情感挑战；external challenge 外部挑战

诵读 This Italian restaurant, which prides itself on strong pasta sales, says it's ready to tackle the challenge. 这家以意大利面销售强劲而著称的意大利餐厅说，他们准备迎接挑战。

champion ['tʃæmpjən] *n.* 冠军

诵读 They have won the table tennis world champions in men and women's singles. 他们获得了男女乒乓球单打世界冠军。

channel ['tʃænl] *n.* 海峡

辨义 *n.* 途径

诵读 They will try to resolve the problem through diplomatic channels. 他们将试图通过外交途径解决问题。

charge [tʃɑːdʒ] *vt.* 控告；充电；收费

搭配 in charge of 负责；free of charge 免费

诵读 I was charged fifty cents for mending a pair of shoes. 我花了50美分修一双鞋。

charm [tʃɑːm] *n.* 吸引力，魅力

巧记 attract 指客观上吸引人的注意力；charm 侧重迷住某人或使之高兴；fascinate 通常含使人无法拒绝、无法摆脱的意味；tempt 强调欲望被唤醒。

诵读 He was a man of great charm and distinction. 他这个人魅力十足，卓尔不群。

chart [tʃɑːt] *n.* 图表

巧记 同义词 graph

诵读 The course of a ship is marked on a chart. 轮船的航线是标在航海图上的。

chase [tʃeɪs] *vt.* 追逐，追求

诵读 The librarians are busy chasing books called for by readers. 图书馆工作人员正忙于寻找读者要借的书。

cheat [tʃiːt] *vt.* 欺骗；作弊

诵读 He cheated me into the belief that he would go away. 他骗我说他要走了。

cheque [tʃek] *n.* 支票；总收入

诵读 He opened him a bad cheque. 他给他开了一张空头支票。

childhood [ˈtʃaɪldhʊd] *n.* 幼年，童年

诵读 A happy childhood helps to give children security. 幸福的童年有助于培养孩子的安全感。

chill [tʃɪl] *n.* 寒冷，寒气，寒战 *v.* 使寒冷

诵读 I was chilled to the bone. 我感到寒气刺骨。

chin [tʃɪn] *n.* 下巴

诵读 His chin was completely covered by his beard. 他的下巴长满了胡子。

choke [tʃəʊk] *v.* 窒息，堵塞，阻塞

诵读 The smoke almost choked me. 烟呛得我几乎透不过气。

chop [tʃɒp] *vt.* 砍，劈

诵读 They chopped a way through the undergrowth. 他们在矮树丛中劈出一条路来。

citizen [ˈsɪtɪzən] *n.* 公民，市民，平民

诵读 Every citizen is entitled to effective and accessible health services. 每个公民都有权获得有效的、可获得的卫生服务。

cigarette [ˌsɪɡəˈret] *n.* 香烟，纸烟，卷烟

诵读 According to the regulation, selling cigarettes and alcohol to minors is banned. 根据该规定，禁止向未成年人出售香烟和酒。

circle [ˈsɜːkl] *n.* 环状物；圈子 *vt.* 围绕，环绕

僻义 *n.* 周期，循环

拓展 circular *a.* 圆的；circus *n.* 马戏团，圆形广场

诵读 He has a large circle of friends. 他交际很广。

cite [saɪt] *vt.* 引用，引证，举（例）

诵读 This paper cites a line of verse. 这篇论文引用了一行诗。

civil [ˈsɪvl] *a.* 公民的，市民的，民间的

拓展 civilian *n.* 平民 *a.* 平民的；civiliza-tion *n.* 文明

诵读 The Chinese civilization is one of the oldest in the world. 中华文明是世界上最古老的文明之一。

classic [ˈklæsɪk] *n.*（*pl.*）杰作，名著 *a.* 第一流的，不朽的

巧记 辨析 classical *a.* 古典的

诵读 There are a great many classic works in China that have prevail over centuries and still resonate emotionally with people. 中国拥有大量的经典作品。它们已经流行了几个世纪，仍能引起人们的情感共鸣。

classify [ˈklæsɪfaɪ] *vt.* 分类

拓展 classification *n.* 分类

诵读 Mail is classified according to the place where it is to go. 邮件按寄送地点分类。

click [klɪk] *n.&vt.* 点击

诵读 Click the square icon again to minimize the window. 再次点击正方形图标，把窗口最小化。

client [ˈklaɪənt] *n.*（律师等的）当事人；顾客

诵读 She can't come to the telephone; she's serving a client. 她不能来接电话，她正在接待一位顾客。

cliff [klɪf] *n.* 悬崖；峭壁

诵读 It's almost impossible to climb up the cliff. 要爬上这个峭壁几乎是不可能的。

climate [ˈklaɪmɪt] *n.* 气候

僻义 *n.* 风气，社会思潮

诵读 Coffee trees will not grow in cold climates. 咖啡树不能生长在寒冷的气候下。

climax [ˈklaɪmæks] *n.* 顶点，高潮

巧记 summit 指山的最顶峰部分，也指通过努力可以达到的最高水平；climax 指临近尾声的精彩部分，戏剧等的高潮；peak 指山峰的全部或上部；top 可指包括人或物或其他任何的最高点或顶点。

诵读 For Pritchard, reaching an Olympics was the climax of her career. 对普里查德来说，参加奥运会是她事业上的巅峰。

cling [klɪŋ] *vi.* 粘住

搭配 cling to 坚持，墨守

诵读 They know scholars reject their legend, but

they still cling to their belief. 尽管他们知道学者们不相信他们的传说，他们还是坚持自己的信仰。

closet [ˈklɒzɪt] *n.* 壁橱 *a.* 私下的

诵读 I'll clear out that closet for you. 我会替你把衣橱清理干净。

clue [kluː] *n.* 线索，暗示

诵读 He worked very hard to find a clue to the problem. 他努力寻找解决问题的线索。

companion [kəmˈpænjən] *n.* 同伴，伙伴

搭配 make a companion of... 与……为友

辨义 *n.* 指南，手册

诵读 The companion volume will soon be published. 这卷书的姊妹篇即将问世。

company [ˈkʌmpəni] *n.* 公司；陪伴 *vt.* 陪伴

搭配 be in good company 与优秀的人在一起；in company 一起

辨义 *n.* 一群人；集会

诵读 Never keep company with dishonest people. 绝不要和不诚实的人来往。

condition [kənˈdɪʃən] *n.* 状况，状态；健康状况

搭配 in/out of condition 健康状况良好或不佳；on condition that... 在……条件下

辨义 *vt.* 限制；使适应

诵读 You can go swimming on condition that you don't go too far from the river bank. 你只有在不远离河岸的条件下才可以去游泳。

connect [kəˈnekt] *vt.* 连接，联结；由……联想到

搭配 be connected with/to... 和……有联系

诵读 High-speed trains that connect Beijing to Zhangjiakou have shrunk travel time from four hours to about an hour. 连接北京和张家口的高铁已将旅行时间从4小时缩短到1小时左右。

consider [kənˈsɪdə] *v.* 考虑 *vt.* 把……看作，认为

搭配 take... into consideration 考虑……

诵读 Perhaps you should consider adopting me as your permanent mentor. 也许你应该考虑下选我当你的终身顾问。

construction [kənˈstrʌkʃən] *n.* 建造，建设

搭配 under construction 修建中

诵读 The new building is a very solid construction. 新建的大楼非常坚固。

contain [kənˈteɪn] *vt.* 包含；容纳

诵读 Whisky contains a large percentage of alcohol. 威士忌的酒精含量很高。

content [ˈkɒntent] *n.* 内容；(*pl.*) 目录

辨义 [kənˈtent] *a.* 满足的 *n.* 满意

搭配 be content with 沉迷于；be content to do sth. 乐于做某事；do sth. to one's heart's content 随心所欲地做某事

诵读 We can swim in the river to our hearts' content. 我们可以在河里尽情地游泳。

continent [ˈkɒntɪnənt] *n.* 洲，大陆

诵读 It's incredible to think that you are now living on another continent. 很难想象你现在生活在另一个洲。

convenient [kənˈviːnjənt] *a.* 方便的，便利的

拓展 convenience store 便利店

诵读 This is a convenient tool for the job. 这个工具用于做这项工作很方便。

corner [ˈkɔːnə] *n.* 角，角落

搭配 around the corner 即将来临，在近处；on every corner 到处；处处

辨义 *n.* 困境 *vt.* 逼入困境

诵读 Experience told him that danger lurked just around the corner. 他凭经验判断出危险就在身旁。

cough [kɒf] *vi.&n.* 咳嗽

诵读 Her huge cough startled me. 她咳嗽的声音很大，吓了我一跳。

count [kaʊnt] *vi.* 数

搭配 count on 依靠，期待，指望

辨义 *vi.* 有价值，有重要意义

诵读 I count myself fortunate in being there. 我认为我能在那里实在很幸运。

course [kɔːs] *n.* 课程；进程，过程

搭配 in the course of... 在……过程中

诵读 The railway is in the course of construction. 铁路正在修建中。

code [kəʊd] *n.* 代码，代号，密码

辨义 *n.* 法典，法规；规划

诵读 Mutual respect is a basic code of behavior for individuals. 相互尊重是个人行为的基本准则。

column [ˈkɒləm] *n.* 柱状物；（报刊中的）专栏

诵读 Wondering what to write about for this column, I made a list of the week's news and events that could be of interest. 考虑本期专栏该写些什么的时候，我把过去一周可能让人感兴趣的新闻和事件写在一份清单上。

combat [ˈkɒmbət] *vt.&n.* 战斗，搏斗

巧记 前缀 com-共同+词根 bat 打击=共同打→战斗

诵读 A bigger army would help, but it will take years to recruit and train new combat units. 更庞大的军队可能有所助益，但招募新兵以及训练出新的战队要花费数年。

comedy [ˈkɒmɪdi] *n.* 喜剧；喜剧性事件

拓展 comic *a.* 喜剧的，滑稽的

巧记 反义词 tragedy *n.* 悲剧

诵读 Life is a comedy to him who thinks and a tragedy to him who feels. 对于理性的人来说，生活是一出喜剧，而对于感性的人来说，生活是一出悲剧。

command [kəˈmɑːnd] *v.* 命令；指挥 *n.* 命令

巧记 前缀 com- 一起+mand 命令=命令，指挥

诵读 He commanded the soldiers to shut the gate. 他命令士兵们把大门关上。

commemorate [kəˈmeməreɪt] *vt.* 纪念，庆祝

巧记 前缀 com-共同+词根 memorate=memory（*n.* 记忆）=大家都记住→纪念

诵读 That is really what I should commemorate. 这才是真正值得庆祝的地方。

commit [kəˈmɪt] *v.* 委托；犯（错误），干（坏事）

搭配 commit crimes 犯罪；commit oneself to 致力于

诵读 He has committed a serious crime. 他犯下了严重罪行。

committee [kəˈmɪti] *n.* 委员会，全体委员

诵读 He had been on the Nobel Prize committee's list of possibles. 他在诺贝尔委员会列出的获奖候选者名单之列。

commodity [kəˈmɒdɪti] *n.* 日用品；商品

诵读 The inspection of commodity is no easy job. 商检工作不是那么简单。

commonplace [ˈkɒmənpleɪs] *a.* 普通的，平庸的 *n.* 寻常之物

巧记 合成词 common 普通的+place 地方→这个地方很普通

诵读 Scientists hope one day 3D food printer will be as commonplace as the microwave oven. 科学家希望有朝一日3D食物"打印机"能跟微波炉一样在日常生活中得到普及。

communicate [kəˈmjuːnɪkeɪt] *v.* 传达，传送

拓展 communications *n.* 电信

诵读 Family therapy showed us how to communicate with each other. 家庭疗法教会了我们彼此之间如何沟通交流。

community [kəˈmjuːnɪti] *n.* 社会；社区

搭配 community service 社区服务

诵读 The Belt and Road Initiative aligns with the concept of a global community of shared future. "一带一路"倡议契合人类命运共同体理念。

comparison [kəmˈpærɪsən] *n.* 比较，类比

拓展 comparable *a.* 可比较的；comparability *n.* 可比性，相似性

诵读 In comparison, at Bank of America Corp., 17% of its total revenue came from credit-card-related services in 2015. 相比之下，2015 年美国银行的信用卡相关业务所创造的收入占该行总收入的 17%。

compensate [ˈkɒmpenseɪt] *vi.* 补偿，赔偿

搭配 compensate for... 为……赔偿

僻义 *vt.* 获得报酬

诵读 If a tax motivates firms to trim health benefits, they should increase salaries to compensate. 如果一项税收促使公司削减员工的健康福利，他们将会以提高工资作为补偿。

compete [kəmˈpiːt] *vi.* 比赛；竞争

巧记 前缀 com-共同+词根 pet追赶=共同为一个目标追赶→竞争

拓展 competent *a.* 有能力的，能胜任的；competition *n.* 竞争，比赛；competitive *a.* 竞争的，（价格等）有竞争力的

诵读 On education, the President said America's ability to compete globally is declining. 在教育问题上，总统说，美国的全球竞争力在下降。

complain [kəmˈpleɪn] *vi.* 抱怨

搭配 complain about/of 抱怨；申诉

拓展 complaint *n.* 抱怨，诉苦

诵读 He who makes constant complaint gets little

compassion. 总是抱怨的人得到的同情也少。

compose [kəmˈpəʊz] v. 组成，构成

巧记 前缀 com-共同+词根 pose 放→把所有的元素都放在一起→组成

搭配 be composed of... 由……组成=consist of...

诵读 Most software programs allow you to compose emails offline. 大部分软件程序允许用户在脱机状态下写电子邮件。

comprehend [ˌkɒmprɪˈhend] vt. 理解，领会

拓展 comprehension n. 理解

辨析 comprehensive 作为形容词既有"理解"的含义，也有"内容广泛的，综合的"的意思，如 comprehensive universities 综合性大学

诵读 They can neither read nor write, nor can they comprehend such concepts. 他们不会读，不会写，也理解不了这样的概念。

compulsory [kəmˈpʌlsəri] a. 强制的；必修的

搭配 compulsory education 义务教育；compulsory courses 必修课

诵读 Free compulsory education became available to all students, urban or rural, throughout the country. 全面实行城乡免费义务教育。

compute [kəmˈpjuːt] vt. 计算，估计

巧记 computer 的动词

诵读 In the days before computers and calculators, a simple equation was more useful because it was easier to compute without errors. 在发明电子计算机和计算器之前，简单方程更有用，因为用它计算起来不易出错。

concentrate [ˈkɒnsəntreɪt] vi. 集中，专心

搭配 concentrate on 集中，专心于

拓展 concentration n. 专心，专注；集中

诵读 They can affect your work performance by making you unable to concentrate and carry out your normal routine. 它们（冬季抑郁）会影响你的工作表现，使你无法集中精力，无法正常进行日常工作。

concept [ˈkɒnsept] n. 概念，观念，设想

巧记 经典教材 New Concept English《新概念英语》

诵读 But this whole concept is new here, and people don't naturally want to share things as much. 但这里的观念跟西方完全不同，人们不喜欢共用东西。

concern [kənˈsɜːn] vt. 涉及，关系到 n. 关心

搭配 be concerned about/with/to... 对……很关心

拓展 concerning prep. 关于，论及

诵读 In recent years, anxiety about job hunting, employment and workplace relationships has become a concern for many young people. 近年来，对求职、就业和职场关系的焦虑已成为许多年轻人关注的问题。

concert [ˈkɒnsət] n. 音乐会，演奏会

拓展 n. 一致

诵读 She told reporters she was looking forward to the concert. 她表示自己很期待这场演唱会。

conclude [kənˈkluːd] v. 结束，下结论

巧记 前缀 con- 全部+clude 关闭→讨论结束了→结束，终止；下结论

拓展 conclusion n. 结论，推论

诵读 They conclude that these genes can make a big difference in a person's intelligence. 他们得出结论是这些基因能使人的智力产生很大的差异。

conduct [kənˈdʌkt] vt. 引导；指挥

僻义 n. 行为，品行

拓展 conductor n. 管理者；领队；指挥

诵读 The city will conduct a comprehensive inspection of potential safety hazards, with particular attention to risks arising from accumulated snow, icy conditions and strong winds. 该市将对潜在的安全隐患进行全面检查，特别关注积雪、结冰和强风带来的风险。

confer [kənˈfɜː] vi. 商讨；授予，颁给

巧记 前缀 con-共同+词根 fer带来=把各自的想法都带过来→讨论

拓展 conference n. 会议；讨论

诵读 He wanted to confer with his colleagues before reaching a decision. 他想与他的同事先商议一下再做决定。

confess [kənˈfes] v. 供认，承认，坦白

巧记 前缀 con-全部+词根 fess说=全都说出来→坦白

诵读 Right off I want to confess that I was wrong. 我立刻就想承认我错了。

confident [ˈkɒnfɪdənt] a. 确信的，自信的

搭配 confidence n. 信心，自信

辨析 同形词 confidential a. 秘密的，机密的

诵读 Two reports show U.S. consumer confidence

dropping to the lowest level ever recorded. 两份经济报告显示，美国消费者信心降至有纪录以来的最低点。

confine [kənˈfaɪn] *vt.* 限制；使不外出

巧记 前缀 con-加强语气+词根 fine 限制=限制

诵读 His genius was not confined to the decoration of buildings. 他的天赋不单体现在建筑物的装饰上。

confirm [kənˈfɜːm] *v.* 证实；确认

巧记 前缀 con-加强语气+词根 firm 坚定

辨析 形近词 conform *vi.* 遵守；使一致

诵读 Earlier reports were unable to confirm that there were any survivors. 早先的报道无法证实是否有幸存者。

conflict [ˈkɒnflɪkt] *n.&vi.* 斗争；冲突

搭配 controversy, argument, dispute 与 conflict 均有"争执，不和"之意

诵读 Employees already are in conflict with management over job cuts. 雇员已经就裁员一事与管理层发生了争执。

confront [kənˈfrʌnt] *vt.* 使面临；面对

巧记 前缀 con-加强语气+词根 front 面→面对

搭配 be confronted with 遇到，遭遇

诵读 In fact, developing countries are confronted with even greater impacts from climate change. 事实上，发展中国家面临的气候变化影响更大。

confuse [kənˈfjuːz] *vt.* 使混乱，混淆

巧记 前缀 con-共同+词根 fuse 流=不同的东西流动到一起→混淆

拓展 confusion *n.* 困惑，糊涂

诵读 To further confuse the issue, there is an enormous variation in the amount of sleep people feel happy with. 使问题进一步复杂化的是，每个人需要的睡眠时间千差万别。

congratulate [kənˈɡrætjʊleɪt] *vt.* 祝贺

拓展 congratulation *n.* 祝贺

诵读 On behalf of the government, I want to extend cordial welcome to all the guests, and warm congratulation to this session! 我代表政府，向各位来宾表示诚挚的欢迎，向大会表示热烈的祝贺！

congress [ˈkɒŋɡres] *n.* 国会，议会

诵读 There were some days to wait before the Congress. 距离大会召开还有几天时间。

conquer [ˈkɒŋkə] *vt.* 征服；占领；克服

拓展 conquest *n.* 征服；战利品

诵读 Wang Jinxi's unyielding spirit to conquer extreme fatigue and physical limits earned him the nickname of "Iron Man". 王进喜克服极度疲劳和身体极限的不屈精神为他赢得了"铁人"的称号。

conscience [ˈkɒnʃəns] *n.* 良心，良知

拓展 conscientious *a.* 认真的，本着良心的

诵读 I have a clear conscience because I am a conscientious worker. 我问心无愧，因为我是一个尽职的员工。

conscious [ˈkɒnʃəs] *a.* 意识到的；神志清醒的

巧记 前缀 con-加强语气+词根 sci 知道+后缀 -ous=意识到

诵读 They are conscious of being watched. 他们意识到有人在监视他们。

consequence [ˈkɒnsɪkwəns] *n.* 结果，后果

拓展 consequently *ad.* 结果，因此，所以

诵读 If you behave so foolishly, you must be ready to take the consequences, and accept what happens as a result. 如果你这样愚昧下去，你必须做好自食恶果的准备。

considerate [kənˈsɪdərɪt] *a.* 考虑周到的，体谅的

拓展 consideration *n.* 需要考虑的事，理由

诵读 It was considerate of you not to play the piano while I was having a sleep. 我睡觉时你没有弹钢琴，你真是考虑得周到。

consistent [kənˈsɪstənt] *a.* 前后一致的

搭配 be consistent with 一致，符合

诵读 He has been a consistent friend to me. 他是我历久不渝的朋友。

constant [ˈkɒnstənt] *a.* 固定的，持续的

诵读 He has been constant in his devotion to scientific studies. 他坚持投身于科学研究。

constitute [ˈkɒnstɪtjuːt] *vt.* 组成；制定；建立

巧记 前缀 con-加强语气+词根 stitute 创立（根据 institute 研究所，机构）

拓展 constituent *n.* 选民；成分 constitution *n.* 构造

诵读 Only people with strong constitutions should climb in the Himalayas. 只有体格健壮的人可以攀登喜马拉雅山。

constrain [kənˈstreɪn] *vt.* 限制，约束；克制，抑制

巧记 前缀 con-加强语气+词根 strain 拉紧=约束

诵读 I feel constrained to apologize to you. 我觉得非向你表示敬意不可。

construct [kənˈstrʌkt] *vt.* 建设，建造

拓展 construction *n.* 建造，构造

诵读 Constructing a new bridge across the river is her dream. 在河上建一座新桥是她的梦想。

consult [kənˈsʌlt] *vt.* 咨询；查阅，查看

搭配 consult sb. about sth. 向某人讨教某事；consult with 商议

拓展 consultant *n.* 顾问

诵读 They consulted long, but could not decide. 他们磋商了很久，但是没能做出决定。

consume [kənˈsjuːm] *vt.* 消耗；吃完，喝光

拓展 consumption *n.* 消费（量），消耗

诵读 He soon consumed his fortune, and spent the money wastefully. 他很快把他的财产挥霍殆尽。

contact [ˈkɒntækt] *vt.&n.* 联系，交往

诵读 Our troops are in contact with the enemy. 我们的部队已与敌军接触。

contend [kənˈtend] *vi.* 坚决主张；竞争

搭配 contend against… 与……争斗；contend with… 与……竞争

诵读 The man contended that he had witnessed the killing of the innocent people by the robber. 那人坚决肯定他亲自看见抢劫犯屠杀无辜群众的情景。

contest [kənˈtest] *n.* 竞争，竞赛，比赛

巧记 前缀 con-共同+词根 test 测试=一起参加测试

诵读 He's contesting the election next week. 他在争取下周当选。

context [ˈkɒntekst] *n.* 上下文；背景

诵读 Can't you guess the meaning of the word from the context? 你不能从上下文猜出此词的意义吗？

continue [kənˈtɪnjuː] *v.* 持续

辨析 continuous *a.* 连续不断的；continual *a.* 频繁的

诵读 Aren't you tired of this continual rain? 雨一直下，你不觉得厌烦吗？

contract [ˈkɒntrækt] *n.* 合同/契约 [kənˈtrækt] *vi.* 缩小

巧记 前缀 con-共同+词根 tract 引，拉=拉到一起→缩小差异，定制合同

搭配 break/breach/violate a contract 违约；cancel a contract 取消合同；carry out/execute a contract 履行合同

诵读 The work will be done by a private contract. 这项工作将包给私人做。

contradict [ˌkɒntrəˈdɪkt] *v.* 反驳；相抵触

拓展 contradiction *n.* 矛盾，不一致

诵读 Your statements today contradicted each other. 你们今天的声明自相矛盾。

contrary [ˈkɒntrəri] *a.* 相反的，矛盾的

搭配 on the contrary 相反

诵读 "Hot" and "cold" are contrary terms. 热与冷是相反之词。

contrast [ˈkɒntrɑːst] *n.* 对比，对照 [kənˈtrɑːst] *v.* 形成对比

搭配 by/in contrast 对比而言

诵读 His white hair was in sharp contrast to his dark skin. 他的白发与他的黑皮肤形成鲜明对比。

contribute [kənˈtrɪbjʊt] *v.* 贡献，捐助

搭配 contribute to 做贡献；导致

拓展 contribution *n.* 贡献；捐款

诵读 Do you consider contributions to the village funds a duty or a pleasure? 你认为捐款给村庄基金是义务还是乐事？

controversy [ˈkɒntrəvɜːsi] *n.* 争论，辩论，争吵

巧记 前缀 contr-相反+词根 vers 转+后缀 -y =转到相反一面→争论，不同意见

拓展 controversial *a.* 引起争论的，有争议的

诵读 The use of facial recognition has sparked controversy in some countries. 人脸识别的使用在一些国家引发了争议。

convention [kənˈvenʃən] *n.* 大会，会议

僻义 *n.* 惯例，常规，习俗

拓展 conventional *a.* 惯例的，常规的

诵读 At the recent convention a declaration was adopted. 在最近举行的大会上通过了一项宣言。

conversely [ˈkɒnvɜːsli] *ad.* 相反地

巧记 前缀 con-加强语气+词根 vers 转=相反

拓展 conversion *n.* 转变，转换；convert *vt.* 变换，转换

诵读 He placed the box conversely. 他把箱子放倒了。

convey [kənˈveɪ] *vt.* 运送；传达，传播

诵读 Every word conveys some meaning. 每一个词都有某种意义。

convince [kənˈvɪns] *v.* 使信服，使确信

搭配 convince sb. of sth. 说服某人相信某事；be convinced that 相信

诵读 I am convinced of his honesty. 我相信他的诚实。

cooperate [kəʊˈɒpəreɪt] *vi.* 合作，协作，相配合

拓展 cooperative *a.* 合作的，协作的

巧记 同义词 coordinate *v.* 协调 *adj.* 同等的

诵读 Everything cooperated to make our holiday a success. 所有的一切相配合使我们的假期圆满结束。

cope [kəʊp] *vi.* 对付，妥善处理

搭配 cope with 处理

诵读 He coped effectively with his opponent. 他有效地应对了他的对手。

core [kɔː] *n.* 果核；中心，核心

诵读 It's important to strengthen innovation capacities in sci-tech and achieve breakthroughs in core technologies in key fields so as to enhance the country's core competitiveness. 重要的是加强科技创新能力建设，在关键领域突破核心技术，提高国家核心竞争力。

corporation [ˌkɔːpəˈreɪʃən] *n.* 公司，企业

诵读 The corporation was founded in 2006. 这家公司成立于 2006 年。

correlate [ˈkɒrɪleɪt] *vi.* 互相关联

搭配 correlate with 与……有联系=be linked with

诵读 These figures seem to correlate. 这些数字看来是相关的。

correspond [ˌkɒrɪsˈpɒnd] *vi.* 符合；类似于

巧记 前缀 cor-共同+词根 respond 做出反应=做出相同的反应→相一致，相符合

搭配 correspond to/with… 与……相符

拓展 correspondence *n.* 符合；通信；correspondent *n.* 记者，通讯员；corresponding *a.* 符合的，相应的

诵读 The house exactly corresponds with my needs. 这房子恰好符合我的需要。

cost [kɒst] *n.* 成本；代价 *vt.* 价值为，花费

搭配 cost price 成本价；at the cost of 以……为代价

拓展 costly *a.* 昂贵的，价值高的

诵读 He built his house without regard to cost, without considering how much money would be needed. 他盖他的房子没有考虑花钱多少。

costume [ˈkɒstjuːm] *n.* （流行的）服饰

诵读 The actor came on in full costume. 那位男演员身穿全套戏装登场。

cosy [ˈkəʊzi] *a.* 暖和舒服的；舒适的

诵读 We spent a cosy evening chatting by the fire. 我们在炉火旁聊天度过了一个舒适的晚上。

council [ˈkaʊnsl] *n.* 理事会，委员会，议事机构

诵读 The matter was debated in the Security Council of the United Nations. 这个问题在联合国安全理事会辩论过。

counsel [ˈkaʊnsəl] *v.* 劝告 *n.* 辩护律师；忠告，辩护人

诵读 I would counsel you to say nothing about the affair. 我劝你对这件事什么也别说。

counter [ˈkaʊntə] *n.* 柜台

僻义 *vt.* 反对，反击

诵读 They countered our proposal with one of their own. 他们提出一项建议以反对我们的建议。

counterpart [ˈkaʊntəpɑːt] *n.* 对应的人（或物）

诵读 LED signs offer more vibrant colors and a softer glow compared with their neon counterparts. 与霓虹灯相比，LED标识提供了更鲜艳的颜色和更柔和的光。

court [kɔːt] *n.* 法院；院子；球场

诵读 The prisoner was brought to court for trial. 那囚犯被带上法庭受审。

courtesy [ˈkɜːtɪsi] *n.* 谦恭有礼；有礼貌的举止

诵读 In fact, it seems that a little more courtesy could save businesses £5 billion every year. 事实表明，对员工以礼相待每年能为公司节省 50 亿英镑的支出。

credit [ˈkredɪt] *n.* 信用；学分；存款数额

僻义 *n.* 赞扬；名誉，名望

搭配 give sb. credit for 称赞某人

诵读 He is a man of the highest credit. 他是一个极有名望的人。

crop [krɒp] *n.* 庄稼；种植 *vi.* 收成

搭配 crop out 露出地面；crop up 意外地出现；a crop of 一大堆；一批

诵读 The annual crop of students brings a new crop of ideas. 每年新生都会带来一些新的想法。

cross [krɒs] *n.* 十字架；苦难 *v.* 穿过，越过

辨义 *a.* 坏脾气的；相反的

搭配 be cross with 生气，发脾气；cross out 删除

诵读 Two of the words have been crossed out. 其中有两个字被删去了。

crack [kræk] *vi.*(使）破裂，砸开；失去控制

巧记 中国人过年放的鞭炮用 cracker 来表示。

诵读 She's calm and strong, and she is just not going to crack. 她镇定而且坚强，绝不会垮掉。

cradle [ˈkreɪdl] *n.* 摇篮；发源地

搭配 from cradle to grave 从摇篮到坟墓

诵读 Now experts fear that global warming linked to carbon emissions will have its worst impact on humanity's cradle. 现在让专家们备感担心的是，与碳排放有关联的全球变暖的趋势将会给这片广袤的大地带来最坏的影响。

craft [krɑːft] *n.* 工艺，手艺，技巧

拓展 crafty *a.* 狡猾的，有手段的

诵读 Many museums now display Aboriginal art and craft as well as musical instruments. 现在有很多博物馆展示土著艺术和手工艺品以及乐器。

crawl [krɔːl] *vi.&n.* 爬行，蠕动

诵读 Baby girls make a beeline for dolls as soon as they can crawl and boys will head for the toy cars. 当女婴刚学会爬的时候，她们通常都会直接爬向娃娃，而男婴则会爬向玩具汽车。

create [kriˈeɪt] *vt.* 创造，创作；造成

拓展 creative *a.* 有创造力的，创造性的

诵读 Having a husband creates an extra seven hours of housework each week for women, according to a new study. 一项最新研究发现，女人有了丈夫后每周得多做七个小时的家务活。

creature [ˈkriːtʃə] *n.* 人，动物，生物

诵读 At first glance it may look like a fearsome snake but this rearing creature is actually a small caterpillar with a cunning means of defense. 第一眼看上去可能会以为它是一条可怕的蛇，但实际上这种饲养的生物是由一只小毛毛虫伪装而成的。

crew [kruː] *n.* 全体船员，全体乘务员

诵读 However, for the crew members involved, it was a labour of love. 而参与这项工作的乘务人员也乐此不疲。

crime [kraɪm] *n.* 罪行，犯罪

拓展 criminal *n.* 罪犯，刑事犯

诵读 The police will continue to heighten its crackdown on the crime of telecom fraud and online gambling. 警方将继续加大对电信诈骗和网络赌博犯罪的打击力度。

crisis [ˈkraɪsɪs] *n.* 危机，紧要关头

搭配 economic crisis 经济危机

诵读 More than 20 million rural migrant workers in the country have lost their jobs and returned to their home villages or towns as a result of the global economic crisis. 受全球经济危机影响，该国有超过 2 000 万外来务工人员失业并返乡。

critic [ˈkrɪtɪk] *n.* 批评家，评论家

拓展 critical *a.* 批评的；criticism *n.* 评论性的文章，评论；criticize *v.* 批评

诵读 Ebert, a Chicago film critic with a nationwide following, had emergency cancer surgery recently. 伊伯特是芝加哥的一位影评人，在美国拥有众多崇拜者。近日，他因患癌症做了急救手术。

crowd [kraʊd] *n.* 人群；一群 *v.* 聚集；挤满

搭配 in a big crowd 在拥挤的环境中

诵读 Many of the villagers gathered in an angry crowd. 许多村民聚集到一起，汇成了愤怒的人群。

crucial [ˈkruːʃəl] *a.* 至关重要的，决定性的

诵读 The crucial point here is whether it's welcomed by the people. 关键是老百姓欢不欢迎。

crude [kruːd] *a.* 天然的；粗鲁的 *n.* 原油；石油

搭配 crude oil 原油

诵读 Crude oil in New York has gained 9 percent since China last increased prices on Oct. 26th. 在中国于 10 月 26 日第二次上涨油价之后，纽约的原油价格上涨了 9 个百分点。

cue [kjuː] *n.* 暗示，提示

诵读 Trading on Wednesday will likely take a cue from what the President says. 周三的交易很可能将受到总统演讲内容的影响。

cultivate [ˈkʌltɪveɪt] *vt.* 耕作；培养，磨炼

诵读 We need to cultivate areas of high consumer demand and expand consumption in new areas. 我们

要深耕消费热点区域,拓展消费新领域。

cunning [ˈkʌnɪŋ] *a.* 狡猾的

诵读 He is as cunning as a fox. 他像狐狸一样狡猾。

curb [kɜːb] *n.* (由条石砌成的)路缘

僻义 *vt.* 制止,抑制

巧记 cur(=curr 跑)+b 不=不能跑了→抑制

诵读 APEC ministers vowed to curb trade barriers and eliminate protectionism on the final day of their two-day meeting. 亚太经合组织(APEC)成员的部长们在两天会晤的最后一天承诺遏制贸易壁垒,消除保护主义。

curiosity [ˌkjʊərɪˈɒsɪti] *n.* 好奇心;古董,古玩

诵读 Science popularization is missioned to light up children's curiosity and to stimulate them to explore science and the unknown. 科普的使命是点燃孩子们的好奇心,激发他们探索科学和未知。

curl [kɜːl] *vt.&vi.* (使)卷曲

诵读 If you find sit-ups difficult, try the reverse curl instead, for it's just as effective but easier on the back. 如果你觉得做仰卧起坐有困难,那就改做反向卷腹吧,因为这同样有效,并且对背部的压力更小。

current [ˈkʌrənt] *n.* 电流;水流,趋势 *a.* 当前的

拓展 currency *n.* 流传,流通;货币

诵读 What is worth studying, or worth hearing, is subject to objective criteria independent of current fashion. 什么是值得研究或倾听的,这要符合不受当前潮流影响的客观标准。

curse [kɜːs] *n.* 诅咒 *v.* 咒骂

诵读 The ancient Egyptian scientists to "the curse" saying, always have other views. 古埃及学家对"诅咒"之说,一向有其他看法。

curve [kɜːv] *n.* 曲线,弯曲(物)

诵读 In other words, current prices—and the steep yield curve—reflect this level of supply.
换言之,当前的价格以及陡峭的收益率曲线反映了这种供应水平。

customary [ˈkʌstəməri] *a.* 习惯的,惯例的

诵读 To prove to a guest that a drink was safe, it became customary for a guest to pour a small amount of his drink into the glass of the host. 为了证实酒是安全的,宾客会把杯中一部分酒倒进主人杯中,这已成为一种习俗。

cycle [ˈsaɪkl] *n.* 自行车;周期,循环 *vt.* 循环

搭配 business cycle 商业周期

诵读 One answer is that the business cycle itself is changing. 答案之一是商业周期本身正在改变。

高 频 词 汇

cave [keɪv] *n.* 洞穴 *v.* 塌落;屈服

诵读 Finally the company caved in to the demands of customers. 最终,公司屈从于顾客们的要求。

cable [ˈkeɪbl] *n.* 电报;电缆

巧记 CNN 的全称为 Cable News Network,美国有线新闻网。

诵读 Not until 1866 was the fully successful transatlantic cable finally laid. 直到 1866 年,第一条横跨大西洋的电缆才铺设成功。

calendar [ˈkælɪndə] *n.* 日历,月历

搭配 Chinese calendar 农历

诵读 Their five-year-old son is able to use the calendar to count how many days it is until his birthday. 他们五岁的儿子能用日历数出离他的生日还有多少天。

cardinal [ˈkɑːdɪnl] *a.* 首要的,基本的

诵读 Doctors commonly view excessive daytime sleepiness as a cardinal sign of disturbed or inadequate sleep. 医生们通常认为白天过度嗜睡是夜晚睡眠时间不足或睡眠紊乱的一个重要信号。

caress [kəˈres] *vt.&n.* 爱抚,抚摸

搭配 caress a pet 爱抚宠物;a tentative caress 勉强的拥抱

诵读 Love is not destroyed by a single failure, nor won by a single caress. 爱情不是因一次失败而毁灭,也不是因一次爱抚而赢得。

cargo [ˈkɑːɡəʊ] *n.* 船货,货物

巧记 合成词 car+go→用车把货物装走

诵读 The cargo was due to be offloaded in Singapore three days later. 货物定于三天后在新加坡卸载。

carve [kɑːv] *vt.* (雕)刻

诵读 The model was carved during the New Kingdom Period but we do not know who it is. 这个模型是在埃及新王国时期雕刻的,但是我们不知道它是谁。

catalogue [ˈkætəlɒg] *n.* 目录

搭配 classified catalogue 分类目录

诵读 We are sending you catalogue under separate cover. 目录将另函寄出。

catastrophe [kəˈtæstrəfi] *n.* 大灾难；结局

巧记 同义词 disaster

诵读 Were they to do so, it would be a catastrophe for the world—causing extraordinary loss of life, and striking a major blow to global peace and stability. 假如他们这么做，将给世界带来巨大的灾难，造成巨大的生命损失，使世界和平与稳定遭受重大的打击。

cellar [ˈselə] *n.* 地窖，地下室

巧记 同义词 basement

诵读 Put down a trail from the basement out to the back yard. Then leave the cellar door open. 从地下室往外铺一条小道直到后院。然后，将地下室的门打开。

cement [sɪˈment] *n.* 水泥；胶泥

辨义 *v.* 巩固，加强

诵读 The report indicates that a bad cement seal on the oil well allowed gas and other liquids to flow up the production pipe. 这份报告表示，油井上一个有问题的水泥塞使得天然气和其他液体通过生产管道涌向海面。

census [ˈsensəs] *n.* 人口普查（调查）

诵读 The census is taken one time every four years in our country. 我国每四年进行一次人口普查。

chamber [ˈtʃeɪmbə] *n.* 房间，室；会议室

巧记 《红楼梦》(Dream of the Red Chamber)

诵读 The design of the chamber is interesting. 房间的设计很有趣。

chaos [ˈkeɪɒs] *n.* 混乱，紊乱

巧记 谐音：吵死了→混乱

搭配 in chaos 处于混乱状态

诵读 The room is of chaos. 那房间太乱了。

charity [ˈtʃærɪti] *n.* 慈善，仁慈，施舍

诵读 He made substantial donations to charity. 他给慈善机构捐了很多钱。

cherish [ˈtʃerɪʃ] *vt.* 珍爱

辨义 *vt.* 怀有（希望等）

诵读 It was a wonderful occasion which we will cherish for many years to come. 那是一个美好的时刻，我们将多年不忘。

chew [tʃuː] *v.* 咀嚼

诵读 You must chew your food well before you swallow it. 你必须充分咀嚼食物再吞下去。

circuit [ˈsɜːkɪt] *n.* 环行，周线，巡回；电路，线路

诵读 We made a circuit of the school campus happily. 我们快乐地绕校园兜了个圈。

clap [klæp] *vi.&n.* 拍手，掌声

诵读 At the end of the performances, the audience clapped. 在演出结束后，观众席掌声不断。

clarity [ˈklærɪti] *n.* 清晰，明晰

巧记 词根clar（=clear）+后缀-ity =清楚

拓展 clarify *v.* 澄清，阐明

诵读 The news commentator analyzed the situation with clarity. 新闻评论员对局势分析得很清楚。

clash [klæʃ] *vi.&n.* 发出碰撞声

巧记 两车 crash（碰撞），相互 crush（挤压），发出 clash（巨大碰撞声）。

诵读 The date clashing with my business, I can't go. 约会与我的工作冲突，我去不成了。

clasp [klɑːsp] *n.* 扣子，钩子 *v.* 扣住，钩住

诵读 Because the clasp has broken, my necklace fell off. 由于项链上的扣子断了，我的项链掉落下来。

clause [klɔːz] *n.* 从句，分句

辨义 *n.*（正式文件或法律文件的）条款

诵读 The sentence consists of a main clause and a subordinate clause. 这句中有一个主句和一个从句。

clay [kleɪ] *n.* 黏土，泥土

诵读 Brick is made from clay. 砖头是由黏土制造的。

clergy [ˈklɜːdʒi] *n.* [总称]牧师，神职人员

诵读 The clergy remain divided on the issue of women priests. 在女性教士的问题上，牧师们意见不一。

clip [klɪp] *n.&vt.* 修剪；夹住

诵读 He is clipping the hedge. 他正在修剪篱笆。

cloak [kləʊk] *n.* 斗篷，披风

辨义 *vt.* 掩盖，掩饰

诵读 She cloaked her sorrow with laughter. 她用笑来掩饰她的悲痛。

clockwise [ˈklɒkwaɪz] *a.& ad.* 顺时针方向

巧记 counter clockwise *a.& ad.* 逆时针方向

诵读 Please turn the key in a clockwise direction. 请顺时针转动钥匙。

clumsy [ˈklʌmzi] *a.* 笨拙的，愚笨的

诵读 His clumsy action made us laugh loudly. 他笨拙的动作把我们逗得大笑。

cluster [ˈklʌstə] *n.* 丛，群，串 *v.* 群集，丛生

诵读 Here and there in the suburbs are newly built houses in clusters. 郊区到处都是新建的住宅区。

coach [kəʊtʃ] *n.* 长途客车；教练 *v.* 训练，指导

诵读 We will leave by coach for Suzhou. 我们将要乘长途汽车去苏州。

coalition [ˌkəʊəˈlɪʃən] *n.* 同盟；联合

巧记 前缀 co-共同+词根 al（=ally 同盟）+后缀-tion→同盟

诵读 The several parties formed a coalition. 这几个政党组成了政治联盟。

coarse [kɔːs] *a.* 粗糙的；粗俗的

诵读 I am sure it must be a coarse imitation. 我肯定这是一个粗糙的仿制品。

cognitive [ˈkɒgnɪtɪv] *a.* 认知的，认识能力的

诵读 This exercise is good for cognitive development. 这项练习有助于认知能力的发展。

cohesive [kəʊˈhiːsɪv] *a.* 黏合性的，有结合力的

诵读 The erosion of cohesive bed is simulated. 模拟了黏性土河床的冲刷特性。

coincide [ˌkəʊɪnˈsaɪd] *vi.* 同时发生；巧合

巧记 前缀 co-共同+in+词根 cide 杀，切=共同切→同时发生

拓展 coincidence *n.* 巧合；同时发生

搭配 coincide with 巧合；相符

诵读 They do not coincide in opinion. 他们的意见不合。

collaborate [kəˈlæbəˌreɪt] *vi.* 协作，合作

巧记 前缀 col- 共同+labor 劳动+ 后缀-ate =合作

搭配 collaborate with sb. in/on…. 与某人合作

诵读 He collaborated on a book with his sister. 他和他的姐姐合著了一本书。

collapse [kəˈlæps] *vi.&n.* 倒塌；崩溃

巧记 同义辨析 collapse 通常指房屋等突然倒塌；fall 一般指由于失去平衡等原因而倒塌

诵读 The roof collapsed under the weight of the snow. 屋顶被雪压塌了。

collide [kəˈlaɪd] *vi.* 互撞，碰撞；冲突，抵触

搭配 collide with… 与……相撞

拓展 collision *n.* 碰撞；冲突，抵触

诵读 Two jets look as though they are about to collide. 两架飞机看起来好像即将发生碰撞。

colony [ˈkɒləni] *n.* 殖民地

拓展 colonize *vt.* 殖民；colonization *n.* 殖民地化；colonial *a.* 殖民地的

诵读 One in ten expect a colony of humans to be living in space in the future. 十分之一的人以为未来会有人移民太空。

commend [kəˈmend] *v.* 称赞，表扬

诵读 We commend the important steps taken by the government to increase protection of workers' rights. 我们对于政府加大员工权利保护的重要措施表示赞赏。

commerce [ˈkɒmɜːs] *n.* 商业，贸易；交际，交往

辨析 同形词 commence *vt.&vi.* 开始

拓展 commercial *a.* 商业的

诵读 Two grocery shops and the general store are the sum total of local commerce. 当地商业总共只有两家杂货店和一家综合商店。

commission [kəˈmɪʃən] *n.* 委员会；委任

巧记 前缀com- 共同 + miss＝mit 送→共同送东西到指定的地方→委托

僻义 *n.* 佣金，手续费

诵读 Are you paid on a salary or a commission basis? 你是按固定薪水算还是按佣金算？

commute [kəˈmjuːt] *vi.* 乘车往返于两地

诵读 We chose to live out of town and commute to work every day. 我们决定住在城外，每天赶路上班。

compact [kəmˈpækt] *a.* 紧密的 *vt.* 使紧凑，压缩

诵读 He looked physically very powerful, athletic in a compact way. 他看上去非常强壮，像个敦实的运动员。

compartment [kəmˈpɑːtmənt] *n.* 车厢；隔间

巧记 前缀 com-共同+part 部分+后缀-ment →几个人共同的部分→隔间

诵读 Six people were travelling in a compartment on a train. 有六个人搭乘火车旅行，坐在同一车厢内。

compassion [kəmˈpæʃən] *n.* 同情；怜悯

巧记 前缀 com-共同+词根 passion 感情=引起共同

感情→同情

诵读 The airline moved quickly to show its compassion for the families of the victims. 航空公司迅速采取行动,对遇难者家属表示同情。

compatible [kəmˈpætəbl] *a.* 兼容的

僻义 *a.* 能和睦相处的,合得来的

诵读 Are your respective career paths compatible? Is either of you going to have to make compromises? Are you prepared to? 你们的职业规划协调一致吗? 是否有人要做出妥协? 你们准备好了吗?

compel [kəmˈpel] *vt.* 强迫,迫使

巧记 前缀 com-共同+词根 pel 推=共同推→强迫

诵读 How will the president compel Americans to buy these cars? 总统将怎样推动美国人买这些汽车?

compile [kəmˈpaɪl] *vt.* 编辑,编制,搜集

巧记 前缀 com-全部+词根 pile 堆=堆到一起→编辑,编制,搜集

诵读 She interviewed 49 couples and 156 other people, and drew on past studies to compile her new book. 为编写新书,她对 49 对夫妇和另外 156 人进行了访问,并借鉴了之前的一些研究成果。

compliment [ˈkɒmplɪmənt] *n.&vt.* 称赞,恭维

巧记 同义词 praise, flattery

辨析 complement *n.* 补足物

诵读 "Since when does he have worldwide influence? It's too big a compliment for him," a netizen said. 一位网友说:"他从什么时候开始具有全球影响力了? 这也太抬举他了。"

comply [kəmˈplaɪ] *vi.* 遵照,照做,应允;顺从

巧记 一起(com)玩(ply)要遵守游戏规则。

搭配 comply with 遵照

诵读 Failure to comply with these conditions will result in termination of the contract. 不遵守这些条件将导致合同终止。

component [kəmˈpəʊnənt] *n.* 组成部分,成分

巧记 前缀 com-共同+词根 pon 放+后缀-ent→把东西放一起

诵读 The menu is all-important. Every component of every meal should create contrasts. 饭菜的安排至关重要。每一顿饭的每一道菜都应该有所不同。

compound [ˈkɒmpaʊnd] *n.* 混合物 *a.* 混合的 *v.* 混合

巧记 compound dictation 复合式听写

诵读 Scientists found "boiled before cut" carrots contained 25% more of the anti-cancer compound than those chopped up first. 科学家发现,"先煮后切"的胡萝卜中所含的抗癌成分,要比"先切后煮"的胡萝卜高出近 25%。

compress [kəmˈpres] *vt.* 压紧,压缩

巧记 前缀 com-共同+词根 press压=一起压→压缩

诵读 They could also convert the gas from the food waste to compressed natural gas, to fuel their trucks. 他们也可以把食物垃圾产生的沼气转换成压缩天然气,给他们的卡车当燃料。

compromise [ˈkɒmprəmaɪz] *n.&vi.* 妥协,折中

巧记 联想记忆:为了对所有人做出妥协,只能一起(com)做出承诺(promise)。

诵读 He would rather shoot himself than compromise his principles. 他宁愿一枪打死自己也不愿违背自己的原则。

conceal [kənˈsiːl] *vt.* 隐藏,隐瞒

诵读 8.7 percent tried to conceal "non-essential" Internet use from family, friends and employers. 8.7% 的受访者不想让家人、朋友和老板知道他们有"不必要的"上网行为。

concede [kənˈsiːd] *vt.* 承认;认输;退让

拓展 concession *n.* 让步,妥协

诵读 This dictionary is generally conceded to be the best in China. 这部词典被公认是中国最好的词典。

conceive [kənˈsiːv] *vi.* 设想,构思;怀胎

诵读 Many people can't conceive of a dinner without meat or fish. 许多人无法想象没有肉和鱼的晚餐。

concise [kənˈsaɪs] *a.* 简明的,简洁的

巧记 前缀con- 共同+cise 切掉→把共同的重复的部分切掉→简洁的

诵读 We felt a need for an up-to-date concise book in this field. 我们认为在本学科领域内需要一本最新的概要书籍。

concrete [ˈkɒnkriːt] *n.* 混凝土

僻义 *a.* 具体的,实质性的 *vt.* 使坚固

诵读 Your decision must be translated into specific, concrete actions. 你的决定必须转化为具体明确的

行动。

condemn [kənˈdem] *vt.* 指责

巧记 前缀 con-加强语气+词根demn（=damn骂人）→指责

诵读 They must unite to condemn the lost of lives. 他们必须联合起来谴责造成人员伤亡的袭击行动。

condense [kənˈdens] *v.* 凝结；浓缩，压缩

巧记 前缀 con-加强语气+词根 dense 密集的，浓厚的=压缩，浓缩

诵读 Cumulus clouds form when humid air cools enough for water vapor to condense into droplets or ice crystals. 当湿润气团冷却到水汽足以冷凝为水珠或冰晶时，便形成积云。

consecutive [kənˈsekjʊtɪv] *a.* 连续的；连贯的

巧记 前缀 con-加强语气+词根 sec 跟随+后缀-utive=一个跟着一个→连续的

诵读 He was reelected for four consecutive terms. 他连任四期。

consensus [kənˈsensəs] *n.* 一致，共识

巧记 前缀 con-共同的+词根 sens 感觉+后缀-us（感觉）=有共同的感觉→共识

诵读 Can we reach a consensus on this issue? 我们能在这个问题上达成一致吗？

consent [kənˈsent] *vi.&n.* 同意，赞成

巧记 前缀 con-共同的+词根 sent=sens 感觉=与……保持相同的感觉→赞成

诵读 Anne's father would not consent to her marrying a foreigner. 安妮的父亲不会答应她嫁给外国人。

conservation [ˌkɒnsəˈveɪʃən] *n.* 保护；保守

拓展 conservative *a.* 保守的，守旧的

诵读 She is interested in environmental conservation. 她对环保感兴趣。

console [kənˈsəʊl] *vt.* 安慰，慰问

巧记 前缀 con-共同+词根 sole 独自=两个个体靠在一起→安慰

诵读 We tried to console her when her husband died. 她的丈夫死后，我们尽力安慰她。

consolidate [kənˈsɒlɪdeɪt] *vt.* 使加固，使加强

巧记 前缀 con-加强语气+词根 solid 固体+后缀-ate =巩固，加强

诵读 We've made a good start, and now it's time to consolidate. 我们有了一个良好的开端，现在应该加以巩固。

conspicuous [kənˈspɪkjʊəs] *a.* 显眼的，明显的

诵读 Traffic signs should be conspicuous. 交通标志应当明显。

conspiracy [kənˈspɪrəsi] *n.* 阴谋，密谋，共谋

巧记 前缀 con-加强语气+词根 spir 呼气+后缀-acy=同呼吸→共谋

诵读 The men were found guilty of conspiracy to murder. 这些人被裁决犯有蓄意谋杀罪。

contaminate [kənˈtæmɪneɪt] *v.* 弄污；染污

巧记 同义词 pollute

诵读 They are contaminating the minds of our young people with these unhealthy ideas. 他们用这些不健康的思想污染我们年轻人的精神。

contemplate [ˈkɒntempleɪt] *vt.* 沉思；注视，凝视

巧记 前缀 con-加强语气+词根 templ 太阳穴+后缀-ate =双手按住太阳穴（联想一休思考动作）

诵读 The possibility of war is too horrifying to contemplate. 要打仗太可怕了，真不堪细想。

contemporary [kənˈtempərəri] *a.* 现代的，当代的

诵读 I intended to deal with contemporary writers in a separate article. 我打算单独写一篇文章论述当代作家。

contempt [kənˈtempt] *n.* 轻视，藐视；受辱，丢脸

巧记 前缀 con-加强语气+词根 tempt 诱惑=一直诱惑别人让人瞧不起

诵读 Such behaviour will bring you into contempt. 这种行为将使你遭受鄙视。

contrive [kənˈtraɪv] *vt.* 谋划，策划；设计

诵读 Can you contrive to be here early? 你能设法早到这里吗？

convict [kənˈvɪkt] *vt.* 宣判……有罪；定罪

搭配 convict sb. of sth. 因为某事宣判某人有罪

拓展 conviction *n.* 定罪，判罪；确信

诵读 I have all the evidences necessary to convict this young criminal now. 我掌握了给这个年轻犯人定罪的所有证据。

copyright [ˈkɒpɪraɪt] *n.&a.* 版权（的）

巧记 复制（copy）别人的东西对（right）吗？因为侵犯了别人的版权。

诵读 Copyright expires 50 years after the death of the author. 版权在作者死后 50 年即行终止。

cordial [ˈkɔːdjɪəl] *a.* 诚恳的，亲切的，热诚的

诵读 He was cordial in all his letters. 他的每封来信都充满热情。

corridor [ˈkɒridɔː] *n.* 走廊，通路

诵读 The corridor opens into Mr. Brown's office. 这条走廊通到布朗先生的办公室。

corrupt [kəˈrʌpt] *vt.* 贿赂，收买 *a.* 腐败的

诵读 Some governmental officials were corrupted. 有些政府官员已被收买。

cosmic [ˈkɒzmɪk] *a.* 宇宙的；巨大的

诵读 From cosmic point of view, nothing is important. 从宇宙的角度来看，没什么事情是重要的。

coward [ˈkaʊəd] *n.* 懦夫，胆怯者

诵读 A coward considers difficulties as a heavy burden on his back, but a valiant fighter turns difficulties into a steppingstone for his advance. 懦弱的人把困难看作沉重的负担，而勇士把困难当作进步的阶梯。

credential [krɪˈdenʃəl] *n.* 文凭；证明；资格

诵读 The security server send back the user's authentication credential, or ticket. 安全服务器返回用户身份验证凭据或票证。

creep [kriːp] *vi.* 爬，爬行；（植物）蔓延

诵读 Back I go to the hotel and creep up to my room. 我回到旅馆，蹑手蹑脚地上楼回到房间。

cripple [ˈkrɪpl] *n.* 跛子，残疾人 *v.* 使残疾

诵读 The oil is beginning to kill wildlife and cripple the tourism and fishing industries. 原油泄漏目前已对当地的野生动物、旅游资源以及捕鱼产业造成了极大的破坏。

criterion [kraɪˈtɪərɪən] *n.* 标准，尺度

巧记 同义词 standard, gauge

诵读 Yet more than a fifth admitted that they used age as a recruitment criterion. 然而，超过五分之一的经理人承认年龄是他们招聘员工的标准。

cruise [kruːz] *v.* 巡航 *n.* 乘船巡游

巧记 联想：与汤姆克鲁斯（Cruise）一起去 cruise 是很多女生的梦想。

诵读 Her parents took a three-day cruise to the Bahamas. 她的父母参加了一个三天的巴哈马游轮旅行。

crust [krʌst] *n.* 外皮；地壳

诵读 Our crust is a little bit thicker, our sauce is a little bit spicier and there are a few more ingredients on the top. 我们比萨饼的面饼表皮显得稍微厚一些，所用调味汁的味道更辛辣，而且面饼上的配料种类更多。

crystal [ˈkrɪstəl] *n.* 水晶 *a.* 水晶的

僻义 *a.* 透明的

搭配 be crystal clear about… 对……了如指掌

诵读 The 4,000-square-meter pavilion, named "Magic Box", is designed to be a metallic square with a crystal cube embedded inside. 这个场馆占地 4 000 平方米，被称为"魔盒"，外部为方形金属结构，内部设有水晶状立方体。

curriculum [kəˈrɪkjʊləm] *n.* 课程

诵读 Two other things I have come to love are the discipline-based approach and the flexible curriculum. 另外两个让我喜欢的是，以学科为基础的教学方式和弹性化的课程体系。

cushion [ˈkʊʃən] *n.* 垫子，软垫

僻义 *vt.* 缓和，减轻

诵读 In order to cushion the impact of the financial crisis on the real economy, we also need to sustain domestic demand and further promote international trade. 为了减少这场金融危机对实体经济的冲击，我们需要维持国内需求并且进一步推动国际贸易。

calamity [kəˈlæmɪti] *n.* 灾祸，灾难

诵读 If we had been careful such a calamity would not have befallen us. 假如我们谨慎的话，这种灾难不会降临到我们的头上。

caption [ˈkæpʃən] *n.* 标题，（图片的）说明文字

诵读 I didn't understand the drawing until I read the caption. 直到看到这幅画的说明，我才明白其意思。

chancellor [ˈtʃɑːnsələ] *n.* （英）大臣；总理

诵读 She said she wanted to be a "chancellor for all Germans, so Germany does better, particularly in a crisis". 她说她想成为"所有德国人的总理，这样德国做得更好，尤其是在危机时刻"。

chronic [ˈkrɒnɪk] *a.* （疾病）慢性的

僻义 *a.* 长期的

诵读 Most of them were chronically ill. 他们中大部分人都有慢性病。

clench [klentʃ] *vt.* 紧握,抓紧;咬紧

诵读 She clenched her teeth and refused to move. 她咬紧牙关不肯挪动一步。

clutch [klʌtʃ] *vt.&vi.* 抓住,紧握

搭配 a clutch of 一群

诵读 The party has attracted a clutch of young southern liberals. 聚会吸引了一群南部的年轻开明人士。

coherent [kəʊˈhɪərənt] *a.* 一致的,协调的

巧记 前缀 co-—起+词根 her 粘贴+后缀-ent→粘贴在一起→一致的

诵读 He has failed to work out a coherent strategy for modernizing the service. 他无法想出一个连贯的策略来实现服务现代化。

conjunction [kənˈdʒʌŋkʃən] *n.* 连接,联合

诵读 The two clauses are joined by a conjunction. 这两个分句由一个连词连在一起。

cord [kɔːd] *n.* 绳,索

拓展 accord *n.* 协议 *vt.* 符合

诵读 They came to an accord that profits should be shared equally. 他们达成协议,收益由大家均分。

cognition [kɒgˈnɪʃən] *n.* [哲] 认识;认识力

诵读 It is a big leap in the process of cognition. 这是认识过程的一次大飞跃。

cohabit [kəʊˈhæbɪt] *vi.* (未婚者) 同居

诵读 She refused to cohabit with him before the wedding. 她拒绝在婚礼前与他同居。

conceit [kənˈsiːt] *n.* 骄傲自大

诵读 Conceit comes from shallowness; arrogance is due to ignorance. 骄傲来自浅薄;狂妄出于无知。

converge [kənˈvɜːdʒ] *vi.* 会于一点,向一点会合

巧记 前缀 con-—起+词根 verge 边缘→从边缘一起向里汇聚

诵读 The roads converged at the stadium. 各条道路在体育场汇聚。

cuisine [kwɪˈziːn] *n.* 烹饪艺术;菜肴

诵读 This book is the definitive guide to world cuisine. 这本书是世界美食的权威指南。

cynical [ˈsɪnɪkəl] *a.* 怀疑的,愤世嫉俗的

诵读 With that cynical outlook, he doesn't trust anyone. 他抱着那种愤世嫉俗的观点,不相信任何人。

cyberspace [ˈsaɪbəˌspeɪs] *n.* 网络空间

damage [ˈdæmɪdʒ] *vt.&n.* 损害,毁坏

辨析 damage 表示部分毁坏;destroy 表示摧毁

搭配 do damage to 破坏

诵读 The storm did great damage to the crops. 那次暴风雨对农作物造成极大的损失。

dawn [dɔːn] *n.* 黎明,拂晓 *vi.* 破晓

搭配 at dawn 在黎明

僻义 *n.* 开端 *vi.* 开始出现

诵读 The truth began to dawn upon him. 他开始明白那个道理。

data [ˈdeɪtə] *n.* (datum 的复数) 资料,数据

拓展 database *n.* 数据库

诵读 Study adds data that vegetables reduce cancer risk. 研究增加了有关蔬菜能降低癌症风险的数据。

decide [dɪˈsaɪd] *vt.* 决定,下决心

拓展 decision *n.* 决定,决心;decisive *a.* 决定性的

诵读 The judge decided the case. 法官已对案件作出判决。

declare [dɪˈkleə] *vt.* 宣布;断言,宣称

拓展 declaration *n.* 宣言,宣布,声明

诵读 The accused man declared that he was not guilty. 被告人声称他无罪。

deed [diːd] *n.* 行为,行动;功绩,事迹

诵读 Deeds are better than words when people are in need of help. 当有人需要帮助时,行动胜过语言。

defeat [dɪˈfiːt] *vt.* 战胜,挫败 *n.* 失败

诵读 This kind of problem always defeats me. 我总

是无法应付这类问题。

defense [dɪˈfens] *n.* 防御，保卫

拓展 self-defense 自我防卫

诵读 I never fight except self-defense. 我除了自卫以外决不言战。

delight [dɪˈlaɪt] *n.* 快乐，高兴

搭配 take delight in... 以……为乐

诵读 The naughty boy takes great delight in pulling the cat's tail. 那顽皮的男孩以扯猫尾巴为乐。

deadline [ˈdedlaɪn] *n.* 最后期限

巧记 合成词：dead 死亡+line 界限→最后期限

诵读 We were not able to meet the deadline because of manufacturing delays. 因为制造方面的延误，我们没能赶上最后期限。

deadly [ˈdedli] *a.* 致命的

巧记 同义词 fatal, mortal

搭配 in deadly haste 火急地

诵读 Passive smoking can be deadly too. 被动吸烟也可能会致命。

deaf [def] *a.* 聋的

搭配 turn a deaf ear to... 对……置之不理

诵读 Now although deaf, Lucy catches mice in the garden, still in good shape and extremely independent. 如今虽然耳朵有些聋，但露西还能在花园捉老鼠，而且身材保持得不错，个性也很独立。

dealer [ˈdiːlə] *n.* 商人

诵读 GM said the new car should arrive in dealer showrooms during the second quarter of this year. 通用公司声称，新车将在本年第二季度经销商展厅亮相。

debate [dɪˈbeɪt] *vt.&n.* 争论，辩论

诵读 The trend has led some experts to debate the reintroduction of compulsory pre-marital health checks which were scrapped in 2003. 由于新生缺陷儿不断增多，一些专家们正在考虑恢复已于 2003 年取消的婚前体检。

debt [det] *n.* 债，债务

诵读 Dentists claimed that massive debt and deficit problems in Ireland have left the country with an increasing number of cases of teeth-grinding. 牙医们声称，爱尔兰的债务危机和赤字问题使得当地人的

磨牙症呈不断攀升的趋势。

decade [ˈdekeɪd] *n.* 十年

诵读 These developments were foreseen in embryo more than a decade ago. 这些发展早在十多年前的萌芽阶段就已预见到。

decent [ˈdiːsənt] *a.* 体面的；正派的；像样的

诵读 It was a decent performance until the second goal. 在丢第二球之前，我们表现很正常。

decline [dɪˈklaɪn] *vi.&n.* 下降；拒绝

巧记 同义词 decrease, descend

诵读 But more important is the decline in birth rates when people leave the countryside. 但更重要的原因是，当人们走出农村，生育率便开始下降了。

decorate [ˈdekəreɪt] *v.* 装饰，装潢，布置

诵读 How are you going to decorate your apartment? 你打算如何装修你的公寓呢？

dedicate [ˈdedɪkeɪt] *vt.* 奉献；献身于

搭配 dedicate oneself to=devote oneself to 献身于

诵读 I'm willing to dedicate myself wholeheartedly to this cause. 我愿意为这项事业献出我的全部心血和精力。

defect [dɪˈfekt] *n.* 过失；缺点，不足

巧记 前缀 de-消极含义+词根 fect 做=有的地方没有做好→过失；缺点

诵读 Lincoln may have had facial defect. 林肯可能有面部缺陷。

define [dɪˈfaɪn] *vt.* 给……下定义

拓展 definition *n.* 定义，解释

诵读 It doesn't define who you are as a woman. 但这并没有规定你应该成为什么样的女人。

definite [ˈdefɪnɪt] *a.* 明确的，一定的

诵读 The case was dismissed in the absense of any definite proof. 此案因缺乏确凿证据而不予受理。

delete [dɪˈliːt] *vt.* 删除

诵读 Several words had been deleted from the letter by the censor. 那封信中有好几个字被审查员删去了。

delicate [ˈdelɪkɪt] *a.* 纤弱的；精致的；微妙的

诵读 The international situation is very delicate at present. 目前的国际形势极其微妙。

delicious [dɪˈlɪʃəs] *a.* 美味的；令人愉快的

诵读 Doesn't it smell delicious? 其味岂不美哉？

deliver [dɪˈlɪvə] *vt.* 递送；发表；接生

拓展 delivery *n.* 递送；交付

诵读 A postman is a man employed to deliver letters and parcels. 邮差就是雇来投递信件和包裹的人。

democracy [dɪˈmɒkrəsi] *n.* 民主

拓展 democratic *a.* 民主的

诵读 The development of AI technology should conform to humanity's common values of peace, development, equity; justice, democracy and freedom. 人工智能技术的发展应符合和平、发展、公平、正义、民主、自由的全人类共同价值。

demonstrate [ˈdemənstreɪt] *vt.* 论证，证实；演示，说明

诵读 The salesman demonstrated the new washing machine. 售货员演示了如何使用新式洗衣机。

denial [dɪˈnaɪəl] *n.* 否认

拓展 deny *vt.* 否认

诵读 The prisoner repeatedly denied the charge brought against him. 该囚犯对于被指控的罪名再三否认。

dense [dens] *a.* 浓厚的，密集的，稠密的

拓展 density *n.* 密集；密度；浓度

诵读 We entered a dense forest. 我们进入一片茂密的森林。

depart [dɪˈpɑːt] *vi.* 离开，起程

拓展 departure *n.* 离开，起程

诵读 Before you depart let me give you a word of advice. 你动身前，我给你一句忠告。

depend [dɪˈpend] *vi.* 取决于，依靠

搭配 depend on 取决于，依靠

拓展 dependent *a.* 依靠的，依赖的，从属的

诵读 Children depend on their parents for food and clothing. 小孩依赖他们的父母供给衣食。

depict [dɪˈpɪkt] *v.* 描绘，描写，描述

巧记 前缀 de-加强语气+词根 pict 画=描绘，描述

诵读 The painting depicts the different attitudes of college students towards campus lectures. 这幅画描绘了大学生对校园讲座的不同态度。

deposit [dɪˈpɒzɪt] *vt.* 存放；使沉淀

巧记 前缀 de-向下+词根 pos 放+后缀-it →放在下面→沉淀

诵读 She deposited papers with one's lawyer. 她将文件交给律师保管。

depress [dɪˈpres] *vt.* 压抑，降低；使沮丧，压下

巧记 前缀 de-向下+词根 press 压=向下压→使沮丧

诵读 Does mass unemployment depress wages? 大规模失业会降低工资吗?

deprive [dɪˈpraɪv] *vt.* 剥夺，夺去

搭配 deprive...of... 从……剥夺……

诵读 What would a student do if he were deprived of his books? 一个学生如果没书该怎么办?

derive [dɪˈraɪv] *vi.* 引申；来自；源自

搭配 derive from 源自

诵读 Thousands of English words derive from Latin. 成千上万的英语单词出自拉丁语。

descend [dɪˈsend] *vi.&vt.* (使) 下降

拓展 descendant *n.* 子孙，后代；descent *n.* 下降

诵读 They descended the slope towards the hamlet. 他们顺坡下山,向那个村子走去。

describe [dɪsˈkraɪb] *v.* 描述，形容

拓展 description *n.* 描写

诵读 Words can't describe the beauty of the scene. 此景之美非语言所能形容。

desert [ˈdezət] *n.* 沙漠，不毛之地

僻义 *vt.* 抛弃，遗弃

辨析 形近词 dessert *n.* 正餐后的水果或甜食

诵读 The village had been hurriedly deserted, perhaps because bandits were in the district. 全村的人匆匆地逃走了,可能因为有土匪到达该地区。

deserve [dɪˈzɜːv] *vt.* 应受，值得

诵读 These people deserve our help. 这些人值得我们帮助。

desirable [dɪˈzaɪərəbl] *a.* 值得拥有的；令人向往的

巧记 词根 desire 渴望+后缀-able→能渴望的→值得拥有的

诵读 The desirable property is to be sold or let. 优质房产将要出售或出租。

despair [dɪsˈpeə] *n.* 绝望

诵读 Your stupidity will drive me to despair. 你的愚笨将会使我绝望。

desperate [ˈdespərɪt] *a.* 拼命的；绝望的；危急的

诵读 The wretched prisoners become desperate in their attempts to escape. 那些该死的囚犯拼命逃亡。

despise [dɪsˈpaɪz] *vt.* 轻视, 蔑视

诵读 Strike breakers are despised by their work-mates. 破坏罢工者为同事所鄙视。

destination [ˌdestɪˈneɪʃən] *n.* 目的地, 终点

诵读 They reached their destination safely. 他们安全到达了目的地。

destiny [ˈdestɪni] *n.* 命运

诵读 It was his destiny to die in a foreign country, far from his family. 天命要他死在异邦, 远离亲人。

detach [dɪˈtætʃ] *vt.* 拆下; 脱离; 派遣

巧记 由attach (贴上, 附上)可知词根tach 意为粘贴; 前缀 de-否定+词根 tach 粘贴 →拆下, 使分离

诵读 They detached their trailer and set up camp. 他们卸下拖车, 架起帐篷。

detail [ˈdiːteɪl] *n.* 细节, 详情 *vt.* 详述

搭配 in detail 详细地

诵读 Don't omit a single detail. 不要遗漏任何一点细节。

detect [dɪˈtekt] *vt.* 察觉, 发觉, 侦察, 探测

拓展 detective *n.* 侦探; detector *n.* 发现者, 侦察器

诵读 Can you detect an escape of gas in this corner of the room? 你能察觉这屋里有煤气泄漏吗?

device [dɪˈvaɪs] *n.* 装置, 设备

拓展 devise *vt.* 设计; 发明; 想出 (办法)

distance [ˈdɪstəns] *n.* 距离, 间隔

僻义 *n.* 疏远, 冷淡

拓展 distant *a.* 远的; 不太友好的

诵读 Keep your distance from him. 和他保持距离。

divide [dɪˈvaɪd] *vt.* 分, 划分

诵读 The English Channel divides England and France. 英吉利海峡把英国和法国隔开。

double [ˈdʌbl] *a.* 两倍的 *vt.* 加倍

僻义 *a.* 两面派的, 虚伪的

诵读 We don't like the man who bears a double face. 我们不喜欢不诚实的人。

down [daʊn] *ad.* 向下 *prep.* 顺……向下

僻义 *a.* 处于低落状态

诵读 He described the subject from the main points down to the minutest details. 他按从重点到细节的顺序来描述这一主题。

diagram [ˈdaɪəɡræm] *n.* 图表; 图解

诵读 The engineer drew a diagram of the bridge. 工程师绘制了大桥的示意图。

dialect [ˈdaɪəlekt] *n.* 方言

诵读 He wrote a play in a local dialect. 他用当地方言写了一个剧本。

dictate [dɪkˈteɪt] *vt.* 口授; (使)听写

僻义 *vt.* 命令

拓展 dictation *n.* 听写; 命令

诵读 He cannot write but he can dictate. 他不会写, 但可以口述。

differ [ˈdɪfə] *vi.* 与……不同; 与……意见不同

诵读 I'm sorry to differ from you on that question. 对不起, 关于那个问题, 我与你看法不同。

differentiate [ˌdɪfəˈrenʃieɪt] *vt.* 区分, 区别

巧记 词根 different 不同+后缀-ate→使不同

诵读 The report doesn't differentiate the two aspects of the problem. 此报告未能将问题的两方面加以区别。

digital [ˈdɪdʒɪtəl] *a.* 数字的

诵读 There's a digital watch on the table. 桌子上有一块数字手表。

dignity [ˈdɪɡnɪti] *n.* 庄严; 尊贵

诵读 A man's dignity depends not upon his wealth or rank but upon his character. 人的真正价值不在财富或地位, 而在品格。

dim [dɪm] *a.* 暗淡的, 模糊的

诵读 His eyesight is getting dim. 他的视力逐渐模糊。

dimension [dɪˈmenʃən] *n.* 尺寸, 尺度; 维

诵读 This adds a new dimension to our work. 这给我们的工作增添了新的内容。

diploma [dɪˈpləʊmə] *n.* 毕业文凭, 学位证书

拓展 diplomatic *a.* 外交的; 策略的, 有手腕的

诵读 She worked hard to earn her music diploma. 她刻苦用功, 以求获得音乐学位。

directory [dɪˈrektəri] *n.* 名址录, 电话号码簿

诵读 Her name is listed in the telephone directory. 她的名字被列在电话簿上。

disaster [dɪˈzɑːstə] *n.* 灾难

拓展 disastrous *a.* 灾难性的

诵读 The election results will bring political disaster.

选举结果将带来政治性灾难。

discipline ['dɪsɪplɪn] *n.* 纪律；训练

释义 *n.* 学科

诵读 The discipline of studying music can help children develop good work habits. 音乐训练可以帮助孩子们培养良好的工作习惯。

disclose [dɪs'kləʊz] *vt.* 揭示，泄露

巧记 前缀 dis-表否定+词根 close 封闭= 揭示

诵读 They contend that the company failed to disclose material information. 他们认为该公司并未透露实质性的信息。

discount ['dɪskaʊnt] *n.* 折扣；贴现

搭配 discount ticket 折扣券

诵读 Participants lined up near the booth where discount theater tickets are sold. 参与人员在出售折扣电影的售票亭附近排队。

discourage [dɪs'kʌrɪdʒ] *v.* 使泄气，使失去信心

巧记 前缀 dis-表否定+词根 courage 勇气→使……失去勇气

诵读 To discourage smokers, Tokyo has raised the price of cigarettes. 为了劝阻吸烟族，东京提高了烟价。

discourse ['dɪskɔːs] *n.* 论文；演讲 *vi.* 论述

巧记 前缀 dis-四处分开+词根 course 课程=四处讲课

诵读 Much of our political discourse, including the debate about climate-change policies, focuses around the question of "what's in it for me?". 我们的许多政治言论，包括关于应对气候变化的政策的辩论，都集中在一个问题上"对我有什么好处？"。

discriminate [dɪs'krɪmɪneɪt] *vi.* 区别对待，歧视

释义 *vi.* 区别，辨别

诵读 You must learn to discriminate between facts and opinions. 你必须学会把事实和看法区分开来。

disgrace [dɪs'greɪs] *n.* 耻辱 *v.* 使蒙受耻辱

巧记 前缀 dis-表否定+词根 grace 优雅的→耻辱

诵读 Many people expressed their disappointment at him for bringing disgrace to the community. 很多人对他的不当行为表示遗憾，认为他给社区抹了黑。

dismay [dɪs'meɪ] *n.* 沮丧；惊慌；失望 *vt.* 使沮丧

诵读 Goderdzi Kasradze looks on in dismay. 卡斯拉泽悲愤地看着这一切。

dismiss [dɪs'mɪs] *v.* 解雇，开除；解散

诵读 A spokesman dismissed any suggestion of a boardroom rift. 发言人的话打消了人们关于董事会不和的猜测。

disorder [dɪs'ɔːdə] *n.* 混乱；骚乱

巧记 前缀 dis-表示否定+词根 order 秩序→混乱

搭配 anxiety disorder 焦虑性障碍；mental disorder 精神障碍

诵读 If you find the winter months tough, you may suffer from Seasonal Affective Disorder. 如果你觉得冬天很难熬，那么你可能患上了季节性情绪失调。

displace [dɪs'pleɪs] *vt.* 转移；取代

诵读 Many feared that radio would displace the newspaper industry. 许多人担心广播将会取代报业。

display [dɪs'pleɪ] *vt.&n.* 陈列，展览

搭配 display interest in... 表现出对……的兴趣

诵读 Any visitor to Chinese Cultural Week would be amazed by the tea, food, Chinese knotting and traditional paper-cutting artworks on display. 参加中国文化周的游客都会对展出的茶、食物、中国结和传统剪纸艺术品感到惊讶。

dispose [dɪs'pəʊz] *vi.* 处理，处置；布置，安排

巧记 前缀 dis-四处分开+词根 pose 放置=处置

搭配 dispose of 处理

拓展 disposal *n.* 处理；disposition *n.* 排列；部署

诵读 The world produces much more garbage that it can dispose of. 全球垃圾产生速度要远远超过垃圾处理速度。

dispute [dɪs'pjuːt] *n.* 争论，争执

诵读 The two countries have settled a long-standing dispute over their shared land border. 两国已经解决了共同陆地边界的一个长期纠纷。

distinct [dɪs'tɪŋkt] *a.* 清楚的；截然不同的

搭配 be distinct from... 与……不同的

拓展 distinction *n.* 区别；特性；声望

诵读 This is a distinction of great importance because it might help direct environmental concern to goals that people can actually achieve. 这是非常重要的区别，因为它也许能使环保工作朝着人们能够实现的目标迈进。

distinguish [dɪs'tɪŋgwɪʃ] *vt.* 区别，辨别

搭配 distinguish... from... 区别，辨别

拓展 distinguished *a.* 杰出的

诵读 Many Americans know their red wines and easily distinguish a Manet from a Monet. 很多美国人对红酒很了解，他们能轻松地区别马奈和莫奈。

distort [dɪsˈtɔːt] *vt.* 扭曲；歪曲（真理、事实等）

诵读 The media distorts reality and categorizes people as all good or all bad. 媒体会歪曲事实，将人分为不是完美无缺，就是一无是处。

distract [dɪsˈtrækt] *vt.* 分散；使分心；打扰

巧记 前缀 dis-四处分开+词根 tract 拉=把精神和注意力拉开→分散；使分心

诵读 A recent Trump TV ad says Biden is attacking him to distract voters' attention away from the economic crisis. 最近的一个特朗普竞选电视广告说，拜登通过攻击他转移选民对经济危机的注意力。

distress [dɪsˈtres] *n.* 苦恼；危难；不幸

巧记 dis 四面八方+stress 压力→多方压力→苦恼

诵读 One in three families have already experienced financial distress this year. 今年有三分之一的家庭已陷入经济困境。

distribute [dɪsˈtrɪbjuːt] *vt.* 分发；分配

联想 同根词 contribute, attribute

诵读 Sony had the right to distribute those recordings through 2015. 索尼有权在 2015 年以前销售这些唱片。

disturb [dɪsˈtɜːb] *vt.* 扰乱，妨碍，使不安

拓展 disturbance *n.* 动乱，骚乱

诵读 Disturb the snake by hitting the grass. 打草惊蛇。

dive [daɪv] *vi.&n.* 潜水；跳水；俯冲

诵读 The largest contributor to the first-quarter dive was the decline in exports which, in turn, drove down private investment. 导致第一季度产量暴跌的最大原因，就是出口的下降，而这又进一步压低了私人投资。

diverse [daɪˈvɜːs] *a.* 多种多样的，不同的

巧记 前缀 di-分开+词根 verse 转→转出花样

拓展 diversion *n.* 转向；divert *vt.* 使转向；转移

诵读 Woodland, Washington is a surprisingly diverse American small town. 华盛顿州的伍德兰是一个高度多元化的美国小镇。

dividend [ˈdɪvɪdend] *n.* 红利，股息

辨析 形近词 divided *a.* 分割的，分开的

诵读 Unveiling a big stock buyback or a dividend would make sense. 进行股票大批回购或分红也会起作用。

division [dɪˈvɪʒən] *n.* 分割；部门；分界线

诵读 We have had an approach from a German company to buy our car division. 一家德国公司已与我们接洽，以购买我们的汽车部门。

divorce [dɪˈvɔːs] *vt.&n.* 离婚，分离

诵读 The global trend toward higher divorce rates has created more households with fewer people. 全球离婚率日益上升导致家庭数量增多，家庭成员减少。

documentary [ˌdɒkjʊˈmentəri] *a.* 文献的 *n.* 纪录片

诵读 Morgan is also working on a documentary on the death of Monroe. 摩根还在制作一部关于梦露之死的纪录片。

domain [dəʊˈmeɪn] *n.* 领域，范围；领地

拓展 dominate *vt.* 支配；dominant *a.* 占优势的

诵读 Cubicles, hallways, elevators, bathrooms—even commuter trains—are not your private domain. 小隔间、走廊、电梯、卫生间甚至通勤火车都不是你的私人领地。

domestic [dəˈmestɪk] *a.* 家里的；本国的

搭配 domestic violence 家庭暴力

诵读 Over the past eight years, 98.99 million impoverished rural residents living below China's domestic poverty line has all been lifted out of poverty. 过去八年来，生活在中国国内贫困线以下的9 899万农村贫困人口全部脱贫。

donate [dəʊˈneɪt] *vt.* 捐赠（金钱等）；赠予

搭配 blood donation 献血

诵读 She would donate the money from the busness to charity. 她打算把做生意挣的钱捐给慈善机构。

doom [duːm] *n.* 厄运，劫数 *v.* 注定，命定

辨析 形近词：boom *n.* 繁荣；dome *n.* 穹顶，圆顶

诵读 Investors turn anxious when there's a sense of impending gloom and doom. 当投资者感到悲观或厄运即将到来时，他们就会感到焦虑。

dorm [dɔːm] *n.* 宿舍（=dormitory）

诵读 Despite this, the dorms are more sedate than

their Japanese versions. 尽管如此，这些寝室的风格要比其日式风格安静稳重得多。

doubt [daʊt] *n.&vt.* 怀疑，疑虑

诵读 There can be little doubt that he will offend again. 毋庸置疑，他还会再犯的。

downward [ˈdaʊnwəd] *a.* 向下的 *ad.* 向下，往下

巧记 合成词：down 朝下+ward 表示方向=向下的

诵读 Despite the excitement the inauguration of the President generated around the world, overseas markets continued their downward slide. 尽管总统的就职宣誓在全球各地都引起了激动和兴奋，但是海外股市还是继续下滑。

doze [dəʊz] *vi.&n.* 瞌睡

巧记 形近词记忆：感冒的时候，服用恰当计量 dose 的感冒药，也会引起瞌睡 doze

诵读 American children are more sleep-deprived than ever, with more than a quarter reporting that they doze off in class at least once a week. 当今的美国青少年比以往任何年代都缺乏睡眠，超过四分之一的高中生每周至少一次在课堂上睡觉。

draft [drɑːft] *n.* 草稿，草案，草图 *vt.* 起草，草拟

搭配 draft a contract 起草合同

诵读 Better to hammer out a rough draft and revise later than spin your wheels for hours. 与其耗费几个小时而没有进展，不如列出一个粗略的草案，再修改。

drag [dræg] *vt.* 拖，拖曳

诵读 As foreclosures increase, they drag the average price of homes in a neighborhood down. 随着丧失抵押品赎回权的增加，它们会拖累同一街区的平均房价。

drain [dreɪn] *n.* 排水管，阴沟；消耗，负担 *v.* 排出

搭配 brain drain 人才流失

诵读 Mismanagement had delayed the evacuation and slowed efforts to drain water from the mine. 管理失误耽误了疏散，并延缓了从煤矿中排水的措施。

drama [ˈdrɑːmə] *n.* 戏剧；戏剧性事件或场面

拓展 dramatic *a.* 戏剧的，戏剧性的；剧烈的

诵读 The Web's encore came at the Inauguration, when streaming video had its most dramatic day up to that point. 在总统就职演讲时，网络的盛况再次上演，视频流量在当天达到了史上最高点。

drastic [ˈdræstɪk] *a.* 激烈的，严厉的

搭配 a drastic rise 急剧的增长

诵读 The country faces the potential risk of drastic economic fluctuation. 这个国家面临经济波动的潜在风险。

drawer [drɔː] *n.* 抽屉

诵读 Keep a bubble wrap in your desk drawer. Press it and feel your stress disappear with the sound of popping bubbles. 在抽屉里放一个气泡膜，挤压它，你就能感觉到压力伴随着气泡的爆破声散去。

dread [dred] *vt.&n.* 恐惧，担心

诵读 And even though we have known this day was coming for some time now, we awaited it with no small amount of dread. 尽管我们彼此都知道这一天终将到来，我们等待着，毫不畏惧。

drip [drɪp] *vi.* 滴下，漏水 *n.* 滴，水滴，点滴

巧记 形近词记忆：一滴（drop）水，滴（drip）下来

诵读 Ethiopia's effort could turn out to be just the first drip in a very large pot. 埃塞俄比亚所付出的努力可能最终只是落入沧海的第一滴水。

drunk [drʌŋk] *a.* 醉酒的；陶醉的 *n.* 酗酒者

搭配 drunk driving 醉酒驾车

诵读 Serious violations including speeding, overtaking, overloading, tired driving and drunk driving should be harshly punished to ensure the safety of people's lives and property. 为了确保人民生命财产安全，对超速、超车、超载、疲劳驾驶、酒驾等严重违法行为要严厉查处。

durable [ˈdjʊərəbl] *a.* 持久的，耐久的

联想 同根词 endurance *n.* 持久力；忍耐力；duration *n.* 持久；持续时间

诵读 The apartment building is resistant to earthquakes, as the stainless-steel structure is more durable than concrete. 由于不锈钢结构比混凝土结构更耐用，该公寓楼具有抗震能力。

dusk [dʌsk] *n.* 薄暮，黄昏

诵读 The lighthouse beam was quite distinct in the gathering dusk. 灯塔的光束在渐浓的暮色中清晰可见。

dynamic [daɪˈnæmɪk] *a.* 充满活力的；动态的

搭配 static and dynamic 静态和动态

诵读 Both teams are fast and very dynamic although

South Korean team is the underdog in this match. 这两个队速度都很快，而且场上表现也很活跃，尽管韩国队在这场比赛中并不被看好。

dull [dʌl] *a.* 单调的；迟钝的；愚笨的

辨义 *vt.* 使不鲜明，使无光泽

诵读 The color of the red flag has been dulled by age. 那面红旗因年深日久而褪色了。

dust [dʌst] *n.* 灰尘，尘土 *v.* 拂，掸

诵读 This is the dust of our ancestors. 这是我们祖先的遗骸。

duty ['djuːti] *n.* 义务，责任；职务；关税

搭配 on duty 值班，上班；off duty 下班

诵读 The committee carried out the duties entrusted to it. 委员会履行了赋予它的职责。

damp [dæmp] *a.* 潮湿的

辨义 *vt.* 抑制；使沮丧

诵读 Don't sleep between damp sheets. 不要睡在潮湿的床单上。

dam [dæm] *n.* 水坝，水闸

诵读 Yichang, Hubei province, is where the Three Gorges Dam, the world's largest hydropower project, is located. 湖北省宜昌市是世界上最大的水电工程——三峡大坝的所在地。

dash [dæʃ] *vi.&n.* 冲，猛冲

诵读 I'm not going to break the 100-meter dash record, but I thought I could break this record. 我不打算打破 100 米短跑的纪录，不过我想这个应该没问题。

dazzle ['dæzl] *vt.* 使惊奇；耀（眼）*n.* 耀眼的光

诵读 The dazzle of the spotlights made him ill at ease. 聚光灯的耀眼强光使他局促不安。

decay [dɪ'keɪ] *n.* 腐烂；衰退 *v.* 破败

诵读 Long before the invention of electric drills and anesthesia early humans drilled teeth to treat decay. 早在电钻和麻醉剂发明之前，早期人类就开始通过在牙齿上钻孔的方法来医治蛀牙。

deceive [dɪ'siːv] *vt.* 欺骗，蒙蔽

拓展 deceit *n.* 欺骗，欺骗行为

诵读 Do not be deceived by claims on food labels like "light" or "low fat". 不要被食品标签上像"少脂"或"低脂"的字样误导。

deduce [dɪ'djuːs] *vt.* 演绎，推断，推论

搭配 deduce... from... 从……推出……

诵读 From the evidence the detective deduced that the servant had done it. 根据证据侦探推断是佣人所为。

deem [diːm] *vt.* 认为，相信

诵读 Without software to help filter and organize based on factors we deem relevant, we'd drown in the deluge. 如果没有软件来帮助我们根据我们认为相关的因素进行过滤和组织，我们就会在信息的洪流中无所适从。

deficiency [dɪ'fɪʃənsi] *n.* 缺乏，不足

巧记 看成 efficiency（效率）的反向构成

诵读 Early iron deficiency can change the neuro-anatomy of the brain. 早期缺铁会使脑部组织发生变化。

deficit ['defɪsɪt] *n.* 赤字；不足，缺乏

诵读 A deficit of 1.05 trillion Yuan has been projected. 今年财政赤字预计将达到 1.05 万亿元。

defy [dɪ'faɪ] *vt.*（公然）违抗，反抗

诵读 People of the world, be courageous, dare to fight, defy difficulties and advance wave upon wave. 全世界人民要有勇气，敢于战斗，不怕困难，前赴后继。

degenerate [dɪ'dʒenəreɪt] *vi.* 衰退，堕落

巧记 前缀 de-表否定+词根 generate 产生→产生的相反就是衰退

诵读 Don't let thrift degenerate into avarice. 不要让节俭变成贪财。

delegate ['delɪɡət] *n.* 代表 ['delɪɡeɪt]*vt.* 授权；委托

诵读 The delegate moved for a reconsideration of the suggestion. 这位代表提议重新考虑这一建议。

deliberate [dɪ'lɪbərɪt] *a.* 故意的

辨义 *a.* 深思熟虑的

诵读 He did it in a deliberate manner. 他做事很谨慎。

denote [dɪ'nəʊt] *vt.* 表示，意味着

巧记 前缀 de-向下+词根 note 笔记 →通过笔记记下来→知道意思是什么

诵读 In algebra the sign "x" usually denotes an unknown quantity. 在代数学中，符号"x"通常代表

一个未知数。

denounce [dɪˈnaʊns] *vt.* 公开指责；谴责

巧记 与 announce（发言）的概念相反

诵读 We should denounce a heresy. 我们应该公开指责异端邪说。

designate [ˈdezɪgneɪt] *vt.* 指明；任命

诵读 The chairman has designated her as his successor. 主席已指定她作为他的接班人。

desolate [ˈdesəlɪt] *a.* 荒凉的；孤独的 *v.* 使荒芜

诵读 The house was desolate, ready to be torn down. 这房子没人居住，准备拆除。

detain [dɪˈteɪn] *vt.* 耽搁；扣押，拘留

诵读 The bad weather detained us for several hours. 恶劣的天气耽搁了我们几个小时。

deteriorate [dɪˈtɪərɪəreɪt] *vi.* 恶化，变坏

诵读 Leather quickly deteriorates in a hot, damp climate. 皮革在闷热而潮湿的气候中极易变坏。

deviate [ˈdiːvɪeɪt] *vi.* 背离，偏离

巧记 前缀 de-表否定+词根 via 通过=通过的方式不对→背离

诵读 The plane had to deviate from its normal flight path. 飞机不得不偏离正常的航线。

diffuse [dɪˈfjuːs] *vi.* 扩散；传播 *a.* 散开的

诵读 Direct light is better for reading than diffuse light. 直射光比漫射光更有利于阅读。

digest [daɪˈdʒest] *vt.* 理解；消化 *n.* 文摘；分解物

诵读 Some foods are digested more easily than others. 某些食物较其他食物易于消化。

dilemma [dɪˈlemə] *n.* （进退两难的）窘境，困境

诵读 You place me in something of a dilemma. 你使我进退两难。

diligent [ˈdɪlɪdʒənt] *a.* 勤奋的，用功的

诵读 Full of youthful vigour he was diligent and modest. 他充满青春活力，既勤奋又谦虚。

discard [dɪsˈkɑːd] *vt.* 丢弃，抛弃，遗弃

巧记 前缀 dis-四处分开+词根 card 纸牌=丢的纸牌到处都是→丢弃

诵读 I discarded my winter underclothing when the weather gets warm. 天气转暖时，我丢弃了冬天穿的内衣。

discern [dɪˈsɜːn] *vt.* 认出；辨别，识别

巧记 前缀 dis-四处分开+词根 cern 切 =切开才能分辨

诵读 We discerned the figure of a man clinging to the mast of the wrecked ship. 我们看出有一个人紧抱着破船的桅杆。

discharge [dɪsˈtʃɑːdʒ] *vt.&n.* 放电

巧记 前缀 dis-四处分开+词根 charge 充电=放电

辨义 *vt.* 卸货；发射；遣散，解雇

诵读 How long will the discharge of the cargo take? 卸货需要多久？

discreet [dɪsˈkriːt] *a.* 谨慎的；慎重的

诵读 Spain's Fernando Torres recently chopped off his highlighted locks, opting for a discreet crop. 西班牙队的费尔南多托雷斯最近也剪掉了他那一头惹眼的长发，选择了谨慎的短发。

discrepancy [dɪsˈkrepənsi] *n.* 相差；差异

巧记 前缀 dis-四处分开+词根 crep 等同于 creep=向四面八方爬行→差异

诵读 We don't know why there is this discrepancy. 我们尚不清楚为什么会存在这种差异。

disguise [dɪsˈgaɪz] *n.&vt.* 假装，伪装

诵读 However, *Prince of Persia* does not disguise its video game origins. 但是，《波斯王子》并没有隐藏其电子游戏的"出身"。

disgust [dɪsˈgʌst] *n.* 厌恶，恶心 *v.* 使厌恶

诵读 East Asians are more likely than Westerners to read the expression for "fear" as "surprise", and "disgust" as "anger". 与西方人相比，东亚人更容易把"恐惧"的表情错认为"惊讶"，把"厌恶"看成"愤怒"。

disperse [dɪsˈpɜːs] *vt.* 分散；散开；疏散

巧记 前缀 dis-四处分开+词根 sper分散=分散，疏散

诵读 Because the town sits in a valley, air pollution is not easily dispersed. 因为小镇坐落在山谷中，空气污染不太容易散去。

disregard [ˌdɪsrɪˈgɑːd] *vt.* 不理会；忽视；漠视

巧记 前缀 dis-表否定+词根 regard 认为，考虑=不理会，忽视

诵读 But cancer experts yesterday urged people not

to disregard the advice of governmeat. 但是癌症专家昨天呼吁人们不要忽视政府的建议。

disrupt [dɪsˈrʌpt] *vt.* 使混乱，使崩溃，使分裂

巧记 前缀 dis-四处分开+词根 rupt 断=断开→使混乱，使崩溃

诵读 We track and freeze, and try to disrupt the assets of many stateless groups. 我们追查、冻结并且争取捣毁许多无国籍的集团资产。

dissipate [ˈdɪsɪpeɪt] *vt.* 驱散

诵读 You must wait till it is digested, and then amusement will dissipate the remains of it. 你要静候它的逝去，再用欢乐的力量将它驱散。

dissolve [dɪˈzɒlv] *vi.&vt.* 溶解；解散，取消

诵读 The resistance would dissolve in places wherever we would attack. 反抗势力会在我们的进攻地点就地解散。

distill [dɪˈstɪl] *vt.* 蒸馏；提取

诵读 Here I have tried to distill this down to its very essence. 在此我想尽可能把这些办法的精髓提取出来。

dose [dəʊs] *n.* 剂量，一剂 *vt.* 给……服药

搭配 a high dose of 大剂量的；a lethal dose of 致命药量的

诵读 If you don't finish the course or take them at reduced dose there is a risk you won't kill all the bacteria. 如果你没有完成治疗疗程，或是减少药量，那么就有可能无法完全消灭病菌。

dot [dɒt] *n.* 点，圆点 *vt.* 在……上打点

巧记 .com 这个常见的网站结尾曾经成为网络经济的代名词，并诞生了 dotcom company 这样一个新词

诵读 Soon they were only dots above the hard line of the horizon. 很快他们就成了地平线上的几个小点了。

drawback [ˈdrɔːbæk] *n.* 欠缺，缺点

巧记 合成 draw 拉，拽+back 往后→把人往回拽的东西→缺点

诵读 Despite that drawback, most food safety advocates support the new law. 尽管存在缺陷，大多数食品安全倡议人士支持新通过的食品安全法。

drift [drɪft] *vi.&n.* 漂，漂流；流动

诵读 The drift to the suburbs has slowed and the city's population is predicted to swell by a further 10%

by 2035. 人往郊区迁移的速度已经放缓，预计到2035年该城市的人口将继续增长10%。

dubious [ˈdjuːbjəs] *a.* 可疑的；不确定的

诵读 The tests have been shown to be of dubious validity. 这些试验的有效性令人怀疑。

dumb [dʌm] *a.* 哑的，无言的

僻义 *a.* 沉默的

辨析 同形词 dump *v.* 丢掉，摆脱 *n.* 垃圾场

诵读 The questions were set up to make her look dumb. 问题这么设计，就是为了让她出丑。

duplicate [ˈdjuːplɪkət] *n.* 复制品 [ˈdjuːplɪkeɪt] *vt.* 复写，使加倍 [ˈdjuːplɪkət] *a.* 复制的，二重的

诵读 Subway stations need to provide convenience for passengers to reduce duplicate security and improve transit efficiency. 地铁站需给乘客提供便利，减少二次安检，提高换乘效率。

dwarf [dwɔːf] *n.* 矮子，侏儒

诵读 The ancient Egyptians looked on dwarfs as magical figures. 侏儒在古埃及人眼中是神奇的人物。

dwell [dwel] *vi.* 住，居留

拓展 dwelling *n.* 住宅，寓所

诵读 Besides, we cannot dwell on our dreams. 此外，我们不能停留在我们的梦境中。

depletion [dɪˈpliːʃən] *n.* 消耗；用尽

诵读 Increased consumption of water has led to rapid depletion of groundwater reserves. 用水量的增加导致了地下水储备迅速枯竭。

despise [dɪsˈpaɪz] *vt.* 鄙视，看不起

巧记 前缀 de-向下+词根 spis 看→往下看→蔑视

诵读 Honest boys despise lies and liars. 诚实的孩子鄙视谎言和说谎者。

diagnose [ˈdaɪəgnəʊz] *vt.* 诊断；判断

拓展 diagnosis *n.* 诊断

诵读 The soldiers were diagnosed as having flu. 这些士兵被诊断为患了流感。

dial [ˈdaɪəl] *vt.* 拨号，打电话

dilute [daɪˈljuːt] *vt.* 稀释，冲淡

诵读 If you give your baby juice, dilute it well with cooled, boiled water. 如果你要喂婴儿果汁，要用凉开水充分稀释。

dislike [dɪsˈlaɪk] *n.&vt.* 不喜欢，厌恶

辨析 unlike *prep.* 不像，unlikely *a.* 不可能的

诵读 They had a snobbish dislike for their intellectual and social inferiors. 他们非常势利，不喜欢智力和社会地位不如自己的人。

document [ˈdɒkjʊmənt] *n.* 公文，文献

divergence [daɪˈvɜːdʒəns] *n.* 分叉；分歧；离题

诵读 There was a divergence of opinion among us. 我们中间出现了意见分歧。

earnest [ˈɜːnɪst] *a.* 热心的，诚挚的

诵读 Remarkably, their earnest attempts to bridge the language barrier were greeted with appreciation from the local community. 值得注意的是，他们在克服语言障碍上所做出的真诚努力得到当地社区的赞赏。

ease [iːz] *vt.* 减轻；使舒适 *n.* 容易；舒适，悠闲

巧记 同义词 lessen，relieve

诵读 I gave him some medicine to ease the pain. 我给他一些药来减轻病痛。

echo [ˈekəʊ] *vi.&n.* 回声，反响，共鸣

诵读 His words aroused echoes in their hearts. 他的话在他们心中引起共鸣。

economy [ɪˈkɒnəmi] *n.* 经济

僻义 *n.* 节约

拓展 economic *a.* 经济学的；economical *a.* 节约的

诵读 The economics of national growth are of great importance to governments at all levels. 国民生产的经济效益对各级政府都非常重要。

edit [ˈedɪt] *vt.* 编辑，校订

拓展 edition *n.* 版本，版次；editor *n.* 编辑，编者；editorial *n.* 社论 *a.* 社论的

诵读 They had edited one hundred famous speeches by the prestigious statesmen throughout the world. 他们已编辑了100篇由世界上声望很高的政客们所做的著名演说词。

effective [ɪˈfektɪv] *a.* 有效的

诵读 That product offers an effective treatment for hair loss. 那个产品能有效治疗脱发。

efficiency [ɪˈfɪʃənsi] *n.* 效率；功效

拓展 efficient *a.* 有效的，效率高的

诵读 These machines have raised efficiency a lot. 这些机器大幅提高了工作效率。

elbow [ˈelbəʊ] *n.* 肘，肘部 *vt.* 用肘推，用肘挤

诵读 He elbowed his way through the crowd. 他从人群中挤过去。

elect [ɪˈlekt] *vt.* 选举

诵读 They elected my brother as chairman. 他们推选我哥当主席。

electrical [ɪˈlektrɪkəl] *a.* 电的，电学的

拓展 electrician *n.* 电学家，电工；electron *n.* 电子；electronic *a.* 电子的

诵读 He is an electrical engineer. 他是一名电气工程师。

elegant [ˈelɪɡənt] *a.* 优雅的；端庄的；雅致的

诵读 His manners are elegant. 他的举止优雅。

element [ˈelɪmənt] *n.* 元素；要素；成分

拓展 elementary *a.* 初步的；基本的；[化]元素

诵读 There is an element of truth in your argument. 你的论点有一定的道理。

elevate [ˈelɪveɪt] *vt.* 举起，提拔

拓展 elevator *n.* 直梯；escalator *n.* 自动扶梯

诵读 He was elevated to the rank of captain. 他被晋升为上尉。

eligible [ˈelɪdʒəbl] *a.* 符合条件的；合格的

巧记 前缀e- 出来+词根 lig 选择+后缀-ible能……=能被挑选出来的→符合条件的

诵读 In accordance with the recent policy, graduates who want to start their own businesses are eligible to apply for interest-free loans. 根据最新政策，想要创业的毕业生有资格申请无息贷款。

elite [eɪˈliːt] *n.* 精英 *a.* 精锐的，出类拔萃的

诵读 Industrial transformation provides opportunities for developing novel and elite small and medium-sized enterprises. 产业转型为培育专精特新中小企业提供了机遇。

electric [ɪˈlektrɪk] *a.* 电的，导电的，电动的

拓展 electricity *n.* 电，电流，电学

诵读 He just bought an electric shaver. 他刚买了个电动剃须刀。

emerge [ɪˈmɜːdʒ] *vt.* 显现，浮现

巧记 前缀 e- 出来+词根 merge 浸没=从浸没中出来→浮现

拓展 emergency *n.* 紧急情况，突然事件

诵读 The sun emerged from behind the clouds. 太阳从云层后面钻出来。

emigrate [ˈemɪɡreɪt] *vi.* 自本国移居他国

巧记 反义词 immigrate *vi.* 从他国移居本国

诵读 In the present difficult conditions, many people are emigrating from Britain. 在当前困难时期，很多人正离开英国，移居国外。

eminent [ˈemɪnənt] *a.* 显赫的；杰出的；有名的

诵读 We are expecting the arrival of an eminent scientist. 我们正期待一位著名科学家的来访。

emit [ɪˈmɪt] *vt.* 发出；散发；发行

巧记 前缀 e- 出来+词根 mit 传输=输出出去→散发，排放

诵读 The chimney emitted smoke. 烟囱冒烟。

emotion [ɪˈməʊʃən] *n.* 情绪，情感，感情

诵读 Love, hatred, and grief are emotions. 爱、恨和悲伤都是感情。

emphasis [ˈemfəsɪs] *n.* 强调，重点

搭配 lay emphasis on 强调

拓展 emphasize *v.* 强调

诵读 The dictionary places an emphasis on chanting examples. 该词典着重强调诵读的重要性。

employment [ɪmˈplɔɪmənt] *n.* 雇用；使用；工作

拓展 employee *n.* 雇员；employer *n.* 雇主

诵读 The employment rate of youths entering the labor market every year influences the potential economic growth to a certain extent. 每年进入劳动力市场的青年的就业率在某种程度上影响着经济的潜在增长率。

enclose [ɪnˈkləʊz] *vt.* 围住，圈起，封入

巧记 前缀 en-进入+词根 close 关闭→关闭在里面→围住

拓展 enclosure *n.* 围住，圈起

诵读 I enclosed a check for $50 with the letter. 我随信寄去 50 美元的支票。

encounter [ɪnˈkaʊntə] *n.&vt.* 遇到，遭遇；邂逅

诵读 He encountered many problems. 他遇到许多问题。

encourage [ɪnˈkʌrɪdʒ] *vt.* 鼓励，怂恿

诵读 The new company has made an encouraging start. 这家新公司开张大吉。

endure [ɪnˈdjʊə] *vt.* 忍受，持久，持续

巧记 endurance *n.* 忍耐力，持久力

诵读 I cannot endure that noise a moment again. 那吵闹声我一分钟也无法忍受下去了。

energetic [ˌenəˈdʒetɪk] *a.* 精力旺盛的；积极的

诵读 Cool autumn days make us feel energetic. 清秋日子使我们精力充沛。

enforce [ɪnˈfɔːs] *vt.* 实施；强制；坚持（要求等）

巧记 前缀 en-在……里面+词根 force力量=(具有力量去)实施，执行

诵读 The new law about seat belts in cars will be difficult to enforce. 关于开车系安全带的新法律会很难实施。

engage [ɪnˈɡeɪdʒ] *vi.* 从事，着手；约定；使订婚

搭配 engage in 从事

拓展 engagement *n.* 约会，约定；婚约

诵读 I can't come tomorrow because I have an engagement. 我明天不能来，因为我有约会。

engine [ˈendʒɪn] *n.* 发动机，引擎

拓展 engineering *n.* 工程学

诵读 Some trains have diesel engines. 有些火车使用柴油发动机。

enhance [ɪnˈhɑːns] *vt.* 提高，增强

诵读 Passing the examination should enhance your chances of getting a job. 通过了考试可以增加你找到工作的机会。

enlarge [ɪnˈlɑːdʒ] *vt.* 扩大

诵读 We are enlarging the vegetable garden to grow more food. 我们正在扩大菜园以生产更多蔬菜。

enlighten [ɪnˈlaɪtən] *vt.* 启发，启蒙，教导

巧记 前缀 en-使……+词根 light 灯光=使点亮，照亮→启发，开导

诵读 The child thought the world was flat until I enlightened him! 在我教这孩子之前，他认为世界是平的!

enormous [ɪˈnɔːməs] *a.* 巨大的，庞大的

巧记 前缀 e- 出来+词根 norm 规范=超出规范的→巨大的

诵读 He watched her with sadness and enormous pity. 他抱以悲哀和极大的同情看着她。

enquire [ɪnˈkwaɪə] *vi.&vt.* 询问，打听；调查

巧记 同 inquire

搭配 inquire into 询问

诵读 He enquired what I wanted. 他问我需要什么。

enrich [ɪnˈrɪtʃ] *vt.* 使富足；使肥沃

巧记 前缀 en- 使…… +词根 rich 富有的= 使富足

诵读 The discovery of oil will enrich the nation. 发现石油将使该国富裕起来。

enroll [ɪnˈrəʊl] *vt.* 招收；登记；入学

巧记 前缀 en-使……+词根 roll 名单 =上了名单→登记

诵读 Please enroll me in the contest. 我报名参加这次比赛。

ensure [ɪnˈʃʊə] *v.* 确保，保证；使安全

巧记 前缀 en-使……+词根 sure 确定= 使……确定→保证，保护

诵读 If you want to ensure that you catch the plane, take a taxi. 如果你想顺利登上飞机，那就乘出租车吧。

entertain [ˌentəˈteɪn] *vt.* 招待；使娱乐

巧记 前缀 enter-在……里面+词根 tain 保持= 保持（在快乐的状态）里→娱乐

拓展 entertainment *n.* 款待；娱乐

诵读 He does most of his entertaining in restaurants. 他大多数情况下在餐厅招待客人。

enthusiasm [ɪnˈθjuːzɪæzəm] *n.* 热情；狂热

拓展 enthusiastic *a.* 热情的，热心的

诵读 The new teacher is full of enthusiasm. 这位新来的老师十分热情。

entitle [ɪnˈtaɪtl] *vt.* 给予权利；给……命名

巧记 前缀 en-在……里面+词根 title标题，名号=给……题名，授权

搭配 be entitled to… 被赋予……

诵读 This ticket doesn't entitle you to travel first class. 你这张票不能坐头等舱。

environment [ɪnˈvaɪərənmənt] *n.* 环境；外界

拓展 environmental *a.* 环境的；environmentalist *n.* 环保主义者

诵读 Some 63% said they approved of a green tax to discourage behavior that harms the environment. 约63%的人表示，他们赞成征收环保税，以阻止损害环境的行为。

envy [ˈenvi] *vt.&n.* 羡慕，忌妒

巧记 同义词 jealousy

诵读 We typically envy our bosses not only for their higher salaries but also for the responsibility and authority they command. 我们通常会羡慕老板，不光是因为他们薪水高，还因为他们承担的责任和拥有的权威。

equal [ˈiːkwəl] *a.* 平等的；对等的

拓展 equality *n.* 同等；平等；equation *n.* （数学）等式，方程式

诵读 Political equality requires democratic political institutions. 政治平等需要民主的政治制度。

equip [ɪˈkwɪp] *vt.* 装备，配备

搭配 be equipped with 装备

诵读 An extra $130 is needed to equip it with third-generation wireless capability. 如配备 3G 无线上网功能则需额外支付 130 美元。

equivalent [ɪˈkwɪvələnt] *a.* 相等的，等价的 *n.* 相等物，等价物

巧记 前缀 equ-相等+i 无意义+词根 val 价值 = 相等的，等价的

搭配 be equivalent to 与……等价，相等的

诵读 China's budgets in these areas would be equivalent to about a quarter of those in the U.S. 中国在这些方面的预算将相当于美国的四分之一左右。

erase [ɪˈreɪz] *vt.* 擦掉；删去

巧记 橡皮擦是 eraser, 去掉词尾 r 就是擦除

诵读 I cannot erase the sight that I saw on the Great Wall. 我无法忘记我在长城亲眼所见的一幕。

erect [ɪˈrekt] *vt.* 建立，使竖立 *a.* 直立的

巧记 前缀 e-出来+词根 rect 正、直=直着走出来

诵读 Offices are increasingly open-plan nowadays,

pushing them to erect new barriers. 如今办公室越来越多地采用开放式设计，迫使他们设置新的隔断。

error ['erə] *n.* 错误，过失

拓展 erroneous *a.* 错误的，不正确的

诵读 There is no successful theory to guide the discovery of these materials, so scientists can only rely on repeated experiments and continuous trial and error, much like finding a needle in a haystack. 因为没有成功的理论来指导这些物质的发现，所以科学家只能依靠反复的实验和不断的试错，就像大海捞针一样。

essence ['esns] *n.* 本质，实质

拓展 essential *a.* 本质的，重要的；essentially 实际上

诵读 *The Dream of Red Chamber* is more like an encyclopedia because it encapsulates the essence of traditional Chinese culture, passed down for centuries. 《红楼梦》更像一部百科全书，它浓缩了几个世纪以来传承下来的中国传统文化的精髓。

establish [ɪsˈtæblɪʃ] *vt.* 建立，设立

拓展 well-established *a.* 完全形成的；沿用已久的；establishment *n.* 建立，设立

诵读 He wants to establish a domestic carbon emissions trading system. 他希望在国内建立碳排放交易体系。

estate [ɪˈsteɪt] *n.* 不动产；所有权；地位

搭配 real estate 房地产

诵读 He had a long career in real estate. 他曾长期从事房地产业。

estimate ['estɪmeɪt] *vt.* 估计 ['estɪmət] *n.* 估计，估价；评估

诵读 A conservative estimate of the bill, so far, is about £22,000. 到目前为止，这笔账单保守估计大约为 2.2 万英镑。

evaluate [ɪˈvæljʊeɪt] *vt.* 估价，评价；求……的值

巧记 前缀 e-出+词根 valu 价值+后缀-ate →算出价值→估价，评价

诵读 After the earthquake, volunteer psychologists arrived at the villages near the epicenter so as to evaluate the mental trauma on the surviors. 震后，心理学志愿者来到震中区附近的村庄，评估幸存者的心理创伤程度。

eventually [ɪˈventʃʊəli] *ad.* 终于，最后

诵读 Curbs targeting China's technology development do not benefit anyone and will eventually backfire. 针对中国科技发展的限制措施对任何人都没有好处，最终会适得其反。

evidence ['evɪdəns] *n.* 证据；明显

拓展 evident *a.* 明显的，明白的

诵读 Policies designed to deal with the threat of dangerous climate change, are lagging "far behind" the scientific evidence. 应对危险气候变化威胁的政策制定远远落后于科学证据。

evil ['iːvəl] *a.* 邪恶的，罪恶的 *n.* 邪恶，罪恶

巧记 不把生活(live)过好就是一种罪恶(evil)

诵读 He's not evil, but he's not Robin Hood either. 他不是恶魔，但也不是侠盗罗宾汉。

evoke [ɪˈvəʊk] *vt.* 唤起(回忆、感情等)；引起

巧记 前缀 e-出+词根 vok 声音=发出声音→唤起

诵读 The performance evoked a profound sense of longing for the homeland. 表演唤起了人们对祖国的深切思念。

evolve [ɪˈvɒlv] *vt.* 发展；进化；进展

巧记 前缀 e-出+词根 vol=旋转而出→发展

拓展 evolution *n.* 进化，演变，发展

诵读 It aims to clarify the evolution of western journalism. 本课程旨在阐明西方新闻事业的演变过程。

excel [ɪkˈsel] *vi.* 胜过其他；擅长 *vt.* 胜过，优于

拓展 excellent *a.* 优秀的

诵读 Designers excel in mastering practical skills and understanding design theory and aesthetics. 设计师擅长掌握实践技能和理解设计理论与审美。

exception [ɪkˈsepʃən] *n.* 例外，除外；反对；异议

巧记 exceptional *a.* 例外的，异常的

辨析 形近词 excerpt *n.&vt.* 摘录

诵读 A future economic landscape, he said, would be characterized by exceptional investor caution. 他表示，未来经济形势的特征就是投资人会格外谨慎。

excess ['ekses] *a.* 过量的，额外的 *n.* 过量；过剩

巧记 前缀 ex-出+词根 cess 走=走到范围之外的→过量；过剩

拓展 excessive *a.* 过多的；过分的；额外

诵读 This study suggests that excess noise exposure

in the workplace is an important occupational health issue. 这项研究表明，嘈杂的工作环境是一个重要的职业健康问题。

exchange [ɪksˈtʃeɪndʒ] *vt.&n.* 交换，兑换；交流
搭配 in exchange for 交换
诵读 The Russian exchange students have come to study in our university. 俄罗斯交换生来到我校交流学习。

exclaim [ɪksˈkleɪm] *vt.&vi.* 呼喊，惊叫，大声说
巧记 前缀 ex-出 +词根 clam 呼喊=呼喊，惊叫
诵读 She exclaimed, "this is the perfect blouse; I'll never part with it." 她兴奋地喊道："这件衬衫真是太完美了，我要把她一直穿在身上！"

exclude [ɪksˈkluːd] *vt.* 拒绝；排斥
巧记 前缀 ex-出 +词根 clud 关闭=关出去→排除
拓展 exclusive *a.* 独占的；排他的
搭配 exclusive news 独家新闻
诵读 Our figure skating club has exclusive use of the rink on Mondays. 我们的花样滑冰俱乐部星期一独家使用这个滑冰场。

execute [ˈeksɪkjuːt] *vt.* 实行；执行；履行；处死
拓展 executive *n.* 总经理 *a.* 执行的，实施的
诵读 Sino-chem has yet to execute a big international deal having failed last year to complete a bid for Australia's Nufarm. 自去年收购澳大利亚 Nufarm 公司以失败告终以来，中化集团尚未进行大规模的国际交易。

exert [ɪgˈzɜːt] *vt.* 尽力，施加
搭配 exert influence on… 对……施加影响
诵读 We want this administration to exert its pressure to finally find out whether it is necessary to implement the new policy. 我们希望政府施压，看看有没有必要实行新政策。

exhaust [ɪgˈzɔːst] *vt.* 使筋疲力尽，耗尽；抽完
诵读 Buying the right gift, saying the right words, even ordering the right dishes—these responsibilities can exhaust me. 买称心的礼物，说对心的话，甚至要点合胃口的菜，这些任务令我难以招架。

expand [ɪksˈpænd] *vt.* 膨胀，扩张；张开
拓展 expansion *n.* 扩张，膨胀
诵读 Health officials are proposing to expand their services by organizing counselling. 卫生官员计划通过组织咨询来扩展他们的服务。

expectation [ˌekspekˈteɪʃən] *n.* 预期，期望
搭配 meet the expectation 达到预期
诵读 Mother-in-law and daughter-in-law conflict often emerges from an expectation that each is criticizing or undermining the other. 婆媳冲突的原因通常是双方都认为对方在指责或贬低自己。

expend [ɪksˈpend] *vt.* 消费，花费
拓展 expense *n.* 花费；expenditure *n.* 经费；消耗
诵读 They don't have enough activity to expend their energy. 他们没有足够多的活动来释放自己的精力。

explode [ɪksˈpləʊd] *vi.* 爆炸，爆发
拓展 explosion *n.* 爆炸，爆发；explosive *a.* 爆炸性的
诵读 The Chinese economy is booming, and China's demand for overseas travel, especially among wealthy people, is about to explode. 中国经济正蓬勃发展，中国人尤其是富人对海外旅游的需求将激增。

exploit [ɪksˈplɔɪt] *vt.* 开拓；开发；剥削
诵读 We have enormous natural resources that we've been able to exploit. 我们有大量的自然资源可以开发利用。

explore [ɪksˈplɔː] *vt.* 勘探，探测，探究，探索
巧记 Internet Explorer: IE 浏览器
诵读 The original deal granted China the right to not only explore the field but to share in the profits. 原始合约规定，中国不但拥有开发油田的权利，同时还可分享获利。

expose [ɪksˈpəʊz] *vt.* 使暴露；使曝光
巧记 前缀 ex-出 +词根 pose 放置=放置在外→暴露
搭配 expose… to… 暴露于……，接触
拓展 exposure *n.* 暴露，揭露
诵读 They will expand work space on the station and allow astronauts to expose experiments to the vacuum of space. 他们将扩展空间站的工作空间，并且让宇航员在真空空间中进行实验。

express [ɪksˈpres] *vt.* 表达，表示
拓展 *a.* 特快的，快速的 *n.* 快车，快运
诵读 Some people consider prolonged eye contact impolite and smile to express a range of emotions. 有些人认为长时间的目光接触是不礼貌的，微笑可以表达很多情绪。

examine [ɪgˈzæmɪn] *vt.* 检查,细查;考核;审查

诵读 She examined the pupils in mathematics. 她考查了学生们的数学知识。

explain [ɪksˈpleɪn] *vt.* 解释,说明

诵读 I don't understand this, but Paul will explain it to us. 这事我不明白,不过保罗会给我们解释的。

extra [ˈekstrə] *a.* 额外的,附加的 *n.* 附加物,额外的东西 *ad.* 特别地,非常

僻义 *n.* 临时工;额外人手

诵读 Breakfast is an extra at this hotel. 这家旅馆早餐要另外收费。

extend [ɪksˈtend] *vt.&vi.* 延长,延伸

拓展 extension *n.* 延长,扩大;extensive *a.* 广泛的

诵读 The hot weather extended into October. 炎热的天气一直持续到10月。

extent [ɪksˈtent] *n.* 程度,限度

诵读 I was surprised at the extent of her knowledge. 我对她的知识广博感到惊讶。

exterior [ɪkˈstɪərɪə] *a.* 外部的,外面的 *n.* 外部

巧记 同义词 external

诵读 The exterior covering of the seed is very hard. 种子的外壳比较硬。

extraordinary [ɪksˈtrɔːdnərɪ] *a.* 异乎寻常的

巧记 合成词:extra 以外的 + ordinary 平常的 →平常之外的→非凡的

诵读 What an extraordinary idea! 多么奇特的想法!

extreme [ɪksˈtriːm] *a.* 极度的 *n.* 极端;最大程度

诵读 Extreme cold will cause the engine to fail. 严寒会导致发动机失灵。

eyesight [ˈaɪsaɪt] *n.* 视力

巧记 合成词:eye 眼睛 +sight 视力

诵读 Her eyesight is improving. 她的视力改善了。

expert [ˈekspɜːt] *n.* 专家,能手

搭配 be expert in 熟练于

诵读 The Egyptians were expert in the working of stone. (古)埃及人以石工技艺见长。

export [eksˈpɔːt] *vt.&n.* 输出,出口 *n.* 出口商品

巧记 反义词 import *n.&v.* 进口

诵读 Purchase tax was not payable on goods for export. 出口商品无须缴纳购置税。

eccentric [ɪkˈsentrɪk] *a.* 古怪的 *n.* 古怪的人

诵读 She is so eccentric that she is regarded as a bit of a curiosity. 她非常古怪,算是个奇人。

edible [ˈedɪbl] *a.* 可食用的

诵读 The difference between edible and poisonous berries is not obvious. 可食用的浆果和有毒浆果之间的区别并不明显。

ego [ˈiːgəʊ] *n.* 自我,自负

诵读 He is absolute ego in all things. 他在所有事情上都绝对自我。

eject [ɪˈdʒekt] *vt.* 喷射,排出;驱逐

巧记 前缀 e-出来+词根 ject 扔, 投=被扔出来→喷射

诵读 The police came and ejected the noisy men from the restaurant. 警察来了,把吵闹的人赶出餐厅。

elaborate [ɪˈlæbəreɪt] *vt.* 详细说明 [ɪˈlæbərət] *a.* 精心制作的;详尽的

巧记 前缀 e-出来+词根 labor 工作+后缀-ate→努力做出来→精心制作

诵读 Just tell us the facts; don't elaborate on them. 只是告诉我们事实,不要加以发挥。

elapse [ɪˈlæps] *vi.* (时间)溜走;(光阴)逝去

巧记 前缀 e-出来+词根 lapse 溜走→时光溜走→逝去

诵读 Four years have elapsed since he went to London. 自从他去了伦敦,已过了四年。

elastic [ɪˈlæstɪk] *a.* 弹性的

巧记 前缀 e-出来+词根 last 延长+ic →能够延长的→有弹力的

诵读 The rules are elastic. 这些规则可以变通。

eliminate [ɪˈlɪmɪneɪt] *vt.* 淘汰;删除

巧记 前缀 e-出来+词根 limi 界限=界限以外→排出

诵读 His job is to eliminate the mistake from your writing. 改正你文章的错误是他的工作。

eloquent [ˈeləkwənt] *a.* 雄辩的;口才流利的

诵读 The defence lawyer made an eloquent plea for his client's acquittal. 被告方的律师为委托人的无罪开释做了强有力的辩护。

embark [ɪmˈbɑːk] *vi.* 上船（或飞机、汽车等）

辨义 *vi.* 着手，从事

诵读 He is about to embark on a new business venture. 他准备开始新的商业投资。

embarrass [ɪmˈbærəs] *vt.* 使困窘；阻碍

巧记 前缀 em-在……里面+词根 bar 栏杆=被拦在栏杆里→阻碍

诵读 I don't like making speech in public, because it is so embarrassing. 我不喜欢在公众面前讲话，太难为情了。

embed [ɪmˈbed] *vt.* 把……嵌（埋、插）入，扎牢

诵读 They embedded the pilings deep into the subsoil. 他们把桩深深打进地基里。

embody [ɪmˈbɒdi] *vt.* 具体表达；包含

诵读 The letter embodied all his ideas. 这封信表达了他的全部看法。

embrace [ɪmˈbreɪs] *vt.* 拥抱；包含；采用

诵读 She embraced her son tenderly. 她温柔地拥抱了儿子。

empirical [ɪmˈpɪrɪkəl] *a.* 经验主义的

诵读 We now have empirical evidence that the moon is covered with dust. 现在我们有实证证据表明月球上布满了灰尘。

endeavor [ɪnˈdevə] *vi.&n.* 努力，尽力

诵读 You must endeavor to improve your work. 你必须努力改进工作。

endow [ɪnˈdaʊ] *vt.* 资助，捐赠；（with）给予，赋予

诵读 The dissemination and sharing of technology can endow competitive power. 技术的传播和共享可以赋予竞争力。

entail [ɪnˈteɪl] *vt.* 使承担；需要

诵读 The work entails precision so you are the very person for it. 这工作需要精确性，你是最合适的人选。

enterprise [ˈentəpraɪz] *n.* 事业，企（事）业单位

辨义 *n.* 事业心，进取心

拓展 entrepreneur *n.* 企业家，主办人

诵读 Do you believe in private enterprise, or in government ownership of industry? 你赞成私人企业还是国有企业？

entity [ˈentɪti] *n.* 实体；组织，机构

搭配 entity shop 实体店

诵读 The policy package will give strong supports to entity economy and private enterprise. 一揽子政策将大力支持实体经济和民营企业。

envisage [ɪnˈvɪzɪdʒ] *vt.* 想象，设想，展望

巧记 前缀 en-表动词+词根 vis 看=使你看到→展望

诵读 Nobody can envisage the consequences of total nuclear war. 没有人能够想象全面核战争的后果。

epidemic [ˌepɪˈdemɪk] *n.* 流行病；蔓延 *a.* 盛行的

辨析 epidemic 通常指疾病的流行；popular 通常指某个人或事物受到青睐

诵读 The mystery of the mass animal death epidemic deepens. 近期频发动物集体死亡事件再添疑云。

episode [ˈepɪsəʊd] *n.* 一段情节；片段

诵读 This episode is as repetitive as the first. 这部电影和第一部一样重复拖沓。

epoch [ˈiːpɒk] *n.* 新纪元；时代

巧记 同义词 era

诵读 A man has passed away thanks to whom a whole new epoch was born. 他走了，他曾经缔造了新纪元。

erosion [ɪˈrəʊʒən] *n.* 腐蚀；削弱，减少

搭配 soil erosion 水土流失；moral erosion 道德沦丧

诵读 Erosion was damaging industrial areas and cities as well as remote rural land. 水土流失正在对工业区、各个城市以及偏远的乡村土地造成破坏。

erupt [ɪˈrʌpt] *vi.* （尤指火山）爆发

巧记 前缀 e-出来+词根 rupt 断裂→断裂而出→爆发

诵读 Unless the government acts very quickly, it will erupt into a tribal war. 除非政府迅速行动，否则将爆发部落战争。

escalate [ˈeskəleɪt] *vt.&vi.* 逐步增长，逐步升级

巧记 前缀 e-出来+词根 scal 规模+后缀-ate=规模逐步增大

诵读 Her fear was escalating into panic. 她的恐惧逐渐升级为恐慌。

escort [ɪˈskɔːt] *vt.* 护送（卫）；陪同 [ˈeskɔːt] *n.* 警卫，护送者

诵读 My sister needed an escort for a company dinner. 我妹妹需要有人陪她参加公司晚宴。

esteem [ɪsˈtiːm] *n.* 尊敬，尊重 *vt.* 尊重，敬重

拓展 self-esteem *n.* 自尊

诵读 Wall Street bankers are not the only figures who have suffered a loss of public esteem. 华尔街银行家并不是唯一失去公众尊重的人物。

eternal [iːˈtɜːnl] *n.* 永久的，永恒的

诵读 We ask in your goodness to give eternal light and peace to all who died here. 我们请求您的慈爱永远照耀那些在这里逝去的人。

ethnic [ˈeθnɪk] *a.* 种族的

诵读 The government says the opposition has been orchestrating the ethnic violence in the region. 政府说，反对党一直在这个地区策动族群暴力事件。

evacuate [ɪˈvækjʊeɪt] *vt.* 撤离，疏散，排泄，剥夺

巧记 前缀 e-出+词根 vac 空的+后缀-uate = 都出去清空里面→撤离，疏散

诵读 Army helicopters tried to evacuate the injured. 军队直升机试图转移伤员。

evade [ɪˈveɪd] *vt.* 逃避，回避；避开，躲避

巧记 前缀 e-出+词根 vade 走=走出去→逃避

诵读 If you try to evade paying your taxes, you risk going to prison. 如果你试图逃税，你就有入狱的危险了。

evaporate [ɪˈvæpəreɪt] *vi.* 蒸发，挥发；发射

巧记 前缀 e-出+词根 vapor 蒸汽+后缀-ate→变成蒸汽→蒸发

诵读 Disinfectants evaporate more quickly in high temperatures. 消毒剂在高温下挥发得更快。

exaggerate [ɪgˈzædʒəreɪt] *vt.* 夸大，夸张

诵读 People are more likely to exaggerate their good points while hiding anything negative. 人们倾向于夸大自己的优点，掩饰自己的缺点。

exceed [ɪkˈsiːd] *vt.* 超过，胜过；越出

巧记 前缀 ex-出+词根 ceed 走→超越

拓展 exceedingly *ad.* 极端地，非常

诵读 Citation should not exceed 2,500 characters or 10 percent of the work. 引用非诗词类作品不得超过2 500字或被引用作品的十分之一。

excursion [ɪksˈkɜːʃən] *n.* 短途旅行，游览

僻义 *n.* 离题；[物理]偏移，漂移

诵读 We also recommend a full-day optional excursion to the upper Douro. 我们还推荐去杜罗河上游的短途自助一日游。

exemplify [ɪgˈzemplɪfaɪ] *vt.* 举例证明

巧记 example 例子，榜样+后缀-ify→例证；示范

诵读 But if there was ever a company that we should expect to exemplify that idea, surely it was Google. 但是，如果我们期待有一家公司去证明这一说法，那这家公司显然就是谷歌。

exempt [ɪgˈzempt] *a.* 免除的 *vt.* 免除 *n.* 免税者；被免除义务者

诵读 It's got an MOT, and it's tax exempt. 它拥有正式牌照，而且免税。

exile [ˈeksaɪl] *n.&vt.* 流放，放逐

诵读 The documents were written while he was in exile on the island. 这些手稿是他被流放到那个岛上时所写。

exotic [ɪgˈzɒtɪk] *a.* 奇异的；异国情调的

诵读 As with exotic cars, someone bought an exotic watch. 像买各式新奇汽车一样，有些人买了一块奇异的手表。

expedition [ˌekspɪˈdɪʃən] *n.* 远征，探险

诵读 The expedition was wrecked by bad planning and poor navigation. 这次探险因计划不周和航行不畅而失败。

expel [ɪksˈpel] *vt.* 把……开除；驱逐；排出

巧记 前缀 ex-出 +词根 pel 推=往外推→驱逐

诵读 They threatened to expel him from his adoptive country. 他们威胁将他驱逐出他的移居国。

expertise [ˌekspɜːˈtiːz] *n.* 专门知识，专长

巧记 expert专家+后缀-ise→"专家所掌握的东西"→专门知识

诵读 The agreement will allow cooperation between organizations with complementary expertise and know-how. 这项协议将允许专业和技能互补的组织进行合作。

expire [ɪksˈpaɪə] *vi.* 期满；终止；断气

巧记 前缀 ex-出 +词根 pir（=spir 呼吸）=呼出最后一口气→断气

诵读 When does your driving licence expire? 你的

驾照什么时候到期?

explicit [ɪksˈplɪsɪt] *a.* 详述的, 明确的

辨义 *a.* 坦率的

诵读 She was very explicit on the issue during her visit to Beijing. 她在访问北京期间对这个问题表达了非常明确的看法。

exquisite [ˈekskwɪzɪt] *a.* 优美的, 高雅的

诵读 We ordered a pan-fried salt and pepper Chilean sea bass that was exquisite and skillfully cooked. 我们点了一份椒盐智利鲈鱼, 菜品精致, 厨艺也不错。

extinct [ɪksˈtɪŋkt] *a.* 灭绝的; 熄灭的

诵读 Dinosaurs have been extinct for millions of years. 恐龙已灭绝数百万年了。

extinguish [ɪksˈtɪŋgwɪʃ] *v.* 熄灭; 消灭

诵读 Nothing could extinguish his faith in human nature. 没有任何东西能使他丧失对人性的信念。

extract [ɪksˈtrækt] *vt.&n.* 拔出, 抽出

辨义 *n.* 精华; 摘录

巧记 前缀 ex-出+词根-tract 拉=往外拉→抽出

诵读 He has extracted out of that pamphlet a few notorious falsehoods. 他已从那本小册子中摘录了几条臭名昭著的谎言。

extravagant [ɪksˈtrævəgənt] *a.* 奢侈的; 过分的

巧记 前缀 extra- 超过 +词根 vag 走= 走过了→过度的, 过分的

诵读 He makes the most extravagant claims for his new system. 他对自己的新系统大肆吹捧。

excitement [ɪkˈsaɪtmənt] *n.* 刺激, 激动

诵读 The happiness and the excitement had been drained completely from her voice. 幸福和激动已经完全从她的声音中消失了。

exhibit [ɪgˈzɪbɪt] *vt.* 展出, 陈列

诵读 His work was exhibited in the best galleries in America, Europe and Asia. 他的作品在美国、欧洲和亚洲顶级的美术馆都展览过。

exit [ˈeksɪt] *n.* 出口, 通道

诵读 He picked up the case and walked toward the exit. 他提起箱子朝出口走去。

enchant [ɪnˈtʃɑːnt] *vt.* 使欣喜; 使心醉

诵读 He was enchanted by the idea. 他听到这个主意后欣喜若狂。

fade [feɪd] *vi.* 褪色; 衰减 *n.* 淡出

诵读 The sound of thunder faded into the distance. 雷声逐渐消失在远处。

failure [ˈfeɪljə] *n.* 失败, 不及格; 故障

诵读 Her plans ended in failure. 她的计划以失败告终。

fair [feə] *a.* 公平的, 合理的

辨义 *n.* 集市, 交易会 (funfair 游乐场)

诵读 It is not fair to kick another player in football. 足球比赛是不允许踢对方球员的。

fairy [ˈfeəri] *a.* 幻想中的; 虚构的 *n.* 仙女; 精灵

诵读 In his dream, he became a fairy. 在梦中, 他变成了一个小精灵。

faithful [ˈfeɪθfʊl] *a.* 守信的, 忠实的

诵读 We are all faithful listeners to the program. 我们都是这档节目的忠实听众。

facility [fəˈsɪlɪti] *n.* 灵巧, 熟练

辨义 *n.* (复数)设备, 设施

拓展 facilitate *v.* 推动; 帮助

诵读 His facility with languages is surprising. 他的语言才能很惊人。

factor [ˈfæktə] *n.* 因素, 要素

诵读 His friendly manners is an important factor in his rapid success. 待人和气是他迅速成功的因素之一。

faculty [ˈfækəltɪ] *n.* 学院, 系; 全体教学人员

辨义 *n.* 才能

诵读 He has the faculty to learn languages easily. 他有学语言的才能。

fake [feɪk] *n.* 假货，赝品 *a.* 假的，冒充的 *vt.* 伪造；伪装

诵读 The antique is a fake. 那古董是一件赝品。

fame [feɪm] *n.* 名声；名望

诵读 She hoped to find fame as a poet. 她希望写诗成名。

familiar [fəˈmɪljə] *a.* 熟悉的

搭配 be familiar with... 对……熟悉

诵读 Are you familiar with football? 你熟悉足球吗?

fancy [ˈfænsi] *n.* 喜欢 *v.* 想象 *a.* 花哨的

拓展 fantastic *a.* 奇异的，幻想的；fantasy *n.* 幻想

诵读 Everyone should indulge in fantasy on occasion. 每个人都应偶尔沉浸在想象之中。

fare [feə] *n.* 车费，船费

僻义 *v.* 过活；进展；经营

诵读 The bus fare has gone up by another one yuan. 公共汽车车票钱又涨了 1 元。

farewell [ˈfeəˈwel] *int.* 再会 *n.* 告别

巧记 海明威的名著 *Farewell to Arms*《永别了，武器》

诵读 His farewell speech marked his exit from politics. 他的告别演说是他退出政界的标志。

fascinate [ˈfæsɪneɪt] *vt.* 迷住，强烈吸引

诵读 I have always been fascinated with astronomy. 我一直对天文学很着迷。

fashion [ˈfæʃən] *n.* 风尚，风气

僻义 *vt.* 形成，制成

拓展 fashionable *a.* 流行的，时髦的

诵读 The long hair among artists is out of fashion. 艺术家留长头发已不流行了。

fault [fɔːlt] *n.* 过失；缺点，毛病

拓展 faulty *a.* 有错误的，有缺点的

诵读 Though no fault of her own she lost her job. 完全不是由于她的过错而她却失去了工作。

favor [ˈfeɪvə] *n.* 恩惠，帮助；好感，喜爱

僻义 *vt.* 赞成，支持

辨析 favorable *a.* 赞许的；有利的；favorite *n.* 最喜欢的人或物

搭配 in favor of 有利于；赞成

诵读 He worked hard to get back in the teacher's favor. 他努力学习想重新赢得老师的喜爱。

feature [ˈfiːtʃə] *n.* 特征；特色；特写

僻义 *v.* 描绘

诵读 Wet weather is a feature of this country. 多雨是这个国家的特征。

federal [ˈfedərəl] *a.* 联邦的

拓展 federation *n.* 同盟；联邦

诵读 What hopes are there for the federation? 这个联盟有些什么希望?

fee [fiː] *n.* 费用

诵读 Does your school charge school fees? 你们学校收费吗?

feedback [ˈfiːdbæk] *n.* 反馈；回馈

诵读 The company welcome feedback from people who use the goods it produces. 该公司欢迎产品用户提供反馈信息。

fellowship [ˈfeləʊʃɪp] *n.* 伙伴关系；联谊会，团体

诵读 It looks that they'll be admitted to the fellowship. 看来他们将获批入会。

female [ˈfiːmeɪl] *n.* 女性 *a.* 女性的；柔弱的

诵读 We only employ female workers. 我们只雇用女工。

feminine [ˈfemɪnɪn] *a.* 女性的；娇柔的

诵读 This is a smart, yet soft and feminine look. 这是一张透着精明的面孔，但是线条柔和，女人味十足。

festival [ˈfestəvəl] *n.* 节日

诵读 The Mid-Autumn Festival is the second most important festival in China after Chinese New Year. 中秋节是中国仅次于农历新年的第二大节日。

fire [ˈfaɪə] *n.* 火 *vt.* 开枪；射击

僻义 *vt.* 解雇

搭配 on fire 点火，着火；set fire to 点燃

拓展 fireman *n.* 消防队员；fireplace *n.* 壁炉

诵读 The manager fired Bob because he was always late for work. 鲍勃因上班总迟到而被经理解雇。

firm [fɜːm] *a.* 坚定的；稳固的 *n.* 公司，商号

僻义 *v.* 巩固，强化

诵读 He reshuffled the cabinet to firm his government. 他重新改组内阁以强化其政府。

fiber [ˈfaɪbə] *n.* 纤维；构造

诵读 Cotton is a natural fiber but nylon is a man-made fiber. 棉花是天然纤维，尼龙是人造纤维。

fiction [ˈfɪkʃən] *n.* 虚构，编造；小说

诵读 The newspaper's account of what happened was a complete fiction. 那家报纸对这件事情的报道纯属虚构。

fierce [fɪəs] *a.* 凶猛的，残忍的

诵读 Because there is so much unemployment, the competition for jobs is very fierce. 由于失业人数众多，找工作竞争十分激烈。

figure [ˈfɪɡə] *n.* 体形；轮廓；数字；图形

搭配 figure out 计算；推测

诵读 I am no good at figures! 我算术不行。

file [faɪl] *n.* 文件，档案 *v.* 锉

诵读 Here is our files on the Middle East. 这是我们有关中东的资料。

finance [faɪˈnæns] *n.* 财政，金融 *vt.* 提供资金

拓展 financial *a.* 财政的，金融的

诵读 State finance has also entered a new stage. 国家财政也进入了一个新阶段。

fitting [ˈfɪtɪŋ] *a.* 适当的，恰当的

僻义 *n.* （复数）配件，附件

诵读 It is fitting that we should remember him on his birthday. 他生日时，我们应有所表示才行。

flaw [flɔː] *n.* 裂缝；缺陷

诵读 The flaws in the contract are quite obvious. 合同上的漏洞非常明显。

flexible [ˈfleksəbl] *a.* 柔韧的，易弯曲的，灵活的

诵读 We can visit you on Saturday or Sunday; our plan is fairly flexible. 我们星期六或星期日都可以看你，我们的计划比较灵活。

flight [flaɪt] *n.* 飞翔，飞行；航班；航程

诵读 There are two flights to Australia. 去澳洲有两个航班。

flavor [ˈfleɪvə] *n.* 风味；韵味

诵读 This movie really catches the flavor of New York. 这部影片真正抓住了纽约的特色。

float [fləʊt] *vi.&n.* 浮动，飘动

诵读 The old man floats from town to town with nowhere to go and nothing to do. 这位老人从一个市镇游荡到另一个市镇，无所事事，也没有目的地。

fresh [freʃ] *a.* 新的，新鲜的

僻义 *a.* 精神饱满的，生气勃勃的

辨析 同形词 flesh *n.* 肉，肌肉

诵读 The old man looks as fresh as a young man. 这位老人看上去像年轻人一样生气勃勃。

frighten [ˈfraɪtən] *vt.* 使恐怖，吓唬

诵读 You'll find that I don't frighten easily. 你会发现我不是轻易就会害怕的。

flu [fluː] *n.* （influenza）流行性感冒

focus [ˈfəʊkəs] *n.* 焦点 *vi.* 使聚集

搭配 focus on 焦点，聚集

诵读 The focus of the U.S. presidential race shifts to the mid-Atlantic region of the country. 美国总统竞选的焦点转移到美国中大西洋地区。

folk [fəʊk] *n.* 人们；民族；亲属 *a.* 民间的

搭配 folk music 民乐；folk art 民间艺术

诵读 Young folk with blue eyes are generally seen as being more flirtatious, sexy and kind. 人们常认为长着蓝色眼睛的年轻人更具诱惑力、更性感、更让人感到亲切。

forbid [fəˈbɪd] *vt.* 禁止

巧记 the Forbidden City 紫禁城

诵读 The bylaws forbid playing ball in the public garden. 地方法规定任何人不得在公园打球或踢球。

forecast [ˈfɔːkɑːst] *vt.&n.* 预测，预报

巧记 前缀 fore-在前面+词根 cast 抛掷=提前说出→预测，预报

搭配 weather forecast 天气预报

诵读 The study also forecast an explosion in the diet soft-drink market. 该研究还预测低糖软饮料市场将迅猛增长。

forehead [ˈfɔːhed] *n.* 前额

foremost [ˈfɔːməʊst] *a.* 最初的；最重要的 *ad.* 首先

巧记 前缀 fore-在前面+词根 most 最高级→最先的；最初的

搭配 first and foremost 最重要的

诵读 Its consequences are universal and will be felt first and foremost by the poorest. 它的影响是全球性的，并且将首先波及极贫困人口。

foresee [fɔːˈsiː] *vt.* 预见，预知

巧记 前缀 fore-在前面+词根 see 看见→预见，预知

诵读 Which of the younger players do you foresee can give you trouble in the near future, if any? 你认为哪

些年轻球员在将来会给你带来麻烦，如果有的话？

formal ['fɔ:məl] *a.* 正式的；形式的

辨析 同形词 former *pron.* 前者

诵读 The authority will issue its first formal apology for past mistreatment. 政府会对过去的过失首次做出正式道歉。

forth [fɔ:θ] *ad.* 向前；向外

搭配 back and forth 来回地

诵读 She passed the needle through the rough cloth, back and forth. 她一针一针地缝那块粗布。

forthcoming [fɔ:θ'kʌmɪŋ] *a.* 即将到来的；准备好的 *n.* 来临

诵读 Many young people will host parties in the forthcoming 7-day holiday. 很多年轻人将在即将到来的7天假期里举行晚会。

fortunate ['fɔ:tʃənɪt] *a.* 幸运的，侥幸的

诵读 I was also fortunate enough to be cherished and encouraged by some strong male role models. 我也很幸运地从一些男性榜样那里得到珍爱和鼓励。

forum ['fɔ:rəm] *n.* 论坛，讨论会

foster ['fɒstə] *vt.* 养育；收养；怀抱 *a.* 收养的

诵读 Fashionable clothing is often an unaffordable dream for young girls who live in foster care. 对那些生活在寄养家庭的女孩来说，时尚服饰通常是一个不可能实现的梦想。

found [faʊnd] *vt.* 建立；创立

拓展 foundation *n.* 基础；建立；基金

诵读 We must lay a new foundation for growth and prosperity. 我们必须为增长和繁荣奠定新的基础。

frequency ['fri:kwənsi] *n.* 频率，周率

拓展 frequent *a.* 经常的

诵读 The frequency is expected to increase during next month's World Cup. 这一频率在下月世界杯期间预计还会增加。

friction ['frɪkʃən] *n.* 摩擦，摩擦力

诵读 There are plenty of potential sources of friction between the two Pacific powers. 在两大太平洋国之间，存在着诸多的潜在摩擦的导火索。

fruitful ['fru:tful] *a.* 多产的；富有成效的

巧记 词根 fruit 果实+后缀-ful 表示充满的形容词后缀＝多产的；富有成效的

诵读 We had a long, happy, fruitful relationship. 我们有过一段长久、愉快而富有成效的关系。

frustrate ['frʌstreɪt] *vt.* 挫败，阻挠，使灰心

诵读 We shall not do anything that may frustrate or endanger the campaign itself. 我们不会做任何阻碍或危及这次行动的事情。

fulfill [fʊl'fil] *vt.* 完成，履行，实践，满足

搭配 fulfill one's dream 实现某人的梦想

诵读 My father was very keen that I should fulfill my potential. 我父亲热切地希望我能够发挥出自身的潜力。

function ['fʌŋkʃən] *n.* 功能，作用 *vi.* 起作用

诵读 His function is vital to the accomplishment of the agency's mission. 要完成该机构的使命，他的作用至关重要。

fund [fʌnd] *n.* 资金，基金

搭配 raise fund 募集资金

诵读 The concert will raise funds for research into AIDS. 这场音乐会将为艾滋病研究筹款。

fundamental [fʌndə'mentəl] *a.* 基础的，基本的

诵读 I am doing so because they are fundamental to our economic growth. 这样做是因为它们是我们经济增长的基础。

fur [fɜ:] *n.* 毛，毛皮

furious ['fjʊərɪəs] *a.* 狂怒的，狂暴的，猛烈的

巧记 气的毛（fur）都竖了起来，相当的愤怒。

诵读 Condemnations of AIG and the bonuses were coming fast and furious. 对 AIG 集团和该集团发放奖金行动的谴责声铺天盖地。

furnish ['fɜ:nɪʃ] *vt.* 供应，提供；装备，布置

诵读 First you must find out the clause of the quality problems and furnish sufficient evidence. 首先你必须查看有关质量问题的条款，并提供足够的证据。

fabricate ['fæbrɪkeɪt] *vt.* 捏造，编造

诵读 The story was fabricated and not completely true. 这篇报道是捏造的，一点都不真实。

fabulous [ˈfæbjʊləs] *a.* 极好的；极为巨大的

巧记 fabul 说+后缀-ous→传说中的，难以置信的

诵读 This is a fabulous sum of money. 这是一笔巨款。

famine [ˈfæmɪn] *n.* 饥荒

巧记 谐音"发米"

诵读 Many people die during famines every year. 每年有很多人死于饥荒。

fasten [ˈfɑːsən] *vt.* 扎牢，使固定

诵读 The door fastens with a hook. 这门是用钩子闩紧的。

fatigue [fəˈtiːg] *n.&vt.*（使）疲劳

诵读 He was pale with fatigue after his sleepless night. 他一夜没睡，脸色苍白，十分疲惫。

feasible [ˈfiːzəbl] *a.* 可行的；切实可行的；行得通的

诵读 This is a feasible scheme. 这是一个切实可行的计划。

feeble [ˈfiːbl] *a.* 虚弱的，无力的

诵读 Grandfather has been getting feeble lately. 祖父近来身体越来越虚弱。

fertile [ˈfɜːtaɪl] *a.* 肥沃的，富饶的

拓展 fertilizer *n.* 肥料

诵读 Some fish are very fertile.They lay thousands of eggs. 有些鱼是非常多产的，它们能产数以千计的鱼卵。

filter [ˈfɪltə] *n.* 滤器，滤纸

诵读 The lake water passes through a filter before it is piped to our homes. 湖水过滤后用管道输送到各家各户。

flame [fleɪm] *n.* 火焰，火苗 *vi.* 发火焰，燃烧

诵读 The candles flamed brighter. 烛光更明亮了。

flash [flæʃ] *n.&vi.* 闪光，闪亮

诵读 A bright light flashed across the sky. 一道亮光从天空掠过。

flatter [ˈflætə] *vt.* 奉承；使高兴

拓展 flattering *a.* 讨人喜欢的

诵读 We flattered her about her cooking. 我们恭维她的烹调技术。

fling [flɪŋ] *vt.*（用力地）扔，抛，丢

诵读 Flinging up his sleeve in impatience, he walked off. 他不耐烦地一甩袖子，就走了。

flock [flɒk] *n.* 一群；大量 *vi.* 群集，成群

搭配 a flock of birds 一群鸟

诵读 Many experts now expect more delegates will flock to Biden. 许多专家认为更多代表会趋之若鹜，支持拜登。

flourish [ˈflʌrɪʃ] *n.&vi.* 繁荣，茂盛，兴旺

诵读 Keep the soil moist, and the seedling will flourish. 保持土壤湿润，那样幼苗就能茁壮成长。

fluctuate [ˈflʌktjʊeɪt] *vi.* 波动；起伏

搭配 fluctuate in 在某方面波动；fluctuate between… and… 在某个区间波动

诵读 There's a great many reasons why a woman's weight may fluctuate. 女性的体重变化受到很多因素的影响。

fluent [ˈfluːənt] *a.* 流利的，流畅的

巧记 词根 flu 流动+ 后缀-ent →流利的

诵读 "I saw her at the exit," he said in nearly fluent English. "我在安全出口处看见她。"他用一口近乎流利的英语说道。

fluid [ˈfluːɪd] *a.* 流动的，液体的 *n.* 流体，液体

巧记 词根 flu 流动+后缀-id 表示状态

诵读 Make sure that you drink plenty of fluids. 务必保证摄入足够的水分。

flush [flʌʃ] *n.* 脸红

僻义 *vt.* 冲洗

诵读 Flush the eye with clean cold water for at least 15 minutes. 用干净冷水冲洗眼睛至少 15 分钟。

forge [fɔːdʒ] *vt.* 锻造，伪造 *n.* 锻工车间；锻炉

巧记 谐音记忆：仿制（forge）

诵读 Let us seize the opportunity to forge ahead, hand in hand, and work together to enhance cooperation as partners. 让我们抓住机遇、携手前行，共同加强伙伴合作。

format [ˈfɔːmæt] *n.* 版式，格式 *vt.* 设计；安排

拓展 formation *n.* 形成；构成

诵读 Despite free elections and the formation of a representative government, instability grew. 尽管伊拉克举行了自由选举，并组成了代表制政府，但动乱在不断加剧。

formidable [ˈfɔːmɪdəbl] *a.* 令人敬畏的；可怕的

诵读 He remained a formidable opponent. 他依然是一个令人敬畏的对手。

formula [ˈfɔːmjʊlə] *n.* 公式；规则；药方

巧记 F1 方程式赛车中的 F 代表 formula

诵读 No adverse reactions have been found so far in patients who took the formula. 迄今为止，使用此方剂的患者尚未出现不良反应。

formulate [ˈfɔːmjʊleɪt] *vt.* 用公式表示；规划；设计

诵读 The meeting promoted consensus on how to formulate a way forward. 会议就如何制订解决方案达成共识。

foul [faʊl] *a.* 污秽的；邪恶的 *vt.* 弄脏

诵读 In the end, you'll learn more and foul up less. 最后，你会学到很多，也不会把事情弄糟。

fraction [ˈfrækʃən] *n.* 碎片，小部分；分数

诵读 It's just ridiculous that the auto industry is getting tormented over getting a fraction of the money we have given Wall Street. 我们要的钱只不过是华尔街得到的零头而已，但是汽车工业为此却倍受指责，简直荒谬。

fracture [ˈfræktʃə] *n.&vi.&vt.* 裂缝；骨折

fragile [ˈfrædʒaɪl] *a.* 易碎的；虚弱的，脆弱的

诵读 He remains the anchor of the country's fragile political balance. 他仍然是维系该国脆弱政治平衡的支柱。

fragment [ˈfrægmənt] *n.* 碎片，小部分，片段

诵读 We now know that this climate change caused the rainforests to fragment into small "islands" of forest. 我们现在了解到此次气候变化将雨林分裂为小型森林"岛"。

fragrant [ˈfreɪɡrənt] *a.* 香的；芬芳的

诵读 They held their wedding in the evening at a hotel in Fragrant Hills on the outskirts of Beijing. 他们的婚礼晚宴是在北京郊外香山的一家宾馆举行的。

frame [freɪm] *n.* 框架；体格；组织 *vt.* 设计；制订

拓展 framework *n.* 构架；框架

诵读 It seems that most designers don't want her to wear their clothes, all thanks to her super-skinny frame. 由于她的体型过于纤瘦，大多数设计师似乎不太乐意让她穿上自己设计的服装。

fraud [frɔːd] *n.* 欺诈，诈骗

诵读 But no link was found between telling porkies and a tendency to cheat in exams or commit fraud in later life. 但撒谎与后来人生中考试作弊或诈骗倾向并无关联。

freight [freɪt] *n.* 货物，货运，运费

诵读 About 20 percent of airline revenues comes from air freight. 航空公司大约 20% 的收入来自航空运输。

fringe [frɪndʒ] *n.* 边缘

frontier [ˈfrʌntɪə] *n.* 国境，边境

诵读 Chongqing is the new frontier for the electronics industry. 重庆是电子工业的新前沿地区。

frown [fraʊn] *vi.* 皱眉

搭配 frown on 对某事表示不认可

诵读 If you frown while you are concentrating at the screen, over time you will inevitably end up with frown lines. 如果你在计算机前专心工作时常常蹙眉，长此以往你的面部必然出现皱纹。

fuse [fjuːz] *n.* 保险丝，导火线

僻义 *vt.&vi.* 熔化，熔合

诵读 Let us now fuse together now as one people who want to do something for the country. 现在让我们融汇在一起，团结起来，成为为国效力的人。

fuss [fʌs] *n.&vi.* 忙乱，大惊小怪

搭配 make fuss over 就某事大惊小怪

诵读 The organization may continue to use the issue to make a fuss. 这个组织可能会继续利用这一问题做文章。

futile [ˈfjuːtaɪl] *a.* 无效的，无用的，无希望的

诵读 The actress has started to realize all efforts to kill the story are futile. 女演员开始意识到扼杀这个故事的企图是无效的。

fabric [ˈfæbrɪk] *n.* 结构；构造

诵读 The fabric of society has been deeply damaged by the previous regime. 社会结构已被上届执政者严重地破坏了。

finite [ˈfaɪnaɪt] *a.* 有限的

诵读 Only a finite number of situations can arise. 只有有限的几种情况可能会出现。

fortnight [ˈfɔːtnaɪt] *n.* 两星期

诵读 You need a break. Why not take a fortnight off from work? 你需要休息，为什么不休假两周呢？

frank [fræŋk] *a.* 坦白的，直率的

搭配 to be frank 老实说

诵读 To be frank, he could also be a bit of a bore. 老实说，他有时也会让人厌烦。

friendly [ˈfrendli] *a.* 友好的，友谊的

诵读 The spokesman said the tone of the letter was very friendly. 发言人说信函的语气非常友好。

gain [geɪn] *vt.* 获得，博得 *n.* 收益；利润

搭配 No pains, no gains. 不经一事，不长一智。

诵读 My watch has gained ten minutes since yesterday. 从昨天开始，我的手表就快了 10 分钟。

game [geɪm] *n.* 游戏，娱乐；比赛

僻义 猎物

诵读 We must obey the game laws. 我们必须遵守游戏规则。

gather [ˈgæðə] *vi.* 聚集，聚拢

诵读 A crowd gathered to see what had happened. 一群人聚集起来，看到底发生了什么事。

gay [geɪ] *n.* 同性恋

僻义 *a.* 快乐的，愉快的

诵读 We were all gay at the thought of the coming holiday. 想到即将到来的假期我们都很高兴。

gap [gæp] *n.* 缺口；差距；空白；缺乏

搭配 generation gap 代沟；income gap 收入差距

诵读 As Japanese industries reel from Chinese export restrictions on rare earth metals, alternative sources are moving in to fill the gap. 当中国的稀土出口限制影响到日本工业界时，其他稀土矿产地在逐渐填补这一缺口。

garment [ˈgɑːmənt] *n.* 衣服

诵读 It is the unique garment monthly published in the area. 这是该地区唯一一本服装月刊。

gasp [gɑːsp] *n.* 喘息，气喘 *v.* 喘息；气喘吁吁地说

诵读 An audible gasp went round the court as the jury announced the verdict. 陪审团宣布判决的时候，听到法庭上有人倒抽了一口气。

gaze [geɪz] *vi.&n.* 凝视，注视

诵读 The interior was shielded from the curious gaze of passers-by. 屋子内部被挡住了，以防路人好奇地张望。

gentle [ˈdʒentl] *a.* 和蔼的，有礼貌的；温柔的

拓展 gentleman *n.* 绅士，先生；gently *ad.* 文雅地，有礼貌地

诵读 My new English teacher is both gentle and encouraging to me. 我的新英文老师很和蔼，还一直鼓励我。

gender [ˈdʒendə] *n.* 性别

诵读 French differs from English in having gender for all nouns. 法语不同于英语，所有的名词都分阴阳性。

gene [dʒiːn] *n.* 基因

拓展 genetic *a.* 遗传的

诵读 It's very difficult to treat genetic diseases. 遗传性疾病治疗起来很困难。

generalize [ˈdʒenərəlaɪz] *vt.* 归纳；推广，普及

巧记 词根 general 概括+后缀-ize→概括

诵读 Our history teacher is always generalizing. He never deals with anything in detail. 我们的历史老师总是泛泛而谈。他从不细说任何事情。

generate [ˈdʒenəreɪt] *vt.* 产生，发生

拓展 generator *n.* 发电机，发生器

诵读 Our electricity comes from a new generating station. 我们的电来自一个新建的发电厂。

generous [ˈdʒenərəs] *a.* 宽宏大量的，慷慨的

诵读 It was very generous of you to lend me your car yesterday. 昨天承蒙你慷慨地把汽车借给我。

genius [ˈdʒiːnjəs] *n.* 天才

诵读 Einstein is a genius. 爱因斯坦是个天才。

gift [gɪft] *n.* 礼品，赠品；天赋，才能

搭配 have a gift for 对……有天赋=have a genius for

诵读 He has a gift for music. 他有音乐天赋。

giant [ˈdʒaɪənt] *n.* 巨人 *a.* 巨大的

诵读 Our country is taking giant strides forward. 我国正以巨人步伐向前迈进。

glad [glæd] *a.* 高兴的，乐意的

搭配 be glad to do... 高兴……；be glad about 对……满意

诵读 I'm glad he got the job. 我很高兴他找到了这个工作。

glance [glɑːns] *vi.* 扫视 *n.* 匆匆看，一瞥，一眼

搭配 glance at/over 扫视

诵读 One glance at his face told me he was ill. 看一眼他的脸，我就知道他病了。

glamor [ˈglæmə] *n.* (glamour) 魅力；魔法 *vt.* 迷惑

诵读 What makes television distinctive is its glamor and its reach. 电视的独特之处在于它的魅力和覆盖面。

glare [gleə] *vi.* 怒目而视；发射强光

僻义 *n.* 强光；怒视

诵读 I started to offer help, but the fierce glare on his face stopped me. 我正想要帮助他，但他脸上凶恶的表情把我吓住了。

glimpse [glɪmps] *n.&vi.* 一瞥，瞥见

诵读 I only caught a glimpse of the thief, so I can't really describe him. 我只是瞥了一眼小偷，因此我无法仔细描述出他的样子。

glitter [ˈglɪtə] *n.* 光辉，灿烂 *vi.* 闪闪发光；闪耀

诵读 The children were attracted by the glitter of the Christmas tree decorations. 那些孩子被圣诞树上闪耀的装饰品所吸引。

globe [gləʊb] *n.* 球体，地球仪；地球，世界

拓展 global *a.* 球形的；全球的

诵读 Look at the globe and point out China. 看地球仪，指出中国。

goal [gəʊl] *n.* 目的，目标；守门员

诵读 We won by three goals to one. 我们以 3 比 1 的比分获胜。

gorgeous [ˈgɔːdʒəs] *a.* 华丽的；灿烂的；美丽的

诵读 The cosmetics industry uses gorgeous women to sell its skincare products. 化妆品行业常找一些性感美女来推销护肤产品。

govern [ˈgʌvən] *vt.* 统治，管理；决定，支配

拓展 governor *n.* 统治者，管理者

诵读 The need for money governs all his plans. 他的计划受制于资金短缺。

gown [gaʊn] *n.* 长袍，特殊场合穿的长服

诵读 She bought an evening gown for the party. 她为这次聚会买了一件晚礼服。

grade [greɪd] *n.* 等级，级别；年级；分数

僻义 *vt.* 分等，分级

诵读 These potatoes have been graded according to size and quality. 这些马铃薯已经按大小和质量进行了分级。

greet [griːt] *vt.* 致敬，敬意

僻义 *vt.* 迎接

拓展 greeting *n.* 问候，致敬

诵读 She greeted us by shouting a friendly "Hello!". 她友好地向我们喊了一声"你好！"。

grey [greɪ] *n.* 灰色，暗淡 *a.* 灰色的；苍白的

ground [graʊnd] *n.* 地面，土地；场所；根据，理由

搭配 on the ground(s) that ... 由于……

诵读 What ground does the boss have for hiring him? 老板为什么雇佣他？

grab [græb] *vt.&n.* 抓住；夺得

诵读 He grabbed the money and ran off. 他抢过钱，撒腿就跑。

grace [greɪs] *n.* 优美，文雅；恩泽

辨析 graceful *a.* 优雅大方的；gracious *a.* 亲切的，仁慈的

诵读 An oilpaper umbrella is more than a piece of art that adds elegance and grace; it is also a means of protection from the rain. 油纸伞不仅是一件增添优雅和风度的艺术品，也可用于挡雨。

gradual [ˈgrædjʊəl] *a.* 逐渐的，逐步的

诵读 There has been a gradual increase in the number of people owning cars. 拥有车的人逐步增加。

graduate [ˈgrædjʊɪt] *n.* 毕业生 *v.* 毕业 *a.* 毕了业的

拓展 undergraduate 本科生；postgraduate 研究生

诵读 He is a graduate of Renmin University of China. 他是中国人民大学的毕业生。

grand [grænd] *a.* 盛大的；重大的，主要的

诵读 He held a grand farewell in a grand hotel. 他在一个豪华的旅店里举行了盛大的告别会。

grant [grɑːnt] *vt.* 同意；授予 *n.* 授予物；津贴

诵读 The boys were granted an extra vacation. 男孩子们被准予额外假期。

grape [greɪp] *n.* 葡萄

搭配 sour grape 酸葡萄

诵读 Grape seeds contain powerful antioxidants. 葡萄籽含有强大的抗氧化剂。

graph [grɑːf] *n.* 图表

拓展 graphic *a.* 绘画似的，图解的，生动的

诵读 The book gave a graphic description of the war. 这本书生动地描述了战争的情况。

grasp [grɑːsp] *vt.&n.* 抓住，抓紧

辨义 *vt.* 掌握，领会

诵读 You should grasp this opportunity, or you will regret. 你应该抓住这次机会，否则你会后悔。

grateful ['greɪfʊl] *a.* 感激的；感谢的

搭配 be/feel grateful to... for... 因……而对……充满感激

拓展 gratitude *n.* 感激，感谢

诵读 I was grateful to John for bringing the books. 我很感激约翰把书带来了。

greenhouse ['griːnhaʊs] *n.* 温室

grief [griːf] *n.* 悲伤，悲痛

辨义 grieve *v.* 使悲伤，使伤心

诵读 It grieves me to see him in such bad health. 他的健康状况如此糟糕，真使我伤心。

grocer ['grəʊsə] *n.* 食品商，杂货商

诵读 Go down to the grocer's and get some sugar. 去杂货店买点糖来。

grope [grəʊp] *n.&vi.&vt.* 摸索，探索

诵读 I grope for the light switch in the dark room. 我在黑暗的房间里摸索着找电灯开关。

gross [grəʊs] *a.* 总的，毛（重）的

辨义 *a.* 粗鲁的，粗俗的

诵读 The RECP agreement covers about 30 percent of the world's gross domestic products, trade and population.《区域全面经济伙伴关系协定》（RECP）覆盖了全球约30%的国内生产总值、贸易和人口。

grown-up ['grəʊnʌp] *a.* 成长的，成人的 *n.* 成年人

guide [gaɪd] *vt.* 领路，引导 *n.* 指南，导游

拓展 guidance *n.* 引导，指导

诵读 She needs some guidance with her studies. 她在学习方面需要指导。

guarantee [ˌgærən'tiː] *n.&vt.* 保证，担保

诵读 I give my guarantee that she will come in five minutes. 我保证她5分钟后会到。

guideline ['gaɪdlaɪn] *n.* 指导方针，准则，标准

巧记 合成词：guide 指导+line 路线→指导方针

诵读 We laid out the economic guidelines and followed it. 我们制定并遵循了经济方针。

guilt [gɪlt] *n.* 罪过，内疚

拓展 guilty *a.* 有罪的，内疚的

诵读 The children behave badly, but the guilt lies with the parents, who don't care about their behavior. 小孩子行为不端，罪责在父母，因为他们不关心子女的行为。

gut [gʌt] *n.* 内脏

辨义 *n.*（复数）胆量，勇气

诵读 Barbara hasn't got the guts to leave her mother. 巴巴拉没有勇气离开妈妈。

guy [gaɪ] *n.* 家伙，人

诵读 He is a nice guy. 他是一个好人。

gallop ['gæləp] *vi.&n.* 奔驰，飞奔

诵读 Small companies gallop to international market. 小公司纷纷向国际市场进军。

gamble ['gæmbl] *n.&vi.* 投机，冒险；赌博

巧记 本来只是游戏（game→gam）的球类（ball→ble）运动，近年来成了赌博的目标

诵读 Alcohol must not be used as an inducement to encourage people to gamble. 不得用酒精吸引顾客赌博。

garbage [ˈɡɑːbɪdʒ] *n.* 垃圾

诵读 He said the envelope was retrieved from his garbage the early Monday. 他说星期一早晨从他的垃圾箱中捡了这封信。

gauge [ɡeɪdʒ] *n.* 标准；规格 *v.* 测量

诵读 To gauge the effect of sound levels on drinking, the team spent three Saturday nights visiting two bars. 为了测量音乐音量对于饮酒的实际影响，研究小组在三个周六对两家酒吧进行了夜访。

genuine [ˈdʒenjʊɪn] *a.* 真正的，名副其实的

诵读 Joan is now a genuine friend. 琼现在是真正的朋友。

germ [dʒɜːm] *n.* 微生物，细菌

gesture [ˈdʒestʃə] *n.* 姿势，姿态，手势 *v.* 做手势

诵读 We invited our new neighbours to dinner as a gesture of friendship. 我们邀请新邻居来吃饭，以示友好。

gigantic [dʒaɪˈɡæntɪk] *a.* 巨大的，庞大的

诵读 It is a gigantic threat to our lives. 这是对我们生命的极大威胁。

giggle [ˈɡɪɡl] *vi.&n.* 痴笑；咯咯地笑

诵读 Her nervous giggles annoyed me. 她神经质的傻笑把我惹火了。

glide [ɡlaɪd] *n.&vi.* 溜，滑行；(时间)消逝

诵读 The boat glided over the river. 船在河上轻快地航行着。

gloomy [ˈɡluːmi] *a.* 阴暗的，阴沉的，令人沮丧的

诵读 It was a gloomy winter's morning. 那是一个阴沉的冬日早晨。

glorious [ˈɡlɔːriəs] *a.* 壮丽的，辉煌的；光荣的

拓展 glory *n.* 光荣，荣誉

诵读 The sunrise of the Mountain Tai is glorious. 泰山日出真是壮丽至极。

glow [ɡləʊ] *vi.* 发热，发光

诵读 The oil lamp gives a soft glow. 油灯发出柔和的光。

glue [ɡluː] *n.* 胶水 *vt.* 胶合，粘贴

诵读 She glued the two pieces of wood together. 她把两块木头粘到一起。

gossip [ˈɡɒsɪp] *n.&vi.* 闲话，闲聊

诵读 Do not tell her anything for she is a gossip. 别告诉她任何事，她是个长舌妇。

grave [ɡreɪv] *n.* 坟墓

僻义 *a.* 严肃的，庄重的

拓展 gravity *n.* 严肃，庄重；重力

诵读 Anything that is dropped falls to the ground, pulled by the force of gravity. 由于地心引力，掉下的任何东西都会落在地面上。

greedy [ˈɡriːdi] *a.* 贪吃的，贪婪的，渴望的

搭配 be greedy for 渴望得到；be greedy of 贪恋

诵读 The greedy little boy ate all the food at the party. 那贪吃的小男孩把聚会上的食品全吃光了。

grim [ɡrɪm] *a.* 严酷的，令人害怕的；不愉快的

诵读 His expression was grim when he told them they had lost their jobs. 当告诉他们已被解雇时，他的表情十分严肃。

grin [ɡrɪn] *n.&vi.* 露齿而笑，咧嘴一笑

诵读 I know she is joking because she has a big grin on her face. 我知道她是在开玩笑，因为她满脸笑容。

grind [ɡraɪnd] *vt.* 磨碎，碾碎

搭配 be ground by... 受……的折磨

诵读 He grinds up the wheat to make flour. 他把小麦磨成面粉。

grip [ɡrɪp] *vt.&n.* 紧握，抓紧；掌握

诵读 The policeman would not loosen his grip on the thief. 警察紧抓着小偷不放手。

groan [ɡrəʊn] *vi.&n.* 呻吟

巧记 和 moan(抱怨，呻吟)一起记忆

诵读 The old man who had been injured in the accident lay groaning beside the road. 在车祸中受伤的老人躺在路边呻吟。

habit ['hæbɪt] *n.* 习惯，习性，脾性

搭配 be in the habit of... 有……的习惯；get/fall into the habit of... 养成……的习惯

诵读 I smoke out of habit, not for pleasure. 我抽烟是出于习惯，而不是为了乐趣。

handsome ['hænsəm] *a.* 漂亮的，英俊的

僻义 慷慨的，数量可观的

诵读 He gave each servant a handsome present of a hundred dollars every year. 他慷慨地每年给每个侍从 100 美元的礼品。

hang [hæŋ] *vt.* 悬挂，垂吊；吊死，绞死

搭配 hang about 闲逛，徘徊；hang on 抓紧不放，等一下；hang up 挂断（电话）

诵读 I was so angry that I hung up on her. 我气得没等她说完话就把电话挂断了。

hardly ['hɑ:dli] *ad.* 几乎不，简直不，仅仅

诵读 Hardly had we started our journey when the car got a flat tire. 我们刚一出发，车胎就爆了。

harvest ['hɑ:vɪst] *n.* 收获；成果 *vt.* 收获，收割

诵读 The new machine is the harvest of two years' research. 这种新型机器是两年研究的成果。

habitat ['hæbɪˌtæt] *n.* 栖息地

诵读 This creature's natural habitat is the jungle. 这种动物的栖息地是丛林。

handbook ['hændbʊk] *n.* 手册，指南

诵读 Will you please pass me that handbook? 把那本手册递给我好吗？

handful ['hændfʊl] *n.* 一把；少数

诵读 I picked up a handful of letters and began to open them. 我拣起一把信，开始拆信。

handle ['hændl] *n.* 把手，拉手 *v.* 处理，对待

诵读 I turned the handle and opened the door. 我转动把手，打开了门。

handwriting ['hændˌraɪtɪŋ] *n.* 笔迹，手迹，书法

巧记 合成词：hand 手+writing 写=笔迹

诵读 She has very clear handwriting. 她的字迹很清晰。

handy ['hændi] *a.* 手边的，近便的；方便的

诵读 The stores are quite handy. 商店就在附近。

harbor ['hɑ:bə] *n.* 海港；避难所 *vt.* 隐匿，窝藏

巧记 网络信号或者 USB 接口的分线器也叫 harbor

诵读 He had jumped overboard in New York harbor and swum to shore. 他在纽约港跳下船，游上了岸。

harden ['hɑ:dn] *vt.&vi.*（使）变硬

巧记 词根 hard 坚硬的+后缀-en，表示"使，强化"→（使）变硬

诵读 Their work is to harden steel. 他们的工作就是使钢淬火。

hardship ['hɑ:dʃɪp] *n.* 艰难，困苦

巧记 词根 hard 艰难的+后缀-ship，表抽象含义→艰难，困苦

诵读 Thirty-two students had to suspend studies this year due to financial hardship. 今年有 32 名学生因经济困难而被迫辍学。

harmony ['hɑ:məni] *n.* 协调，和谐；融洽

诵读 As they smiled at each other, harmony was restored again. 他们彼此微笑的时候，又恢复了往日的和睦。

haste [heɪst] *n.* 匆忙，急速；草率

巧记 More haste, less speed. 欲速则不达。

拓展 hasty *a.* 匆忙的，仓促的

诵读 In her haste to complete the work on time, she made a number of mistakes. 她急于按时完工，结果出了不少错。

hatred ['heɪtrɪd] *n.* 憎恨，憎恶

诵读 Her hatred of them would never lead her to murder. 她虽说仇恨他们，但绝不至于去杀人。

hazard ['hæzəd] *n.* 危险，冒险，危害

诵读 Growing levels of pollution represent a serious health hazard to the local population. 日益严重的污染对当地人的健康构成重大威胁。

headmaster ['hed'mɑ:stə] *n.* 校长

healthy ['helθi] *a.* 健康的；有益健康的，卫生的

诵读 We breathe the healthy country air. 我们呼吸

着有益于健康的乡间空气。

hero [ˈhɪərəʊ] *n.* 英雄；男主人公

拓展 heroic *a.* 英雄的，英勇的，崇高的

诵读 The hero gets the girl at the end of the film. 电影结尾男主角和那位姑娘在一起了。

heal [hi:l] *vt.* 治愈，愈合

诵读 Time is a physician that heals every grief. 时间是治愈一切伤痛的良药。

heel [hi:l] *n.* 脚后跟

巧记 Achilles' heel 阿基里斯之踵→致命弱点

诵读 There'll be coats with rips in the pockets and shoes scuffed at the heel—lasting traces of the items' previous owners. 口袋开裂的外套，鞋跟磨损的鞋子，这些都是它们前任主人留下的痕迹。

heighten [ˈhaɪtən] *vt.* 提高，升高

巧记 height 高度+后缀-en，表示"使……，强化"→提高，升高

诵读 Physicians need to heighten their awareness that older individuals can well have risk factors for HIV infection. 医生需要增强意识：年龄较大的人也很可能感染艾滋病。

helpful [ˈhelpfʊl] *a.* 有帮助的，有益的，有用的

巧记 help 帮助+后缀-ful→有帮助的

搭配 be helpful to 对……有帮助的

诵读 A hotel receptionist needs to be welcoming, friendly and helpful. 酒店前台应该热情、友善和乐于助人。

heroin [ˈherəʊɪn] *n.* 海洛因

辨析 同形词 heroine *n.* 女英雄；女主角

诵读 Alcohol is more dangerous than illegal drugs like heroin and crack cocaine. 酒精的危害性极大，甚至超过海洛因和可卡因等非法毒品。

hesitate [ˈhezɪteɪt] *vi.* 犹豫，踌躇

诵读 Some parents hesitate to take these steps because they suspect that their child is exaggerating. 一些家长不愿意采取这些措施，因为他们怀疑自己的孩子在夸大其词。

hire [ˈhaɪə] *n.&vt.* 雇佣，租借

诵读 He makes a living by working for hire. 他以当雇工谋生。

hit [hɪt] *vt.* 打击；碰撞；到达，完成 *n.* 击中

僻义 轰动一时的人或事物，流行一时的东西

诵读 The play was quite a hit in New York. 这话剧在纽约曾轰动一时。

highlight [ˈhaɪlaɪt] *vt.* 使显著，使突出；强调

巧记 合成词：high 高的+light 光→使显著，使突出

诵读 I would like to highlight a few features of life in the western area. 我想简单谈谈西部地区人们生活方式的一些特点。

hijack [ˈhaɪdʒæk] *vt.* 劫持，劫机

诵读 Somali pirates hijacked a Panama-flagged ship with 23 crew members Monday, maritime official confirmed. 海事官员证实，索马里海盗在星期一劫持了一艘载有 23 名巴拿马船员的船。

hike [haɪk] *n.* 徒步旅行 *vt.* 增加，提高

诵读 We hiked in the dark for an hour and a half. 我们摸黑跋涉了一个半小时。

hint [hɪnt] *n.* 暗示，提示，线索 *vt.* 暗示，示意

诵读 Armies of Terra Cotta Soldiers are hint to the warrior heritage of the Qin Dynasty. 兵马俑是秦朝崇武精神的体现。

hip [hɪp] *n.* 臀部

historian [hɪsˈtɔːriən] *n.* 历史学家

historic [hɪsˈtɒrɪk] *a.* 有历史意义的；历史的

辨析 同形词 historical *a.* 历史的

诵读 China issues memorial stamps for Historic Monuments of Dengfeng. 中国发行了一套关于登封历史建筑群的纪念邮票。

hitherto [ˌhɪðəˈtuː] *ad.* 到目前为止，迄今

诵读 The clearing of sea ice will permit oil-drilling in places hitherto off-limits. 海冰融化使人们能在原本无法开采石油的地方进行石油勘探和开采。

home [həʊm] *n.* 家

搭配 home and abroad 国内外；at home 在家，在国内；自在，自如

诵读 Just make yourself at home. 请自便。

honor [ˈɒnə] *n.* 尊敬，敬意；荣誉，光荣

搭配 in honor of 为纪念，向……表示敬意

拓展 honorable *a.* 可敬的；荣誉的，光荣的

诵读 The party in honor of the visiting president will be held at the hall. 为向来访总统表示敬意而举行的欢迎宴会将在大厅举行。

hobby [ˈhɒbi] *n.* 业余爱好，嗜好，兴趣

诵读 He entered into politics as a hobby. 他参加政治活动是作为一种业余爱好。

hollow [ˈhɒləʊ] *a.* 空的；空洞的，空虚的 *v.* 挖空

诵读 It would be a hollow victory. 这种协议只能是徒有虚名。

hopeful [ˈhəʊpfʊl] *a.* 给人希望的，抱有希望的

诵读 I have never been more hopeful than I am tonight that we will get there. 但我从未像今晚这样对美国满怀希望，我相信我们会实现这个目标。

horizon [həˈraɪzən] *n.* 地平线；眼界，见识

拓展 horizontal *a.* 地平线的；水平的

诵读 The sun had already sunk below the horizon. 太阳已经落到了地平线下面。

horror [ˈhɒrə] *n.* 恐怖，战栗

拓展 horrible *a.* 令人恐惧的，可怕的

诵读 Shocked residents and tourists at the city's luxury hotels watched in horror as the scene unfolded. 受到惊吓的居民和这座城市的几个豪华酒店的游客恐惧地目睹了这幕惨剧。

host [həʊst] *n.* 主人；主持人

搭配 a host of 一大群

拓展 hostess *n.* 女主人，女主持人

诵读 China announced it is hosting the next round of international talks on Iran. 中国宣布主办下一轮有关伊朗问题的国际谈判。

hospitality [ˌhɒspɪˈtælɪti] *n.* 好客，殷勤，款待

巧记 反义词 hostile *a.* 敌对的；敌意的

诵读 The response of the audience varied from outright rejection to warm hospitality. 观众反应不一，有人完全不能接受，也有人拍手叫好。

household [ˈhaʊshəʊld] *n.* 家庭 *a.* 家庭的

诵读 The beauty industry shows no sign of slowing down as beauty and personal care products have become "must have" items in every household. 美容业的增长势头丝毫没有减缓，因为美容类和个人护理类产品已成为每家每户的"必需品"。

hunger [ˈhʌŋgə] *n.* 饥饿；渴望 *vi.* 挨饿，渴望

搭配 hunger after/for 渴望

诵读 She hungers for fame. 她渴望出名。

husband [ˈhʌzbənd] *n.* 丈夫

僻义 *vt.* 节约

humanity [hjuːˈmænɪti] *n.* 人类，人性，人情

诵读 We admire her dedication to the cause of humanity. 我们敬佩她对人类事业的献身精神。

humble [ˈhʌmbl] *a.* 谦卑的，恭顺的；地位低下的

诵读 A maths genius is living with his mother in a humble flat in St Petersburg. 一位数学天才目前和母亲住在圣彼得堡的一个简陋公寓里。

humid [ˈhjuːmɪd] *a.* 湿的，湿气重的

巧记 词根 hum 泥土+后缀-id 表示特征=潮湿的土地

拓展 humidity *n.* 湿气，湿度

诵读 The city is also hot and humid, so windows are left open or air-conditioners whirr away day and night。而当地天气湿热，窗户常常大开，空调日夜运转。

humiliate [hjʊˈmɪlɪeɪt] *v.* 使羞辱，使丢脸

诵读 There are people who want to humiliate you and grind you down. 有些人想让你难堪，欺负你。

humor [ˈhjuːmə] *n.* 幽默，诙谐

拓展 humorous *a.* 富于幽默感的，幽默的；滑稽的

诵读 I think humor is a great lubricant for life. 我认为幽默是人生的润滑剂。

hunt [hʌnt] *vi.&vt.&n.* 打猎，猎取

搭配 hunt for 搜索

诵读 Police have launched a massive hunt for a man suspected of killing eight people. 警方已经开始大规模搜捕一名涉嫌杀死八人的男子。

hail [heɪl] *vi.* 下雹

僻义 *vt.* 向……欢呼

搭配 hail from 来自

诵读 It was so fine this morning. Who would have thought it would hail in the afternoon! 早上天气还挺好的，不料下午竟下起了冰雹。

halt [hɔːlt] *n.&vi.&vt.* 止步，(使)停止

诵读 The car came to a halt just in time to prevent an accident. 汽车及时停住，避免了一场车祸。

hamper [ˈhæmpə] *vt.* 妨碍，阻碍，牵制

诵读 The snow hampered my movements. 大雪阻碍

了我的行动。

handicap [ˈhændɪkæp] *vt.* 妨碍 *n.*（身体或智力方面的）缺陷；不利条件

诵读 Lack of money handicapped him badly. 资金短缺对他造成不利影响。

harassment [ˈhærəsmənt] *n.* 骚扰，扰乱；烦恼，烦乱

诵读 Sexual harassment is a common problem. 性骚扰是个普遍的问题。

harsh [hɑːʃ] *a.* 粗糙的；刺耳的；苛刻的，严酷的

诵读 One New Jersey Senator had earlier pushed for harsh punishment. 新泽西州一位议员此前呼吁从严惩罚。

headquarters [ˈhedˈkwɔːtəz] *n.* 司令部；总部

诵读 In the United States, the lights went out at the Coca-Cola headquarters in Atlanta. 美国亚特兰大的可口可乐公司总部在当晚熄灭了灯光。

heap [hiːp] *n.* 堆，大量，许多 *vt.* 堆，堆起

搭配 heap up 堆，堆起

诵读 There is heaps of time before the plane leaves. 在飞机起飞前还有很多时间。

heave [hiːv] *vt.&n.* 举起

巧记 形近记忆：东西太沉（heavy）了，实在提（heave）不起来

诵读 Now that your daughter is out of college, you can heave a sigh of relief. 你的女儿大学毕业了，你可以松一口气了。

heir [eə] *n.* 继承人

herd [hɜːd] *n.* 群 *vt.* 放牧，群集

诵读 They are individuals; they will not follow the herd. 他们是独立的个体，不愿随大流。

heritage [ˈherɪtɪdʒ] *n.* 遗产，继承物

巧记 词根 her粘贴+ it表动词+后缀-age=与生俱来→遗产，继承物

搭配 cultural heritage 文化遗产

诵读 The Opera House has been included on Australia's National Heritage List. 悉尼歌剧院已被列入澳大利亚国家遗产名单。

hinge [hɪndʒ] *n.* 合页，铰链

搭配 *vi.* 依……而定（on）

诵读 Does not success or failure hinge on this? 成败之机，其在斯乎？

hoist [hɔɪst] *vt.* 举起，升起，吊起

诵读 The cargo was hoisted by crane. 起重机将货物吊起。

holy [ˈhəʊli] *a.* 神圣的，圣洁的

巧记 假期 holiday 的来源 holy day，所以星期日还有礼拜天的叫法。

诵读 The Indians think of him as a holy man, a combination of doctor and priest. 印度人把他视为圣人，他既是医生又是僧侣。

homogeneous [ˌhɒməˈdʒiːnjəs] *a.* 同性质的

巧记 前缀 homo-相同+词根 gene 基因 →同类的

诵读 They are homogeneous people. 他们是同类人。

hook [hʊk] *n.* 钩，吊钩，钩状物 *vt.* 钩住

诵读 They intend to get their way, by hook or by crook. 为达到目的，他们不择手段。

hover [ˈhɒvə] *vi.*（鸟）盘旋，翱翔；徘徊

诵读 Just as at the turn of the century, we hover between great hopes and great fears. 正如世纪之交时那样，我们再次在巨大的希望和忧虑之间彷徨不定。

howl [haʊl] *n.&vi.* 怒吼，咆哮

诵读 A dog will not howl if you beat him with a bone. 骨头打狗狗不叫。

huddle [ˈhʌdl] *n.&vi.* 拥挤；聚集

诵读 They huddle around laptops and desktop computers, often writing code until 7 a.m. 他们坐在笔记本电脑和台式计算机前写程序代码，经常写到早上 7 点。

hug [hʌg] *vt.&n.* 热烈拥抱，紧抱

诵读 Go to that person and hug him every day because he might be gone tomorrow. 每天去拥抱父亲吧，因为他明天可能就离开人世了。

hurl [hɜːl] *vt.* 猛投，力掷

诵读 He was accused of hurling abuse at the referee. 他被指控辱骂裁判。

hypothesis [haɪˈpɒθɪsɪs] *n.* 假说，假设，前提

诵读 According to the hypothesis, the high cost of living is caused by increased wages. 根据这个假定说法，生活费用高是由于工资增长。

hysterical [hɪsˈterɪkəl] *a.* 歇斯底里的

诵读 The doctor slapped the hysterical child to make him calm. 医生拍了拍这位情绪激动的小孩以使他安静下来。

ideal [aɪˈdɪəl] *a.* 理想的 *n.* 理想

诵读 It is an ideal weather for a holiday. 这是度假的理想天气。

identical [aɪˈdentɪkəl] *a.* 同一的, 同样的

搭配 be identical to/with... 与……一致

诵读 Their opinions are identical with mine. 他们的意见和我的完全一样。

identify [aɪˈdentɪfaɪ] *vt.* 识别, 确认

拓展 identification *n.* 识别, 鉴别

诵读 Could you identify him among the cheering crowd? 你能在欢呼的人群中认出他吗?

identity [aɪˈdentɪti] *n.* 身份; 一致

诵读 They have reached an identity of views. 他们已经取得一致的看法。

ignorant [ˈɪɡnərənt] *a.* 无知的; 不知道的

拓展 ignorance *n.* 无知, 愚昧; 不知道

诵读 Authors are famously ignorant about the realities of publishing. 作者们不了解出版界的实际情况, 这是人所共知的。

illness [ˈɪlnɪs] *n.* 病, 疾病

诵读 She was very weak from a long illness. 因为长期生病, 她身体非常虚弱。

image [ˈɪmɪdʒ] *n.* 形象; 印象; 图像

诵读 The vivid images whether of film or novel evoke emotional responses from the reader. 那些生动的形象, 不论是电影中的还是小说中的, 都会引起读者的情感反应。

imagine [ɪˈmædʒɪn] *vt.* 想象

辨析 imaginary *a.* 想象的, 虚构的; imaginative *a.* 富有想象力的

拓展 imagination *n.* 想象 (力)

诵读 The events described in the news are imaginary. 那条新闻里所描写的事件是虚构的。

imitate [ˈɪmɪteɪt] *vt.* 模仿, 仿效

拓展 imitation *n.* 模仿, 仿效

诵读 He wanted to imitate Hemingway style, but was not successful. 他想模仿海明威的风格, 但没有成功。

immediate [ɪˈmiːdɪət] *a.* 立即的, 即时的

诵读 That requires immediate action. 那需要立即采取行动。

immense [ɪˈmens] *a.* 广大的, 巨大的

诵读 Ships sail on the immense sea. 船在无边无际的海上航行。

immerse [ɪˈmɜːs] *vt.* 使沉浸在; 使浸没

诵读 He immersed his head in the water. 他把头浸入水中。

immune [ɪˈmjuːn] *a.* 免疫的, 有免疫力的

搭配 immune system 免疫系统; be immune from... 不受……的影响

诵读 He has had the disease once, so he should be immune from it now. 他曾经得过这种病, 现在该对这种病有免疫力了。

impact [ˈɪmpækt] *n.* 冲击, 碰撞; 影响

诵读 The specific impact of the greenhouse effect is unknowable. 温室效应的具体影响尚不可知。

impatient [ɪmˈpeɪʃənt] *a.* 不耐烦的, 急躁的

巧记 i 前缀 im-表否定+词根 patient 耐心 →不耐烦的

诵读 They are impatient to wait for him in the diner. 他们在小饭店不耐烦地等着他。

imply [ɪmˈplaɪ] *v.* 意指, 含……意思, 暗示

拓展 implication *n.* 含义, 暗示

诵读 Her smile implied that she had not worried about it anymore. 她的微笑说明她不再为此事着急了。

import [ˈɪmpɔːt] *vt.&n.* 进口, 输入

诵读 The police caught a young man trying to import a huge quantity of cars. 警方抓到了一个试图走私大量汽车的年轻人。

impose [ɪmˈpəʊz] *vt.* 征税; 把……强加给

巧记 前缀 im-加强语气+词根 pose 放置 →放在上面→把……强加于

诵读 He imposed a heavy tax on cigarettes. 他对香

烟征收重税。

impress [ɪmˈpres] *vt.* (on)印，盖印；留下印象

巧记 前缀 im-加强语气+词根 press 压 →压在上面→留下印象

拓展 impression *n.* 印象；impressive *a.* 给人深刻印象的，感人的

诵读 He impressed a few words on the paper. 他在纸上印了几个字。

impulse [ˈɪmpʌls] *n.* 推动；冲动，刺激

诵读 Many people act on impulse without counting the cost. 很多人不考虑后果就莽撞行事。

incidence [ˈɪnsɪdəns] *n.* 影响范围；发生率

诵读 The incidence of that disease was very high in that district. 此种病在那个地区的发病率很高。

incident [ˈɪnsɪdənt] *n.* 事件，事变

拓展 incidentally *ad.* 附带地，顺便提及

诵读 I must go now; incidentally if you want that magazine I'll bring it next time. 我必须走了。另外说一句，如果你要看那本杂志，我下次给你带来。

increasingly [ɪnˈkriːsɪŋli] *ad.* 不断增加地，日益

诵读 The situation there has become increasingly grave in the last few weeks. 最近几个星期，那里的形势日益严重。

incredible [ɪnˈkredəbl] *a.* 不可思议的

巧记 前缀 in-表否定+词根 cred 可信的→不可思议的

诵读 Old superstitions seem incredible to educated young men. 对受过教育的年轻人来说，旧时的迷信似乎是不可思议的。

independence [ˌɪndɪˈpendəns] *n.* 独立，自主

拓展 independent *a.* 独立的，自主的

诵读 Having a job gives him financial independence. 工作使他实现经济上独立。

indicate [ˈɪndɪkeɪt] *vt.* 指出，指示；表明，暗示

拓展 indication *n.* 指出，指示；indicative *a.* 指示的，暗示的

诵读 Snow indicates the advent of spring. 飞雪迎春到。

indifferent [ɪnˈdɪfrənt] *a.* 冷漠的，不关心的

诵读 I was so excited to see ice that I was indifferent to the cold. 我见到冰非常兴奋，以至于忘记了寒冷。

individual [ˌɪndɪˈvɪdjʊəl] *a.* 个人的 *n.* 个人

诵读 Would you show individual concern for him?你愿单独照顾他一下吗?

industrial [ɪnˈdʌstriəl] *a.* 工业的，产业的

拓展 industrialize *v.* 工业化

诵读 The gross value of industrial output reach 5 billion yuan. 工业总产值达到 50 亿元。

inevitable [ɪnˈevɪtəbl] *a.* 不可避免的，必然发生的

诵读 We have inevitable responsibilities of taking care of our parents. 照顾父母是我们无法推卸的责任。

infant [ˈɪnfənt] *n.* 婴儿，幼儿

诵读 The sole survivor of the crash was an infant. 这次车祸的唯一幸存者是一个婴儿。

infect [ɪnˈfekt] *vt.* 传染，感染；影响(思想等)

拓展 infectious *a.* 传染的，传染性的，有感染力的

诵读 You can not find any infectious hospital in this area. 在这一地区找不到一家传染病医院。

infer [ɪnˈfɜː] *vt.* 推论，推断

拓展 inference *n.* 推论，推理

诵读 The judge inferred from the testimony that the defendant was lying. 法官从证词推断出被告在撒谎。

inferior [ɪnˈfɪəriə] *a.* 下等的；劣等的

搭配 be inferior to 劣于

诵读 His style was either neglected or held to be innately inferior. 他的风格要么被人忽视，要么被认为天生低劣。

infinite [ˈɪnfɪnɪt] *a.* 无限的，无穷的 *n.* 无限

诵读 Light does not travel with infinite velocity. 光并不是以无限的速度传播的。

inflation [ɪnˈfleɪʃən] *n.* 通货膨胀

influence [ˈɪnflʊəns] *vt.&n.* 影响

拓展 influential *a.* 有影响的；有权势的

诵读 My advice has no influence on him. 我的劝告对他毫无作用。

inform [ɪnˈfɔːm] *vt.* 通知，告诉，报告

搭配 inform sb. of sth. 告知某人某事

诵读 He informed me that if he could not finish his work in time he would be fired. 他告诉我说，如果他不能按时完成工作，他会被开除。

information [ˌɪnfəˈmeɪʃən] *n.* 通知，报告；信息

辨义 *n.* 情报，资料

诵读 We received information that he had been married. 我们得知他已经结婚了。

insist [ɪnˈsɪst] *vi.* 坚决要求，坚决主张，坚持

诵读 The man insisted that he was quite innocent. 那人坚持认为自己无罪。

instruction [ɪnˈstrʌkʃən] *n.* 用法说明；指导

诵读 Some children in the mountain village did not receive the slightest instruction. 山村的一些孩子没有受过任何教育。

interest [ˈɪntrɪst] *n.* 兴趣，关心

辨义 *n.* 利息；(*pl.*)利益，利害

搭配 be interested in doing sth. 对某事感兴趣

诵读 He began to be interested in dictionary-making 20 years ago, and since then has worked at it gladly and never tired. 20 年前他对编词典产生了兴趣，从此乐此不疲。

introduce [ˌɪntrəˈdjuːs] *vt.* 介绍

辨义 *vt.* 引进；提出；采用

诵读 It is introduced that children should have more time controlled by themselves. 据介绍，孩子应该有更多自由支配的时间。

invite [ɪnˈvaɪt] *vt.* 邀请，招待

诵读 I was invited to give my opinion by the chairman. 主席邀请我发言。

inhabit [ɪnˈhæbɪt] *vt.* 居住于，存在于；栖息于

拓展 inhabitant *n.* 居民；住户

区分 同形词：inhibit *vt.* 抑制，约束

辨析 citizen 指公民；civilian 指相对于军人或官员的平民百姓；inhabitant 一般指常住居民；resident 多指长期居住或暂时居住的居民，有时也指旅居者；native 指土生土长的本地居民。

诵读 Large animals that inhabit the desert have evolved a number of adaptations for reducing the effects of extreme heat. 生活在沙漠中的大型动物已经进化出许多适应能力，以减少极端高温的影响。

injure [ˈɪndʒə] *vt.* 损害，损伤，伤害

拓展 injury *n.* 伤害，损害

诵读 Some toys have parts that could be easily torn off and potentially injure children. 有些玩具的部分零件很容易损坏，会对儿童造成潜在伤害。

inner [ˈɪnə] *a.* 内部的，里面的；内心的

诵读 Dreams are reflections of humans' inner spaces and a connection between human subconscious-ness and consciousness. 梦反映出人类内心世界，以及潜意识和意识之间的联系。

innocent [ˈɪnəsnt] *a.* 单纯的，无知的

辨义 *a.* 清白的，无罪的

搭配 be innocent of 清白的

诵读 The foreign minister said he is innocent of any wrongdoing, and predicted that he will return. 外交部部长说他自己是无辜的，没有做错任何事情，并预言将会回来。

innovation [ˌɪnəʊˈveɪʃən] *n.* 改革，革新

巧记 前缀 in-朝里面+词根 nov 新的→改革，革新

诵读 The introduction of the new foldable CityCar heralds an innovation in car design. 新款可折叠电动微型车的推出预示着汽车设计的创新。

innumerable [ɪˈnjuːmərəbl] *a.* 无数的，数不清的

诵读 You have innumerable number of books in this world which will answer all your "How to?". questions. 世界上有无数书籍可以回答你"如何做？"的问题。

inquiry [ɪnˈkwaɪəri] *n.* 询问，打听，调查

诵读 Britain's fashion industry launched an inquiry Monday aimed at establishing health guidelines for supermodels. 英国时装业于本周一发起一项调查，旨在为超级模特制订健康指南。

insect [ˈɪnsekt] *n.* 昆虫

insight [ˈɪnsaɪt] *n.* 洞察力，见识

诵读 The depth and breadth of insight from our research demonstrates how passionate and opinionated people are about life in the UK. 调查所得见解的深度和广度表现了人们对英国生活充满热情，并且对生活有自己的看法。

inspect [ɪnˈspekt] *vt.* 检查，调查，视察

诵读 The bill gives the government broad new powers to inspect processing plants. 这项法案赋予了政府监督检查食品加工企业的广泛权力。

inspire [ɪnˈspaɪə] *vt.* 鼓舞，激起

巧记 前缀 in-朝里面+词根 spir 呼吸+e→注入一些新的气息→使产生灵感

拓展 inspiration *n.* 灵感；鼓舞，激励

诵读 Many people assume that charismatic leadership is a good thing—using a strong personality to inspire loyalty in others. 许多人认为有魅力的领导作风是件好事——用人格魅力激发员工的忠诚。

install [ɪnˈstɔːl] vt. 安装,设置

拓展 installation n.安装,设置;installment n. 分期付款

诵读 The innovative installation, dark for most of the time, only lights up when two people kiss under the tree. 这个颇有创意的装置大部分时间处于不亮状态,只有两人在树下接吻时才能将它点亮。

instant [ˈɪnstənt] a. 立即的;速溶的 n. 瞬间,时刻

巧记 instant noodles 方便面

拓展 instantaneous a. 瞬间的,即刻的

诵读 Companies in the U.S. and Canada that added the words "Oil" or "Petroleum" to their names got an instantaneous 8% boost to stock performance. 在公司名中加入"石油"字样的美国和加拿大公司的股价瞬时飙升 8%。

instinct [ˈɪnstɪŋkt] n. 本能,直觉,天性

搭配 by instinct 本能地

诵读 Children do not know by instinct the difference between right and wrong. 孩子们并非生来就能明辨是非。

institute [ˈɪnstɪtjuːt] n. 研究所;学院 v. 设立

拓展 institution n. 协会;研究所;制度

诵读 Individuals can enrol on self-study courses in the university's language institute. 人们可以在大学的语言学院注册学习自学课程。

insure [ɪnˈʃʊə] vt. 保险,给……保险;保证

拓展 insurance n. 保险,保险费

辨析 assure 用来表示向某人保证某事将要发生;ensure是指确保某事发生;insure是指为防不测向保险公司付钱投保

诵读 The government has acted to insure that private investments in infrastructure projects that require years to complete would be secure. 政府已经采取行动,确保基础建设的私人投资不会因工期时间长而泡汤。

intellectual [ˌɪntɪˈlektʃʊəl] n. 知识分子 a. 智力的

诵读 The offspring of the mothers who had received iron and folic acid during pregnancy through three months postpartum had improved intellectual functioning. 在怀孕期间直到产后三个月内补充铁质和叶酸的母亲,她们的孩子智力发育比较好。

intelligence [ɪnˈtelɪdʒəns] n. 智力,聪明;理解力

辨析 intelligent a. 聪明的,明智的;intelligible a. 可理解的,明白易懂的

诵读 The problem is not with intelligence but with skill development. 这个问题不在于智力而是在于技能的培养。

intend [ɪnˈtend] vt. 想要,打算,企图

拓展 intention n. 意图,意向

诵读 The writer clearly intends his readers to identify with the main character. 作者显然是想让读者跟主人公产生共鸣。

intense [ɪnˈtens] a. 强烈的,剧烈的;热烈的

拓展 intensity n. 强烈,剧烈;intensive a. 加强的,集中的

诵读 Male births have outnumbered female ones for years, which has resulted in intense competition for brides. 多年来,男孩出生率一直高于女孩出生率,这已经加剧了男性求偶的竞争。

interact [ˌɪntərˈækt] vi. 互相作用,互相影响

巧记 前缀 inter-相互的+词根 act 作用→互相作用

诵读 Our findings suggest that online communication is not supplanting face-to-face interactions between friends, family and colleagues. 我们的研究表明,网络沟通并没有取代朋友、家人和同事间的面对面交流。

intercourse [ˈɪntəkɔːs] n. 交流,交往

巧记 前缀 inter-相互的+词根 course 过程→交流

诵读 The magazine becomes a cultural medium of intercourse between the two peoples. 该杂志成为两个民族间文化交流的媒介。

interpret [ɪnˈtɜːprɪt] vt. 解释,说明

诵读 What can you do to recall your dreams more often and interpret them more clearly? 为了更轻易回忆起梦境并阐释梦境的意义,你应该怎么做才好呢?

interrupt [ˌɪntəˈrʌpt] vt. 中断,遮断,阻碍;打断

巧记 前缀 inter-中间+rupt 破→中断;打断(话)

诵读 The only time the Queen has had to interrupt an overseas tour was in 1974 during a tour of Australia and Indonesia. 女王唯一一次中断海外出访是 1974 年访问澳大利亚和印度尼西亚期间。

intersection [ˌɪntəˈsekʃən] *n.* 相交，交叉；道路交叉口，十字路口

interval [ˈɪntəvəl] *n.* 间隔；间歇
搭配 at intervals 不时，相隔一定距离
诵读 This usually happened when the interval reached around 50 milliseconds. 这通常发生在间隔时间达到 50 毫秒左右时。

intervene [ˌɪntəˈviːn] *vi.* 干涉，干预；插入，介入
巧记 前缀 inter-中间+词根 ven 走，来→来到中间→干涉
诵读 Some parents just give up intervening or intervene inconsistently, leaving the field wide open for the bully sibling. 于是一些家长放弃调停，或者减少调停的次数，致使以大欺小的现象屡屡发生。

interview [ˈɪntəvjuː] *vt.&n.* 面试
巧记 前缀 inter-相互+词根 view 看→会面，面试
诵读 And no matter where the interview is running, there are three things you need to know about. 不管你的采访是在什么地方进行的，有三件事情是你需要了解的。

intimate [ˈɪntɪmət] *a.* 亲密的，密切的 *n.* 熟人
辨析 同形词 intimidate *vt.* 胁迫，威胁
诵读 The COVID-19 pandemic has shone a light on the intimate and delicate links between humans, animals and the environment. 新冠肺炎疫情揭示了人类、动物和环境之间密切而微妙的关系。

intuition [ˌɪntjʊˈɪʃən] *n.* 直觉，直观
诵读 In general you want to look for more analytical approaches than just your intuition. 通常来讲，你应该寻求分析方法，而不是仅仅依靠直觉。

invaluable [ɪnˈvæljʊəbl] *a.* 非常宝贵的，无价的
巧记 前缀 in-不+词根 value 价值→价值没有办法计算的→无价的
诵读 But no matter how long or short the list of appreciated qualities, moral values are invaluable. 但是不论这张品格表是多长或多短，道德价值都是无价的。

investigate [ɪnˈvestɪgeɪt] *vt.* 调查，调查研究
诵读 Investigate who in your profession or related profession could be good to know, and learn more about them. 调查在你的专业领域或相关领域里有谁比较值得结交，然后了解他们的情况。

invisible [ɪnˈvɪzəbl] *a.* 看不见的，无形的
巧记 前缀 in-表否定+词根 vis 看→看不见的
诵读 There is an invisible barrier that keeps women out of top jobs. 有一种无形的障碍将女性挡在高层职位之外。

involve [ɪnˈvɒlv] *vt.* 卷入；包含，涉及
巧记 前缀 in-进入+词根 volv 旋转→卷入，陷入
诵读 Some teachers just stood in front of the room and just talked and didn't really like to involve you. 有些老师只不过是照本宣科，他们根本就不在乎你是否能听得进去。

isolate [ˈaɪsəleɪt] *vt.* 隔离，孤立
诵读 New-born babies must be isolated from possible contamination. 新生儿必须隔离，以免受感染。

issue [ˈɪsjuː] *n.* 问题，争端，发行（物），期号
僻义 *vt.* 发行，流出
诵读 A sound of laughter issued from the inside room. 屋里传来一阵笑声。

item [ˈaɪtəm] *n.* 条（款），项目
诵读 All the items that were found were sent to the Museum. 被发现的全部物品都送到了博物馆。

ignite [ɪgˈnaɪt] *vt.* 点火，引燃
僻义 *vt.* 引起
诵读 There was one teacher who really ignited my interest in words. 曾经有一位老师真正激起了我对文字的兴趣。

invent [ɪnˈvent] *vt.* 发明，创造
拓展 invention *n.* 发明，创造
诵读 His father had helped invent a whole new way of doing business. 他父亲帮助创造了一套全新的生意经。

invest [ɪnˈvest] *vt.* 投资，投入（精力、时间等）
拓展 investment *n.* 投资
僻义 *v.* 赋予
诵读 The buildings are invested with a nation's history. 这些建筑承载着国家的历史。

illusory [ɪˈluːsəri] *a.* 虚幻的
诵读 It seemed to be an idealistic and illusory dream. 那似乎是个不切实际、理想主义的美梦。

inflict [ɪnˈflɪkt] *vt.* 把……强加给；使遭受
诵读 Mary inflicted her children on her mother for the weekend. 周末玛丽硬把孩子们交给母亲照料。

idle [ˈaɪdl] *a.* 空闲的；闲置的；懒散的 *vi.* 虚度

诵读 We should not live idle lives. 我们不该过悠闲的生活。

illegal [iˈliːgəl] *a.* 不合法的，非法的

巧记 前缀 il-表否定+词根 legal 合法的 =不合法的

诵读 It is illegal to park your car in the street. 在这条街上停车是违法的。

illiterate [ɪˈlɪtərɪt] *a.* 文盲的，未受教育的

巧记 前缀 il-表否定+词根 literate 文学→不识字的

诵读 There are a lot of illiterate people in this area. 这一地区有大量的文盲。

illuminate [ɪˈljuːmɪneɪt] *vt.* 照亮，照明

诵读 The little oil lamp poorly illuminated an old man. 那盏小小的油灯惨淡地照在一个老人身上。

illusion [ɪˈluːʒən] *n.* 幻想；幻觉，假象

诵读 The sun appears to go round the Earth, but it's an illusion. 太阳看起来好像绕着地球转，但这只是个错觉。

illustrate [ˈɪləstreɪt] *vt.* 举例说明，阐明；图解

拓展 illustration *n.* 说明；例证

诵读 The flow of a river is a beautiful illustration of the law of obedience. 河水顺流而下，是顺应自然法则最好的说明。

impair [ɪmˈpeə] *vt.* 损害，损伤；削弱，减少

巧记 前缀 im-表否定+词根 pair 一对=不再是一对→削弱

诵读 He impaired his health by overwork. 由于工作过度他的健康受损了。

impart [ɪmˈpɑːt] *vt.* 传授，给予；告知，通知

诵读 A teacher's aim is to impart knowledge. 教师的职责就是传授知识。

imperative [ɪmˈperətɪv] *n.* 命令 *a.* 强制的；紧急的

诵读 It is imperative that every one of us remould his world outlook. 我们每个人都必须改造自己的世界观。

implement [ˈɪmplɪmənt] *vt.* 贯彻，实现

巧记 前缀 im- 使……+ple 满+后缀-ment→使圆满，使生效→实施

诵读 Leadership is about the ability to implement change. 领导才能就是要有实施变革的能力。

implicit [ɪmˈplɪsɪt] *a.* 含蓄的

诵读 The way in which he expresses feelings is implicit. 他表达感情的方式很含蓄。

incentive [ɪnˈsentɪv] *n.* 刺激；动力；鼓励；诱因

巧记 前缀 in-加强语气+词根 cent 声音=号召→激励

诵读 A little bonus will give the employees an incentive to work harder. 一点奖金就可以激励雇员更加努力地工作。

incline [ɪnˈklaɪn] *vt.&vi.* 倾斜；倾向于 *n.* 斜坡

诵读 The partly deaf man inclined forward to hear what others said clearly. 耳朵有点聋的人俯身向前，想把别人说的话听得更清楚。

inclusive [ɪnˈkluːsɪv] *a.* 包括的

诵读 There were fifty people present, inclusive of the students. 包括学生在内，共有 50 人出席。

incorporate [ɪnˈkɔːpəreɪt] *vt.* 合并，纳入，结合 *a.* 合并的

诵读 The range of the scene is broadened to incorporate past, present and future. 把这段戏的范围推而广之，使过去、现在和未来浑然成为一体。

incur [ɪnˈkɜː] *vt.* 招致，惹起，遭受

诵读 He incurred a heavy loss through you. 他因为你而遭受重大损失。

indignant [ɪnˈdɪgnənt] *a.* 愤慨的，愤慨不平的

拓展 indignation *n.* 愤怒，愤慨

诵读 He was very indignant with me for my doing that. 由于我那样做，他对我非常恼火。

indispensable [ˌɪndɪsˈpensəbl] *a.* 必不可少的

诵读 Book knowledge is an indispensable mental food to us. 书本知识是我们必不可少的精神食粮。

induce [ɪnˈdjuːs] *vt.* 引诱，劝使；引起

诵读 Nothing could induce me to fool about. 任何事都不能诱使我去虚度时光。

indulge [ɪnˈdʌldʒ] *vt.* 放任，纵容，沉溺

诵读 He no longer indulged himself in smoking. 他不再过度抽烟了。

infrastructure [ˈɪnfrəˌstrʌktʃə] *n.* 基础结构

巧记 前缀 infra-在下部 +词根 structure 结构 =下面的机构→基础结构

诵读 Vast sums are needed to maintain the infrastructure. 保养基础设施需要大量资金。

ingenious [ɪnˈdʒiːnjəs] *a.* 机敏的；有独创性的

诵读 The ingenious boy finished the experiment by himself. 这个机灵的男孩独立完成了实验。

ingredient [ɪnˈgriːdjənt] *n.* 组成部分，配料

诵读 Speed is the essential ingredient of all athletics. 速度是所有田径运动项目的关键要素。

inhale [ɪnˈheɪl] *vt.&vi.* 吸入（气体等），吸（烟）

巧记 前缀 in-朝里面+词根 hale 呼吸 = 吸气

诵读 Exhale through the right nostril, inhale through the right nostril, then pause and switch to exhale through the left nostril. 用右鼻孔呼气后再吸气，然后停住，再换到左鼻孔呼气。

inherent [ɪnˈhɪərənt] *a.* 固有的，内在的，天生的

巧记 前缀 in-朝里面+词根 her黏着= 黏着在里面的 →固有的

诵读 Lying may seem to be an inherent part of human nature and it's an important part of social interaction. 说谎似乎是人性中固有的部分，也是社交中不可或缺的一部分。

inherit [ɪnˈherɪt] *vt.* 继承；经遗传获得

巧记 前缀 in-朝里面+词根 her黏着→附着在内部→继承，遗传

诵读 The children of these couples will tend to inherit both qualities, building a genetic link over successive generations between them. 这些夫妇生下来的孩子通常会继承他们的优点，这种基因联系经历数代后将被强化。

initial [ɪˈnɪʃəl] *a.* 最初的，开头的；词首的 *n.* 词首大写字母

拓展 initiate *vt.* 开始；initiative *a.* 创始的 *n.* 倡议

诵读 My initial reaction was to decline the offer. 我的第一反应是拒绝这个提议。

inject [ɪnˈdʒekt] *vt.* 注射（药液等）；注入

巧记 前缀 in-朝里面+词根 ject 扔→注射

诵读 The plan will inject new money into efforts to reform education. 这项计划会给教育改革注入新的资金。

insert [ɪnˈsɜːt] *vt.* 插入，嵌入 *n.* 插入物

巧记 前缀 in-朝里面+词根 sert 插→插入

诵读 The newspaper had an insert of pages of pictures. 该报带有数页插图。

instrument [ˈɪnstrʊmənt] *n.* 工具；器械；乐器

僻义 *n.* 手段，方法

拓展 instrumental *a.* 器械的；乐器的；起作用的

诵读 He said in the fight against illegal immigration, there are a lot of instruments at our disposal. 他说，在打击非法移民的行动中，我们掌控很多手段。

insulate [ˈɪnsjʊleɪt] *vt.* 隔离；使绝缘，使绝热

辨析 isolate 侧重指完全分离、隔开，也指人或物处于完全孤立的状态；separate 指一般意义上的分开或隔开；insulate 指隔开、分离，尤指用某种东西阻挡从里面逃出或从外面进入的东西

搭配 insulate...from... 把……和……隔离开

诵读 We must now take action on the global financial recession because no country can insulate itself from it. 我们现在必须就应付全球金融衰退采取行动，因为没有一个国家能不受到影响。

insult [ɪnˈsʌlt] *vt.&n.* 侮辱，凌辱

诵读 In some countries, whistling by listeners is a sign of approval while in other countries it is a form of insult. 在一些国家，听众吹口哨是表示赞许，而在另一些国家，却是一种侮辱。

intact [ɪnˈtækt] *a.* 完整无缺的，未经触动的，未受损伤的

巧记 前缀 in- 否定+词根 tact 触摸→未经触动的

诵读 They were intact and had not been shot. 它们完好无损，没有被射杀的痕迹。

integral [ˈɪntɪgrəl] *a.* 构成整体所必需的；完整的

诵读 His visage is an integral part of company's image and his departure is symbolic, according to analysts. 分析家们认为他的形象已是公司整体形象的一部分，而他的离开是有标志意义的。

integrate [ˈɪntɪgreɪt] *v.* 使成为一体；融入

搭配 integrate into/with... 与……成为一体

拓展 integrity *n.* 完整；正直

诵读 They understood instinctively that integrity means having a personal standard of morality and ethics. 他们本能的理解是，正直意味着具备个人的伦理道德标准。

interfere [ˌɪntəˈfɪə] *vi.* 干涉，干预；妨碍，打扰

拓展 interference *n.* 干涉，干预

诵读 Environmentalists threw bottles and other interference with the implementation of whaling activities. 环保主义者对捕鲸船实施了投掷瓶子等干扰活动。

interim [ˈɪntərɪm] *a.* 暂时的，临时的 *n.* 过渡期

巧记 前缀 inter-相互的+词根 im 在中间的→中间的，暂时的

搭配 interim government 是指"临时政府"，也称"过渡政府"。

诵读 The guys from London are being coached by an interim manager. 来自伦敦的小伙子们正由一位临时经理人指导。

interior [ɪnˈtɪərɪə] *a.* 内部的，里面的 *n.* 内部

巧记 前缀 inter-内部+后缀-ior→内部的，里面的

搭配 The late afternoon sun brightened the interior of the church. 傍晚的夕阳照亮了教堂内部。

intermediate [ˌɪntəˈmiːdɪət] *a.* 中间的 *n.* 媒介

诵读 You're able to classify people into very low risk, low risk, intermediate, and high risk for these events based upon test result. 根据测试结果，可以把人分为极低、低、中和高风险等级。

internal [ɪnˈtɜːnəl] *a.* 内部的；国内的，内政的

巧记 inter-内部+后缀-nal→内部的

诵读 A combination of internal and external factors caused the company to close down. 内因和外因共同致使公司倒闭。

intricate [ˈɪntrɪkɪt] *a.* 复杂的；难以理解的

辨析 complex 侧重指内在关系的复杂；complicated 与 complex 的含义接近，但语气更强；sophisticated 侧重指事物发展到或达到高级的程度所体现出的复杂；intricate 着重指错综复杂，令人迷惑。

诵读 He knows his way around the intricate maze of European law. 他通晓错综复杂的欧洲律法。

intrigue [ɪnˈtriːg] *n.* 阴谋 *v.* 密谋，私通

诵读 These results really surprised and intrigued us. 研究结果让我们很惊讶，同时也引起了我们的兴趣。

intrinsic [ɪnˈtrɪnsɪk] *a.* 固有的，本质的，内在的

诵读 Fights and disagreements are apparently intrinsic to all relationships of marriage. 争吵和分歧显然是婚姻关系中固有的。

intrude [ɪnˈtruːd] *vi.* 闯入，侵入

巧记 前缀 in-进入+词根 trude 突然→闯入，侵入

诵读 There are times when personal feelings cannot be allowed to intrude. 有些时候是不允许夹杂个人感情的。

invade [ɪnˈveɪd] *vt.* 入侵，侵略

巧记 前缀 in-里面+词根 vad 走→侵略

拓展 invasion *n.* 入侵，侵略，侵犯

诵读 If you notice warning signs of trouble, then you might want to invade your child's privacy until you get to the heart of the problem. 如果你注意到一些问题的信号，你可能会介入孩子的隐私直到了解问题的实质。

invalid [ɪnˈvælɪd] *n.* 病弱者 *a.* 伤残的；无效的

巧记 前缀 in-不+词根 valid 有效的→无效的

诵读 Their church weddings are legally invalid because the vicars who married them used the wrong form of words. 他们在教堂举行的婚礼在法律上是无效的，因为主持婚礼的牧师念的证婚词有误。

invariably [ɪnˈveərɪəbli] *ad.* 不变地，永恒地，总是

巧记 前缀 in-不+词根 vary 变化+形容词后缀-able+副词-ly→*ad.* 不变地

诵读 Those aged 35－44 invariably hit a mid-life crisis when their happiness level plunges lower than at any other age. 35～44 岁之间的男人总是会遭遇中年危机，他们此时的幸福感比其他任何年龄段都要低。

inventory [ˈɪnvəntəri] *n.* 详细目录，财产清册

诵读 The online companies manage supply by purchasing only those that customers have ordered, minimizing inventory costs. 在线公司只采购顾客订购的那些货物，将库存成本降至最低。

inverse [ɪnˈvɜːs] *a.* 相反的，倒转的 *n.* 相反之物

巧记 前缀 in-反+词根 vers-转动→转过来→相反的

拓展 invert *vt.* 倒置，倒转

诵读 A study showed an inverse correlation between sleep duration and obesity in high-school-age students. 一项研究显示，高中生的睡眠时间与肥胖程度呈反比。

irony [ˈaɪərəni] *n.* 反话，讽刺，讽刺之事

诵读 The irony is that this is the place where people with clear thinking and action have their best chance of achieving performance success. 具有讽刺意味的是，正是在这一领域，具有清晰的思维和行动的人最有机会在业绩上获得成功。

irrespective [ˌɪrɪsˈpektɪv] *a.* 不顾的，不考虑的

诵读 Heavy drinking is risky irrespective of social support level. 不论社会支持程度如何，酗酒是很危险的。

irrigate [ˈɪrɪˌɡeɪt] *vt.* 灌溉，修水利 *vi.* 进行灌溉

irritate [ˈɪrɪteɪt] *vt.* 激怒，恼火，使急躁

诵读 He was irritated against his son because the little fellow didn't know the importance of study. 他对儿子非常生气，因为这个小家伙不知道学习的重要性。

impetus [ˈɪmpɪtəs] *n.* 推动，促进

巧记 前缀 im-往里+词根 pet追

诵读 The impetus for change came from lawyers. 促进转变的动力来自律师们。

idol [ˈaɪdl] *n.* 偶像

诵读 Blind worship of this idol must be ended. 对偶像的盲目崇拜应该结束了。

introvert [ˈɪntrəˌvɜːt] *n.* 性格内向的人

诵读 That young man is an introvert. 那个年轻人的性格很内向。

jealous [ˈdʒeləs] *a.* 妒忌的

搭配 be jealous of… 对……妒忌

诵读 He was jealous of his friend's reputation. 他妒忌他朋友的名声。

jeans [dʒiːnz] *n.* 牛仔裤

诵读 A woman in blue jeans walked into the store. 一个穿蓝色牛仔裤的妇女走进商店。

joint [dʒɔɪnt] *n.* 接合处

僻义 *a.* 联合的，共同的

诵读 Before we discuss the joint practice, let me be clear about what the practice is and is not. 在我们讨论联合实践之前，让我先说明什么是实践，以及什么不是实践。

journal [ˈdʒɜːnl] *n.* 杂志；日志

拓展 journalist *n.* 记者，新闻工作者

诵读 Did you keep a journal of the time when you study last week? 你把上星期的学习时间记下来了吗？

journey [ˈdʒɜːni] *n.* 旅行，旅程

诵读 I don't envy your journey in this bad weather. 我并不羡慕你在这样恶劣的天气里旅行。

judgement [ˈdʒʌdʒmənt] *n.* 判决；看法

诵读 Don't let your personal feelings cloud your judgement. 不要让个人感觉干扰你的判断。

junior [ˈdʒuːnjə] *a.&n.* 年少的，低年级的；大三学生

诵读 She was displaced by her junior clerk. 她被下级职员顶替了。

justice [ˈdʒʌstɪs] *n.* 公正

巧记 词根 just 公正的+名词后缀-ice →正义，公正

拓展 justify *v.* 证明……正当，为……辩护

诵读 She argued with her brother about the justice of equal pay for women. 她同哥哥就男女同酬是否公平的问题进行了争论。

juvenile [ˈdʒuːvɪnaɪl] *n.* 青少年

僻义 *a.* 幼稚的

诵读 For a grown man he acted in a very juvenile manner. 作为成年人，他的行为举止显得十分幼稚。

jam [dʒæm] *n.* 果酱

僻义 *n.&vt.* 阻塞

诵读 The traffic was jammed for an hour. 交通阻塞了一个小时。

jacket [ˈdʒækɪt] *n.* 短上衣，夹克衫

诵读 It's in my jacket pocket. 它在我上衣口袋里。

jazz [dʒæz] *n.* 爵士乐

诵读 I like classical music, but I also like jazz. 我喜欢古典音乐，但也喜欢爵士音乐。

jewel [ˈdʒuːəl] *n.* 宝石

拓展 jewelry *n.*（总称）珠宝

诵读 He spent important money on a small jewel for his wife. 他花大价钱购买了一颗小宝石给太太。

jog [dʒɒg] *vi.* 慢跑

诵读 The car jogged along the rough track. 汽车在崎岖的小道上缓缓行驶。

judicial [dʒuːˈdɪʃəl] *a.* 司法的，审判的

巧记 词根 jud 评判+后缀-ic+后缀-ial

诵读 The White House says the meeting was about judicial nominations, not arms control. 白宫声称这次会谈是关于法官提名的，不是军备控制。

junk [dʒʌŋk] *n.* 废物

诵读 What about junk food? 垃圾食品怎么样？

jury [ˈdʒʊəri] *n.* 陪审团

诵读 The jury listened to counsel on both sides. 陪审团听取了双方律师的意见。

keen [kiːn] *a.* 锋利的；敏锐的；热心的

搭配 be keen on 热衷于，喜爱

诵读 He wasn't keen on buying a car, but we talked him into it. 他虽不迫切想买车，但最终我们说服了他。

kidnap [ˈkɪdnæp] *vt.* 绑架，劫持

诵读 Terrorists kidnaped their baby and demanded $100,000 from them for its release. 恐怖分子绑架了他们的小孩，要求他们付十万美金才释放小孩。

kindness [ˈkaɪndnɪs] *n.* 仁慈；好意

诵读 He did it all out of kindness, not in the hope of reward. 他做此事完全是出于仁慈之心，不希望接受报酬。

kit [kɪt] *n.* 成套工具，工具箱

诵读 This furniture comes as a kit. 这是一套组合家具。

kneel [niːl] *vi.* 跪，下跪

诵读 He knelt down to look for a coin he had dropped. 他跪下找他掉了的硬币。

knit [nɪt] *v.* 编织；接合

诵读 She was knitting stockings out of wool. 她正在用羊毛线织长袜。

knock [nɒk] *vi.* 敲打 *n.* 敲击

搭配 knock down 撞倒，击倒；knock out 击倒，击昏

诵读 He was knocked out by a stone from the other side of the road. 他被路对面的一块石头击昏了。

knowledge [ˈnɒlɪdʒ] *n.* 知识；了解

搭配 in the knowledge of 知道

区分 acknowledge *vt.* 承认，鸣谢

诵读 My knowledge of French is poor. 我的法语不太好。

keyboard [ˈkiːbɔːd] *n.* 键盘

巧记 计算机各部件：鼠标 mouse，无线鼠标 wireless mouse，显示屏 screen

诵读 I bought a keyboard in the supermarket yesterday. 昨天我在超市买了键盘。

kid [kɪd] *n.* 小孩

僻义 *vt.* 戏弄

诵读 They kidded him because he grew a beard. 他们戏弄他，因为他长着大胡子。

kin [kɪn] *n.* 家族，亲属

拓展 kinship *n.* 亲属关系

诵读 We are near kin. 我们是近亲。

kindergarten [ˈkɪndəˌgɑːtən] *n.* 幼儿园

诵读 Little children play in kindergarten. 小孩在幼儿园玩耍。

labor [ˈleɪbə] *n.* 劳动 *vi.* 苦干

诵读 He labored at the English course for three years. 他刻苦攻读了 3 年英语。

lack [læk] *n.* 缺乏 *vt.* 不足

搭配 for lack of... 因没有……

诵读 Several research institutions were closed down for lack of fund. 由于缺乏资金，好几家研究所被迫关门了。

land [lænd] *n.* 土地 *vi.* 着陆

拓展 landlord *n.* 房东，地主

搭配 land off 飞机落地

诵读 The passengers landed as soon as the ship reached harbor. 船刚一抵港，乘客们迅速上岸。

lay [leɪ] *vt.* 放；下（蛋）

搭配 lay aside 搁置一边；lay off 解雇；lay out 安排

诵读 He tried his best to lay out his first printed page. 他尽最大努力设计他的第一幅印刷版面。

lecture [ˈlektʃə] *n.* 演讲 *vt.* 讲课

僻义 *vt.* 责备

诵读 He lectured me heatedly for a few minutes. 他激烈地训了我几分钟。

length [leŋθ] *n.* 长度；一段

搭配 at length 终于；详细地

诵读 I looked into the case at length. 我详细地调查了这件事。

let [let] *vt.* 让；假设

搭配 let alone 更不用说；let sb. down 使失望；let go 放开，松手

诵读 You ought to be fined for this break of rules, but I will let you off this time. 你违反规定应该被罚款，但这次我就饶了你。

lab [læb] *n.*（laboratory）实验室

诵读 In order to use a lab, the teacher had to be well trained or highly experienced. 为了能使用实验室，教师必须训练有素或经验丰富。

label [ˈleɪbəl] *n.* 标签

僻义 *vt.* 把……称为

诵读 When you are travelling you should put labels on your luggage. 旅行时你应该在行李上贴上标签。

large [lɑːdʒ] *a.* 广大的，大规模的

拓展 largely *ad.* 主要地，基本上

搭配 at large 逍遥法外；详细地

诵读 The president's powers under the act would be very large. 根据这一法案，总统的权力会很大。

latter [ˈlætə] *a.* 后者的

诵读 In the latter part of May she announced that she was going for a fortnight's holiday to the seaside. 五月下旬她宣布将到海边度假两周。

laughter [ˈlɑːftə] *n.* 笑

搭配 burst into laughter 大笑

诵读 You know by the boy's loud laughter that he is enjoying the joke. 从这个男孩响亮的笑声你可以知道，他很喜欢这个笑话。

launch [lɔːntʃ] *vt.* 发射；开展

诵读 The Americans have launched many rockets into space. 美国人已向太空发射了许多火箭。

lead [liːd] *vt.* 领导

拓展 leadership *n.* 领导；leading *a.* 领导的，最主要的

搭配 lead to 导致

诵读 Now they lead in the manufacture of chips. 现在他们在芯片制造方面领先。

leap [liːp] *vi.* 跳，跳跃

诵读 Look before you leap. 三思而后行。

learned [ˈlɜːnɪd] *a.* 博学的，有学问的

拓展 learning *n.* 学问；学习

诵读 There was no person learned enough in the town to understand it. 在这个城市里没有人如此博学，能够理解它。

legal [ˈliːgəl] *a.* 法律的，合法的

巧记 词根 leg 法律+后缀-al=合法的

诵读 The judge's daughter hopes to enter the legal profession. 这个法官的女儿想从事法律行业。

legislation [ˌledʒɪsˈleɪʃən] *n.* 法律；立法

诵读 The most prominent new legislation is to

introduce an element of a "European passport" system, the equivalent of business license. 新立法最突出的一项内容就是引入了"欧盟护照"机制，相当于营业执照。

legitimate [lɪ'dʒɪtɪmɪt] *a.* 合法的；合理的

拓展 legitimacy *n.* 合法性

诵读 The two countries have to find a delicate balance between the free flow of commerce and legitimate securities concerns. 两国必须在商业自由流动和合理安全关切之间找到微妙的平衡。

leisure ['leʒə] *n.* 空闲，闲暇

诵读 Don't squander your leisure time hanging around doing nothing. 别在业余时间无所事事。

lest [lest] *conj.* 唯恐，免得

诵读 Read in a good light lest it should hurt your eyes. 到明处看书，以免损伤你的视力。

liberal ['lɪbərəl] *a.* 慷慨的；自由的

拓展 liberate *vt.* 解放，释放；liberty *n.* 自由，自由权

诵读 New York's social circle was far too liberal for her taste. 纽约的社交圈过于开放，不合她的胃口。

likely ['laɪkli] *a.* 很可能的 *ad.* 大概地

拓展 likelihood *n.* 可能性

搭配 be likely to 很有可能

诵读 Blacks who smoke up to a pack a day are far more likely than whites who smoke similar amount to develop lung cancer. 每天吸一包烟的黑人比每天吸一包烟的白人更容易患肺癌。

likewise ['laɪkwaɪz] *ad.* 同样地

诵读 She mentioned how her uncle likewise had been questioned by the police. 她提到叔叔同样也被警察盘问过。

limitation [ˌlɪmɪ'teɪʃən] *n.* 限制，局限性

拓展 limited *a.* 有限的，被限制的

诵读 Through the Internet, we can make friends from different countries, despite space limitation. 通过互联网，我们可以和不同国家的人交朋友，不受空间限制。

linger ['lɪŋɡə] *vi.* 逗留，徘徊

诵读 An increasing body of evidence shows little particles of virus can linger on tabletops, telephones and other surfaces. 越来越多的证据表明，微小的病

毒颗粒会残留在桌面、电话和其他物体的表面。

linguistic [lɪŋ'ɡwɪstɪk] *a.* 语言的，语言学的

诵读 The Linguistic Society of America has not taken a position on whether Ebonics is a language. 美国语言学学会并没有肯定"黑人英语"是一门语言。

link [lɪŋk] *v.* 连接，联系 *n.* 环节

搭配 be linked to… 与……有联系

诵读 A five-year study found no link between drinking green tea and reducing a person's risk of cancer. 为期五年的实验表明，喝绿茶与抗癌竟毫无关系。

literacy ['lɪtərəsi] *n.* 有文化，有读写能力

搭配 scientific literacy 科学素养

诵读 This program is a part of an effort to promote financial literacy for young people. 这个项目旨在提升年轻人的财务素养。

literally ['lɪtərəli] *ad.* 照字面意义，逐字地

诵读 He says you have to read it literally. 他说你必须逐字阅读。

literary ['lɪtərəri] *a.* 文学上的，文学的

诵读 He is known as a literary person who cares about social events. 他是一个关心社会大事的文人。

local ['ləʊkəl] *a.* 地方的，当地的

拓展 locate *vt.* 位于；location *n.* 位置，场所

搭配 be located at 坐落于

诵读 You can change your sterling into the local currency at the airport. 你可以在机场把英镑兑换成当地的货币。

logic ['lɒdʒɪk] *n.* 逻辑

巧记 谐音记忆：逻辑

拓展 logical *a.* 逻辑的，符合逻辑的

诵读 This is the area of the brain where logic and reasoning tasks are carried out. 这里是大脑中用于逻辑推理的区域。

lower ['ləʊə] *a.* 较低的

僻义 *vt.* 降低

诵读 Positive emotions can actually lower people's blood pressure. 乐观的情绪可以降低血压。

loyal ['lɔɪəl] *a.* 忠诚的，忠贞的

拓展 loyalty *n.* 忠诚，忠心

诵读 This woman is a complex combination of being vain and insecure, loyal and self-serving. 这个

女人是虚荣与不安全、忠诚与自私的复杂结合体。

lure [lʊə] *n.* 魅力 *vt.* 引诱

拓展 luring *a.* 具有诱惑力的

诵读 Foreign educational institutions are holding seminars and exhibitions to lure more Chinese youngsters to study abroad. 国外的教育机构举办各种研讨会和展览来吸引中国年轻人到国外学习。

luxury [ˈlʌkʃəri] *n.* 奢侈 *a.* 奢华的

巧记 luxurious *a.* 奢侈的

诵读 Wealthy tourists are expected to spend a billion pounds on luxury goods during the sales. 预计富有的游客将在促销期花费10亿英镑购买奢侈品。

lag [læg] *vi.&n.* 落后

搭配 lag behind 落后

诵读 Bad weather caused a lag in the scheduled activities. 恶劣的天气使事先安排好的活动推迟了。

lane [leɪn] *n.* 小路，小巷

lantern [ˈlæntən] *n.* 灯，灯笼

搭配 Lantern Festival 元宵节

诵读 The child next door carried a lantern. 隔壁的小孩提一个灯笼。

lap [læp] *n.* 大腿，（跑道的）一圈

搭配 laptop 笔记本电脑

诵读 She was sitting with her hands on her lap. 她坐着，把手放到膝上。

lapse [læps] *n.* 小错，疏忽；流逝，丧失

搭配 a lapse of the tongue (pen) 口（笔）误；lapse of concentration 走神

诵读 New products and production processes are transferred to the developing countries only after a substantial amount of time has lapsed. 新的产品和生产工序要经过一段相当长的时间后才能向发展中国家转移。

layman [ˈleɪmən] *n.* 外行

诵读 Where the law is concerned, I'm only a layman. 谈到法律，我不过是个外行。

leak [liːk] *vt.* 泄漏 *n.* 漏洞

诵读 Who leaked the news to the press? 谁将消息泄

漏给新闻界的？

lean [liːn] *vi.* 倾斜 *a.* 瘦的

诵读 He leant out of the window to see the magnificent scene. 他探出窗外，欣赏壮丽的景色。

lease [liːs] *vt.* 出租 *n.* 租借

搭配 a new lease of life 新的生机和活力；焕然一新

诵读 When does the lease expire? 租约何时期满？

leather [ˈleðə] *n.* 皮革

诵读 This book is bound in leather. 这本书是用皮革装订的。

legacy [ˈlegəsi] *n.* 遗产，遗赠

巧记 词根 leg-法律+acy =根据法律（从父母那获得的）东西→遗产，遗赠

诵读 We will maintain this legacy. 我们会致力保留这个优良传统。

liable [ˈlaɪəbl] *a.* 有……倾向的；可能遭受……的

拓展 liability *n.* 责任；（pl.）债务

搭配 be liable to 有……倾向；易于

诵读 We might be more liable to spree when financially squeezed: under stress we can feel driven to hoard. 当经济紧缩时，我们可能会变得更加疯狂：在压力之下，我们会被迫囤积东西。

license [ˈlaɪsəns] *n.* 许可证，执照

搭配 driving license 驾照

诵读 Certain amount of alcoholic beverages is good for health, but that's no license to go crazy though. 适当饮酒对健康有益，但这绝不意味着可以疯狂地喝酒。

lightning [ˈlaɪtnɪŋ] *n.* 闪电

辨析 同形词：lighten *vt.&vi.* 发光，使更明亮

巧记 lightning marriage 闪婚

诵读 Suddenly a bolt of lightning crackled through the sky. 突然，一道闪电划破长空。

liquid [ˈlɪkwɪd] *n.* 液体 *a.* 液体的

诵读 You have added too much liquid to the mixture. 你给这混合物加了过多的液体。

litter [ˈlɪtə] *n.* 垃圾 *vt.* 使杂乱

诵读 Don't litter the ground with paper. 勿随地乱扔纸屑。

loan [ləʊn] *n.* 贷款 *vt.* 借出

诵读 On the other hand some researchers support the use of loan words. 另一方面，一些研究人员支持使

用外来语。

lodge [lɒdʒ] *vt.* 给……提供住宿 *n.* 传达室

诵读 I drove out of the gates, past the keeper's lodge. 我驶出大门，经过守门人的小屋。

lofty ['lɒfti] *a.* 崇高的，高尚的

诵读 Virtue is lofty, but it requires you to give. 美德是高尚的，但美德需要付出和给予。

loose [luːs] *a.* （宽）松的；散漫的

拓展 loosen *vt.* 解开，放松

诵读 You should wear loose-fitting clothing to keep cool in summer. 你应该穿宽松的衣服，这样夏天能保持凉爽。

lubricate ['luːbrɪkeɪt] *vt.* 润滑，行贿

诵读 Mineral oils are used to lubricate machinery. 矿物油可用来润滑机器。

luggage ['lʌgɪdʒ] *n.* 行李

诵读 The girl simply walked out of the building with her friend concealed in her luggage. 女孩慢慢走出了大楼，此时她的朋友正藏在行李中。

lump [lʌmp] *n.* 团 *vt.* （使）成团

搭配 lump together 把……合在一起（考虑）

诵读 The artist shaped and squeezed a lump of clay into a graceful shape. 艺术家把一大块黏土塑型，压成漂亮的形状。

lunar ['luːnə] *a.* 月亮的，阴历的

巧记 Chinese Lunar New Year 中国农历新年

诵读 Generally, December 22nd marks Dong Zhi, or the Winter Solstice Festival, according to the Chinese lunar calendar. 一般来说，12 月 22 日是中国农历冬至，也叫冬至节。

material [mə'tɪəriəl] *n.* 材料 *a.* 物质的

搭配 raw material 原材料

诵读 This will give your promotional material individuality and style. 这会让你的促销品显得个性十足、格调高雅。

mathematics [ˌmæθɪ'mætɪks] *n.* （maths）数学

machinery [mə'ʃiːnəri] *n.* （总称）机器，机械

诵读 In 1976, the Big Ben stopped when a piece of its machinery broke. 1976 年，由于一小片零件出了故障，大本钟也一度停摆。

maintain [meɪn'teɪn] *vt.* 维修，保养

拓展 maintenance *n.* 维修，保养

诵读 It's best to maintain at least an arm's-length distance when talking to someone who shows signs of infection. 当和有感染症状的人交谈的时候，最好保持一臂远的距离。

major ['meɪdʒə] *a.* 主要的，主修课程 *vi.* 主修

拓展 majority *n.* 多数，大多数

诵读 The major you choose is more important than the overall ranking of your university. 你所选择的专业比你大学的综合排名更为重要。

male [meɪl] *n.&a.* 男性；男性的

巧记 反义词 female *n.&a.* 女性；女性的

诵读 I realize there's no consensus on what are male or female values. 我意识到人们对男性价值观和女性价值观的定义并无共识。

manage ['mænɪdʒ] *vt.* 经营，管理

搭配 manage to do sth. 做成某事

拓展 management *n.* 经营；manager *n.* 经理，管理人

诵读 He manages the hotel very well. 他把这家酒店管理得井井有条。

mankind [mæn'kaɪnd] *n.* 人类

诵读 Mankind has always struggled forward no matter what difficulty lies in its way. 不管道路上有任何困难，人类总是要奋勇前进。

manner ['mænə] *n.* 方式；举止

诵读 I love duck cooked in Chinese manner. 我爱吃中式做法的鸭。

manual ['mænjʊəl] *a.* 手的，体力的

巧记 词根 manu 手+后缀-al→ 手工的

诵读 All we have ever got was manual labour and illness. 我们所得到的只有体力劳动和疾病。

manufacture [ˌmænjʊˈfæktʃə] *vt.* 制造，加工

巧记 词根manu（=man手）+fact制作+后缀-ure→用手制作→可制造的，可加工的

诵读 The factory is now trying to manufacture a new model. 这家工厂正在试制一种新产品。

margin [ˈmɑːdʒɪn] *n.* 页边，边缘

僻义 *n.* 盈余，利润

拓展 marginal *a.* 边缘的

诵读 Students have played an important role in the past, but for the moment, they're on the margins. 学生曾经发挥了重要的作用，不过现在他们变得无足轻重了。

mark [mɑːk] *n.* 痕迹 *vt.* 标记

诵读 The enemy's retreat left marks of haste. 敌人留下了仓皇退去的痕迹。

market [ˈmɑːkɪt] *n.* 市场

拓展 marketing *n.* 营销

诵读 Farmers go to the market to buy and sell vegetables. 农夫们到市场上买卖蔬菜。

marriage [ˈmærɪdʒ] *n.* 结婚

拓展 married *a.* 已婚的

诵读 The story begins with their marriage. 故事以他们的婚姻开始。

marvel [ˈmɑːvəl] *vi.* 感到惊奇

搭配 marvel at... 对……感到惊奇

拓展 marvelous *a.* 惊人的，奇迹般的

诵读 The creation by the workers is marvelous. 工人们的创造是惊人的。

mask [mɑːsk] *n.* 面具

僻义 *v.* 掩饰

诵读 We tore from them the mask of democracy. 我们撕下了他们民主的假面具。

mature [məˈtjʊə] *a.* 成熟的 *vi.* （使）成熟

诵读 He is a mature man. 他是成年人。

mean [miːn] *vt.* 意味着

僻义 *a.* 卑鄙的，吝啬的

辨析 means *n.* 方法，手段

诵读 In running a company, strict financial management means everything. 经营一家公司，严格的财务管理是至关重要的。

merit [ˈmerɪt] *n.* 优点 *vt.* 值得

搭配 merits and demerits 优缺点

诵读 He was awarded a first-class merit in the War of Liberation. 他在解放战争中荣立一等功。

message [ˈmesɪdʒ] *n.* 消息，要旨

拓展 messenger *n.* 送信者，使者

诵读 Did you catch the message of this book? 你领会这本书的要旨了吗？

meantime [ˈmiːntaɪm] *n.* （meanwhile）其时 *ad.* 同时地

诵读 Put the kettle on to boil and in the meantime we will cut the bread. 把壶放在火上烧开，同时我们来切面包。

measure [ˈmeʒə] *vt.* 测量 *n.* 尺寸

诵读 I continued to measure his progress against the charts in the doctor's office. 我根据医生办公室里的图表继续估量他的进展。

mechanic [mɪˈkænɪk] *n.* 技工，机修工

拓展 mechanical *a.* 机械的；mechanism *n.* 机械装置，机构

诵读 If you smell something unusual, take the car to your mechanic. 如果你闻到了异味，就把车开动修理工那里。

medal [ˈmedəl] *n.* 奖章，勋章

诵读 The war hero received many medals for bravery. 那位战斗英雄由于英勇获得了许多奖章。

medium [ˈmiːdjəm] *n.* 媒体，介质 *a.* 中等的

拓展 复数形式是 media

诵读 There has to be a medium between good and bad. 在好与坏之间必然存在一个中间状态。

melt [melt] *vt.&vi.* （使）融化，（使）熔化

巧记 兼收并蓄、海纳百川是现阶段美国文化的显著特征。因此，美国也被称为大熔炉（the melting pot）。

诵读 Salt melts in water. 盐在水中溶解。

membership [ˈmembəʃɪp] *n.* 会员资格，成员资格

诵读 Xiao Li applied for Party membership. 小李申请入党。

memorial [mɪˈmɔːrɪəl] *a.* 纪念的 *n.* 纪念碑

诵读 Building a memorial to Columbus has been his lifelong dream. 建一座哥伦布纪念碑是他一生

的梦想。

merchant [ˈmɜːtʃənt] *n.* 商人，零售商

拓展 merchandise *n.* 商品，货物

诵读 Any knowledgeable wine merchant would be able to advise you. 任何一位懂行的葡萄酒商人都能为你提出建议。

mercy [ˈmɜːsi] *n.* 仁慈，怜悯

搭配 at the mercy of... 由……处理

诵读 They meant to finish her off, swiftly and without mercy. 他们打算毫不留情地迅速解决了她。

mere [mɪə] *a.* 纯粹的；仅仅

拓展 merely *ad.* 仅仅

诵读 Sixty percent of teachers are women, but a mere five percent of women are principals. 60%的教师是女性，但只有5%的女性是校长。

mind [maɪnd] *n.* 头脑 *vt.* 注意

搭配 come to one's mind 被某人想起；bear/keep in mind 记住；make up one's mind to do sth. 下决心做某事

诵读 She did not come because she was ill, but I did not have it in mind. 她没来，因为她病了。但我把这事儿给忘了。

minute [ˈmɪnɪt] *n.* 分

僻义 *a.* 微小的

诵读 The doctor made a minute study of the illness. 医生对病情进行了细致的检查。

minor [ˈmaɪnə] *a.* 较小的 *n.* 兼修学科

拓展 minority *n.* 少数，少数民族

诵读 She is known in Italy for a number of minor roles in films. 她因担任电影中一些配角而闻名意大利。

miss [mɪs] *n.* 小姐 *vt.* 错过

搭配 miss one's way 迷路；miss out 漏掉，省去

诵读 You have missed out one word. 你漏掉了一个词。

mistake [mɪsˈteɪk] *n.* 错误 *vt.* 弄错

搭配 by mistake 错误地；mistake...for... 把……误认为……

诵读 The bird mistook the pebble for an egg and tried to hatch it. 这鸟错把卵石当作蛋来孵化。

mild [maɪld] *a.* 温和的，轻微的

诵读 We have a very mild climate. 我们这里的气候很温和。

military [ˈmɪlɪtərɪ] *a.* 军事的，军用的

诵读 He has a lot of military experience. 他军事经验丰富。

minimize [ˈmɪnɪmaɪz] *vt.* 使减少到最少

巧记 词根 mini 小+ mize-动词词根→使减少到最小，使降到最低

拓展 minimum *n.* 最小值

诵读 The explorers tried their best to minimize the dangers of their trip. 探险家们极力把探险途中的危险降到最低。

miracle [ˈmɪrəkl] *n.* 奇迹，令人惊奇的人（或事）

诵读 The doctor said that her recovery was a miracle. 医生说她能康复真是个奇迹。

mirror [ˈmɪrə] *n.* 镜子

僻义 *vt.* 反映

诵读 Before going out, she surveyed herself in the mirror. 出门之前，她在镜子中审视自己。

miserable [ˈmɪzərəbl] *a.* 痛苦的，悲惨的

拓展 misery *n.* 痛苦，悲惨，不幸

诵读 You are looking very miserable. 你看起来很痛苦的样子。

misfortune [mɪsˈfɔːtʃən] *n.* 不幸，灾祸

巧记 前缀 mis-错误+词根 fortune运气→不幸，灾难

诵读 Jack had the misfortune to be ill on the day of the party. 不幸的是杰克在开晚会那天生病了。

mislead [ˌmɪsˈliːd] *vt.* 误导，使误入歧途

诵读 The travellers were misled by the guide. 旅游者们被向导领错路了。

misunderstand [ˌmɪsʌndəˈstænd] *vt.* 误解，误会

巧记 前缀 mis-错误+词根 understand理解→误解，误会

诵读 Some experts cautioned that the general public could misunderstand the meaning of the study. 一些专家警告说，公众可能会对这项研究产生误解。

mixture [ˈmɪkstʃə] *n.* 混合；混合物

巧记 词根 mix 混合+后缀-ture→混合；混合物

诵读 They looked at him with a mixture of horror, envy and awe. 他们看他时的表情夹杂着害怕、羡慕和敬畏。

modern [ˈmɒdən] *a.* 现代的

拓展 modernization *n.* 现代化

诵读 In this part of the city, you can see ancient and modern buildings next to each other. 在这一城区，你可以看见古建筑和现代建筑并存。

moment [ˈməʊmənt] *n.* 片刻

搭配 for a moment 片刻，一会儿；in a moment 立刻，马上；the moment 一………就……

诵读 The enemy plane was shot down the moment it intruded into the country's air space. 这架敌机一侵入该国领空就被击落。

monitor [ˈmɒnɪtə] *n.* 班长 *vt.* 监控

诵读 You will have to monitor your eating constantly. 你一定要经常注意控制饮食。

mode [məʊd] *n.* 方式，式样

诵读 It should be done only once for each mode. 此操作对于每个模式来说只进行一次。

moderate [ˈmɒdərɪt] *a.* 中等的，温和的

诵读 Contrary to the popular belief, moderate exercise actually decreases your appetite. 与通常的看法相反，适度的运动事实上会降低食欲。

modest [ˈmɒdɪst] *a.* 谦虚的

拓展 modesty *n.* 谦虚

诵读 Modesty helps one advance, whereas conceit makes one fall behind. 谦虚使人进步，反之，骄傲使人落后。

modify [ˈmɒdɪfaɪ] *vt.* 更改，修改

巧记 词根 mod（=mode 样式）+后缀-ify→变成某种样式→更改，修改

诵读 The club members did agree to modify their recruitment policy. 俱乐部成员确已同意修改纳新政策。

monetary [ˈmʌnɪtəri] *a.* 金融的，货币的

巧记 词根 mone（=money）+ 后缀-tary→金融的，货币的

搭配 monetary policy 货币政策

诵读 China is to shift to prudent monetary policy next year. 中国明年将转向实行稳健的货币政策。

monument [ˈmɒnjʊmənt] *n.* 纪念碑，纪念馆

诵读 The soldier's name was inscribed on a monument. 那名战士的名字被刻在纪念碑上。

moral [ˈmɔːrəl] *a.* 道德（上）的

拓展 morality *n.* 道德，美德

辨析 mortal *a.* 致命的

诵读 Some voices, though, are calling Americans back to traditional moral values. 有些人在呼吁美国人回到传统的道德价值观上。

motive [ˈməʊtɪv] *n.* 动机 *a.* 运动的

巧记 mot 动+iv+动词后缀-ate→激励

拓展 motivate *vt.* 激励，作为……的动机；motion *n.* 运动

诵读 You have first got to motivate the children and then to teach them. 你首先得激发孩子们的学习兴趣，然后再去教他们。

mood [muːd] *n.* 心情，情绪

诵读 He is clearly in a good mood today. 显然，他今天心情不错。

mostly [ˈməʊstli] *ad.* 几乎全部地；主要地

诵读 I am working with mostly highly motivated people. 我正与积极性很高的人共事。

mount [maʊnt] *vt.* 登上 *vi.* 增加

诵读 For several hours, tension mounted. 几个小时中，紧张局势加剧了。

must [mʌst] *modal.* 必须，应当

辨义 *n.* 必须做的事，必不可少的事物

诵读 Warm clothes are a must in the mountains. 到山区去必须穿暖和的衣服。

multiple [ˈmʌltɪpl] *a.* 多样的 *n.* 倍数

巧记 multiple choice 选择题

拓展 multiply *vi.&vt.*（by）乘；倍增

诵读 French women seem to have it all: multiple children, a job and, often, a figure to envy. 法国女性似乎样样不缺，她们有一群孩子，有一份工作，往往还有一副令人羡慕的好身材。

multitude [ˈmʌltɪtjuːd] *n.* 众多，大量

诵读 The full-service stores have a multitude of uses. 这家全服务型商店有多种功能。

muscle [ˈmʌsl] *n.* 肌肉，体力

拓展 muscular *a.* 肌肉的；强健的

诵读 Keeping your muscles strong and in tone helps you to avoid back problems. 保持肌肉强壮健康有助于避免患上背疾。

musical [ˈmjuːzɪkəl] *a.* 音乐的 *n.* 音乐片

拓展 musician *n.* 音乐家，乐师

诵读 We have a wealth of musical talents in this region. 我们在该地区有大量的音乐人才。

mutual [ˈmjuːtʃʊəl] *a.* 相互的；共同的

搭配 mutual understanding 相互理解

诵读 The East and the West can work together for their mutual benefit and progress. 东西方可以为互惠进步而合作。

mystery [ˈmɪstəri] *n.* 神秘

巧记 mysterious *a.* 神秘的，可疑的

诵读 The source of the gunshots still remains a mystery. 枪弹来自何处依然是一个谜。

myth [mɪθ] *n.* 神话；虚构的理论

诵读 His story about being very wealthy was a complete myth. 关于他非常富有的说法完全是捏造出来的。

magic [ˈmædʒɪk] *n.* 魔术，魔（魅）力

诵读 This enchanting film captures the magic of a very special place. 这部迷人的电影捕捉到了一个非常特别的地方的魔力。

magnet [ˈmæɡnɪt] *n.* 磁体，磁铁

拓展 magnetic *a.* 磁的，有吸引力的

诵读 Placing a magnet on your head can temporarily turn you from a right-hander to a left-handed person. 在脑袋上放置一块磁铁能将人暂时从"右撇子"变成"左撇子"。

magnify [ˈmæɡnɪfaɪ] *vt.* 放大，扩大；夸大

搭配 magnifying glass 放大镜

拓展 magnificent *a.* 华丽的，高尚的

诵读 She is inclined to magnify her troubles. 她喜欢夸大她的困难。

magnitude [ˈmæɡnɪtjuːd] *n.* 巨大，庞大；重要性

诵读 There is mounting evidence that the frequency and magnitude of landsliding is changing in many parts of the world in response to climate change. 越来越多的证据表明，受气候变化影响，世界各地滑坡发生的频率和程度正在发生改变。

maneuver [məˈnuːvə] *n.* 机动，移动

诵读 She tried to maneuver her body into a more comfortable position. 她试着把身子挪了挪，换了一个较为舒服的姿势。

manifest [ˈmænɪfest] *vt.* 表明，显示 *a.* 明白的

巧记 词根 mani（=man 手）+词根 fest→用手打出手势→表明

诵读 These newly unearthed cultural objects manifest the intelligence of the working people of ancient China. 这些新出土的历史文物显示了古代中国劳动人民的聪明才智。

manipulate [məˈnɪpjʊleɪt] *vt.* 操纵，控制

巧记 词根 mani（=man 手）+词根 pul=pull 拉+后缀-ate→用手拉→操纵，控制

诵读 Do you know how to manipulate a computer? 你知道怎样操作计算机吗？

manuscript [ˈmænjʊskrɪpt] *n.* 手稿，原稿

巧记 词根 manu（=man 手）+script 稿子

诵读 This is a manuscript bearing a title as *Ruth*. 这是一篇题为《鲁思》的手稿。

masculine [ˈmɑːskjʊlɪn] *a.* 男性的，阳刚的

巧记 女性通常认为肌肉（muscle）发达的男性比较有男人味（masculine）

诵读 He was handsome and strong, and very masculine. 他英俊强壮，富有男子汉气概。

massive [ˈmæsɪv] *a.* 大而重的，大规模的

巧记 词根 mass 大量+后缀-ive

诵读 Four massive pillars support the roof. 四根大柱子支撑着屋顶。

masterpiece [ˈmɑːstəpiːs] *n.* 杰作，名著

巧记 合成词：master 精通+piece 片，篇

诵读 This painting is a masterpiece of Leonardo da Vinci. 这幅画是达·芬奇的杰作。

mate [meɪt] *n.* 伙伴，配偶

诵读 The little girl is looking for a mate for her female cat. 小女孩正在为她的母猫找配偶。

maximum [ˈmæksɪməm] *n.* 最大值 *a.* 最大的

巧记 词根 maxi 最大+词缀-mum→最大化，最佳化

诵读 The law provides for a maximum of two years in prison. 法律规定监禁最长两年。

meditate [ˈmedɪˌteɪt] *vi.* 考虑，沉思

拓展 meditation *n.* 熟虑；默想

诵读 On the day her son began school, she meditated

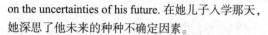

on the uncertainties of his future. 在她儿子入学那天，她深思了他未来的种种不确定因素。

melody ['melədi] *n.* 旋律；悦耳的音乐

诵读 He played an Irish melody on the harp. 他用竖琴演奏了一首爱尔兰曲调。

menace ['menəs] *n.* 威胁 *v.* 威吓

巧记 under menace 在恐吓之下

诵读 In my view, you are a menace to the public. 在我看来，你对公众是一个威胁。

merge [mɜːdʒ] *vt.&vi.* (使)结合，(使)合并

诵读 The two countries merged into one. 这两个国家合二为一了。

merry ['meri] *a.* 欢乐的，愉快的

巧记 Merry Christmas 圣诞快乐

诵读 Signs of merry life could be seen everywhere after the bumper harvest. 丰收以后到处可以看到一片欢乐景象。

mess [mes] *n.* 混乱 *vt.* 弄脏

诵读 The hall was a mess after the party. 晚会之后，大厅一片狼藉。

metropolitan [ˌmetrə'pɒlɪtən] *a.* 大都市的

诵读 Metropolitan residents are used to fast rhythm. 大都市的居民习惯了快节奏。

midst [mɪdst] *n.* 中间，当中

诵读 I saw her in the midst of the crowd. 我从人群中看见了她。

migrate [maɪ'greɪt] *vt.* 迁移，移居(国外)

诵读 Mr Smith migrated to China to find work. 史密斯先生为了找工作而移居中国。

minus ['maɪnəs] *a.* 负的 *prep.* 减去

诵读 One minus one is zero. 一减一等于零。

mischief ['mɪstʃɪf] *n.* 损害；恶作剧

巧记 前缀 mis-错误+词根 chief 首领→首领出现错误→带来巨大损害

诵读 He is sorry for having told lies but the mischief has been done and cannot be undone. 他因为撒谎而后悔，但危害已造成，无法弥补了。

mingle ['mɪŋgl] *vi.* (使)混合

诵读 Go out of your way to mingle with others at the wedding. 在婚礼上你要主动和别人交际。

miniature ['mɪnɪtʃə] *n.* 缩小的模型，缩图

诵读 This is a miniature of the map of China. 这是一幅中国地图的缩图。

ministry ['mɪnɪstri] *n.* 政府部门；牧师

拓展 minister *n.* 部长，大臣

诵读 He began his diplomatic career as an interpreter at the Ministry of Foreign Affairs. 他在外交部当了一名译员，开始了他的外交生涯。

moan [məʊn] *n.* 呻吟声 *vi.* 悲叹

诵读 You clearly need to be able to moan about him from time to time. 你显然需要偶尔抱怨他几句。

mobile ['məʊbaɪl] *a.* 可动的，活动的，运动的

巧记 mobile phone 手机

拓展 mobilize *vt.* 动员

诵读 A growing number of students are cheating in their exams, with many using mobile phones to boost their marks. 考试作弊的学生数量呈上涨趋势，其中有很多学生利用手机作弊，以提高考试成绩。

mock [mɒk] *vt.&vi.* 嘲笑 *a.* 模拟的

诵读 In the mock drama Austria defeated the Netherlands in the final. 在这部炮制的纪录片中，奥地利队在决赛中击败了荷兰队。

momentum [məʊ'mentəm] *n.* 动力，要素

诵读 This campaign is really gaining momentum. 这场运动确实势头正猛。

monopoly [mə'nɒpəli] *n.* 垄断，独有

巧记 前缀 mono-单一的+词根 poly 起作用→只有一家起作用→垄断

诵读 Women do not have a monopoly on feelings of betrayal. 背叛感并非是女人独有的。

monotonous [mə'nɒtənəs] *a.* 单调的，无变化的

巧记 前缀 mono-单一的+词根 ton 语调+形容词后缀-ous→一个语调说话→单调的

诵读 This could be anything ranging from a boring lecture, to a monotonous conversation with people. 这可以是任何事，一次枯燥的演讲，或者是人们单调乏味的一段对话。

mortgage ['mɔːgɪdʒ] *n.&vt.* 抵押(借款)

诵读 The President is set to unveil a $75 billion mortgage relief plan. 总统将宣布一项 750 亿美元的抵押贷款减免计划。

mould [məʊld] *n.* (mold) 模子 *vt.* 造型

诵读 He could never be accused of fitting the mould. 他永远都不可能被指责属于这个类型。

mourn [mɔːn] *vt.&vi.* 哀悼，忧伤

诵读 We mourn for our fallen soldiers. 我们哀悼牺牲的兵士。

model [ˈmɒdəl] *n.* 模范；模型 *v.* 模仿

name [neɪm] *n.* 名字 *vt.* 取（或命）名

僻义 *n.* 名声，名望

搭配 be worthy of the name 名副其实

诵读 He had a name for good judgement. 他以精准判断而闻名。

narrow [ˈnærəʊ] *a.* 狭窄的，狭隘的

搭配 narrow escape 九死一生

诵读 The gate is too narrow for a car to pass; we will have to walk through. 这门太窄了，汽车通不过，我们得走过去。

nation [ˈneɪʃən] *n.* 民族，国家

拓展 national *a.* 民族的，国家的；native *a.* 本地的 *n.* 本地人；nationality *n.* 国籍，民族

诵读 A native of London, Mr. Green lives mostly in Leeds. 格林先生出生于伦敦，但他大部分时间住在里兹。

nature [ˈneɪtʃə] *n.* 自然，本质

拓展 natural *a.* 自然的，天赋的

搭配 by nature 就本质而言，天生地

诵读 She had a natural gift for teaching. 她有当老师的天赋。

namely [ˈneɪmlɪ] *ad.* 即，也就是

诵读 Only one person can answer the question, namely, you. 只有一个人能回答这个问题，那就是你。

narrative [ˈnærətɪv] *a.* 叙述性的 *n.* 叙述

诵读 Neither author was very strong on narrative. 两位作者在叙述方面都不强。

nasty [ˈnɑːstɪ] *a.* 肮脏的，令人厌恶的

诵读 In this area the weather is usually nasty in winter. 这里冬天的天气通常非常恶劣。

neat [niːt] *a.* 整洁的，优美的

诵读 It was really a neat party; I enjoyed myself. 那是一次非常好的晚会，我玩得很高兴。

necessary [ˈnesɪsəri] *a.* 必需的

僻义 *n.* 必需品

拓展 necessitate *vt.* 使成为必要，需要

搭配 not necessary 不必要；not necessarily 不一定

诵读 We packed those necessaries for future use. 我们把这些必需品包起来备用。

need [niːd] *v.* 需要 *n.* 必要

搭配 in bad/great need of 急需

诵读 Many families are in great need. 许多家庭生活极端贫困。

nearly [ˈnɪəli] *ad.* 差不多，几乎

诵读 Nearly 20 percent of U.S. workers are unemployed. 美国近20%的劳动力失业。

negative [ˈnegətɪv] *a.* 否定的，消极的

诵读 The self-esteem of older people rose after they read a negative article about younger people. 在读完有关年轻人的负面文章后，老年人的自信心会有所上升。

neglect [nɪˈglekt] *vt.&n.* 忽视

巧记 同义词：ignore, overlook

拓展 negligible *a.* 可忽略不计的，微不足道的

诵读 Don't neglect your duty. 不要玩忽职守。

negotiate [nɪˈgəʊʃieɪt] *vi.* 谈判，交涉

诵读 The government will not negotiate with the terrorists. 政府决不与恐怖分子谈判。

neighborhood [ˈneɪbəˌhʊd] *n.* 邻居；街道

诵读 Neighborhood may help prevent childhood obesity. 家庭周边环境可能有助于预防青少年肥胖。

neither [ˈniːðə] *a.* 两者都不的 *ad.* 也不 *conj.* 也不

诵读 Neither the father nor the son is interested in the film. 父子俩对这部电影都不感兴趣。

nerve [nɜːv] *n.* 神经

辨义 *n.* 胆量

拓展 nervous *a.* 神经的；紧张不安的

诵读 It takes a bit of nerve to transport explosives.运输炸药要有点胆量。

network [ˈnetwɜːk] *n.* 网络

诵读 The nervous system is the network of nerves in the body. 神经系统就是人体内部的神经网。

neutral [ˈnjuːtrəl] *a.* 中立的；中性的

搭配 remain neutral 保持中立

诵读 "I know you," he said flatly, matter-of-fact, neutral in tone. "我认识你。"他平淡地说道，就事论事，不带任何感情。

nevertheless [ˌnevəðəˈles] *ad.* 仍然；然而

巧记 同义词：nonetheless *ad.* 虽然如此，但是

诵读 The news may be unexpected. Nevertheless, it is true. 这个消息可能是出乎意料，然而是真实的。

noble [ˈnəʊbl] *a.* 高尚的 *n.* 贵族

诵读 He was an upright and noble man who was always willing to help in any way he could. 他是一个正直、高尚的人，总是愿意尽其所能帮助别人。

nod [nɒd] *vi.* 点头

note [nəʊt] *n.* 笔记 *vt.* 记下

搭配 take notes 记笔记

拓展 notable *a.* 值得注意的，显著的；notebook 笔记本

诵读 Having visited a city, he noted down his impressions of the city. 访问一个城市后，他写下了对这座城市的印象。

nothing [ˈnʌθɪŋ] *n.* 没有东西

搭配 nothing but 只有，仅仅

诵读 Don't worry for my illness; what I need is nothing but a few days' rest. 不要为我的病担心，我只要稍微休息两天就会好的。

notice [ˈnəʊtɪs] *n.* 通知 *vt.* 注意到

搭配 take notice of 注意到

拓展 noticeable *a.* 显而易见的，重要的；notify *v.* 通知，告知

诵读 He slipped off when I was not noticing. 他趁我不注意时溜走了。

now [naʊ] *ad.* 现在 *conj.* 既然

拓展 nowadays *ad.* 如今，现在

搭配 now that 既然，由于；every now and then 有时，时时，偶尔；now and then 时而，不时

诵读 Now that you mention it, I do remember seeing you at the theatre. 经你一提，我记得的确在剧院里见到过你。

noisy [ˈnɔɪzi] *a.* 吵闹的，喧闹的

诵读 The food was monotonous and the dining room was too noisy. 饭很单调而且餐厅太吵闹。

nominal [ˈnɒmɪnəl] *a.* 名义上的

巧记 词根 nom（=name名字，名义）+in在……里面+后缀-al→名义上的

拓展 nominate *vt.* 提名，任命

诵读 He was elected as the nominal leader of the party. 他被选为这个政党的名义领袖。

nonsense [ˈnɒnsəns] *n.* 胡说，废话

诵读 You mustn't chatter about nonsense on serious diplomatic occasions. 在严肃的外交场合，你可不能唠唠叨叨地胡说一气。

noodle [ˈnuːdl] *n.*（常用复数）面条

norm [nɔːm] *n.* 准则，规范，平均数

拓展 normalization *n.* 正常化，标准化；normal *a.* 正常的，标准的

诵读 Normal working hours here are from 9 a.m. to 5 p.m. 正常的工作时间是上午 9 点到下午 5 点。

notion [ˈnəʊʃən] *n.* 概念，观点

巧记 词根 not 知道+后缀-ion→概念

诵读 They have no notion of time. 他们没有时间概念。

novel [ˈnɒvəl] *n.*（长篇）小说 *a.* 新奇的

巧记 词根 nov 新+后缀-el→新奇的

拓展 novelty *n.* 新奇，新颖

诵读 He likes to read the novels of Dickens. 他喜欢读狄更斯的小说。

nurture [ˈnɜːtʃə] *n.&vt.* 养育 *n.* 营养品

诵读 One of the best ways to nurture trust is to ask for help. 培养信任最好的方法之一是寻求帮助。

nutrition [njuːˈtrɪʃən] *n.* 营养，营养学

诵读 This food provides nutrition for you. 这种食物能为你提供营养。

naive [naːˈiːv] *a.* 天真的；幼稚的

诵读 She's surely not so naive as to believe his story. 她肯定不会轻信他编造的故事。

nap [næp] *n.* 小睡，打盹

诵读 I might take a little nap. 我可能会打个盹儿。

navy [ˈneɪvɪ] *n.* 海军

拓展 naval [ˈneivəl] *a.* 海军的，军舰的

诵读 Her own son was also in the navy. 她自己的儿子也曾在海军服役。

navigation [ˌnævɪˈgeɪʃən] *n.* 航海，航空；导航，领航

巧记 词根 navi（=navy 海军）+gat 通道→航海通道

诵读 There has been an increase in navigation through the Suez Canal. 通过苏伊士运河的船只增加了。

nearby [ˈnɪəbaɪ] *a.* 附近的 *prep.* 在……附近

诵读 He's been accused of stealing speed-boats to travel to nearby islands to plunder empty homes. 他被指控涉嫌盗用快艇前往邻近岛屿，洗劫无人住宅。

nightmare [ˈnaɪtmeə] *n.* 噩梦；无法摆脱的恐惧

诵读 I had a nightmare about being drowned in a lake. 我做了个噩梦，梦见淹死在湖里。

notorious [nəʊˈtɔːrɪəs] *a.* 臭名昭著的，声名狼藉的

诵读 The notorious gangster was arrested yesterday. 那个臭名昭著的歹徒于昨天被逮捕了。

nuisance [ˈnjuːsəns] *n.* 讨厌的人或事

诵读 The mosquitoes are a nuisance. 蚊子非常令人讨厌。

numb [nʌm] *a.* 麻木的，失去感觉的

诵读 His fingers were numb with cold. 他的手冻得发麻。

numerical [njuːˈmerɪkəl] *a.* 数字的

辨析 numerous *a.* 众多的，许多的

搭配 That kind of bird has become more numerous around here lately. 近来这种鸟在这一带多了起来。

notwithstanding [ˌnɒtwɪθˈstændɪŋ] *prep.&ad.* 尽管

诵读 They travelled on, notwithstanding the storm. 尽管有暴风雨，他们仍然继续赶路。

nourish [ˈnʌrɪʃ] *v.* 养育，怀有（希望，仇恨等）

搭配 nourish the soil 给土地施肥

诵读 They need good food to nourish their bodies. 他们需要好的食物来滋补身体。

obey [əʊˈbeɪ] *vt.* 服从；听由

拓展 obedient *a.* 顺从的；obedience *n.* 服从，顺从

诵读 I have modified a word in obedience to a suggestion of your own. 我按照你的建议改正了一个词。

object [ˈɒbdʒɪkt] *n.* 物体 *vi.* 反对

拓展 objection *n.* 反对；objective *a.* 客观的，真实的

搭配 object to 反对

诵读 A bright moving object appeared in the sky at sunset. 日落时，天空中出现一个发光的移动物体。

oblige [əˈblaɪdʒ] *vt.* 强迫

巧记 前缀 ob-加强语气+词根 lig选择→被迫选择→强迫做某事

僻义 *vt.* 感激 be obliged to sb.

拓展 obligation *n.* 义务

诵读 Your bad behaviour obliges me to dismiss you. 你的品行很坏，我不得不开除你。

observe [əbˈzɜːv] *vt.* 观察；遵守；评述

拓展 observation *n.* 观察；观点

诵读 He observed the stars all his life. 他毕生都在观察星球。

obstacle [ˈɒbstəkl] *n.* 障碍

巧记 前缀 ob-加强语气+词根 sta 站立+后缀-cle→

站着挡路→障碍

诵读 Ignorance is an obstacle to progress. 无知是进步的障碍。

obtain [əbˈteɪn] vt. 获得，得到

诵读 We wish to obtain first-hand information. 我们希望得到一手信息。

obvious [ˈɒbvɪəs] a. 明显的，显而易见的

诵读 He was very obvious in his distrust of us. 他明显对我们不信任。

occur [əˈkɜː] vi. 发生；想起

搭配 It occurs to sb. that… 某人突然意识到……

拓展 occurrence n. 发生，事件

诵读 It occurred to me that she didn't know our new address. 我突然想到她还不知道我们的新住址。

occasion [əˈkeɪʒən] n. 场合，时节

拓展 occasional a. 偶然的，临时的

诵读 A birthday is no occasion for tears. 生日可不是哭鼻子的时候。

occupy [ˈɒkjʊpaɪ] v. 占用；使从事

拓展 occupation n. 占领；职业

诵读 My time is fully occupied by my daily work. 我的时间都被日常事务占去了。

odd [ɒd] a. 奇数的，奇怪的

辨义 a. 临时的

拓展 odds n. 概率，可能性

诵读 It makes no odds whether he comes or not. 他来不来都没有什么关系。

offer [ˈɒfə] vt. 提供 n. 提议；录取通知书

诵读 She has received an offer of marriage. 她接受了求婚的请求。

officer [ˈɒfɪsə] n. 官员；工作人员

拓展 official n. 官员 a. 官方的

诵读 They made an official visit to the king. 他们对国王进行了正式拜访。

offspring [ˈɒfsprɪŋ] n. 子孙，后代

巧记 前缀 off-离开+ 词根 spring 泉水 →泉水往下流就像子孙后代的延续→孩子，子女

诵读 She is a mother of numerous offspring. 她是一位多子女的母亲。

operate [ˈɒpəreɪt] vi. 运转，动手术

拓展 operation n. 运转，操作；operational a. 操作的，运转的；operator n. 操作人员，(电话)接线员

搭配 come into operation 开始运转

诵读 The machine is operating properly. 这台机器运转正常。

opinion [əˈpɪnjən] n. 意见，主张

诵读 Public opinion is against the proposed change. 公众舆论反对提出的变更。

opposite [ˈɒpəzɪt] a. 对面的，对立的 ad. 在对面

搭配 on the opposite 对面；be opposite to 与……对立

拓展 oppose vt. 反对，使对立

诵读 The snow on the opposite mountain hasn't melted yet. 对面高山上的残雪还没有完全消融。

opening [ˈəʊpənɪŋ] n. 空缺 a. 开始的

诵读 The book lay open on the table. 书打开着放在桌子上。

opportunity [ˌɒpəˈtjuːnɪti] n. 机会

诵读 There may be an opportunity for you to see the manager this afternoon. 今天下午你可能有机会见到经理。

optimistic [ˌɒptɪˈmɪstɪk] a. 乐观主义的

巧记 前缀 op-相反的+词根 timis=timid 胆怯的+后缀-tic

诵读 The president says she is optimistic that an agreement can be worked out soon. 总统说，她对很快能达成协议持乐观态度。

order [ˈɔːdə] n. 命令；次序，顺序

搭配 in order to 以便；in order that 以便；out of order 发生故障，失调

拓展 orderly a. 整齐的，有秩序的

诵读 We should put the society in order. 我们必须整顿社会秩序。

ordinary [ˈɔːdɪnəri] a. 普通的，平凡的

诵读 The speaker was ordinary and tiresome. 发言人讲得平淡乏味。

oral [ˈɔːrəl] a. 口头的

诵读 The manager gave oral instructions to his staff. 经理向职员们做口头指示。

organize [ˈɔːɡənaɪz] vt. 组织，编组

拓展 organization n. 组织，团体

诵读 Organize it, and tie up all loose ends possible. 整理好工作，将所有松懈的事项整理好。

orient [ˈɔːriənt] *n.* 东方 *vt.* 使适应

拓展 oriental *a.* 东方的 *n.* 东方人；orientation *n.* 方向，定位，倾向性

搭配 market-oriented economy 市场经济

诵读 The union is oriented towards welfare capitalism. 工会以福利资本主义为其奋斗目标。

original [əˈrɪdʒɪnəl] *a.* 最初的，新颖的

拓展 originate *vi.* 起源；origin *n.* 起源

搭配 originate from 起源于

诵读 This is one of my favorite original sound tracks. 这是我最喜欢的电影原声音乐之一。

otherwise [ˈʌðəwaɪz] *ad.&conj.* 要不然，否则

诵读 Leave now, otherwise you will be late. 现在就走，否则你要迟到了。

outdoors [ˈaʊtdɔːz] *ad.* 户外 *a.* 室外的

诵读 There is an outdoors concert in the park tonight. 今晚在公园里有一场户外音乐会。

outbreak [ˈaʊtbreɪk] *n.* 爆发，发作

巧记 来自词组：break out 爆发

诵读 Outbreaks of rain are expected in the afternoon. 预计下午将会有暴雨。

outcome [ˈaʊtkʌm] *n.* 结果，成果

诵读 She was satisfied with the outcome of her efforts. 她对自己努力的结果很满意。

outer [ˈaʊtə] *a.* 外部的，外面的

搭配 outer space 外太空

诵读 The outer door was wide open but the inner one was locked. 外边的门敞开着，但里面的门锁着。

outline [ˈaʊtlaɪn] *n.* 轮廓，大纲

巧记 组合词：out 外面+line 线→用线画出外观→轮廓；大纲

诵读 These reports give an outline rather than the details. 这些报告只给了一个大纲，没有提供细节。

outlook [ˈaʊtlʊk] *n.* 景色；展望

巧记 组合词：out 外面+look 看→向外看到风景

诵读 The economic outlook is bright. 经济前景非常光明。

output [ˈaʊtpʊt] *n.* 产量，输出（量）

巧记 组合词：out 外面+put 放置→放出来的→产量

诵读 The measures will enable us to double our output of bicycles. 这些措施能使我们的自行车产量加倍。

outrage [ˈaʊtreɪdʒ] *n.* 愤慨 *v.* 激怒

巧记 合成词：out 出来+rage 愤怒→愤怒发出来

诵读 Would the use of H-bombs be an outrage against humanity? 使用氢弹是否违背人道？

outset [ˈaʊtset] *n.* 开始，开端

巧记 来自词组：set out 出发，开始

诵读 At the outset, it looked like a nice day. 一开始，天气很晴朗。

outskirts [ˈaʊtskɜːts] *n.* 郊区

诵读 They mostly live on the outskirts of a town. 他们大多住在近郊。

outstanding [ˌaʊtˈstændɪŋ] *a.* 显著的，杰出的

巧记 来自词组：stand out 突显

诵读 She is an outstanding actress. 她是一个杰出的演员。

outward [ˈaʊtwəd] *a.* 外面的 *ad.* 向外

诵读 MPs kept up their outward allegiance to the parties they belonged to. 议员们对各自所属的党派保持表面上的忠诚。

overall [ˈəʊvərɔːl] *a.* 全面的 *n.*（*pl.*）工作服

巧记 合成词：over 完全的+all 全部的→全面的，综合的

诵读 The overall situation is worsening. 整体形势在日益恶化。

overcome [ˌəʊvəˈkʌm] *vt.* 战胜，克服

诵读 India has sufficient food to overcome drought shortages. 印度有足够的粮食度过干旱。

overlook [ˌəʊvəˈlʊk] *vt.* 俯瞰；看漏，忽视

巧记 合成词：over 从上面+look 看→从上往下看→俯瞰；看个大概

诵读 The monument overlooks the square. 纪念碑高耸在广场之上。

overnight [ˌəʊvəˈnaɪt] *a.* 通宵的 *ad.* 一夜工夫

诵读 The actor became famous overnight. 那位演员声名鹊起。

overtime [ˈəʊvətaɪm] *a.* 超时的 *ad.* 加班

巧记 组合词：over 从上面+time 时间→时间上已经超过

诵读 They were paid extra for overtime. 他们拿到了

考研英语高频词汇 **2618**

加班费。

owing ['əʊɪŋ] *a.* 欠的，未付的

诵读 I have got $200 owing to me for a job I did last week. 上周工作挣的 200 美元还未付给我。

ownership ['əʊnəʃɪp] *n.* 所有权，所有制

诵读 There was a quarrel over the ownership of the land. 对那块土地的所有权存在争执。

obsession [əb'seʃən] *n.* 迷住，困扰

拓展 obsess *vt.* 迷恋

诵读 With him, gambling is an obsession. 对于他来说，赌博是无法摆脱的。

obsolete [ˌɒbsə'liːt] *a.* 已废弃的，过时的

巧记 前缀 ob-加强语气+词根 sol 独自+后缀-ete→就剩一个→已经过时

诵读 That word is obsolete; do not use it. 这个词已被废弃，不要再用了。

obstruct [əb'strʌkt] *vt.* 阻隔 *n.* 阻碍物

巧记 前缀 ob-加强语气+词根 struct 建造→建造出来挡路→阻碍

拓展 obstruction *n.* 妨碍，障碍物

诵读 Drivers who park their cars illegally, particularly obstructing traffic flow, deserve to be punished. 非法停车的司机，尤其是那些阻碍交通的，应当予以惩处。

offend [ə'fend] *vt.&vi.* 犯罪，违反

拓展 offensive *a.* 冒犯的

诵读 People who offend against the law must be punished. 违法者必究。

offset ['ɒfset] *n.* 补偿 *v.* 抵消

诵读 Prices have risen in order to offset the increased cost of materials. 为补偿原料成本增加，价格提高了。

omit [əʊ'mɪt] *v.* 省略，删去

诵读 The cost may be omitted from the account. 这笔费用可以不入账。

ominous ['ɒmɪnəs] *a.* 不吉的，不祥的

诵读 Those black clouds look ominous for our picnic. 那些乌云对我们的野餐来说是个不祥之兆。

opponent [ə'pəʊnənt] *n.* 对手，敌手

巧记 前缀 op-相反的+词根 pon（=pose放置）+后缀-ent→放在相反位置→对手

诵读 She defeated her opponent in the tennis match. 她在网球赛中击败了对手。

oppress [ə'pres] *vt.* 压迫，压制

诵读 The rich oppress the mass by their control of the political and judicial system. 有钱人靠控制政治和司法来压迫贫苦大众。

opt [ɒpt] *vi.* 抉择，选择

拓展 option *n.* 选择；optional *a.* 可以任选的，随意的，非强制的

搭配 optional course 选修课

诵读 I have no option. 我没有选择的余地。

organ ['ɔːgən] *n.* 器官；机关

拓展 organic *a.* 器官的；有机的；organism *n.* 生物体，有机体

诵读 He was lucky that the bullet hadn't entered a vital organ. 他很幸运，子弹没有伤到身体的要害部位。

ornament ['ɔːnəmənt] *vt.* 装饰 *n.* 装饰物

诵读 The clock is simply for ornament; it doesn't work any more. 这架时钟纯属摆设，它再也不走了。

ordeal [ɔː'diːl] *n.* 折磨；煎熬

诵读 Being lost in the wilderness for a week was an ordeal for me. 在荒野里迷路一星期对我来说真是一场磨难。

overflow [ˌəʊvə'fləʊ] *v.* 溢出

巧记 合成词：over 从上面+flow流动→外溢

诵读 The crowd overflowed the theater into the street. 戏院里人多得容纳不下而被挤到街头。

overhear [ˌəʊvə'hɪə] *vt.* 偶然听到

巧记 合成词：over 从上面+hear 听到→偶然听到

诵读 You overhear the two middle-aged men in front: "Good morning." 无意中你听到前面两个中年人在说："早晨好。"

overlap [ˌəʊvə'læp] *vt.&vi.* 重叠

巧记 合成词：over 从上面+lap 膝盖→一只脚盖在另一只脚上

诵读 Obviously, the two sets of policies overlap and can complement each other. 显然，两套政策有重复的地方，也可以互相补充。

090

overpass [ˈəʊvəpɑːs] *n.* 过街天桥

巧记 合成词：over 从上面+pass 通过→从马路上方通过的通道→过街天桥

诵读 Yell English on an overpass right now！现在就在天桥上大声练英语！

overseas [ˌəʊvəˈsiːz] *a.* 外国的 *ad.* 在海外

诵读 He has returned to South Africa from his long overseas trip. 他结束了漫长的海外旅行，回到了南非。

overthrow [ˌəʊvəˈθrəʊ] *vt.&n.* 推翻，颠覆

巧记 合成词：over从上面+throw扔掉→推翻，颠覆

诵读 Fascism had lawlessly overthrown the democratic government. 法西斯非法推翻了民主政府。

overturn [ˌəʊvəˈtɜːn] *n.* 倾覆 *vt.* 打翻

诵读 Some high-ranking officers plotted to overturn the government. 有几名高级军官策划推翻政府。

overwhelm [ˌəʊvəˈwelm] *v.* 淹没，压倒

拓展 overwhelming *a.* 势不可挡的，压倒的

诵读 The defense was overwhelmed by superior numbers. 防守被优势兵力摧垮了。

pain [peɪn] *n.* 痛苦；(*pl.*)努力

搭配 take pains 尽力，煞费苦心

拓展 painful *a.* 疼痛的，使痛苦的

诵读 She takes great pains in educating her children. 她费尽心血教育她的孩子。

paint [peɪnt] *n.* 油漆 *vt.* 描绘

拓展 painting *n.* 绘画，油画

诵读 His letters painted a wonderful picture of his life in Italy. 他的信把他在意大利的生活描绘得很美好。

particular [pəˈtɪkjʊlə] *a.* 特别的，特定的

搭配 in particular 特别地，尤其

诵读 He stressed that point in particular. 他特别强调了那一点。

partly [ˈpɑːtli] *ad.* 部分地，不完全地

诵读 Partly by industry, partly by good luck, he became rich. 他发财的原因一是因为他勤劳，二是由于他运气好。

party [ˈpɑːti] *n.* 聚会；党派

诵读 England was a party to the Treaty of Berlin. 英国是柏林条约的缔约国。

pass [pɑːs] *vi.* 经过，传递

拓展 passage *n.* 通过；段落

搭配 pass away 去世，逝世；pass off 中止，停止

诵读 The fog began to pass off when we started. 我们动身时雾开始消散。

pay [peɪ] *vt.&vi.* 支付 *n.* 工资

搭配 pay back 偿还，回报；pay off 还清；pay up 全部付清

拓展 payment *n.* 支付

诵读 The efforts pays off in the long run. 这种努力最终会有好结果的。

pace [peɪs] *n.* 步伐

巧记 keep pace with… 保持和……的步调

诵读 There were perhaps ten paces between me and the bear. 在我和熊之间相距大约有十步。

palm [pɑːm] *n.* 手掌，掌状物

巧记 palm reader 算命先生

诵读 She placed the money in his palm. 她把钱放在他的手心里。

panic [ˈpænɪk] *n.&a.* 恐慌

诵读 It initially looked quite lethal, and caused panic. 最初它看上去非常致命，并造成了恐慌。

paradox [ˈpærədɒks] *n.* 悖论，矛盾，似非而是的话

诵读 The answer to the question is full of paradox. 对这个问题的回答矛盾百出。

parallel [ˈpærəlel] *a.* 平行的 *n.* 类似

巧记 前缀 para-旁边，llel 想成有三条平行的 l→平行的

诵读 It's an ecological disaster with no parallel anywhere else in the world. 这是一场世界上任何地方均无先

例的生态灾难。

partial [ˈpɑːʃəl] *a.* 部分的，不公平的

诵读 The film was only a partial success. 这部电影仅仅是部分成功。

participate [pɑːˈtɪsɪpeɪt] *vi.* 参与，参加

搭配 participate in 参与

拓展 participant *n.* 参加者，参与者

诵读 The company encourages its employees to participate directly in philanthropic projects on company time. 公司鼓励员工在上班时间直接参与公益项目。

partner [ˈpɑːtnə] *n.* 合作者，合伙人

诵读 Are you sure that you want him for your partner for life? 你确定要他做你的终身伴侣吗？

passerby [ˈpæsəˌbaɪ] *n.* 过路人

诵读 Passersby could hear our rising voices. 过路行人可以听到我们的声音越来越高。

passion [ˈpæʃən] *n.* 热情，激情

拓展 passionate *a.* 热情的

诵读 His passion for soccer drives him to finish the tsunami recovery. 对足球的热爱让他从海啸造成的创伤中逐渐恢复过来。

passive [ˈpæsɪv] *a.* 被动的，消极的

搭配 passive smoking 被动吸烟

诵读 WHO says 600,000 die from passive smoking globally. 世界卫生组织表明全球每年 60 万人死于二手烟。

patent [ˈpeɪtənt] *a.* 专利的 *n.* 专利

诵读 He held a number of patents for his many innovations. 他拥有多项创新专利。

pattern [ˈpætən] *n.* 式样 *vt.* 仿制

诵读 All three attacks followed the same pattern. 三次袭击都是同一模式。

pave [peɪv] *vt.* 铺砌，铺（路）

拓展 pavement *n.* 人行道

诵读 The street is paved with asphalt. 街道铺着柏油。

peace [piːs] *n.* 和平；平静

拓展 peaceful *a.* 和平的；平静的，安宁的

搭配 at peace 处于和平状态

诵读 He lives at peace with his neighbors. 他与邻居和睦相处。

per [pɜː] *prep.* 每；经，由

僻义 *prep.*（表示根据）依照，根据

拓展 percent *n.* 百分之……

诵读 How much fuel does it consume per a hundred kilometres. 这车每百公里耗油是多少？

perfect [ˈpɜːfɪkt] *a.* 完善的 *vt.* 使完美

拓展 perfection *n.* 完美

诵读 He endeavored to perfect himself in English. 他努力提高英语水平。

perform [pəˈfɔːm] *vt.* 表演；履行

僻义 *vi.* 起作用

拓展 performance *n.* 表演

诵读 He failed in the performance of his duties. 他没能履行自己的职责。

perhaps [pəˈhæps] *ad.* 也许，大概

诵读 In the end they lose millions, perhaps billions. 最终他们损失了数百万元，也许数亿元。

period [ˈpɪərɪəd] *n.* 时期

拓展 periodical *n.* 期刊，杂志

诵读 The library subscribes to scores of periodicals. 图书馆订了数十种期刊。

permit [pəˈmɪt] *vt.* 许可，允许

拓展 permission *n.* 许可

诵读 I would like to do it with you, but I am not sure whether my parents permit. 我愿意和你一起做，但不知我父母是否允许。

personal [ˈpɜːsənəl] *a.* 个人的，人身的

诵读 That's my personal opinion. 这是我的个人意见。

拓展 personality *n.* 人格，个性

辨析 形近词 personnel *n.* 全体人员；人事

诵读 The boy is developing a fine personality. 那男孩正在培养良好的个性。

peep [piːp] *vi.* 偷看，窥视

诵读 Now and then she peeped to see if he was noticing her. 她时不时地偷看他是否在注意自己。

peer [pɪə] *n.* 同辈 *vi.* 凝视

诵读 He peered at his father's face. 他凝视着父亲的脸。

penalty [ˈpenəlti] *n.* 处罚，刑罚

诵读 Carrying fire arms is forbidden under a heavy penalty. 禁止携带枪支，违者重罚。

pension [ˈpenʃən] *n.* 养老金

诵读 Full pension is 250 dollars a week. 最高的养老金是每周 250 美元。

permanent [ˈpɜːmənənt] *a.* 永久的，持久的

诵读 We all hope for permanent peace. 我们都希望持久和平。

perpetual [pəˈpetʃʊəl] *a.* 永久的，永恒的

诵读 I'm tired of your perpetual nagging. 我对你那没完没了的唠叨感到厌倦。

persevere [ˌpɜːsɪˈvɪə] *vi.* 坚持，坚忍

诵读 Persevere with an arduous task. 坚持完成这项艰巨的工作。

persist [pəˈsɪst] *vi.* 坚持，持续

诵读 The snow persists in the valley. 山谷里的雪始终没有化。

perspective [pəˈspektɪv] *n.* 透视；远景；观点

巧记 前缀 per—一致+词根 spect 看+后缀-ive→一直看→看透

诵读 Primitive artists often paint without perspective. 早期的画通常不用透视法创作。

persuasion [pəˈsweɪʒən] *n.* 说服，说服力

诵读 He won their support by persuasion, not force. 他通过劝说，而不是强迫赢得了他们的支持。

pessimistic [ˌpesɪˈmɪstɪk] *a.* 悲观的

诵读 There is no reason to be pessimistic about the future. 没有理由对未来悲观。

phase [feɪz] *n.* 阶段，状态，时期

诵读 We entered upon the second phase of the research. 我们进入了研究的第二阶段。

phenomenon [fɪˈnɒmɪnən] *n.* 现象

诵读 A rainbow is one of the most beautiful phenomena of nature. 彩虹是最美丽的自然现象之一。

philosophy [fɪˈlɒsəfi] *n.* 哲学，哲理

拓展 philosopher *n.* 哲学家

诵读 He believed in the philosophy of Russell. 他信奉罗素的哲学。

physics [ˈfɪzɪks] *n.* 物理（学）

拓展 physical *a.* 物质的；身体的

辨析 physicist *n.* 物理学家；physician *n.* 内科医生；physiological *a.* 生理学的，生理学上的

诵读 The physical world is full of wonders. 物质世界充满了奇迹。

pick [pɪk] *vt.* 采，摘

搭配 pick out 选出，挑出；pick up 拾起，学会

诵读 He picked up English while living in London. 在伦敦居住期间，他学会了英语。

picture [ˈpɪktʃə] *n.* 图片

僻义 *n.&vt.* 描绘

诵读 I'll try and give you a better picture of what the boys do. 我会试着更清楚地向你描述这些男孩子都干些什么。

piece [piːs] *n.*（一）件

僻义 *vt.* 拼合

诵读 The policeman tried to piece together the facts. 警察试图把事实拼聚在一起。

pickup [ˈpɪkˌʌp] *n.* 拾起，获得

诵读 If you can't handle me at my worst, then you sure as well don't deserve me at my best. 如果你不能应付我最差的一面，你也不值得得到我最好的一面。

picnic [ˈpɪknɪk] *n.* 野餐 *vi.*（去）野餐

诵读 They picnicked in the woods. 他们在树林里野餐。

plain [pleɪn] *a.* 平常的；平凡的

诵读 Most of my friends are just plain folk. 我的朋友多半都是普通人。

plan [plæn] *n.&vt.* 计划

诵读 She hasn't planned for so many guests. 她并没有计划请那么多客人。

plant [plɑːnt] *n.* 植物 *vt.* 栽种

拓展 plantation *n.* 种植园

诵读 This is the pine tree planted by the mayor's own hand last year. 这就是去年市长亲手栽种的松树。

play [pleɪ] *vt.* 表演 *n.* 游戏

搭配 fair play 公平的竞赛；play with 以……为消遣，玩弄

拓展 playground *n.* 运动场，游戏场

诵读 You should observe the spirit of fair play. 你们应该遵循公平竞赛的原则。

plenty [ˈplenti] *n.* 丰富，大量

搭配 plenty of 很多，大量

拓展 plentiful *a.* 富裕的，丰富的

诵读 There is plenty of coal in this area. 这个地区有

丰富的煤矿资源。

plot [plɒt] *n.* 秘密计划；情节

诵读 His plot against the king was discovered. 他反对国王的阴谋被发觉了。

plunge [plʌndʒ] *vi.* 投入，猛冲

僻义 *vt.* 投身，从事

诵读 Take the opportunity to plunge yourself into your career. 抓住机会投身到事业中。

plus [plʌs] *prep.* 加上 *a.* 加的

诵读 Typing is a requirement for the job, but knowing shorthand would be a plus factor. 打字是这项工作的要求，可是速记就是额外的要求了。

pocket [ˈpɒkɪt] *n.* 衣袋 *a.* 袖珍的

诵读 The man stole a pen from my pocket. 那人从我口袋里偷去了一支笔。

point [pɔɪnt] *n.* 要点，论点 *vt.* 指向

搭配 come to the point 说到要点，扼要地说；on the point of 即将……的时候；point out 指出；to the point 切中要害，切题

诵读 He didn't speak for long, but he spoke very much to the point. 他说得不多，可句句切中要害。

pole [pəʊl] *n.* 杆；地极

搭配 South and North Poles 南北极

拓展 polar *a.* 两极的，极地的

诵读 Their political beliefs are at opposite poles. 他们的政治信仰完全不同。

pool [puːl] *n.* 水池

僻义 *vt.* 聚拢

诵读 We pooled ideas and information. 我们集思广益，共享信息。

position [pəˈzɪʃən] *n.* 位置；姿势

搭配 in a position to 能够

诵读 Before the debate, both sides made their positions clear. 辩论前，双方都阐明了各自的立场。

possess [pəˈzes] *vt.* 占有，拥有

拓展 possession *n.* 持有，拥有；财产，财富

搭配 in possession of 拥有，持有

诵读 I am in possession of a number of splendid suits. 我拥有许多奢华的衣服。

pound [paʊnd] *n.* 磅

僻义 *vt.* （连续）猛击

诵读 He pounded the door with his fist. 他用拳头猛击门。

poet [ˈpəʊɪt] *n.* 诗人

拓展 poetry *n.* 诗歌，诗集

诵读 It was important for poets to write about their own memories. 诗人应该写下自己的记忆。

poison [ˈpɔɪzən] *n.* 毒物，毒药

拓展 poisonous *a.* 有毒的，恶意的

诵读 The food was analyzed and found to contain small amounts of poison. 对这种食物进行了分析，发现其中含有少量毒物。

policy [ˈpɒləsɪ] *n.* 政策，方针

搭配 policy maker 政策制定者

诵读 The most common complaint centres on foreign policy. 最常见的抱怨集中在外交政策上。

polish [ˈpɒlɪʃ] *vt.* 磨光，擦亮

诵读 Each morning he shaved and polished his shoes. 他每天早晨都刮胡子、擦皮鞋。

polite [pəˈlaɪt] *a.* 有礼貌的，客气的

诵读 His polite manners bespoke the gentleman. 他那彬彬有礼的举止显出他是个绅士。

politician [ˌpɒlɪˈtɪʃən] *n.* 政治家，政客

拓展 politics *n.* 政治，政治学

诵读 Popular support is music to the ears of any politician. 大众的支持对任何一名政界人士来说都是佳音。

poll [pəʊl] *n.* 民意测验 *vt.* 对……进行民意测验

诵读 More than 18,000 people were polled. 18 000 多人接受了民意测验。

pollute [pəˈluːt] *vt.* 弄脏，污染

拓展 pollution *n.* 污染

诵读 Bicycle is a good exercise; moreover, it does not pollute the air. 骑自行车是很好的运动；而且不污染空气。

portion [ˈpɔːʃən] *n.* 一部分，一份

诵读 A significant portion of tax revenues will not come back, unless new sources of economic growth are found. 找不到新的经济增长点，相当部分的税收就不会恢复。

portray [pɔːˈtreɪ] *vt.* 描写，描述

拓展 portrait *n.* 肖像，画像

诵读 It is not easy to portray the surprise of the Indians at this discovery. 印第安人见到这种情况，其惊异之情真是难以形容。

pose [pəʊz] *vt.* 提出 *vi.* 摆姿势

巧记 照相的时候摆造型，称为摆 pose

拓展 posture *n.* 姿势

诵读 The president must now put necessity aside and pose two fundamental questions. 现在总统必须将必要性放在一边，提出两个基本问题。

positive [ˈpɒzɪtɪv] *a.* 肯定的，积极的

诵读 Her husband became much more positive and was soon back in full-time employment. 她丈夫变得积极多了，并且很快又干起了全职工作。

possibility [ˌpɒsəˈbɪlɪti] *n.* 可能，可能性

诵读 There were several possibilities open to each manufacturer. 每个制造商都有几种可能的选择。

post [pəʊst] *n.* 邮政；职位

拓展 postage *n.* 邮费；poster *n.* 海报；postman *n.* 邮递员

诵读 After a six-month probationary period, she was confirmed in her post. 经过六个月的试用期，她获准正式任职。

postpone [ˌpəʊstˈpəʊn] *vt.* 推迟，延期

巧记 前缀 post-后+词根 pone（=pose 放）→往后放→推迟

诵读 It won't hurt to postpone the matter for a few days. 把此事搁置几天并无妨碍。

potential [pəˈtenʃəl] *a.* 潜在的 *n.* 潜能

诵读 The company has identified 60 potential customers. 该公司已确定了 60 位潜在客户。

poverty [ˈpɒvəti] *n.* 贫穷，贫困

诵读 Extreme poverty had reduced them to a state of apathy. 极端的贫困使他们万念俱灰。

powerful [ˈpaʊəful] *a.* 强大的，有力的

巧记 词根 power 威力+形容词后缀-ful→强大的

诵读 You're a powerful man—people will listen to you. 你是个有影响力的人，人们会听你的。

practice [ˈpræktɪs] *n.* 实践，实际 *v.* 练习

搭配 bring/put... into practice实施，实行；in practice 实际上

诵读 We declare that the decision shall not be brought into practice. 我们宣布这个决议将不能实施。

press [pres] *vt.* 压，按 *n.* 出版社

诵读 The police pressed the crowd back behind the barriers. 警察迫使人群退到路障后面。

pretend [prɪˈtend] *vt.* 假装，装扮

诵读 He does not pretend to be an expert. 他没有冒充专家。

pretty [ˈprɪti] *a.* 漂亮的 *ad.* 相当地

诵读 Pretty soon the peach trees would be in bloom. 桃树很快就要开花。

price [praɪs] *n.* 价格 *vt.* 标价

诵读 They won the battle, but at the price of many lives. 他们打赢了这一仗，但牺牲了许多人。

pride [praɪd] *n.* 自豪，自尊心

搭配 take pride in ... 为……感到骄傲

诵读 She is the joy and pride of her parents. 她是父母的快乐和自豪。

print [prɪnt] *vt.* 印刷

诵读 All today's newspapers have printed the minister's speech in full. 今天所有报纸都全文刊登了部长的讲话。

produce [prəˈdjuːs] *vt.* 生产，出示

拓展 production *n.* 产量；产品

诵读 She produced her passport. 她出示了护照。

pronounce [prəˈnaʊns] *vt.* 宣布，发音

拓展 pronunciation *n.* 发音

诵读 The doctor pronounced the man dead. 医生宣告那人已经死亡。

proper [ˈprɒpə] *a.* 适合的，恰当的

诵读 Complaints must be made through proper channels. 投诉必须通过正当途径。

pray [preɪ] *vi.* 请求，祈祷

拓展 prayer *n.* 祈祷，祷文

诵读 He took beads from his pocket and began to pray silently. 他从口袋中取出念珠，开始默默祈祷。

precious [ˈpreʃəs] *a.* 珍贵的，贵重的

诵读 Along with the elapsing of year, this book will be more precious. 随着岁月的流逝，这本书将更为珍贵。

precise [prɪˈsaɪs] *a.* 精确的，准确的

拓展 precision *n.* 精确，精确度

诵读 I can remember the precise moment when my daughter came to see me and her new baby brother in the hospital. 我还记得女儿来医院看望我和她刚出生的弟弟的那一刻。

predict [prɪˈdɪkt] *vt.* 预言，预测

巧记 前缀 pre-前+词根 dict 说→提前把事情说出来→预测

诵读 The latest opinion polls are predicting a very close contest. 最新的民意测验预言将会有一场势均力敌的竞赛。

predominant [prɪˈdɒmɪnənt] *a.* 占优势的；主要的

巧记 predominant over 占优势

诵读 Mandy's predominant emotion was confusion. 曼迪的主导情绪是困惑。

prepare [prɪˈpeə] *vt.* 准备，预备

拓展 preparation *n.* 准备，预备

诵读 Some authors make thorough mental preparation before they put pen to paper. 有些作者在下笔之前已经完全打好了腹稿。

presence [ˈprezəns] *n.* 出席，到场

拓展 present *a.* 出席的，现在的 *n.* 现在，礼物 *vt.* 赠送，提出

诵读 They argued that his presence in the town could only stir up trouble. 他们认为他在城里出现只会搅起麻烦。

preserve [prɪˈzɜːv] *vt.* 保护，维持

诵读 People smoke fish to preserve them. 人们把鱼熏制一下以便保存。

preside [prɪˈzaɪd] *v.* 主持

巧记 前缀 pre-前+词根 sid（=sit 坐）→坐在前面主持

拓展 president *n.* 总统，校长，会长，主席

诵读 Who is to preside over the meeting hasn't been decided. 这个会议要谁来主持还未决定。

pressure [ˈpreʃə] *n.* 压力

诵读 If the pressure builds up excessively, the pressure valve opens to relieve the pressure. 如果油箱内压力过高，则压力阀会开启，以降低压力。

prime [praɪm] *a.* 首要的；最好的，一流的 *n.* 青春，全盛期

拓展 primary *a.* 首要的，主要的

诵读 His prime task is to lower the tax rate. 他的首要任务是降低税率。

primitive [ˈprɪmɪtɪv] *a.* 原始的，远古的

诵读 It's a complete reversion to primitive superstition. They are confusing cause and effect. 这完全是倒退回了原始的迷信，他们把因果关系弄混淆了。

principal [ˈprɪnsəpəl] *n.* 校长

僻义 *a.* 最重要的，主要的

诵读 Today the principal tools for prospecting the brain are electrical. 当今探查大脑的主要工具是用电的。

principle [ˈprɪnsəpl] *n.* 原理，原则

诵读 Buck never allowed himself to be bullied into doing anything that went against his principles. 巴克从不允许自己受迫做任何违背原则的事。

prior [ˈpraɪə] *a.* 优先的，在前的

拓展 priority *n.* 优先，重点

搭配 prior to… 在……之前

诵读 He claimed he had no prior knowledge of the protest. 他声称事先对那次抗议一无所知。

private [ˈpraɪvɪt] *a.* 私人的，个人的

拓展 privacy *n.* 隐私

诵读 Everyone nodded agreement save Fee, who seemed intent on some private vision. 每个人都点头表示同意，除了菲以外，她看上去正沉湎于个人的梦幻里。

privilege [ˈprɪvɪlɪdʒ] *n.* 特权，优惠

诵读 The Russian Federation has issued a decree abolishing special privileges for government officials. 俄罗斯联邦已颁布了一条取消政府官员特权的法令。

probable [ˈprɒbəbl] *a.* 很可能的，大概的

拓展 probability *n.* 可能性，概率

诵读 It seems to me much more probable that he will refuse. 照我看，他多半会拒绝。

product [ˈprɒdʌkt] *n.* 产品，产物

拓展 productive *a.* 能产的；productivity *n.* 生产率

诵读 Our car is a product of that factory. 我们的车是那个厂生产的。

profession [prəˈfeʃən] *n.* 职业，专业

拓展 professional *a.* 职业的 *n.* 专业人员

诵读 She intends to make teaching her profession. 她

打算以教书为业。

profit ['prɒfɪt] *n.* 利润

拓展 profitable *a.* 有利可图的，有益的

诵读 We made a profit of $5,000 in those shares. 我们从那些股票中赚了 5 000 美元。

profound [prə'faʊnd] *a.* 深刻的；渊博的

诵读 The doctor's discovery will have a profound influence on mankind. 这名医生的发现将对人类产生深远影响。

progressive [prə'gresɪv] *a.* 进步的，先进的

诵读 Jim is a man of progressive views. 吉姆是个有进步观点的人。

prohibit [prə'hɪbɪt] *vt.* 禁止，不准

诵读 Picking flowers in the park is prohibited. 公园里禁止摘花。

project [prə'dʒekt] *n.* 工程 *v.* 投射

拓展 projector *n.* 幻灯机，投影仪

诵读 The project was estimated to have cost £100,000. 这项工程估计已经耗费 10 万英镑。

prolong [prə'lɒŋ] *vt.* 拉长，延长

巧记 前缀 pro-向前+long 长→向前拉→延长

诵读 The train made a prolonged stop at the station. 火车在站上停了很久。

promote [prə'məʊt] *vt.* 促进，发扬

诵读 We should promote world peace. 我们应该促进世界和平。

prompt [prɒmpt] *a.* 迅速的，即刻的

诵读 Thank you for your prompt attention to the matter. 谢谢你及时关注这件事。

prone [prəʊn] *a.* 倾向于

诵读 For all her experience as a television reporter, she was still prone to camera nerves. 尽管有丰富的电视记者经验，她在镜头前仍然紧张。

proof [pru:f] *n.* 证据，证明

诵读 His finger prints were a proof of his guilt. 他的指纹是他的罪证。

proponent [prə'pəʊnənt] *n.* 支持者，拥护者

诵读 Halsey was identified as a leading proponent of the values of progressive education. 哈尔西被认为是进步教育价值观的主要拥护者。

propose [prə'pəʊz] *vt.* 提议，建议

拓展 proposal *n.* 提议；proposition *n.* 主张，建议

诵读 We proposed to make a change. 我们建议做改变。

prospect ['prɒspekt] *n.* 景色；前景

巧记 前缀 pro-向前+词根 spect 看→前景

拓展 prospective *a.* 预期的

诵读 From the top of the hill there is a beautiful prospect over the valley. 从山顶望去，山谷呈现出一片美丽的景色。

prosper ['prɒspə] *vi.* 成功，兴隆

拓展 prosperity *n.* 繁荣；prosperous *a.* 繁荣的

诵读 Our great motherland is prospering with each passing day. 我们伟大的祖国蒸蒸日上。

protect [prə'tekt] *vt.* 保护，保卫

搭配 protect...from... 保护

诵读 I will protect you from danger. 我会保护你免遭危险。

provide [prə'vaɪd] *vt.* 提供，供给

搭配 provide sb. with sth. 为某人提供某物

拓展 provided *conj.* 倘若；provision *n.* 供应，条款

诵读 The provision of a new and larger library has been of great educational advantage to the students. 新建的大型图书馆对学生的教育大有好处。

purchase ['pɜːtʃəs] *vt.* 买，购买

诵读 We purchased a new car. 我们买了一辆新车。

pure [pjʊə] *a.* 纯洁的

僻义 *a.* 完全的

拓展 purify *vt.* 使纯净，提纯

诵读 He is an adventurer, pure and simple. 他是个十足的冒险家。

pursue [pə'sju:] *vt.* 追赶；继续

拓展 pursuit *n.* 追赶；职业

诵读 She felt their eyes pursuing her. 她觉得他们一直在盯着她。

puzzle ['pʌzl] *n.* 难题 *vt.* (使)迷惑

诵读 The murder case was a puzzle to the detective. 这件谋杀案对那个侦探来说是个难题。

pale [peɪl] *a.* 苍白的；暗淡的

pardon [ˈpɑːdən] *vt.* 饶恕，赦免

诵读 We should pardon him for his little faults. 我们应该宽恕他的那些小过失。

passenger [ˈpæsɪndʒə] *n.* 乘客，旅客

pause [pɔːz] *vi.* 中止，暂停

诵读 He paused to look around. 他停下来环顾一下四周。

pack [pæk] *vt.* 打包 *n.* 包裹

拓展 package *n.* 包装，包裹

诵读 He packed his clothes into a trunk. 他把衣服装进皮箱。

pact [pækt] *n.* 合同，条约

诵读 This led to a non-aggression pact between the two countries. 这使两国签订了互不侵犯的协议。

panel [ˈpænəl] *n.* 控制板，仪表盘

辨义 *n.* 专门小组

诵读 A panel discussion was held on abortion. 就堕胎问题举行了小组讨论会。

pant [pænt] *n.* 喘气 *vi.* 气喘吁吁地说

诵读 Before he reached the top, he was already sweating and panting. 他还没有爬到山顶就已经浑身出汗，气喘吁吁了。

paperback [ˈpeɪpəbæk] *n.* 平装本，简装本

巧记 合成词：paper 纸+back 面→纸质的封面→平装本，简装本

诵读 In the paperback edition of *My Life,* former President Clinton acknowledges that his memoir may have been too long. 美国前总统克林顿在平装版《我的生活》中首次公开承认自己的回忆录可能写得太长了。

paralyze [ˈpærəˌlaɪz] *vt.* 使瘫痪；使丧失作用

诵读 All the opinions and analysis will paralyze anyone who is not up to the task. 所有的意见和分析都会使那些没有参与这项任务的人感到不知所措。

parcel [ˈpɑːsəl] *n.* 包裹 *vi.* 打包

诵读 The two big nations parceled out the little country between them. 这两个大国把那个小国瓜分了。

parliament [ˈpɑːləmənt] *n.* 国会，议会

passport [ˈpɑːspɔːt] *n.* 护照

搭配 合成词：pass 通过+port 海关→通过海关的时候需要具备护照

诵读 A person who travels abroad must carry a passport. 出国旅行要携带护照。

paste [peɪst] *n.* 糨糊 *vt.* 粘

诵读 Posters were pasted up on the bulletin board. 布告栏上贴了一些海报。

pastime [ˈpɑːstaɪm] *n.* 消遣，娱乐

巧记 合成词：past 过去+time 时间→度过时间

诵读 India was named the best place to fly a kite as the pastime is a daily activity for many Indians. 在印度，放风筝是很多印度人日常生活消遣的活动，所以印度被评为最适合放风筝的国家。

patch [pætʃ] *n.* 碎片小块 *vt.* 修补

诵读 We decided to patch up our differences and become friends again. 我们决定消除分歧，重归于好。

patriotic [ˌpætrɪˈɒtɪk] *a.* 爱国的

诵读 Twenty percent blamed a broken society for their lack of patriotism, while half said they had been patriotic in the past. 20%的人认为社会分裂是导致人们缺乏爱国心的主因，一半的人称自己过去很爱国。

peak [piːk] *n.* 山顶

辨义 *n.* 最高点

诵读 This year the stock market reached its peak in September. 今年的股票市场在 9 月达到最高点。

peculiar [pɪˈkjuːljə] *a.* 古怪的，异常的

诵读 He is very peculiar in his behaviour. 他行为异常。

pedestrian [pɪˈdestrɪən] *n.* 步行者

辨义 *a.* 平淡无奇的

搭配 His style is so pedestrian that the book becomes a real bore. 他的文风十分平庸，以至于那本书乏味至极。

peel [piːl] *vt.* 削皮，剥皮

诵读 Mother is peeling the potatoes. 母亲在削土豆皮。

penetrate ['penɪtreɪt] *vt.* 穿过，渗入

诵读 The rain has penetrated his coat. 雨水淋湿了他的外衣。

perceive [pə'siːv] *vt.* 察觉，感知

巧记 perception *n.* 知觉，观念

诵读 I perceived a car coming toward me. 我发觉有一辆车朝我驶来。

perplex [pə'pleks] *vt.* 使困惑，使费解

诵读 This problem is hard enough to perplex even the teacher. 这个问题够难的，连老师也答不出来。

persecute ['pɜːsɪkjuːt] *vt.* 迫害

诵读 The reformers were terribly persecuted for their new ideas. 改革者因其新观点而遭到严重迫害。

pervade [pə'veɪd] *vt.* 遍及；弥漫

诵读 A retrospective influence pervaded the whole performance. 怀旧的氛围弥漫了整个演出。

pile [paɪl] *vt.* 堆积

诵读 His debts are piling up. 他债台越筑越高。

pierce [pɪəs] *vt.* 刺穿，刺破

诵读 The nail pierced through the sole of his shoe. 钉子刺穿了他的鞋底。

pill [pɪl] *n.* 药丸

诵读 Bitter pills may have wholesome effects. 良药苦口。

pit [pɪt] *n.* 坑，陷阱

诵读 A fall in the pit, a gain in your wit. 吃一堑，长一智。

plague [pleɪg] *n.* 瘟疫，灾害

诵读 Floods are a plague in this district. 洪水是这一地区的祸害。

plastic ['plæstɪk] *n.* 塑料

诵读 Plastics don't rust like metal. 塑料不像金属那样生锈。

platform ['plætfɔːm] *n.* 平台；站台

诵读 Nick finished what he was saying and jumped down from the platform. 尼克讲完话，从讲台上跳了下来。

plausible ['plɔːzəbl] *a.* 看似合理的；可信的

诵读 Her story sounded perfectly plausible. 她的说辞听起来言之有理。

plea [pliː] *n.* (法律) 抗辩；请求

拓展 plead *vi.* 恳求；为……辩护

搭配 Mr. Nicholas made his emotional plea for help in solving the killing. 尼古拉斯先生恳请帮助以解决这起凶杀案。

pledge [pledʒ] *n.* 誓约 *vt.* 发誓

诵读 The athletes made a solemn pledge. 运动员们作了庄严的宣誓。

ponder ['pɒndə] *vi.* 沉思，考虑

诵读 They would do well to pause and ponder upon their new responsibilities. 人们最好还是停一停，好好地想一想所肩负的新责任。

pop [pɒp] *a.* 流行的

僻义 *vi.* 突然出现

诵读 The girl's eyes almost popped out of her head with excitement. 小女孩兴奋得把眼睛睁得大大的。

porter ['pɔːtə] *n.* 搬运工

拓展 portable *a.* 轻便的，手提 (式) 的

诵读 I can construct bridges which are very light, strong and very portable. 我能建造轻便、坚固、搬运便利的桥梁。

precaution [prɪ'kɔːʃən] *n.* 预防，谨慎

巧记 前缀 pre-在……之前+caution 小心→预防，谨慎

诵读 Could he not, just as a precaution, move to a place of safety? 他难道不能作为预防措施搬到一个安全的地方去吗？

precede [ˌprɪ'siːd] *vt.* 领先于，在……之前

巧记 前缀 pre-在……之前+词根 ced 走→走在……之前

拓展 precedent *n.* 先例；preceding *a.* 在前的，在先的

诵读 The earthquake was preceded by a loud roar and lasted 20 seconds. 地震之前有一声巨响，持续了20秒。

preclude [prɪ'kluːd] *vt.* 排除，阻止

巧记 前缀 pre-前+词根 clud (=close 关闭)→提前关闭→排除和阻止意外发生

诵读 John feels his age precludes too much travel. 约翰感觉到年龄不允许经常旅行。

predecessor ['priːdɪsesə] *n.* 前辈，前任

巧记 前缀 pre-前+de 向下+cess 走+or 人→在向下

走的人之前的那些人→前辈

诵读 He maintained that he learned everything he knew from his predecessor. 他坚称他所知道的一切都是从前任那儿学到的。

preferable [ˈprefərəbl] *a.* 更可取的，更好的

搭配 preferable to 更可取的

拓展 preference *n.* 偏爱；优先选择

诵读 The rule of law is preferable to that of a single citizen. 法治优于人治。

prejudice [ˈpredʒʊdɪs] *n.* 偏见；损害

巧记 前缀 pre-前+词根 jud 判断→提前做出判断→偏见

诵读 I want to make it clear that I have no prejudice against you. 我要表明对你没有偏见。

preliminary [prɪˈlɪmɪnəri] *a.* 预备的，初步的

巧记 前缀 pre-前+词根 limi 界限+nary 形容词后缀→在界限前准备→预备

诵读 He has easily won the preliminary contest for the high jump. 他轻松地通过了跳高预赛。

premise [ˈpremɪs] *n.* 前提 *vt.* 假定

诵读 A fundamental premise of the market system is that it allows for both failure and success. 市场机制的一个根本前提是，既允许失败，也允许成功。

premium [ˈpriːmɪəm] *n.* 额外费用，奖金

诵读 Such hours attract a pay premium. 这种工时需偿付加班津贴。

prescribe [prɪˈskraɪb] *vt.* 规定；开（药）

巧记 医生的药方上有个大写字母，是这个单词中的第二个字母 R。

拓展 prescription *n.* 药方，处方

诵读 The physician examines the patient then diagnoses the disease and prescribes medication. 内科医生检查了病人，然后对疾病作出诊断，并开出药方。

prestige [presˈtiːʒ] *n.* 声望，威望

拓展 prestigious *a.* 有威望的

诵读 At the time, however, it wasn't prestige or power I wanted. It was money. 不过，在当时，我要的既不是名，也不是权。我要的是钱。

presume [prɪˈzjuːm] *vt.* 假定，假设

拓展 presumably *ad.* 推测起来，大概

诵读 I presume that you are hungry, so I'm making you some sandwiches. 我估计你饿了，所以打算给你做些三明治。

pretext [ˈpriːtekst] *n.* 借口，托词

诵读 They wanted a pretext for subduing the region by force. 他们需要一个用武力征服那个地区的托词。

prevail [prɪˈveɪl] *v.* 取胜，占优势

巧记 前缀 pre-前+词根 vail（=val 力量）→力量在别人前面的→占优势

拓展 prevalent *a.* 流行的，普遍的

诵读 Good will prevail over evil. 善良将战胜邪恶。

prey [preɪ] *n.* 被掠食者 *vi.* 捕食

诵读 The effect was to disrupt the food chain, starving many animals and those that preyed on them. 后果是破坏食物链，使许多动物和捕食它们的动物饿死。

probe [prəʊb] *vt.&vi.* 探查 *n.* 探究

诵读 He used a stick as a probe to test the ice on the lake. 他用棍棒试探湖面冰的厚薄。

proceed [prəˈsiːd] *vi.* 进行；发生

拓展 procedure *n.* 程序；process *n.* 过程，进程；procession *n.* 队伍，行列

诵读 The work is proceeding rapidly. 工作正在迅速进行。

proclaim [prəˈkleɪm] *vt.* 宣告，声明

诵读 The colony proclaimed its independence. 这片殖民地宣告独立。

proficiency [prəˈfɪʃənsi] *n.*（in）熟练，精通

诵读 I have already mentioned four ways of improving general oral proficiency. 我已经介绍了四种方式来提高口语水平。

profile [ˈprəʊfaɪl] *n.* 侧面（像）；轮廓

诵读 He drew her profile. 他给她画侧面像。

prominent [ˈprɒmɪnənt] *a.* 突起的，凸出的

诵读 The insect has prominent eyes. 那昆虫有一对凸起的眼睛。

promising [ˈprɒmɪsɪŋ] *a.* 有希望的，有前途的

诵读 The weather looks promising. 看来会有个好天气。

propaganda [ˌprɒpəˈgændə] *n.* 宣传

搭配 These reports clearly contain elements of propaganda. 这些报告明显带有一些宣传的意味。

propel [prəˈpel] *v.* 推进，推动

巧记 前缀 pro-向前+词言 pel 推→向前推→推动

诵读 a ship propelled by steam 蒸汽船

property [ˈprɒpəti] *n.* 财产，资产

诵读 Richard could easily destroy her personal property to punish her for walking out on him. 理查德可以轻而易举地毁掉她的私有财产作为对她背叛的惩罚。

prophet [ˈprɒfit] *n.* 预言家；先知

proportion [prəˈpɔːʃən] *n.* 比例；部分

搭配 in proportion 相应地,恰如其分地

诵读 The proportion of men to women in the population has changed. 人口中男女的比例已经改变。

prosecute [ˈprɒsɪkjuːt] *vt.* 实行,起诉

诵读 The police have decided not to prosecute because the evidence is not strong enough. 警方已决定不起诉,因为证据不够充分。

protein [ˈprəʊtiːn] *n.* 蛋白质

protest [ˈprəʊtest] *vi.&n.* 抗议，反对

诵读 They protested to the President but in vain. 他们向总统提出抗议,但无济于事。

province [ˈprɒvɪns] *n.* 省；领域

provoke [prəˈvəʊk] *vt.* 挑动；激发

巧记 前缀 pro-向前+词根 vok（=voc 声音）→人群前大声说话→激起

诵读 His foolish behaviour provoked laughter. 他的愚蠢行为引起哄堂大笑。

prudent [ˈpruːdnt] *a.* 谨慎的；顾虑周到的

辨义 *a.* 节俭的

搭配 a prudent housekeeper 一个节俭（谨慎）的管家

诵读 It is always prudent to start any exercise programme gradually at first. 刚开始进行一项锻炼时,循序渐进总是明智的。

publish [ˈpʌblɪʃ] *vt.* 出版,刊印

拓展 publication *n.* 出版；publicity *n.* 公开, 宣传

诵读 They only publish novels which cater to the mass market. 他们只出版迎合大众市场的小说。

pulse [pʌls] *n.* 脉搏，脉冲

诵读 The doctor felt his pulse. 医生为他诊脉。

punctual [ˈpʌŋktʃʊəl] *a.* 准时的，正点的

诵读 He is always punctual for appointment. 他赴约总是很准时。

超高频词汇

quality [ˈkwɒlɪti] *n.* 品质，特性

辨义 *a.* 上流社会的

拓展 qualitative *a.* 性质上的, 定性的；qualification *n.* 资格,合格

诵读 She brought many quality people to her wedding. 她邀请许多上流社会的人们参加婚礼。

quantity [ˈkwɒntɪti] *n.* 量；大量

拓展 quantify *vt.* 确定数量；quantitative *a.* 数量的, 定量的

诵读 Test your quantitative judgement by guessing how many beans are in the jar. 使用猜坛子中有多少颗豆子的方法测试你在数量方面的判断力。

question [ˈkwestʃən] *vt.* 询问 *n.* 问题

搭配 in question 正在考虑

诵读 This is the document in question. 这就是那份有争议的文件。

quiet [ˈkwaɪət] *a.* 安静的，平静的 *vt.* 使安静

诵读 The city quieted down. 城市安静下来了。

quarterly [ˈkwɔːtəli] *a.* 每季的 *n.* 季刊

诵读 We've walked a quarter of the distance now. 我们已经走了全程的 1/4 了。

quit [kwɪt] *vt.* 离开, 辞职

诵读 The guard did not quit his post all night long. 卫兵整晚都没有离开过岗位。

quiz [kwɪz] *n.* 小型考试, 问答比赛

诵读 She took part in a television quiz and won a lot of prizes. 她参加了一次电视问答比赛并赢得了许多奖品。

quota [ˈkwəʊtə] *n.* 配额，限额

诵读 The government set a quota on the annual number of immigrants from Italy. 政府规定了每年接受意大利移民的限额。

quote [kwəʊt] *vt.* 引用，援引

搭配 a passage quoted from the editorial 一篇引自社论的文章

高 频 词 汇

queer [kwɪə] *a.* 奇怪的，古怪的

诵读 She looked a bit queer, as if she knew something. 她看上去有点儿古怪，就好像她知道什么似的。

quench [kwentʃ] *vt.* 熄灭，扑灭

诵读 Water will quench a fire. 水可以灭火。

quest [kwest] *n.* 探寻，探求

诵读 Man will suffer many disappointments in his quest for truth. 人类在探索真理过程中必然会遭受挫折。

questionnaire [ˌkwestʃəˈneə] *n.* 调查表，问卷

诵读 We returned the questionnaire as instructed. 我们依照指示交回了调查表。

queue [kjuː] *n.* 行列，长队

诵读 She joined the queue of people waiting for the bus. 她加入等公共汽车的行列。

quilt [kwɪlt] *n.* 被子

quiver [ˈkwɪvə] *vi.&n.* 颤抖，抖动

诵读 His clothes quivered in the cold wind. 他的衣服在寒风中抖动。

超 高 频 词 汇

raise [reɪz] *vt.* 提高，提出

诵读 One of the members raised a new point. 其中一位会员提出了一个新观点。

rapid [ˈræpɪd] *a.* 快的，急的

诵读 He walked at a rapid pace along Charles Street. 他沿着查尔斯大街快步行走。

race [reɪs] *n.* 赛跑；人种

拓展 racial *a.* 种的，种族的

诵读 Our race horse was gaining on the favorite. 我们的马正逼近那匹大家都认为会获胜的马。

radical [ˈrædɪkəl] *a.* 激进的；基本的，重要的

诵读 Meanwhile, the justice system is to undergo a radical transformation. 同时，司法系统将要经历一场根本性的改革。

radioactive [ˌreɪdɪəʊˈæktɪv] *a.* 放射性的

巧记 radio 无线电 + active 活跃的

诵读 The government has been storing radioactive waste at Fernald for 50 years. 该政府 50 年来一直在弗纳德储存放射性废物。

rail [reɪl] *n.* 栏杆；铁路

拓展 railroad *n.* 铁路

诵读 The President wants the country to have an extensive high-speed rail system. 总统希望该国开发一套广阔的高速铁路系统。

range [reɪndʒ] *vt.&n.* 领域，排列

诵读 They ranged themselves with the workers. 他们站在工人一边。

rank [ræŋk] *n.* 社会阶层 *vt.* 分等级

诵读 Hong Kong beat Singapore again to rank as the freest economy in the world for the 17th consecutive year. 香港再次打败新加坡，连续 17 年当选全球最自由的经济体。

rare [reə] *a.* 稀有的，难得的

拓展 rarely *ad.* 很少，难得

诵读 These animals in China are rare, too. 在中国这些动物也很稀少。

rate [reɪt] *n.* 速率

搭配 interest rate 利率；growth rate 增长率

僻义 *vt.* 估价

诵读 She spoke with feeling about the high rate of unemployment. 她针对失业率之高慷慨陈词。

rational [ˈræʃənl] *a.* 理性的，合理的

诵读 We talk through things in a more rational fashion. 我们有理有据地讨论各个部分。

realize [ˈrɪəlaɪz] *vt.* 实现，认识到

诵读 You're luckier than most women, and I hope you realize it. 你比大多数妇女都幸运，我希望你能认识到这一点。

recent [ˈriːsnt] *a.* 最近的

regard [rɪˈɡɑːd] *n.* 敬重 *vt.* 把……看作为

搭配 as regards 关于，至于；with/in regard to 对于，就……而论

诵读 In regard to your problem, I would like to make a suggestion. 就你的问题，我愿意提出一个建议。

relation [rɪˈleɪʃn] *n.* 关系；亲属

搭配 in/with relation to 关系到

诵读 Father spoke about school in relation to finding a job when we are older. 父亲谈起上学与我们长大以后找工作之间的关系。

remain [rɪˈmeɪn] *vt.* 剩下，余留

诵读 Much remains to be settled. 待解决的事尚多。

remind [rɪˈmaɪnd] *vt.* 提醒某人，使想起

搭配 remind sb. of… 使某人想起……

诵读 This picture reminds him of his mother. 这张照片使他想起母亲。

reply [rɪˈplaɪ] *vi.* 回答；以……作答

诵读 The man failed to reply to the questions. 那人无法回答这些问题。

republic [rɪˈpʌblɪk] *n.* 共和国，共和政体

request [rɪˈkwest] *vt.* 要求，请求

诵读 Mr. Dennis said he had requested access to a telephone. 丹尼斯先生说他已要求使用电话。

require [rɪˈkwaɪə] *vt.* 需要，要求

诵读 All passengers are required to show their tickets before they get off the bus. 所有的旅客在下车前都必须出示车票。

respect [rɪsˈpekt] *n.* 尊重，问候

搭配 with respect to 关于
辨义 *n.* 方面

诵读 Please send my respect to your father. 请代我向你父亲表达我对他的敬意。

react [rɪˈækt] *vi.* 反应，起作用

搭配 react against 反对，起反作用
拓展 reaction *n.* 反应

诵读 Finally, such a failure would certainly react violently upon the Russian situation. 最后这种失败必将严重影响俄罗斯的局势。

readily [ˈredɪli] *ad.* 容易地；乐意地

诵读 Particular benefits are not readily apparent. 服务的具体收益并不是显而易见的。

reality [rɪˈælɪti] *n.* 现实，实际

拓展 realistic *a.* 现实（主义）的

诵读 Police have to be realistic about violent crime. 警察对暴力犯罪不得不采取务实的态度。

reasonable [ˈriːzənəbl] *a.* 合理的，有道理的

巧记 词根 reason 理由+后缀-able→有道理的
拓展 reason *n.* 原因 *vt.* 推理

诵读 Most programs can make a reasonable substitution. 大多数程序可以找到更合理的替代方式。

receive [rɪˈsiːv] *vt.* 接收；接待

拓展 receipt *n.* 收据，收条；recipient *a.* 接受的 *n.* 接受者；reception *n.* 接待

诵读 Many notables attended the reception. 许多著名人士参加了招待会。

recognize [ˈrekəɡnaɪz] *vt.* 认出，承认

拓展 recognition *n.* 认出；承认

诵读 Shape is the primary way we recognize what an object is. 形状是我们辨识物体的最主要方式。

recollect [ˌrekəˈlekt] *vt.* 回忆，想起

巧记 前缀 re-重新+词根 collect 搜集→重新收集记忆→回忆

诵读 He tried hard to recollect the old scenes of his hometown. 他努力回忆家乡旧时的情景。

recommend [ˌrekəˈmend] *vt.* 推荐，介绍

拓展 recommendation *n.* 推荐

诵读 Businesses have considerable freedom to advertise and recommend pesticides to the farmer. 商家向农民宣传并推荐杀虫剂时有很大的自由。

record [rɪˈkɔːd] *vt.* 录音 [ˈrekɒd] *n.* 记录

拓展 recorder *n.* 记录员；录音机

诵读 A record of each child's birth was kept in the camera. 每个孩子的出生都用相机记录了。

recover [rɪˈkʌvə] *vi.* 恢复 *vt.* 重新找到

拓展 recovery *n.* 痊愈，恢复

巧记 re 回复+cover 覆盖+后缀-age→痊愈，复原

诵读 Economic recovery is supposedly getting underway. 经济复苏应该已经开始了。

recycle [ˌriːˈsaɪkl] *v.&n.* 再循环，重复利用

巧记 前缀 re-反复+词根 cycle 圈→反复的转圈→再循环；重复利用

诵读 This recycle of waste materials is a way of reducing pollution. 这种废材料的循环使用是减少污染的途径之一。

reduce [rɪˈdjuːs] *vt.* 减少，缩小

拓展 reduction *n.* 减小，缩小

诵读 Cost reduction programs are often triggered by a drop in profits. 利润下降常常导致减支计划的出台。

refer [rɪˈfɜː] *vi.* 提交；参考

搭配 refer to 查阅，涉及；refer to ... as ... 称为

拓展 reference *n.* 涉及；参考

诵读 Often, the meeting is recorded on audio or video media for later reference. 通常这种会议会以视频或者音频形式记录下来，供以后查阅。

refine [rɪˈfaɪn] *vt.* 精制，提纯

巧记 前缀 re- 反复+fine 界限→不断地缩小界限→精炼，精制

诵读 Surgical techniques are constantly being refined. 外科手术技术正在不断得到完善。

reflect [rɪˈflekt] *vt.* 反射，反映

拓展 reflection *n.* 映像；反省

搭配 reflect on 反思

诵读 They reflect legal or constitutional norms. 它们反映了法律或宪法准则。

reform [rɪˈfɔːm] *vt.&n.* 改革，改造

巧记 前缀 re- 重新+词根 form 形式→改变形式→改革

诵读 The policy will promote rather than hinder reform. 这项政策将促进改革而不是妨碍改革。

refuse [rɪˈfjuːz] *vt.* 拒绝

拓展 refusal *n.* 拒绝，回绝

诵读 Her country suffered through her refusal to accept change. 她的国家因为她拒绝接受变革而遭受重创。

regarding [rɪˈɡɑːdɪŋ] *prep.* 关于，有关

诵读 He set up a new opinion regarding the project. 他就这个规划提出了新的看法。

regardless [rɪˈɡɑːdlɪs] *a.&ad.* 不管，不顾

搭配 regardless of 不管，不顾

诵读 They catered for everyone regardless of social rank. 他们为所有人服务，不论社会地位如何。

region [ˈriːdʒən] *n.* 地区，地带

诵读 The plan will cost in the region of six million dollars. 这项计划将花费大约 600 万美元。

register [ˈredʒɪstə] *n.&vi.* 登记，注册

诵读 Attendance figures normally include only the people who actually register for the convention. 出席人数一般只包括实际登记参加会议的人。

regulate [ˈreɡjʊleɪt] *vt.* 调节，校准

拓展 regulation *n.* 规则，规章；调整

诵读 Private schools regulate the behavior of students. 私立学校规范学生行为。

reject [rɪˈdʒekt] *vt.* 拒绝，抵制

巧记 前缀 re-往回+词根 ject 投掷→扔回来→拒绝

诵读 The proper time to reject changes is when the changes are made. 拒绝修改的最合适时刻是做出修改时。

relate [rɪˈleɪt] *vt.* 联系

搭配 be related to ... 与……有联系

拓展 relationship *n.* 关系，联系

诵读 Trainees should be invited to relate new ideas to their past experiences. 应鼓励实习生把新想法与以往经历联系起来。

relative [ˈrelətɪv] *a.* 相对的 *n.* 亲戚

拓展 relativity *n.* 相关（性）；相对论

诵读 Because of their relative rarity, they are often missed. 因为相对少见，它们常被忽视。

relax [rɪˈlæks] *vt.&vi.* （使）松弛，放松

诵读 Massage is used to relax muscles, relieve stress and improve the circulation. 按摩可以使肌肉放松，缓解压力和促进血液循环。

religion [rɪˈlɪdʒən] *n.* 宗教，信仰

拓展 religious *a.* 宗教的，信教的

诵读 Christianity and Islam are two different religions. 基督教与伊斯兰教是两种不同的宗教。

rely [rɪˈlaɪ] *vi.* 依赖

搭配 rely on 依赖

拓展 reliable *a.* 可靠的，可信赖的；reliance *n.* 依靠

诵读 We must rely on our own efforts. 我们必须依靠自己的努力。

remain [rɪˈmeɪn] *vi.* 留下，保持

拓展 remains *n.* 剩余；remainder *n.* 剩余物

诵读 I will go ahead with three of you, and the remainder can wait here. 我将和你们中的三个人一起往前走，其余的人可以在这儿等待。

remark [rɪˈmɑːk] *n.* 评语 *vt.&vi.* 评论

搭配 make a remark on 就……发表意见；remark on/upon 谈论，评论

拓展 remarkable *a.* 值得注意的；显著的

诵读 He remarked on the difference in security measures at the two airports. 他谈到了两座机场安全措施的不同。

remote [rɪˈməʊt] *a.* 远的，遥远的

搭配 remote control 遥控器

诵读 He said the old man was his remote relative. 他说这位老人是他的一位远亲。

renew [rɪˈnjuː] *vt.* 更新，恢复

诵读 It is very difficult to renew our library cards. 更换我们的图书卡十分困难。

repeat [rɪˈpiːt] *vt.&n.* 重复

拓展 repetition *n.* 重复，反复；repeatedly *ad.* 重复地，再三地

诵读 I've repeatedly told you to keep the door shut. 我再三告诉你要把门关上。

replace [rɪˈpleɪs] *vt.* 取代，替换

拓展 replacement *n.* 取代，替换

诵读 When you have finished using the axe, please replace it. 用完斧子时，请将它放回原处。

represent [ˌreprɪˈzent] *vt.* 描述，代表

拓展 representative *n.* 代表，代理人

诵读 This painting represents a storm. 这幅画描绘了一场暴风雨。

rescue [ˈreskjuː] *vt.&n.* 营救，援救

诵读 We rescued the boy who fell into the deep lake. 我们营救了那个掉入深湖中的小孩。

reserve [rɪˈzɜːv] *vt.* 保留，预定

拓展 reservation *n.* 保留；预定

搭配 reserve…for 替……保留；without reserve 毫无保留地

诵读 We must reserve our energies for the task that lies ahead. 我们必须积蓄力量以完成将来的任务。

residence [ˈrezɪdəns] *n.* 住处，住宅

拓展 resident *n.* 居民，常住者

诵读 His office is in town, but he has a residence in the country. 他的办公室在城内，但他在乡间有住所。

resign [rɪˈzaɪn] *vi.* 辞职，使顺从

巧记 前缀 re-再次+词根 sign签字→入职签字，再次签字→辞职

诵读 He has resigned from his position as a teacher. 他已经辞去了教师职务。

resist [rɪˈzɪst] *vt.* 抵抗，反抗

拓展 resistance *n.* 抵抗，反抗；resistant *a.* 有抵抗力的

诵读 Lack of proper nourishment reduces their power to resist disease. 营养不良降低了他们抵抗疾病的能力。

resolve [rɪˈzɒlv] *vt.* 决心；决议

拓展 resolute *a.* 果断的；resolution *n.* 决议，决心

搭配 resolve to do 决心做

诵读 She resolved to report the matter to the hospital's nursing supervisor. 她决定向医院的护士长汇报这件事。

resort [rɪˈzɔːt] *vi.* 求助，诉诸

搭配 resort to 采取，求助于

诵读 If other means fail, we shall resort to force. 如果其他手段均不成功，我们将诉诸武力。

resource [rɪˈsɔːs] *n.* 资源，财力

诵读 The treaty makes the moon's natural resources "the common heritage of mankind". 条约规定月球的自然资源为"人类共同的遗产"。

respective [rɪsˈpektɪv] *a.* 各自的，各个的

诵读 All of us were given work according to our respective abilities. 我们每一个人都按各自的能力分工。

respond [rɪˈspɒnd] *vi.* 回答，响应

拓展 response *n.* 回答，反应；responsible *a.* 应负责的；responsibility *n.* 责任

诵读 I offered him a drink but he did not respond. 我请他喝酒，可他却没有回答。

result [rɪˈzʌlt] *n.* 结果，成绩 *vi.* 导致

搭配 result in 导致；result from 由于

诵读 The speeches obtained good results. 演说获得了好效果。

reveal [rɪˈviːl] *vt.* 展现，显示

拓展 revelation *n.* 揭示，揭露

诵读 The mask of benevolence fell and the real man was revealed. 这个人揭掉了慈善的假面具，露出了真面目。

revenue [ˈrevənjuː] *n.* 财政收入，税收

诵读 A government's revenue and expenditure should be balanced. 政府的财政收入和支出要平衡。

reverse [rɪˈvɜːs] *n.* 相反；背面 *a.* 相反的

诵读 Edwin is afraid of Angela, but the reverse is also true. 艾德温惧怕安琪拉，但反过来说也对。

review [rɪˈvjuː] *vt.* 回顾，复习 *n.* 回顾；审查

诵读 The speaker presented a review of recent developments in the Middle East. 发言人回顾了中东近期的发展情况。

revise [rɪˈvaɪz] *vt.* 修订，校订

巧记 前缀 re-再次+词根 vis看→回看→校订

诵读 Ben Johnson tells us that Shakespeare never had to revise a manuscript. 本·琼森告诉我们，莎士比亚从来不必修改原稿。

revive [rɪˈvaɪv] *vt.* 恢复；复苏

巧记 前缀 re-再次+词根 viv生命→再次获得生命

诵读 The fresh air soon revived him. 新鲜的空气使他很快苏醒过来。

revolt [rɪˈvəʊlt] *vi.&n.* 反抗，起义

诵读 The peasants' revolt was put down by the dictator's troops. 农民起义被独裁者的军队镇压下去了。

reward [rɪˈwɔːd] *n.* 报酬，赏金

诵读 He got a reward of $900 for catching the criminal. 他因抓获罪犯而获得 900 美元的酬金。

rid [rɪd] *vt.* 摆脱，去掉 *a.* 得到解脱的

搭配 get rid of 取消

诵读 The doctor rid him of his pain. 医生使他摆脱了痛苦。

risk [rɪsk] *n.* 冒险；风险

搭配 at the risk of… 冒……的风险

诵读 You could never eliminate risk, but preparation and training could attenuate it. 风险不可能完全消除，

但防范和培训可以降低风险。

rival [ˈraɪvəl] *n.* 竞争者，对手

诵读 China is outpacing its rivals in the race to develop new carbon capture technologies, as it pushes forward with plans to achieve carbon neutrality before 2060. 随着推进2060年前实现碳中和这一计划，中国在开发新型碳捕获技术方面超越了竞争对手。

root [rʊt] *n.* 根本，根源

搭配 take root in 生根，扎根

诵读 The root of the problem lay in the seizure of the land of Ireland by the English ruling class. 那问题的根源在于英吉利统治阶级对爱尔兰岛的强占。

rob [rɒb] *vt.* 抢劫，盗取

搭配 rob sb. of sth. 非法剥夺

诵读 Two thieves robbed a man at knifepoint to steal his jeans and shoes. 两名歹徒持刀抢走一名男子的牛仔裤和鞋子。

robust [rəʊˈbʌst] *a.* 强健的，雄壮的

巧记 乐百氏英文标识 robust

诵读 The once robust economy now lies in ruins. 曾经强健的经济现已崩溃。

role [rəʊl] *n.* 角色，作用

搭配 play a role in 起……作用

诵读 The UN would play a major role in monitoring a ceasefire. 联合国在监督停火方面会发挥重要作用。

romance [rəʊˈmæns] *n.* 传奇，爱情故事

巧记 谐音记忆：罗曼史 romance

拓展 romantic *a.* 浪漫的，传奇式的；不切实际的，好幻想的

诵读 Nearly three-quarters said they did not have to keep their romance a secret but 7 percent said they had left a job due to an office romance. 近四分之三的人称自己的办公室恋情不用保密，而 7%的人则因此而离职。

rope [rəʊp] *n.* 绳，索

route [ruːt] *n.* 路线，路程

诵读 The route was designed to relieve traffic congestion. 这条路是为缓解交通拥挤而设计的。

rude [ruːd] *a.* 粗鲁的；猛烈的

诵读 I was often rude and ungracious in refusing help. 我拒绝接受帮助的时候时常显得粗鲁无礼。

ruler [ˈruːlə] *n.* 统治者

诵读 In Greek myths, Zeus was the ruler of gods and men. 在希腊神话中,宙斯是神与人的主宰。

rumor [ˈruːmə] *n.* 传闻,谣言

诵读 Rumor has it that the defence minister will soon resign. 据传闻,国防部长不久就要辞职。

rural [ˈrʊərəl] *a.* 乡下的,田园的

诵读 Many development strategies now give priority to agricultural and rural development. 现在,许多发展战略都把农业和农村的发展放在优先地位。

rage [reɪdʒ] *n.* 愤怒

诵读 He was red-cheeked with rage. 他因愤怒而满脸通红。

raid [reɪd] *n.&vt.* 袭击,搜查

诵读 The rebels attempted a surprise raid on a military camp. 反叛者们曾经试图对兵营发动一场突然袭击。

rally [ˈræli] *vi.* 召集,集合 *n.* 聚集、集会

诵读 Journalists said there was a virtual news blackout about the rally. 记者们说,有关这场集会的新闻实际上被封锁了。

random [ˈrændəm] *a.* 随机的,随意的

搭配 at random 随机地

诵读 The survey used a random sample of two thousand people across the Midwest. 这项调查在中西部随机抽取了2 000人作为样本。

rap [ræp] *n.* 叩击 *vt.* 敲,拍

诵读 They rap about life in the inner city. 他们用说唱形式展现了市中心的生活。

rape [reɪp] *n.&vt.* 掠夺,强奸

诵读 Gender-based violence, including rape, is an increasingly familiar weapon of war. 包括强奸在内的基于性别的暴力是人们越来越熟悉的战争武器。

rash [ræʃ] *a.* 轻率的,鲁莽的

诵读 In a rash moment he removes ten thousand dollars from the company safe. 一时冲动,他从公司的保险柜里取出了1万美元。

ratio [ˈreɪʃɪəʊ] *n.* 比,比率

诵读 As a result, a more even air-fuel ratio is maintained. 因此,能保持更均匀的空燃比。

raw [rɔː] *a.* 未煮过的,生的

搭配 raw material 原材料;raw meat 生肉

诵读 Coal, oil and minerals are the raw materials of industry. 煤、石油和矿产品都是工业原料。

regret [rɪˈgret] *v.* 懊悔 *n.* 遗憾

诵读 I regret to say I cannot come. 很抱歉我不能来了。

revolution [ˌrevəˈluːʃən] *n.* 旋转;革命

拓展 revolve *v.* 旋转

诵读 The earth makes one revolution around the sun in about 365 days. 地球绕着太阳公转一周需要约365天。

reap [riːp] *vt.* 收割,收获

诵读 Giant machines reap the wheat grown in the Mid-western United States. 大型机器收割种植在美国中西部的小麦。

rear [rɪə] *n.* 后面 *vt.* 抚养

诵读 He settled back in the rear of the taxi. 他在出租车后座,往后靠着坐好了。

reassure [ˌriːəˈʃʊə] *vt.* 使安心,使放心

巧记 前缀 re- 反复+前缀 as- 加强语气+词根 sure 确定→反复确定→使安心,使放心

诵读 He was looking for someone conservative enough to reassure the Congress. 他要物色一个保守到足以使国会放心的人。

rebel [ˈrebəl] *vi.* 反抗 *n.* 叛逆者

拓展 rebellion *n.* 叛乱,起义

诵读 He was charged with inciting people to rebel. 他被控煽动民众叛乱。

recall [rɪˈkɔːl] *vt.* 回忆,回想

巧记 前缀 re- 重新+词根 call 唤起→回忆

诵读 No other creature except man can recall the past at will. 除了人类以外,没有任何一种生物能随意回忆过去。

recede [rɪˈsiːd] *vi.* 退回,后退

巧记 前缀 re- 往回+词根 cede 走→往回走→后退;收回

诵读 Luke's footsteps receded into the night. 卢克的

脚步声渐渐消失在夜色中。

reckless [ˈreklɪs] *a.* 大意的；鲁莽的

诵读 He was not really reckless, at any rate in his relations to society. 他至少对社会关系不是轻率的。

reckon [ˈrekən] *vt.* 估算，认为

诵读 Don't reckon upon the weather being fine for your garden party. 不要指望你们举行游园会那天天气良好。

reclaim [rɪˈkleɪm] *vt.* 要求归还；收回

巧记 前缀 re- 往回+词根 claim 宣称→要求拿回

诵读 You may be entitled to reclaim some of the tax you paid last year. 你或许有权要求退回去年交付的部分税金。

reconcile [ˈrekənsaɪl] *vt.* 使和好，调解

诵读 She had reconciled herself to never seeing him again. 她接受了再也不和他见面的事实。

recreation [ˌrekrɪˈeɪʃn] *n.* 娱乐，消遣

诵读 Saturday afternoon is for recreation and outings. 周六下午是娱乐和外出的时间。

recruit [rɪˈkruːt] *vt.* 征募（新兵）*n.* 新成员

诵读 The recruit was all eagerness to go to the front. 新入伍的战士迫切盼望上前线。

rectangle [ˈrektæŋgl] *n.* [数]矩形，长方形

巧记 词根 rect 正+词根 angle 角度 →四角都是直角

诵读 Cloth diaper may be folded in a triangle or a rectangle. 用布做的尿布可以叠成三角形或长方形。

recite [rɪˈsaɪt] *vt.* 背诵，朗诵

诵读 Each child had to recite a poem to the class. 每个孩子都得在班上背诵一首诗。

rectify [ˈrektɪfaɪ] *vt.* 纠正，整顿

巧记 词根 rect 正+后缀-ify→使变成正的→纠正

诵读 Of course, to rectify the economic order, we must straighten out the price system. 当然，为了理顺经济秩序，我们必须调整价格体系。

recur [rɪˈkɜː] *vi.* （尤指不好的事）一再发生；重现

诵读 It is clear that the same difficulties will recur in all the towns of the favoured state. 显然，在受青睐的州的所有城镇中，同样的困难都会再次出现。

redundant [rɪˈdʌndənt] *a.* 多余的；被解雇的

诵读 Nearly all the redundant workers have been absorbed into other departments. 几乎所有冗员，都已调往其他部门任职。

refrain [rɪˈfreɪn] *vi.* 节制；避免

搭配 refrain from smoking 禁止吸烟

诵读 They agreed to maintain production and refrain from severe wage reductions. 他们同意维持生产，禁止大量削减工资。

refresh [rɪˈfreʃ] *vt.*（使）精神振作，（使）精力恢复

巧记 前缀 re- 重新+词根 fresh 新鲜的→精神振作

拓展 refreshment *n.* (*pl.*) 点心；精力恢复

诵读 Further, we provide plenty of means for the mind to refresh itself from business. 此外，我们提供多种方法，使人从纷繁的事务中恢复放松。

refund [riːˈfʌnd] *n.* 归还 *vt.* 退还

巧记 前缀 re- 往回+词根 fund 资金→归还，偿还

诵读 Needless to say, we shall refund any expenses you may incur. 不用说，我们将会偿还你所负担的任何费用。

refute [rɪˈfjuːt] *vt.* 反驳，驳斥

诵读 It was the kind of rumour that it is impossible to refute. 这是那种不可能推翻的谣言。

reign [reɪn] *n.&vi.* 支配 *n.* 统治时期

巧记 reign＝reg 统治

诵读 The mobile phone was invented as a tool for facilitating our life, rather than reigning. 手机的发明是为了方便我们的生活，而不是统治我们的生活。

rein [reɪn] *n.* 统治，支配 *vt.* 驾驭

诵读 What the company has to do is to keep a very tight rein on its spending until the financial situation improves. 公司需要做的是在财务状况好转之前，严格控制支出。

reinforce [ˌriːɪnˈfɔːs] *vt.* 增援；加强

巧记 前缀 re-反复+前缀 in-里面+词根 force 力量→增援，加强

诵读 Public reaction will reinforce it. 公众反应会进一步增强它的作用。

rejoice [rɪˈdʒɔɪs] *vi.*（使）欣喜，（使）高兴

巧记 飘柔洗发水的英文商标就是 Rejoice

诵读 We rejoice at every victory won by your people. 我们为贵国人民取得的每一个胜利感到高兴。

release [rɪˈliːs] *vt.* 释放，解放

诵读 Four dangerous prisoners were released. 四名危险的囚犯被释放了。

relevant ['reləvənt] *a.* 有关的，中肯的

诵读 The judge said that the evidence was not relevant to the case. 法官裁决这证据与案件无关。

relief [rɪ'li:f] *n.* (痛苦等)减轻，救济

拓展 relieve *vt.* 缓解

诵读 A doctor's task is to work for the relief of suffering. 医生的任务是为病人解除痛苦。

reluctant [rɪ'lʌktənt] *a.* 不愿的，勉强的

诵读 The little girl was reluctant to leave her mother. 这个小女孩不愿意离开她的母亲。

remedy ['remɪdi] *vt.* 治疗，纠正

巧记 前缀 re-反复+词根 med 药物→反复使用药物→治疗，医治

诵读 You have to remedy your fault. 你必须纠错。

removal [rɪ'mu:vəl] *n.* 移动，迁居

诵读 That man said that his company did removals. 那个人说他的公司提供搬家服务。

render ['rendə] *vt.* 致使；提出

诵读 My grandfather always taught me to render good for evil. 我的祖父常常教导我要以德报怨。

renovate ['renəveɪt] *vt.* 更新，修复

巧记 前缀 re-重新+词根 nov新+后缀-ate →重新修复一新

诵读 The teacher and his students purchased a run-down house and practiced self-reliance by renovating it. 那个老师与学生们买了一间废弃的房子，然后自己动手重新修复。

rent [rent] *vt.* 租赁 *n.* 租金

诵读 My father rents an office in city. 我父亲在城里租了间办公室。

repay [ri:'peɪ] *vt.* 偿还，报答

诵读 I can never repay you for your kindness. 你的好意，我永远也报答不清。

reputation [ˌrepjʊ'teɪʃən] *n.* 名誉，名声

诵读 She is a scientist of international reputation. 她是一个有国际声望的科学家。

resemble [rɪ'zembl] *vt.* 像，类似

拓展 resemblance *n.* 相似，相似性[点，物]

诵读 She resembles her mother in the way she moves her hands when she talks. 她说话时打手势的动作像她妈妈。

resent [rɪ'zent] *vt.* 对……表示愤恨，怨恨

诵读 He resented his friend's remark. 他怨恨朋友所说的话。

restless ['restlɪs] *a.* 得不到休息的；不平静的

诵读 The soldiers have spent many restless nights. 战士们已经度过了许多个不眠之夜。

restore [rɪ'stɔ:] *vt.* 恢复，使恢复

巧记 前缀 re-再次+词根 store 储存→再次储存满→恢复

诵读 The old building had become a ruin but the people of the town restored it. 这座老建筑已经成为一片废墟，但镇上的人们对它进行了修复。

restrain [rɪs'treɪn] *vt.* 抑制，制止

巧记 前缀 re-反复+词根 strain 拉住→反复拉住→限制

拓展 restraint *n.* 抑制，制止

诵读 I can't restrain my anger when I hear of people being cruel to animals. 当我听说有人虐待动物时，我抑制不住愤怒。

restrict [rɪs'trɪkt] *vt.* 限制，约束

诵读 They became more and more restricted in their freedom of action. 他们在行动自由上受到的限制越来越多。

resume ['rezjumei] *n.* 个人简历 [rɪ'zju:m] *vt.* 再继续

诵读 We resumed our work after a rest. 休息过后，我们重新开始工作。

retail ['ri:teɪl] *n.* 零售

诵读 He opened a small retail business. 他开了一家小型零售店。

retain [rɪ'teɪn] *vt.* 保持，保留

诵读 She is 90 but still retains the use of all her faculties. 她已是 90 岁高龄，但她的器官功能仍未衰退。

retention [rɪ'tenʃən] *n.* 保留，保持

诵读 They advocate the retention of our nuclear power plants. 他们主张保留我们的核电厂。

retire [rɪ'taɪə] *vi.* 退休，引退

诵读 He retired from the business when he was 65. 他 65 岁的时候退休了。

retort [rɪ'tɔ:t] *n.&vt.* 报复，反击

巧记 前缀 re-往回+词根 tort 弯曲→弯回来→回嘴

诵读 His sharp retort clearly made an impact. 他尖刻的反驳显然起了作用。

retreat [rɪˈtriːt] *vi.* 撤退，退却

诵读 The soldiers had to retreat when they were beaten in battle. 士兵们在战斗中受挫时不得不退却。

retrieve [rɪˈtriːv] *vt.* 重新得到，取回

诵读 He is the one man who could retrieve that situation. 他是唯一能挽回局面的人。

retrospect [ˈretrəspekt] *v.&n.* 回顾，回想

巧记 前缀 re-往回+词根 tro (=try 试着) +词根 spect 看→试着回头看→回顾

诵读 Review one's work of the past years in retrospect. 回顾个人过去几年的工作。

revenge [rɪˈvendʒ] *n.* 报复，复仇

搭配 take revenge on sb. for sth. 向某人报仇

诵读 I broke Mary's pen by accident, and in revenge she tore up my school work. 我不小心弄坏了玛丽的钢笔，她出于报复撕坏了我的作业本。

ridiculous [rɪˈdɪkjʊləs] *a.* 荒谬的，可笑的

诵读 Don't be ridiculous. You can't walk outside in the storm. 不要干傻事。暴风雨天你不能在外面走。

rigid [ˈrɪdʒɪd] *a.* 刚性的；刻板的

诵读 A rigid diet seemed as effective as cholesterol-lowering pills. 严格的饮食似乎与降低胆固醇的药物一样有效。

rigorous [ˈrɪɡərəs] *a.* 严格的，严厉的

诵读 He made a rigorous study of the plants in the area. 他对该地的植物进行了仔细的研究。

rough [rʌf] *a.* 粗略的，大致的

诵读 It's only a rough translation of the poem. 这只是这首诗的粗略翻译。

row [rəʊ] *n.* (一)行

辨义 *n.* 激烈的争吵

诵读 They have won five championships in a row. 他们已经赢得了五连冠。

roar [rɔ:] *n.&vi.* 吼叫，怒号

诵读 Her voice was drowned by the roar of the traffic. 她的说话声被车辆的轰鸣声压倒了。

rot [rɒt] *vi.* 腐烂，腐朽

拓展 rotten *a.* 腐烂的，腐朽的

诵读 If we don't unload it soon, the grain will start rotting in the storehouse. 如果我们不马上卸货，这些粮食将在仓中腐烂。

rotate [rəʊˈteɪt] *vt.&vi.* (使)旋转

拓展 rotary *a.* 旋转的

诵读 The earth rotates from west to east. 地球自西向东旋转。

ruin [ˈruːɪn] *vt.* 毁灭，破坏

诵读 That rich man was ruined by this law case. 那个富翁被这场官司搞得倾家荡产。

rust [rʌst] *n.&vi.* 生锈

诵读 The certificate indicates that some of the rollers are rusted. 商检证书上表明有些滚筒生锈了。

ruthless [ˈruːθlɪs] *a.* 残酷的，无情的

诵读 The president was ruthless in dealing with any hint of internal political dissent. 这位总统对任何内部政治分歧的苗头都毫不留情。

商业化和安全化。

safe [seɪf] *a.* 安全的，牢靠的；可靠的

辨义 *n.* 保险箱

拓展 safeguard *v.* 维护，保护 *n.* 安全措施

诵读 Rock'n'roll has become so commercialized and safe since punk. 自从朋克乐流行以来，摇滚乐变得

satisfy [ˈsætɪsfaɪ] *vt.* 使……满意，使满意

搭配 be satisfied with… 对……感到满足

拓展 satisfaction *n.* 满足，愉快

诵读 Cheap goods are available, but not in sufficient quantities to satisfy demand. 有一些廉价的商品，但是数量不足以满足需求。

say [seɪ] *vt.* 说

僻义 *vi.* 比方说

搭配 have a final say in... 在……有最终发言权

诵读 To see the problem here more clearly, let's look at a different biological system, say, an elephant. 为更清晰地理解此处的问题，我们来看一种不同的生物系统，比如说大象。

sack [sæk] *n.* 袋，包

僻义 *vt.* 解雇

诵读 Other industries have had to sack managers to reduce administrative costs. 其他行业不得不精简管理人员以减少行政开支。

sacrifice [ˈsækrɪfaɪs] *n.* 牺牲，牺牲品 *vt.* 牺牲，献出

搭配 sacrifice... for... 牺牲，献出

诵读 He said the task of reconstruction would demand much patience, hard work and sacrifice. 他说重建任务需要付出极大的耐心、艰辛和牺牲。

sake [seɪk] *n.* 缘故，理由

搭配 for the sake of 由于……的缘故；for one's sake 看在某人份上，为了某人

诵读 Let's assume for the sake of argument that we manage to build a satisfactory database. 为了便于讨论，不妨假定我们成功地建立了一个令人满意的数据库。

sane [seɪn] *a.* 心智健全的，神志清醒的，明智的

拓展 sanely *ad.* 心智健全地，稳健地

诵读 Did he come across as a sane rational person? 他看起来是一个正常而理智的人吗？

sarcastic [sɑːˈkæstɪk] *a.* 讽刺的，挖苦的

拓展 同义词 ironic

诵读 A sarcastic remark was on the tip of her tongue. 挖苦的话到了她嘴边却没说出来。

savage [ˈsævɪdʒ] *a.* 野蛮的，残暴的 *n.* 野人

僻义 *vt.* 激烈抨击

拓展 savagery *n.* 野蛮，荒凉的状态

诵读 Such a savage punishment is abhorrent to a civilized society. 对于文明社会来说，如此野蛮的惩罚是可惜的。

second [ˈsekənd] *a.* 第二的；次要的 *n.* 秒

僻义 *vt.* 支持

拓展 secondary *a.* 次要的

诵读 All this, needless to say, had been culled second-hand from radio reports. 不用说，所有这些都是从电台报道中采集来的二手材料。

secret [ˈsiːkrɪt] *n.* 秘密

拓展 secretly *ad.* 秘密地，偷偷地

诵读 The exact locations are being kept secret for reasons of security. 确切地点因为安全原因要保密。

see [siː] *vt.* 看见，理解，访问

拓展 seeable *a.* 看得见的

搭配 see off 给……送行；see through 看穿，识破；干完，干到底

诵读 Specialists see various reasons for the recent surge in inflation. 专家们认为目前通货膨胀加剧有多种原因。

seize [seɪz] *vt.* 抓住，占领

诵读 Seize the day, boys. Make your lives extraordinary. 要抓住每一天，孩子们，让你们的生活变得非凡起来。

seldom [ˈseldəm] *ad.* 很少，难得

诵读 He had seldom seen a child with so much talent. 如此有天赋的孩子他以往没见过几个。

self [self] *n.* 自我，本人

诵读 He is being treated for a self-inflicted gunshot wound. 他因开枪自残受伤正在接受治疗。

settle [ˈsetl] *vt.* 安顿；解决，调停

拓展 settlement *n.* 解决，住宅区

搭配 settle down 定居，过安定的生活

诵读 They agreed to try to settle their dispute by negotiation. 他们同意通过谈判来解决纠纷。

scale [skeɪl] *n.* 比例，规模 *vt.* 测量，攀登

诵读 The scale of migration took a quantum leap in the early 1970s. 20 世纪 70 年代初，移民的规模骤然扩大。

scan [skæn] *vt.* 细看，扫描 *n.* 扫描，浏览

拓展 scannable *a.* 可校验的，能扫描的

诵读 He was rushed to hospital for a brain scan. 他被火速送往医院做脑部扫描。

scarce [skeəs] *a.* 缺乏的，罕见的

拓展 scarcely *ad.* 几乎不；scarcity *n.* 稀缺

诵读 This scarcity is inevitable in less developed countries. 这一匮乏在欠发达国家不可避免。

scatter [ˈskætə] *vt.&vi.* 散开，驱散；散布

诵读 The white clouds mass and scatter. 白云舒卷。

schedule [ˈʃedjuːəl] *n.* 时间表 *vt.* 安排，预定

诵读 He had been unable to keep to his schedule. 他没能遵循自己的计划。

scheme [skiːm] *n.* 计划，方案 *vi.* 计划，图谋

诵读 He reckoned the odds are against the scheme going ahead. 他认为这项计划的成功希望渺茫。

scholar [ˈskɒlə] *n.* 学者，奖学金获得者

拓展 scholarship *n.* 奖学金；学问，学识

诵读 He came to Oxford as a Rhodes scholar and studied law. 他作为罗兹奖学金的获得者来到牛津学习法律。

scold [skəʊld] *vt.* 责骂，训斥

诵读 Don't scold her; she's nothing but a child. 不要责骂她，她只不过是个孩子。

scope [skəʊp] *n.* （活动）范围；见识，领域 *v.* 审视

诵读 There is still scope for new writers to break through. 仍有一些领域需要新作家们去开拓。

scorn [skɔːn] *vt.&n.* 轻蔑，鄙视

诵读 Researchers greeted the proposal with scorn. 研究员们对这个建议嗤之以鼻。

screw [skruː] *n.* 螺旋，螺丝（钉）*vt.* 拧紧，扭曲

诵读 A screw had worked loose from my glasses. 我眼镜上有一颗螺丝松了。

script [skrɪpt] *n.* 脚本，手迹 *vt.* 为电影写剧本，编造

诵读 They stopped you as soon as you deviated from the script. 一旦你偏离了剧本的内容，他们就会喊停。

scrutiny [ˈskruːtɪnɪ] *n.* 细看，监视

诵读 The President promised a government open to public scrutiny. 总统承诺政府将接受公众监督。

sculpture [ˈskʌlptʃə] *n.* 雕刻品，塑像 *v.* 雕刻

诵读 He studied sculpture because he enjoyed working with clay. 他学习雕塑是因为喜欢玩黏土。

seaside [ˈsiːˌsaɪd] *n.* 海滨，海边 *a.* 海滨的，海边的

诵读 Ischia is a popular seaside holiday resort. 伊斯基亚是个很受欢迎的海滨度假胜地。

section [ˈsekʃən] *n.* 节，部分，部门

拓展 sector *n.* 部门，部分

诵读 I'll just flick through the pages until I find the right section. 我会快速地翻页，直到找到要找的那一部分。

secure [sɪˈkjʊə] *a.* 安全的，放心的 *vt.* 防护，担保

拓展 security *n.* 安全，防御，保证

诵读 I couldn't remember ever having felt so safe and secure. 我从未有过如此安全的感觉。

seemingly [ˈsiːmɪŋli] *ad.* 表面上，貌似

诵读 The Bundesbank's seemingly impregnable position has begun to weaken. 德国联邦银行看似不可撼动的地位开始削弱了。

select [sɪˈlekt] *vt.* 选择，挑选 *a.* 精选的，苛责的

拓展 selection *n.* 选择，挑选

诵读 The floorcovering you select will need to be impervious to water. 挑选的地板材料必须是防水的。

selfish [ˈselfɪʃ] *a.* 自私的，利己的

诵读 They painted him to be indecisive, negative, and selfish. 他被描绘成一个优柔寡断、消极又自私的人。

semester [sɪˈmestə] *n.* 学期，半学年

诵读 A student will probably attend four or five courses during each semester. 每个学生一学期可能要修四五门课程。

senior [ˈsiːnjə] *a.* 年长的；资深的 *n.* 大四学生

诵读 Senior officers could be considering a coup to restore authoritarian rule. 高官们可能会策划一场政变来复辟独裁统治。

sense [sens] *n.* 感觉，意识，观念 *vt.* 理解，领会

拓展 sensation *n.* 感觉，知觉；sensible *a.* 明智的，达理的；sensitive *a.* 敏感的，灵敏的

诵读 Behind the mocking laughter lurks a growing sense of unease. 嘲笑声的背后潜伏着一种越来越强烈的不安。

sentence [ˈsentəns] *n.* 句子

僻义 *n.&vt.* 宣判，判决

诵读 He stood emotionless as he heard the judge pass sentence. 他面无表情地站在那里，听法官宣布判决。

sentiment [ˈsentɪmənt] *n.* 感情，情绪，观点，意见

诵读 Political life has been infected by growing nationalist sentiment. 政治生活已受到了不断高涨的民族主义情绪的影响。

sequence [ˈsiːkwəns] *n.* 顺序；连续，数列 *vt.* 安排顺序

诵读 The book is more satisfying if you read each chapter in sequence. 这本书依次读各章会更好。

serial [ˈsɪərɪəl] *n.* 连载小说，连续剧；连载刊物 *a.* 连续的，连载的

诵读 It's a film about a serial killer and not for the faint-hearted. 这部电影是讲一个连环杀手的，不适合胆小的人看。

series [ˈsɪəriːz] *n.* 系列，连续；丛书

诵读 Customs officials have made a series of contradictory statements about the equipment. 海关官员们对这种设备做出了一系列互相矛盾的陈述。

session [ˈseʃən] *n.* 会议，一段时间

诵读 Charles and I were closeted in his study for the briefing session. 我和查尔斯在他的书房里闭门开简报会。

setback [ˈsetbæk] *n.* 挫折，阻碍，倒退

巧记 同义词 barrier, obstacle

诵读 The move represents a setback for the Middle East peace process. 这个行动意味着中东和平进程受挫。

set [ˈset] *vt.* 放，安排，设立

拓展 setting *n.* 环境，装置，背景

诵读 The secret to happiness is to keep setting yourself new challenges. 幸福的秘诀就是要不停地给自己设定新的挑战。

severe [sɪˈvɪə] *a.* 严厉的；剧烈的，苛责的

诵读 We are in one of the most severe recessions in modern times. 我们正在经历现代最严重的一段经济衰退。

shade [ʃeɪd] *n.* 阴影，遮光物 *vt.* 遮蔽，遮光

拓展 shady *a.* 成荫的，可疑的，靠不住的

诵读 Umbrellas shade outdoor cafes along winding cobblestone streets. 在曲折蜿蜒的鹅卵石街道两边，一把把阳伞为露天咖啡馆遮阴挡阳。

shame [ʃeɪm] *n.* 羞耻 *vt.* 使羞愧，玷辱

拓展 shameful *a.* 可耻的，丢脸的

诵读 You've no reason to reproach yourself, no reason to feel shame. 你没有理由自责，也没有理由感到惭愧。

sharp [ʃɑːp] *a.* 锋利的 *ad.* 猛烈地，尖锐地

诵读 Futures prices recovered from sharp early declines to end with moderate losses. 期货价格在早盘深幅下跌后出现反弹，收盘时未见严重损失。

shoot [ʃʊt] *vt.* 拍摄，射击 *n.* 嫩枝，摄影

诵读 If raging inflation returns, then interest rates will shoot up. 如果再发生严重的通货膨胀，那么利率就会迅速上调。

show [ʃəʊ] *vt.* 呈现，证明 *n.* 展览，演出

搭配 show off 炫耀；show up 使呈现，使醒目；出席，到场

诵读 The evening show was terrible, with hesitant unsure performances from all. 晚上的演出很糟，所有人都缩手缩脚，显得很不自信。

shabby [ˈʃæbi] *a.* 破旧的，卑鄙的，低劣的

诵读 It was hard to say why the man deserved such shabby treatment. 真搞不懂为什么这个人就该受到如此恶劣的待遇。

shadow [ˈʃædəʊ] *n.* 影子

诵读 The light from my candle threw his elongated shadow on the walls. 我的烛光将他拉长的影子投射在墙上。

shallow [ˈʃæləʊ] *a.* 浅的，浅薄的 *n.* 浅滩，浅处 *v.* 使变浅

诵读 The shallow seabed yields up an abundance of food. 浅海床提供了丰富的食物。

shape [ʃeɪp] *n.* 形状，状态，身材

僻义 *vt.* 塑造，形成

诵读 She even had plastic surgery to change the shape of her nose. 为改变鼻子的形状，她甚至接受了整形手术。

share [ʃeə] *vt.* 分配，共用；分担

僻义 *n.* 份额；股份

诵读 There are intangible benefits beyond a rise in the share price. 除股价上升之外还有无形利益。

shatter [ˈʃætə] *n.* 碎片；粉碎 *vt.* 粉碎；损坏

诵读 A failure would shatter the hopes of many people. 一次失败会使很多人希望破灭。

sheer [ʃɪə] *a.* 纯粹的，全然的，险峻的

诵读 Talent, hard work and sheer tenacity are all crucial to career success. 事业要成功，才能、勤奋和

顽强的意志都至关重要。

shell [ʃel] *n.* 壳,贝壳

诵读 The solid feel of the car's shell is impressive. 这辆汽车的外壳坚固感十足,令人印象深刻。

shelter [ˈʃeltə] *n.* 掩蔽处,保护 *vt.* 掩蔽,庇护

诵读 When it rained I rigged up a partial shelter with a tarpaulin. 下雨的时候,我用油布草草搭了一个能简单避雨的棚子。

shield [ʃiːld] *n.* 防护物,盾 *vt.* 保护,防护

诵读 The gunman used the hostages as a human shield. 持枪歹徒用人质作人体盾牌。

shipment [ˈʃɪpmənt] *n.* 装船,装运;装载的货物

诵读 The goods are ready for shipment. 货物备妥待运。

shiver [ˈʃɪvə] *vi.&n.* 战栗,发抖

诵读 A sudden gust of cold wind made me shiver. 一股突然刮来的冷风吹得我打哆嗦。

shopkeeper [ˈʃɒpˌkiːpə] *n.* 店主

诵读 That shopkeeper is a scoundrel in the town. 那家商店的老板是这个镇上的地头蛇。

shortage [ˈʃɔːtɪdʒ] *n.* 不足,缺少

拓展 shortcoming *n.* 短处,缺点;shorthand *n.* 速记;shortcut *n.* 捷径

诵读 Any shortage could push up grain prices. 任何一种短缺都会抬高粮食价格。

shoulder [ˈʃəʊldə] *n.* 肩 *vt.* 肩负,承担

搭配 shoulder to shoulder 肩并肩地,齐心协力地

诵读 He was wounded in the shoulder by a ricochet. 他被一颗跳弹打伤了肩膀。

shrink [ʃrɪŋk] *vi.* 缩水

僻义 *vi.* 收缩,减少

诵读 Washing wool in hot water will shrink it. 在热水中洗毛织品会使其缩水。

sink [sɪŋk] *vi.* (使)下沉,下落

诵读 In a naval battle your aim is to sink the enemy's ship. 在海战中,你的目标就是击沉敌船。

sigh [saɪ] *n.&vi.* 叹息,叹气

诵读 The country's politicians are already heaving a collective sigh of relief. 该国的政界人士均已松了口气。

sightseeing [ˈsaɪtˌsiːɪŋ] *n.* 观光,游览

诵读 Sightseeing is best done either by tour bus or by bicycles. 最好的观光方式是乘坐旅游巴士或骑自行车。

signal [ˈsɪgnəl] *n.* 信号,暗号 *vi.* 发信号

诵读 The transmitters will send a signal automatically to a local base station. 发射台会自动将信号发射到地方基站。

signature [ˈsɪgnɪtʃə] *n.* 签名;签字;鲜明特色

诵读 Rabbit stew is one of chef Giancarlo Moeri's signature dishes. 炖野兔是厨师詹卡洛·莫里的招牌菜之一。

significance [sɪgˈnɪfɪkəns] *n.* 意义,含义;重要性

拓展 significant *a.* 有意义的;重大的,重要的

诵读 Ideas about the social significance of religion have changed over time. 关于宗教的社会意义的看法已经随着时间的变迁而改变。

signify [ˈsɪgnɪfaɪ] *vt.* 表示,有重要性

诵读 It doesn't signify, so you needn't worry about it. 这无所谓,你不必担心。

simplicity [sɪmˈplɪsɪti] *n.* 简单,朴素;直率

拓展 simplify *vt.* 简化;simply *a.* 简单地;完全,简直;仅仅

诵读 Using plastic to pay for an order is simplicity itself. 用信用卡支付订单是很简单的事。

simulate [ˈsɪmjʊleɪt] *vt.* 模仿,冒充

巧记 simulated test 模拟测试

辨析 同形词 stimulate *v.* 刺激,激励,鼓舞

诵读 Smoke was used to simulate steam coming from a smashed radiator. 用烟来模拟从撞碎的散热器中冒出的蒸汽。

simultaneous [ˌsɪməlˈteɪnjəs] *a.* 同时的

诵读 The conference hall is provided with facilities for simultaneous interpretation in five languages. 这个会议大厅配有五种语言的同声传译设备。

sin [sɪn] *n.* 罪恶 *vi.* 犯罪

诵读 The Vatican's teaching on abortion is clear: it is a sin. 罗马教廷对堕胎的教义非常清楚:这是罪过。

sincere [sɪnˈsɪə] *a.* 诚挚的,真实的

诵读 There was a sincere expression of friendliness on both their faces. 他们俩的脸上都流露出真挚友好

的表情。

single [ˈsɪŋgl] *a.* 单人的，单个的；未婚的

拓展 singular *a.* 非凡的，卓越的；单数的

诵读 He was single-mindedly devoted to the hastening of freedom for the oppressed. 他一心一意致力于让被压迫者早日获得自由。

site [saɪt] *n.* 位置，场所，地点

诵读 A guide gives a brief talk on the history of the site. 导游简要地介绍了那个遗址的历史。

situated [ˈsɪtjʊeɪtɪd] *a.* 坐落在……的

诵读 The new store is better situated to attract customers. 新店所处的位置优越，更能吸引客源。

skeptical [ˈskeptɪkəl] *a.* 怀疑的

搭配 be skeptical about… 对……表示怀疑

诵读 They are skeptical about how much will be accomplished by legislation. 他们对于立法成效心存疑虑。

skilled [skɪld] *a.* 熟练的，有技能的

拓展 skillful *a.* 灵巧的，娴熟的

诵读 He is a hard worker and a skilled gardener. 他工作很努力，对园艺很在行。

skim [skɪm] *vi.* 轻轻掠过

诵读 It's important for you to skim through the text. 浏览课文对你来说很重要。

skip [skɪp] *vi.* 略过，跳过 *n.* 跳跃 *vt.* 故意忽略

诵读 The parents want their child to skip to the second grade. 这家父母希望他们孩子能跳级到二年级。

slave [sleɪv] *n.* 奴隶 *vt.* 做苦工，拼命地干

诵读 Liverpool grew fat on the basis of the slave trade. 利物浦是靠奴隶贸易肥起来的。

slack [slæk] *a.* 懈怠的；萧条的 *n.* 淡季；便裤

诵读 He had never let a colleague see him slacking. 他从未在哪个同事面前表现出丝毫懈怠。

sly [slaɪ] *a.* 狡猾的，偷偷摸摸的

诵读 He's a sly old beggar if ever there was one. 他确确实实是个老奸巨猾的家伙。

smart [smɑːt] *a.* 漂亮的，聪明的；巧妙的

诵读 Investors are playing it cautious, and they're playing it smart. 投资者审慎精明地行事。

smell [smel] *n.* 气味，嗅觉 *v.* 闻到

诵读 I could smell the honeyed ripeness of melons and peaches. 我能闻到瓜桃熟透了的香甜味道。

smooth [smuːð] *a.* 光滑的，平稳的，顺利的

诵读 The ride was smooth until they got into the merchant ship's wake. 航行一直很顺利，直到他们碰上了商船的尾流。

smash [smæʃ] *vt.&n.* 打碎，粉碎

诵读 He was near to death after a car smash. 他差点在一场撞车事故中丧命。

snap [snæp] *vt.* 咬住，折断 *a.* 匆忙的 *n.* 匆忙

僻义 snap decision 仓促的决定

诵读 I could obtain with the snap of my fingers anything I chose. 我不费吹灰之力就可以得到我看中的任何东西。

snatch [snætʃ] *n.&vt.* 攫取，抢夺

诵读 She managed to snatch the gun from his hand. 她设法从他手里夺过了枪。

society [səˈsaɪəti] *n.* 社会，团体；协会

拓展 social *a.* 社会的；socialism *n.* 社会主义

诵读 She had an entree into the city's cultivated society. 她进入了该城的上流社会。

soft [sɒft] *a.* 软的；温柔的；不含酒精的

诵读 The President could continue to bash Democrats as being soft on crime. 总统可能会继续抨击民主党人对待犯罪活动心慈手软。

solid [ˈsɒlɪd] *a.* 固体的，结实的，可靠的 *n.* 固体

拓展 solidarity *n.* 团结

诵读 The car park was absolutely packed solid with people. 停车场被人挤得水泄不通。

soak [səʊk] *vt.&vi.* 浸泡，浸湿，浸透

搭配 soak up 吸收

诵读 The cells will promptly start to soak up moisture. 细胞会立即开始吸收水分。

sober [ˈsəʊbə] *a.* 清醒的；认真的，冷静的

诵读 He was left to sober up in a police cell. 他被留在一间拘留室里醒酒。

sociable [ˈsəʊʃəbl] *a.* 好交际的，友好的，合群的

诵读 She's a sociable child who'll talk to anyone. 她是个合群的孩子，跟谁都有话说。

soil [sɔɪl] *n.* 泥土，土地

僻义 *vt.* 弄脏

诵读 The soil washed from the hills is silting up the

hydroelectric dams. 从山上冲刷下来的泥土就要让水电大坝淤塞了。

solar [ˈsəʊlə] *a.* 太阳的，日光的

诵读 Saturn is the second biggest planet in the solar system. 土星是太阳系中的第二大行星。

sole [səʊl] *a.* 单独的，唯一的

诵读 The current sole superpower is far from being a disinterested observer. 当前唯一的超级大国远不是一个公正的旁观者。

solitary [ˈsɒlɪtəri] *a.* 独自的，独立的；单一的

诵读 His evenings were spent in solitary drinking. 他晚上的时间都是靠独自喝闷酒打发。

solemn [ˈsɒləm] *a.* 庄严的，隆重的

诵读 Erica was solemn, pulling at her blonde curls. 埃丽卡表情严肃，扯着自己卷曲的金发。

sore [sɔː] *a.* 疼痛的；痛心的 *n.* 痛处，疮口

诵读 Sore throats may be relieved by cold compresses. 冷敷能缓解喉咙痛。

sound [saʊnd] *n.* 声音 *v.* 响，听上去

辨义 *a.* 完好的；正当的

搭配 safe and sound 安然无恙的

诵读 This may sound trivial, but I assure you it is quite important! 这听上去也许微不足道，但是，相信我，它十分重要！

source [sɔːs] *n.* 源泉；来源

诵读 We're interested in the source of these fictitious rumours. 我们对这些子虚乌有的谣言从何而来很感兴趣。

special [ˈspeʃəl] *a.* 特殊的；附加的

拓展 specialize *vi.* 专门从事；speciality *n.* 专长；特产

诵读 A special locking system means the door cannot be opened accidentally. 特殊的锁控系统使门不会被意外打开。

speech [spiːtʃ] *n.* 演讲，言语

诵读 He went even further in his speech to the conference. 他在大会发言中作了更进一步的阐述。

speed [spiːd] *n.* 速度，迅速 *vt.&vi.* 急行；加速

搭配 speed up 加速；at the speed of…以……的速度

诵读 He pushed everyone full speed ahead until production hit a bottleneck. 他催促所有人拼命干活，直到生产遭遇瓶颈。

spirit [ˈspɪrɪt] *n.* 精神，志气，情绪，烈酒

拓展 spiritual *a.* 精神的

诵读 I like to think of myself as a free spirit. 我愿意把自己看成是个无拘无束的人。

splendid [ˈsplendɪd] *a.* 壮丽的，极好的

诵读 The house commanded some splendid views of Delaware Bay. 从这座房子可以俯瞰特拉华湾壮丽的景致。

spoon [spuːn] *n.* 匙，调羹

诵读 Smooth the mixture with the back of a soup spoon. 用汤勺的背面把混合料抹平。

sport [spɔːt] *n.* 运动

诵读 I don't think it has fundamentally altered the sport. 我认为它并没有从根本上改变这项运动。

spread [spred] *vt.&n.* 散布，传播

诵读 The conditions are ripe for the spread of disease. 这种疾病传播的条件已经成熟。

spring [sprɪŋ] *n.* 春天，跳，泉

辨义 *vi.* 跳跃

诵读 The blustery winds of spring had dropped to a gentle breeze. 呼啸的春风已经减弱，成了习习的微风。

spacious [ˈspeɪʃəs] *a.* 广阔的，宽敞的

巧记 词根 space 空间+后缀 -ious

诵读 They specified a spacious entrance hall. 他们专门指定要一个宽敞的大门厅。

specific [spɪˈsɪfɪk] *a.* 明确的，特定的

拓展 specification *n.* 详述；规格，说明书，规范

诵读 Your decision must be translated into specific, concrete actions. 你的决定必须转化为具体明确的行动。

specimen [ˈspesɪmən] *n.* 标本，样本

诵读 Job applicants have to submit a specimen of handwriting. 求职者必须要提交一份笔迹样本。

spectacle [ˈspektəkl] *n.* 眼镜，景象；奇观

拓展 spectacular *a.* 壮观的，引人注目的

诵读 It was a spectacle not to be missed. 这是个不容错过的奇观。

speculate [ˈspekjʊleɪt] *vi.&vt.* 思索；推测

诵读 It is premature to speculate about the resumption

of negotiations. 现在猜测谈判是否会重新开始还为时过早。

sphere [sfɪə] *n.* 球，范围，领域

诵读 This area was formerly within the sphere of influence of the U.S. 这一地区先前属于美国的势力范围。

spill [spɪl] *vt.* 溢出，溅出 *n.* 摔下，跌下

诵读 it is no use crying over the spilt milk. 覆水难收。

spoil [spɔɪl] *vt.* 损坏，搞错；宠坏

诵读 It's important not to let mistakes spoil your life. 重要的是不要让错误毁了你的生活。

spokesman [ˈspəʊksmən] *n.* 发言人

诵读 The spokesman said the tone of the letter was very friendly. 发言人说信函的语气非常友好。

sponsor [ˈspɒnsə] *n.* 发起人 *vt.* 发起；赞助

拓展 spontaneous *a.* 自发的，自然产生的

诵读 We have to make the states that sponsor terrorism pay a price. 我们必须让那些支持恐怖主义的国家付出代价。

sprout [spraʊt] *v.* 发芽 *n.* 新芽，嫩苗

巧记 春天(spring)里，树木花草都露出(out)新芽

诵读 When you sprout seeds their nutritional content increases. 让种子发芽后，营养含量会提高。

spur [spɜː] *n.* 靴刺，刺激 *vt.* 刺激，激励

诵读 It wasn't a spur-of-the-moment decision. We discussed it in detail beforehand. 这可不是头脑一热做出的决定。我们事先仔细地讨论过。

spy [spaɪ] *n.* 间谍 *vt.* 刺探；发现

squeeze [skwiːz] *vt.* 压榨，挤 *n.* 榨取，勒索

诵读 The Government's financial squeeze had killed the scheme off. 政府的财政困难已使这个计划成为泡影。

stand [stænd] *vi.* 站立 *n.* 台，座

辨义 *vt.* 坚持，忍受

搭配 stand for 代替，代表；stand out 突出，显眼；stand up to 勇敢地面对，坚持抵抗，经得起

诵读 You have to know where to stand for a good viewpoint. 你得知道站在哪里观察角度比较理想。

standard [ˈstændəd] *n.* 标准，规则 *a.* 标准的

诵读 The standard of living today is on the edge of subsistence. 现在的生活水平几乎快要无法维持生计。

state [steɪt] *n.* 状态，州 *vt.* 陈述，说明

拓展 station *n.* 车站，站，局，地位；statement *n.* 声明，陈述；statesman *n.* 政治家

诵读 The government decreed a state of emergency. 政府下令进入紧急状态。

storm [stɔːm] *n.* 暴风雨

诵读 The worst of the storm is yet to come. 最猛烈的暴风雨就要来了。

storey [ˈstɔːri] *n.* 楼层

诵读 The multi-storey pagoda came to Japan from china in the sixth century. 公元 6 世纪，多层宝塔从中国传入日本。

straight [streɪt] *a.* 整齐的；正直的 *ad.* 直接

诵读 He finished his conversation and stood up, looking straight at me. 他说完话站起来，直视着我。

strength [streŋθ] *n.* 实力，力量

诵读 Torn muscles retract, and lose strength, structure, and tightness. 撕裂的肌肉会收缩，丧失原来的力量、结构和紧实度。

strict [strɪkt] *a.* 严格的，严谨的，精确的

搭配 be strict with sb. 对某人很严厉

诵读 All members of the association adhere to a strict code of practice. 协会的所有成员都遵守严格的行为规范。

strike [straɪk] *vt.* 撞；罢工；打动；发现 *n.* 罢工

诵读 The strike has taken on overtones of a civil rights campaign. 罢工带上了民权运动的意味。

struggle [ˈstrʌgl] *n.&vi.* 斗争，奋斗，努力

诵读 It's a constant struggle to try to keep them up to par. 要让他们达标，需要不断努力。

stable [ˈsteɪbl] *a.* 稳定的，安定的 *n.* 马厩，马棚

拓展 stability *n.* 稳定，安定；a stable of 一群，一批

诵读 As chief executive, he assembled a polished stable of celebrities. 作为首席执行官，他手下云集了一批优雅的名人。

stack [stæk] *n.* 堆 *vt.* 堆积，堆起

诵读 He ordered them to stack up pillows behind his back. 他命令他们把几个枕头叠放在自己的背后。

staff [stɑːf] *n.* 全体职工

诵读 Free room and board are provided for all hotel staff. 宾馆的所有员工都可享受免费膳宿。

stain [steɪn] *n.* 污点，瑕疵 *vt.* 沾污；染色

诵读 A dark red stain was spreading across his shirt. 一块深红色的污渍正在他的衬衫上渗开。

standpoint [ˈstændpɔɪnt] *n.* 立场，观点

诵读 He will never be bullied into any change of his standpoint. 要想硬逼他改变自己的立场是办不到的。

stare [steə] *vi.* 盯，凝视

搭配 stare at 盯着，凝视

诵读 With a glazed stare she revived for one last instant. 她最后清醒了一会儿，眼神呆滞。

startle [ˈstɑːtl] *vt.* 惊吓，使吃惊

诵读 They have nightmares, they startle easily. 他们常做噩梦，且经常从梦中惊醒。

statistical [stəˈtɪstɪkəl] *a.* 统计的，统计学的

诵读 We need to back that suspicion up with statistical proof. 我们需要用统计数据来证实那一猜测。

statue [ˈstætjuː] *n.* 塑像，雕像

诵读 A small crowd attempted to pull down a statue. 一小伙人试图推倒一尊塑像。

status [ˈsteɪtəs] *n.* 地位，身份，状况

诵读 Despite her status, the Duchess will not be given preferential treatment. 虽然地位显赫，但是公爵夫人并不会得到优待。

statute [ˈstætjuːt] *n.* 法令，法规，规则，条例

诵读 Penalties are laid down in the statute. 法规中有关惩罚措施的规定。

steady [ˈstedi] *a.* 稳定的，坚定的 *vt.*(使)稳固

诵读 It's been hard to get a steady fix on what's going on. 要对正在发生的事情保持持续的关注和了解并不容易。

steep [stiːp] *a.* 陡峭的；险峻的

诵读 She started once again on the steep upward climb. 她又开始沿着陡峭的山路往上爬。

steer [stɪə] *vt.* 驾驶，引导

诵读 The chairman was able to steer the committee towards a decision. 主席能引导委员会做出决定。

stem [stem] *n.* 茎，干

搭配 stem from 起源于

诵读 He told the magazine in an exclusive interview: "All my problems stem from drink." 他在接受一家杂志社的独家采访时说："我所有的问题都是饮酒造成的。"

stick [stɪk] *n.* 棍，棒 *vt.* 刺，扎

拓展 sticky *a.* 黏性的；棘手的；泥泞的

诵读 She poked and shifted things with the tip of her walking stick. 她用手杖尖翻拨挪动东西。

stiff [stɪf] *a.* 硬的，拘谨的；艰难的

诵读 A stiff knee following surgery forced her to walk with a limp. 手术后她的膝盖活动不便，走路时一瘸一拐。

stir [stɜː] *vt.* 搅拌，摇动；激动，鼓动

诵读 Stir the sauce and pour it over the top. 搅拌调味汁，把它浇在上面。

stock [stɒk] *n.* 库存，股票，公债 *vt.* 储存

拓展 stocking *n.* 长(筒)袜

诵读 She built up her fortune by cannily playing the stock market. 她炒股有方，发了大财。

storage [ˈstɔːrɪdʒ] *n.* 贮藏，保管；库房

诵读 The space underneath could be used as a storage area. 底下的空间可用作储藏区。

straightforward [streɪtˈfɔːwəd] *a.* 简单的 *ad.* 坦率地

诵读 It was not as straightforward as we were led to believe. 这事并非如我们所误以为的那样简单。

strain [streɪn] *vt.* 拉紧；扭伤 *n.* 拉紧；负担

诵读 There was a strain of bitterness in his voice. 他的声音听起来有些愤愤不平。

stranger [ˈstreɪndʒə] *n.* 陌生人

诵读 Telling a complete stranger about your life is difficult. 要对一个素昧平生的人谈自己的生活经历是比较困难。

strategy [ˈstrætɪdʒi] *n.* 战略，对策，政策

诵读 Yesterday's meeting was intended to plot a survival strategy for the company. 昨天的会议旨在制订公司的生存策略。

straw [strɔː] *n.* 稻草，吸管

诵读 I stumbled through mud to a yard strewn with straw. 我跌跌撞撞地趟过泥地来到一个铺满稻草的场院。

stream [striːm] *n.* 小河，溪流 *vi.* 涌出

拓展 streamline *a.* 流线型的 *vt.* 使成流线型；使合理化

诵读 There was a small stream at the end of the garden. 花园的尽头有一条小河。

strengthen [ˈstreŋθn] *vt.* 加强，巩固

诵读 His visit is intended to strengthen ties between the two countries. 他此次访问旨在增进两国间的关系。

stress [stres] *n.* 压力；重要性

辨义 *vt.* 强调

诵读 Stress may act as a trigger for these illnesses. 压力可能会成为引发这些疾病的原因。

striking [ˈstraɪkɪŋ] *a.* 显著的；惹人注目的

诵读 I believe we are within striking distance of an agreement. 我相信我们即将达成协议。

string [strɪŋ] *n.* 弦，线，细绳 *vt.* 缚，捆

诵读 The band was forced to cancel a string of live dates. 乐队被迫取消了一系列的现场表演。

strive [straɪv] *vi.* 奋斗，努力

诵读 We encourage all members to strive for the highest standards. 我们鼓励所有成员为达到最高标准而努力。

stroke [strəʊk] *n.* 报时的钟声；中风；举动，（突发的）好事 *vt.* 抚摸

诵读 It didn't rain, which turned out to be a stroke of luck. 天没下雨，结果成了件幸事。

structure [ˈstrʌktʃə] *n.* 结构，构造 *vt.* 构造，建造

诵读 The theatre is a futuristic steel and glass structure. 这家剧院是钢筋和玻璃结构的未来派建筑。

stubborn [ˈstʌbən] *a.* 顽固的，倔强的

诵读 His opponents viewed him as stubborn, dogmatic, and inflexible. 反对者们认为他固执、教条、僵化。

stuff [stʌf] *n.* 原料，东西 *vt.* 填满，塞满

诵读 I don't want any more of that heavy stuff. 我再也不想碰那种麻烦事了。

succeed [səkˈsiːd] *vi.* 成功 *vt.* 接替

诵读 He was too inexperienced and too inexpert to succeed. 他太缺乏经验，太不熟练，难以成功。

suppose [səˈpəʊz] *vt.* 料想，以为

诵读 In a way, I suppose I'm frightened of failing. 我想我有点惧怕失败。

surface [ˈsɜːfɪs] *n.* 表面，外表

诵读 Rumours of financial scandals have come bubbling back to the surface. 有关财务丑闻的谣言接连不断地冒出来。

subjective [sʌbˈdʒektɪv] *a.* 主观（上）的，个人的

诵读 We know that taste in art is a subjective matter. 我们知道艺术品位因人而异。

submarine [ˈsʌbməriːn] *n.* 潜水艇 *a.* 海底的

巧记 前缀 sub-在下方+词根 marine 水=水下方

诵读 We were trying to plot the course of the submarine. 我们试图标绘出潜艇的航线图。

submerge [səbˈmɜːdʒ] *vt.* 沉没，潜入

诵读 The waters were rising about the rock and would soon submerge it. 水快涨到跟岩石一样高了，很快就会淹没它。

submit [səbˈmɪt] *vi.* 使服从 *vt.* 呈送

巧记 前缀 sub-在下方+词根 mit 传送→从下面呈送上来

搭配 submit to 屈服

诵读 He was losing the fight but he would not submit. 他战败了，但不屈服。

subsidy [ˈsʌbsɪdi] *n.* 补助金；津贴费

诵读 There were also pledges to soften the impact of the subsidy cuts on the poorer regions. 他们还承诺要减轻削减补贴给较贫困地区带来的影响。

substance [ˈsʌbstəns] *n.* 物质，本质；主旨，资产

拓展 substantial *a.* 实质的；相当的；显著的

诵读 This substance has now been cloned by molecular biologists. 该物质现在已被分子生物学家克隆。

substitute [ˈsʌbstɪtjuːt] *n.* 替身；代用品 *vt.* 代替

搭配 substitute (...) for 代替，替换

诵读 Reduced-calorie cheese is a great subs tute for crean cheese. 低卡路里干酪是奶油干酪的极好替代品。

subtle [ˈsʌtl] *a.* 精巧的，微妙的

诵读 I even began to exploit him in subtle ways. 我甚至开始巧妙地利用他。

subtract [səbˈtrækt] *vt.* 减去

搭配 subtract... from... 减去

诵读 Please subtract a quarter of the money for your own use. 请从这些钱里减去四分之一，留给你自己使用。

suburb [ˈsʌbɜːb] n. 市郊，郊区

诵读 It had become almost a dormitory suburb of the city. 它几乎成为城市的一个市郊住宅区。

succession [səkˈseʃən] n. 连续，系列，继承

拓展 successive a. 接连的，连续的；successor n. 接替的人或事物，继任者

诵读 The road is a succession of hairpin bends, hills, and blind corners. 这条路上急转弯、坡道和死拐角一个接一个。

suck [sʌk] vt.&n. 吸，舐

诵读 Bees suck honey from flowers. 蜜蜂从花中吸吮蜜汁。

sue [sjuː] vt. 控告，起诉

诵读 She sued the company for racial discrimination. 她以种族歧视为由对公司起诉。

suffice [səˈfaɪs] vi. 足够，足以

拓展 sufficient a. 足够的，充分的

诵读 Suffice to say, it was more than a couple of years ago! 我只想说，那是几年前的事了！

suicide [ˈsjuɪsaɪd] n. 自杀

诵读 They say it would be political suicide for the party to abstain. 他们说这个政党弃权无异于自毁政治前程。

sum [sʌm] n. 总数，金额；要旨 vi. 合计，总计

拓展 summarize v. 概括；summary n. 摘要 a. 概括的

搭配 to sum up 总之

诵读 The sum of evidence points to the crime resting on them. 所有证据表明该起犯罪乃他们所为。

summit [ˈsʌmɪt] n. 顶，巅峰

诵读 Never before has a summit had such a crowded agenda. 以前从来没有一次峰会的日程排得这么满。

summon [ˈsʌmən] vt. 召唤；传讯，鼓起（勇气）

诵读 The oddest events will summon up memories. 那些最稀奇古怪的事情会唤起人们的记忆。

sunrise [ˈsʌnraɪz] n. 日出，朝霞

诵读 There was a spectacular sunrise yesterday. 昨天的朝霞很绚烂。

superb [ˌsjuːˈpɜːb] a. 极好的，华丽的

诵读 It makes a superb filling for cakes and sponges. 它非常适合做蛋糕和软布丁的馅儿。

superficial [ˌsjuːpəˈfɪʃəl] a. 表面的；肤浅的

诵读 Their arguments do not withstand the most superficial scrutiny. 他们的论据经不起一点推敲。

superfluous [sjuːˈpɜːfluəs] a. 多余的，过剩的

诵读 I rid myself of many superfluous belongings and habits that bothered me. 我把很多无用的物品都丢掉了，并且改掉了一些让我烦心的习惯。

superior [sjuːˈpɪərɪə] a. 优良的 n. 上级；长者

拓展 superiority n. 优势，高傲，傲慢

诵读 Our superior technology is our ace in the hole. 我们卓越的技术是我们的法宝。

supervise [ˈsjuːpəvaɪz] vt. 管理，监督

巧记 前缀 super-超，高+词根vis看=从上看→监督

诵读 I supervise the packing of all mail orders. 我负责监督所有邮购商品的包装过程。

supplement [ˈsʌplɪment] n. 增刊；附录，补充 vt. 补充

诵读 Some people may be entitled to a housing benefit supplement. 有些人可能有资格拿到住房补贴。

suppress [səˈpres] vt. 压制，忍住；查禁

诵读 He continued to suppress the people and serve the imperialists. 他继续镇压人民，为帝国主义效劳。

supreme [sjuːˈpriːm] a. 最重要的；最高的

诵读 Sovereign power will continue to lie with the Supreme People's Assembly. 主权将继续掌握在最高人民议会手中。

surge [sɜːdʒ] vi. 汹涌；蜂拥而至 n. 巨浪；彭湃

诵读 Specialists see various reasons for the recent surge in inflation. 专家们认为目前通货膨胀加剧有多种原因。

surgeon [ˈsɜːdʒən] n. 外科医生

拓展 surgery n. 外科，外科学；手术室，诊疗室

诵读 Only your family doctor can refer you to a surgeon. 只有你的家庭医生才能把你转诊给外科医生。

surname [ˈsɜːneɪm] n. 姓

诵读 The majority of British women adopt their husband's surname when they marry. 大多数英国女性结婚后随夫姓。

surpass [səˈpɑːs] vt. 超过，胜过

诵读 He hopes one day to surpass the world record. 他希望有一天能刷新世界纪录。

surplus [ˈsɜːpləs] *n.* 剩余，余额 *a.* 剩余的

诵读 Japan is in the enviable position of having a budget surplus. 日本的预算盈余令人羡慕。

survey [səˈveɪ] *vt.&n.* 俯瞰；调查；勘定

诵读 Our survey revealed that these allergies were mainly one-offs. 我们的调查显示这些过敏多为一次性反应。

survival [səˈvaɪvəl] *n.* 幸存，幸存者，残存物

诵读 If cancers are spotted early there's a high chance of survival. 如果癌症在早期发现的话，存活的概率会很高。

suspect [səˈspekt] *vt.* 猜想；怀疑 *a.* 可疑的 *n.* 嫌疑犯

拓展 suspicion *n.* 怀疑，猜疑；suspicious *a.* 可疑的，多疑的，疑心的

诵读 I suspect he isn't altogether unhappy about my absence. 我猜想他对我的缺席并没有感到很不高兴。

suspend [səˈspend] *vt.* 悬，挂；暂停，取消；推迟

诵读 Ministers took the floor to denounce the decision to suspend constitutional rule. 几位部长发言谴责暂停宪制的决定。

sustain [səˈsteɪn] *vt.* 支撑；维持，经受，忍耐

诵读 There's a sufficiency of drama in these lives to sustain your interest. 这些人的生活充满了戏剧性，总能让你兴趣盎然。

sweep [swiːp] *vt.* 打扫，席卷；扫过

诵读 Get a broom and sweep up that glass, will you? 拿扫帚把那些玻璃清扫干净好吗？

swallow [ˈswɒləʊ] *n.* 燕子

僻义 *v.* 轻信；忍受

诵读 I too found this story a little hard to swallow. 我也觉得这件事有点难以置信。

swarm [swɔːm] *n.* 蜂群；一大群 *vi.* 挤满；云集

诵读 A swarm of people encircled the hotel. 一大群人围住了这个酒店。

sweat [swet] *n.* 汗 *vi.&vt.* （使）出汗

诵读 He awoke from his sleep in a cold sweat. 他从睡梦中醒来，浑身冒着冷汗。

swell [swel] *n.&vi.* 膨胀；增大

诵读 The human population swelled, at least temporarily, as migrants moved south. 随着移居者南移，人口出现膨胀，至少是暂时性膨胀。

swift [swɪft] *a.&ad.* 快的（地）；敏捷的（地） *n.* 雨燕

诵读 He is very sharp, a quick thinker and swift with repartee. 他非常机敏，反应很快，并且能说会道。

sympathetic [ˌsɪmpəˈθetɪk] *a.* 有同情心的

拓展 sympathize *vi.* 同情；共鸣，赞成；sympathy *n.* 同情，赞同，慰问

诵读 Build her up with kindness and a sympathetic ear. 用友善和富有同情心的倾听来重拾她的信心。

symphony [ˈsɪmfəni] *n.* 交响乐，交响曲

诵读 The symphony does require a largish group of players. 这首交响曲确实需要为数不少的一组演奏者。

symposium [sɪmˈpəʊziəm] *n.* 讨论会，专题报告会；专题论文集

诵读 The symposium on AIDS research lasted two days. 这场关于艾滋病研究的报告会持续了两天。

symptom [ˈsɪmptəm] *n.* 症状；征兆

诵读 It is probable that the medication will suppress the symptom without treating the condition. 这种药物有可能治标不治本。

systematic [ˌsɪstəˈmætɪk] *a.* 系统的，有组织的

诵读 They had not found any evidence of a systematic attempt to rig the ballot. 他们没有发现任何证据证明有人企图全面操纵投票。

sample [ˈsɑːmpl] *n.* 样品，实例

诵读 We're giving away 2,000 free samples. 我们正在赠送 2 000 件免费样品。

satisfactory [ˌsætɪsˈfæktəri] *a.* 令人满意的

拓展 satisfaction *n.* 满意

诵读 Theirs had been a happy and satisfactory marriage. 他们的婚姻曾经一直幸福美满。

scene [siːn] *n.* 景色，景象

诵读 You can just picture the scene, can't you? 你完全能想象出那个画面，对吗？

score [skɔː] *n.* 得分；二十

僻义 *v.* 判分

诵读 The weakest students can end up with a negative score. 最差的学生可能会以负分收场。

social [ˈsəʊʃəl] *a.* 社会的；交际的

拓展 sociology *n.* 社会学

诵读 He wants companies to follow the European model of social responsibility. 他希望各公司能够以欧洲公司为榜样，承担社会责任。

solve [sɒlv] *vt.* 解决，解答

拓展 solution *n.* 解答，解决办法

诵读 I dreamed up a plan to solve both problems at once. 我想出了一个方案，可以同时解决两个问题。

sophomore [ˈsɒfəmɔ:] *n.* 二年级学生

spare [speə] *a.* 多余的 *vt.* 节约

诵读 He could have taken a spare key. 他原本可以带上一把备用钥匙的。

sparkle [ˈspɑ:kl] *vi.* 闪耀

诵读 The jewels on her fingers sparkled. 她手指上的珠宝闪闪发光。

specialist [ˈspeʃəlɪst] *n.* 专家

诵读 The peasants looked upon him as a specialist. 农民们把他看作专家。

species [ˈspi:ʃi:z] *n.*（物）种，种类

诵读 Pandas are an endangered species. 大熊猫是濒危物种。

specify [ˈspesɪfaɪ] *vt.* 指定，详细说明

诵读 Each recipe specifies the size of eggs to be used. 每种食谱都具体说明了所用鸡蛋的大小。

spectator [spekˈteɪtə] *n.* 观众，旁观者

巧记 词根 spect看+后缀-ate+or 人

诵读 Thirty thousand spectators watched the final game. 三万观众观看了那场决赛。

speed [spi:d] *n.* 速度

spell [spel] *vt.* 拼写，招致

拓展 spelling *n.* 拼法，拼写法

style [staɪl] *n.* 风格，文体

subsequent [ˈsʌbsɪkwənt] *a.* 随后的，后来的

诵读 There was an increase of population in subsequent years. 随后几年出现人口增长。

suffer [ˈsʌfə] *vi.* 遭受；忍受

搭配 suffer from 遭受

诵读 Millions more suffer from serious sleep deprivation caused by long work hours. 还有数百万人由于工作时数长导致严重睡眠不足。

surroundings [səˈraʊndɪŋz] *n.* 周围的事物，环境

诵读 Schumacher adapted effortlessly to his new surroundings. 舒马赫毫不费力地适应了新环境。

survive [səˈvaɪv] *vi.* 幸免于，幸存

辨义 *vt.* 战胜

诵读 Those organisms that are most suited to the environment will be those that will survive. 最适应环境的将是那些存活下来的生物。

symbol [ˈsɪmbəl] *n.* 符号，标志

诵读 A symbol appears in an upper quadrant of the screen. 一个符号出现在屏幕上方的象限里。

system [ˈsɪstəm] *n.* 系统，体系

拓展 systematic *a.* 系统的

诵读 The new system is still in the planning stages. 新体系仍处于规划阶段。

高 频 词 汇

sacred [ˈseɪkrɪd] *a.* 神圣的；宗教的

诵读 The couple hold the unfashionable view that marriage is a sacred union. 夫妇俩对婚姻的看法很传统，认为婚姻是神圣的结合。

salute [səˈlu:t] *vt.&n.* 敬礼；迎接，欢迎

诵读 Merchant ships salute each other by dipping the flag. 商船互相点旗致敬。

salvation [sælˈveɪʃən] *n.* 拯救，救助

诵读 The church's message of salvation has changed the lives of many. 基督教中耶稣拯救灵魂的教义改变了很多人的生活。

sanction [ˈsæŋkʃən] *n.* 处罚，制裁

诵读 The Security Council will consider taking future actions against sanction-busters. 安理会考虑未来采取措施打击破坏制裁的人。

saturate [ˈsætʃəreɪt] *vt.* 浸透，使饱和 *a.* 浸透的

诵读 Saturate the meat in the mixture of oil and herbs. 把肉浸泡在油和作料混合成的卤汁里。

scandal [ˈskændl] *n.* 丑闻，诽谤，耻辱

诵读 The government began to unravel because of a banking scandal. 政府由于一起金融丑闻而开始瓦解。

scar [skɑ:] *n.* 疤，伤痕 *vt.* 使留下伤痕，结疤

诵读 Her face was disfigured by a long red scar. 脸上一条红色长疤使她破相了。

scenery [ˈsi:nəri] *n.* 风景，舞台布景

诵读 The higher we climbed, the more awe-inspiring the scenery became. 我们爬得越高，风景越是让人叹绝。

seam [si:m] *n.* 缝，接缝 *vt.* 裂开，缝合

诵读 Use vinyl seam adhesive where vinyls overlap. 塑料布相叠处用塑料封口胶粘起来。

segment [ˈsegmənt] *n.* 段落，部分 *vt.* 分割，划分

诵读 The company dominates this segment of the market. 这家公司控制着这一部分市场。

segregate [ˈsegrɪgeɪt] *vt.* 使……分开，隔离

诵读 They segregate you from the rest of the community. 他们把你与社团的其他成员隔离开。

semiconductor [ˌsemɪkənˈdʌktə] *n.* 半导体

巧记 前缀 semi-半+ 词根 conduct 引导

诵读 This is a semiconductor integrated circuit. 这是一个半导体集成电路。

sham [ʃæm] *n.* 赝品，骗子 *vi.* 假装 *a.* 虚假的

诵读 The latest crime figures are a complete sham. 最新的犯罪统计数字完全是捏造的。

shave [ʃeɪv] *vt.* 剃，刮，刨，削 *n.* 刮脸，剃胡子

shed [ʃed] *n.* 棚，小屋

shove [ʃʌv] *vt.&n.* 猛推

诵读 She will not shove the heavy load onto others. 她不愿意把重担推给别人。

shrewd [ʃru:d] *a.* 机灵的，敏锐的；精明的

诵读 He enjoyed the play's shrewd and pungent social analysis. 他喜欢剧中尖锐机敏、一针见血的社会分析。

shrug [ʃrʌg] *vt.&n.* 耸肩

诵读 He gave a self-deprecating shrug. 他自谦地耸耸肩。

shuttle [ˈʃʌtl] *n.* 往返汽车、列车、飞机；穿梭 *v.* 往返穿梭

诵读 UN mediators are conducting shuttle diplomacy between the two sides. 联合国调解员在双方之间进行穿梭外交。

sip [sɪp] *vt.* 小口地喝 *n.* 一小口的量

诵读 She took a sip of water to moisten her dry throat. 她抿了一口水，润一下发干的喉咙。

skate [skeɪt] *vi.* 溜冰，滑冰 *n.* 冰鞋

诵读 They were picked to skate against the visiting team. 他们被选出来与客队进行滑冰比赛。

skeleton [ˈskelɪtn] *n.* 骨骼，框架；梗概

诵读 A skeleton staff of 20 is being kept on. 留下了20名骨干人员。

sketch [sketʃ] *n.* 素描；略图，梗概 *vt.* 绘略图

诵读 The sketch should be a kind of rehearsal for the eventual painting. 草图应该是最终绘画的某种演练。

ski [ski:] *n.* 雪橇 *vi.* 滑雪

诵读 There are countless small ski areas dotted about the province. 该省内遍布着许多小型滑雪场。

slam [slæm] *vt.* 砰地关上 *n.* 猛关的声音

诵读 Politically, this issue is a slam dunk for the party. 在政治上，这一议题是这个党的一张胜券。

slaughter [ˈslɔ:tə] *n.&vt.* 屠杀，宰杀

诵读 The barbaric slaughter of whales is unnecessary and inhuman. 野蛮屠杀鲸鱼既不必要也不人道。

slender [ˈslendə] *a.* 修长的，苗条的；微小的

诵读 My idea of physical perfection is to be very slender. 在我看来，要拥有完美身材就要非常苗条。

slice [slaɪs] *n.* 薄片，切片，部分

搭配 a slice of 一些

诵读 For breakfast I had a thick slice of bread and syrup. 早餐我吃了一片厚厚的涂了糖浆的面包。

slide [slaɪd] *vi.* (使)滑动 *n.* 滑坡，滑道，滑动

诵读 Eric lost his footing and began to slide into the pit. 埃里克一脚踩空，开始往坑里滑。

slight [slaɪt] *a.* 轻微的，纤细的，瘦弱的

诵读 Symptoms are a slight fever, headache and loss of appetite. 症状包括低烧、头痛和食欲不振。

slim [slɪm] *a.* 苗条的 *vt.* 变苗条

诵读 He was a slim, solemn, darkly handsome young man. 他是个身材修长、表情庄重、皮肤黝黑的帅小伙。

slip [slɪp] *vi.* 滑倒，溜走 *n.* 疏忽，小错

诵读 Emergency workers fear that the burning ship

could slip its moorings. 急救人员担心燃烧着的船只可能会脱链滑走。

slit [slɪt] *vt.* 切开，截开 *n.* 缝隙

诵读 She watched them through a slit in the curtains. 她透过窗帘上的一道窄缝注视着他们。

slogan [ˈsləʊɡən] *n.* 标语，口号

诵读 The Socialists tried to trump this with their slogan. 社会主义者设法用他们的口号胜过这一点。

slope [sləʊp] *n.* 斜坡，倾斜，斜度 *v.*（使）倾斜

诵读 The slope increases as you go up the curve. 上了弯道以后，路越来越陡。

slot [slɒt] *n.* 狭缝；空位 *vt.* 把……纳入

诵读 Insert coins into the slot and press for a ticket. 把硬币放进投币口，按钮取票。

sneak [sniːk] *vt.* 偷偷地做

诵读 Sometimes our expectations sneak up on us unawares. 有些时候，我们期待的事情不期而至。

sniff [snɪf] *vi.* 嗅，抽鼻涕，蔑视

诵读 Take a sniff at everything and distinguish the good from the bad. 对任何东西都要用鼻子嗅一嗅，以鉴别其好坏。

solo [ˈsəʊləʊ] *n.* 独奏 *a.&ad.* 单独的(地)

诵读 The piece segues into his solo with the strings. 手曲转入弦乐伴奏下的独奏。

soluble [ˈsɒljʊbl] *a.* 可溶的

诵读 The red dye on the leather is water-soluble. 皮革上的这种红色染料可溶于水。

sophisticated [səˈfɪstɪkeɪtɪd] *a.* 复杂的，先进的；老练的

诵读 Some sign languages are very sophisticated means of communication. 有些手语可以表达非常复杂的内容。

sovereign [ˈsɒvrɪn] *a.* 独立的，有主权的 *n.* 君主

诵读 A preemptive strike against a sovereign nation raises moral and legal issues. 对一个主权国家进行先发制人的攻击会引起道德和法律上的争议。

span [spæn] *n.* 跨度

搭配 life span 生命期

诵读 They have extended the potential life span of humanity everywhere. 他们延长了世界各地人们的预期寿命。

spark [spɑːk] *n.* 火花，火星 *vi.* 发火花

诵读 A mischievous spark glinted in his eyes. 他眼中闪现出一丝顽皮的神情。

spin [spɪn] *vi.&vt.* 旋转；纺纱；织网

搭配 spin out 拖延……的时间

诵读 The Government will try to spin out the conference into next autumn. 政府会竭力将会议拖延到下个秋季。

spine [spaɪn] *n.* 脊柱，刺；书脊

诵读 The emptiness here sent shivers down my spine. 这里的空寂让我脊梁骨发凉。

spiral [ˈspaɪərəl] *a.* 螺旋形的 *n.* 螺旋，螺线 *v.* 盘旋

诵读 The birds circled in a slow spiral above the house. 鸟儿在房子上空缓缓盘旋。

spit [spɪt] *vi.* 吐痰 *n.* 唾液

诵读 The gang thought of hitting him too, but decided just to spit. 那伙人也想过要揍他，但最后只是啐了他一口。

splash [splæʃ] *vt.* 溅，泼 *n.* 飞溅声

诵读 Let them splash around in the pool for a while. 让他们在水池里扑腾一会儿吧。

split [splɪt] *vt.* 劈开；分裂 *n.* 分化，裂口

诵读 The Republicans were deeply split between progressives and conservatives. 共和党分裂成激进派和保守派。

spot [spɒt] *n.* 斑点；地点 *vt.* 认清，发现；玷污

诵读 He wears a cap to cover a spot of baldness. 他戴帽以遮斑秃。

spouse [spaʊz] *n.* 配偶

诵读 Her spouse will come to see her on Sunday. 她的配偶星期天要来看她。

spray [spreɪ] *n.* 喷雾，浪花 *vt.* 喷，喷射

诵读 The moon was casting a rainbow through the spray from the waterfall. 月亮在瀑布溅起的水雾上照出了一道彩虹。

sprinkle [ˈsprɪŋkl] *n.* 洒，喷，淋

诵读 Sprinkle some water before you sweep. 先泼点儿水再扫。

stab [stæb] *vt.&n.* 刺，戳

搭配 have a stab at sth. 尝试

诵读 Several tennis stars have had a stab at acting.

好几位网球明星都尝试过演戏。

stagger [ˈstæɡə] *vi.&n.* 摇晃着移动；蹒跚

诵读 The unexpected blow did not stagger his resolution. 这个意外打击并没有动摇他的决心。

stake [steɪk] *n.* 桩

辨义 *n.* 利害关系；风险

搭配 at stake 处于成败关头

诵读 At stake is the success or failure of world trade talks. 世界贸易谈判的成败正处在关键时刻。

stale [steɪl] *n.* 变质的，陈旧的

诵读 The Government, he said, were/was sticking to stale ideas. 他说政府仍在抱残守缺。

stalk [stɔːk] *n.* 茎，梗

辨义 *vt.* 悄悄地跟踪

诵读 The lion will often stalk its prey for hours. 狮子经常悄然跟踪猎物达几个小时。

stall [stɔːl] *n.* 货摊

诵读 He sold boots on a market stall. 他在集市上摆摊卖靴子。

starve [stɑːv] *vi.* 饿死，挨饿

诵读 The animals were left to starve to death. 那些动物只能等着饿死。

static [ˈstætɪk] *a.* 静态的

拓展 stationary *a.* 静止的，固定的

诵读 Prices on the stock market, which have been static, are now rising again. 股市价格一直停滞不动，现在又在上涨了。

stationery [ˈsteɪʃənəri] *n.* 文具

诵读 I loved stationery and all the accoutrements of writing. 我喜爱信笺信封和所有文房用具。

stereo [ˈstɪəriəʊ] *n.* 立体声音响；立体声装置

拓展 stereotype *n.* 陈规，老套，模式化

诵读 The personal stereo has a water-resistant outer case. 这款随身听的外壳是防水的。

stern [stɜːn] *n.* 船尾

辨义 *a.* 严厉的，坚定的

诵读 He was a stern critic but an extremely kindly man. 他是个苛刻的批评家，但却是个非常善良的人。

sting [stɪŋ] *vt.&n.* 刺痛，剧痛；叮

诵读 This won't hurt—you will just feel a little sting. 这不痛——你只会感觉到像被轻轻叮了一下。

stoop [stuːp] *vi.&n.* 弯腰，俯身

诵读 They will stoop to every low-down trick. 他们什么卑劣的手段都使得出来。

strenuous [ˈstrenjʊəs] *a.* 费力的，艰辛的；奋发的

诵读 The strenuous exercise undergone could balance out the increased calories. 所进行的剧烈运动可以消耗掉增加的热量。

stretch [stretʃ] *vt.&n.* 伸展，延伸

诵读 I stopped at the square and got out to stretch my legs. 我在广场处停下来，下车活动活动腿脚。

stride [straɪd] *vi.&n.* 大踏步走；跨越一大步

诵读 He's still learning and when he hits his stride, he'll be unstoppable. 他仍旧处在学习阶段，一旦驾轻就熟后将势不可挡。

strife [straɪf] *n.* 争吵；冲突，斗争

诵读 The country was torn apart by strife. 这个国家被内部纷争搞得四分五裂。

strip [strɪp] *vt.* 剥 *n.* 窄条，条纹

诵读 Sensitive Cream will not strip away the skin's protective layer. 敏感肌肤专用面霜不会破坏皮肤表面的保护层。

stripe [straɪp] *n.* 长条，条纹

诵读 Each white petal had a stripe of red. 每一片白色的花瓣上都有一条红色的条纹。

studio [ˈstjuːdiəʊ] *n.* 画室；播音室

诵读 The brothers usually roll into their studio around midday. 兄弟几个总是要到正午前后才姗姗来到工作室。

stumble [ˈstʌmbl] *n.&vi.* 跌倒，绊倒

诵读 The sudden weakness in her legs made her stumble. 她突然两腿发软踉跄了一下。

stun [stʌn] *vt.* 使……失去知觉，使吃惊

诵读 Many cinema-goers were stunned by the film's violent and tragic end. 许多来看电影的人都被这部影片暴力而悲惨的结局所震惊。

subordinate [səˈbɔːdɪnət] *a.* 次要的，从属的

巧记 前缀 sub-在下方+词根ord顺序+in 在里面=顺序在下面→次要的

诵读 Women were regarded as subordinate to free men. 过去女人被视为从属于自由男性。

subscribe [səbˈskraɪb] *vi.* 订阅，同意 *vt.* 赞助

搭配 subscribe to 订购，同意（观点建议）

诵读 I've personally subscribed to the view that either sex is superior to the other. 我个人从不同意性别有优劣之分的观点。

supersonic [ˌsjuːpəˈsɒnɪk] *a.* 超声波的 *n.* 超声波

诵读 There was a huge bang; it sounded like a supersonic jet. 传来一声巨响，听起来像是超音速喷气式飞机的声音。

superstition [ˌsjuːpəˈstɪʃən] *n.* 迷信

诵读 It's all rubbish and superstition, and there's nothing in it. 这都是废话和迷信，不是真的。

surrender [səˈrendə] *vi.&n.* 投降，屈服

拓展 surround *vt.* 包围，环绕 *n.* 环绕物

诵读 General Martin Bonnet called on the rebels to surrender. 马丁·邦尼特将军呼吁反叛者投降。

susceptible [səˈseptəbl] *a.* 易受影响的

搭配 be susceptible to 受到……的影响

诵读 Young people are the most susceptible to advertisements. 年轻人最容易受广告的影响。

sway [sweɪ] *vt.* 摇动；倾斜 *n.* 摇动

诵读 His speech failed to sway his colleagues into supporting the plan. 他的一番话没能使他的同事支持这项计划。

swear [sweə] *vi.* 诅咒，发誓

诵读 He has been brought up not to swear in front of women. 他从小就被教育不要在女性面前说脏话。

swing [swɪŋ] *vi.&vt.* 摇摆，旋转 *n.* 秋千；摇摆

诵读 The balance continues to swing away from final examinations to continuous assessment. 教育重心继续从期末考试向持续评估转移。

switch [swɪtʃ] *n.&vi.* 转换

诵读 The spokesman implicitly condemned the United States policy switch. 发言人含蓄地谴责了美国政策上的转变。

symmetry [ˈsɪmɪtri] *n.* 对称；匀称

巧记 前缀 sym-同+词根metr测量=距离相同→对称

诵读 The superpowers pledged to maintain symmetry in their arms shipments. 超级大国承诺在武器运输方面要保持数量均衡。

syndrome [ˈsɪndrəʊm] *n.* 综合症状；典型表现

诵读 Built-up static contributes to sick building syndrome. 静电积累会造成建筑综合征。

synthetic [sɪnˈθetɪk] *a.* 合成的，人造的；综合的

拓展 synthesis *n.* 综合，合成

诵读 Boots made from synthetic materials can usually be washed in a machine. 用合成材料做成的靴子通常可以在机器里洗。

scare [skeə] *vt.* 惊吓，受惊

诵读 The prospect of failure scares me rigid. 失败的前景使我胆战心惊。

salary [ˈsæləri] *n.* 薪金，薪水

so-called [ˈsəʊˈkɔːld] *a.* （贬）所谓的，号称的

soar [sɔː] *vi.* （指鸟等）高飞，飞涨

诵读 Shares soared on the New York stock exchange. 纽约证券交易所股票暴涨。

tale [teɪl] *n.* 故事，传说

搭配 fairy tale 童话

诵读 She was like a princess in a fairy tale. 她就像童话里的公主。

tap [tæp] *n.* 塞子，龙头；轻叩，轻拍 *v.* 轻扣，轻敲

僻义 *vt.* 利用，开发

诵读 The country must tap new resources of energy. 该国必须开发新能源。

tape [teɪp] *n.* 胶带，录音带，磁带 *vt.* 录音；系，捆

诵读 The tape had run to the end but recorded nothing. 磁带已经转到头了，但是什么也没录上。

task [tɑːsk] *n.* 任务，作业，工作

诵读 We will train you first before we set you a task.

我们在给你分派任务之前会先对你进行培训。

tackle ['tækl] *vt.* 处理，解决；抓住

诵读 Ecological groups say that nothing is being done to tackle the problem. 环境保护组织称之前并未采取任何行动处理这个问题。

tactic ['tæktɪk] *n.* 策略，战术

诵读 Fires were started by the prisoners as a diversionary tactic. 犯人纵火以转移注意力。

talent ['tælənt] *n.* 才能，天资；人才

巧记 选秀节目可以用 talent show 来表达

诵读 I believe I have the talent to make it. 我相信自己有成功的天分。

target ['tɑːɡɪt] *n.* 目标，对象，靶子 *vt.* 瞄准

搭配 on target 击中目标

诵读 This is a target which is surely within the realm of possibility. 这是一个完全有可能实现的目标。

taste [teɪst] *vt.* 品尝 *n.* 滋味；味觉

诵读 I like the taste of wine and enjoy trying different kinds. 我喜欢葡萄酒的味道，喜欢品尝不同的口味。

tax [tæks] *n.* 税，负担 *vt.* 对……征税

诵读 Is a tax increase still out of the question? 增加税收仍然是不可能的事吗？

technology [tek'nɒlədʒi] *n.* 科学技术

拓展 technician *n.* 技术员，技师，技工

诵读 New technology should provide a secure firewall against hackers. 新技术应该能提供安全可靠的防火墙抵御黑客袭击。

technique [tek'niːk] *n.* 技术，技能；工艺

诵读 Scientists are becoming increasingly unsure of the validity of this technique. 科学家们越来越拿不准这一技术是否正当合法。

term [tɜːm] *n.* 学期

巧记 同义词 semester

僻义 *n.* 条件

搭配 in terms of 依据，按照；用……措辞

诵读 The agreement should have very positive results in the long term. 从长远来看，这个协议将会产生非常积极的影响。

teenager ['tiːneɪdʒə] *n.* 青少年

诵读 She was the ideal American teenager, both on and off screen. 无论是在荧幕上还是生活中，她都是人们心中完美的美国少女。

temperature ['temprɪtʃə] *n.* 温度，体温

诵读 She was admitted to hospital with a soaring temperature. 她因发高烧被送进医院。

temple ['templ] *n.* 庙宇

僻义 *n.* 太阳穴

诵读 She caught a clear view upwards of the spotlit temple. 她抬头清楚地看到了被聚光灯照得通明的寺庙。

tempo ['tempəʊ] *n.* 节奏

诵读 They waltz to the tempo of the music. 他们跟着音乐的节奏跳华尔兹舞。

temporary ['tempərəri] *a.* 暂时的，短暂的

巧记 词根 tempo 节奏+后缀-rary=节奏一样的→短暂的，暂时的

拓展 temporarily *ad.* 暂时地，临时地

诵读 If there was any disappointment it was probably temporary. 即便有点儿失望，也肯定是暂时的。

tempt [tempt] *vt.* 诱惑，引诱

搭配 tempt sb. to do sth./into doing sth. 引诱某人做某事

拓展 temptation *n.* 引诱，诱惑

诵读 Don't succumb to the temptation to have just one cigarette. 不要经不住诱惑，只抽一支烟也不行。

tend [tend] *vi.* 趋向，往往是

拓展 tendency *n.* 趋势，趋向；倾向

搭配 tend to do 倾向于，往往会；have a tendency to do 倾向做

诵读 I tend to get very uptight during a match. 比赛时我总会紧张得不行。

terror ['terə] *n.* 恐怖；可怕的人(事)

拓展 terrorist *n.* 恐怖分子；terrify *v.* 使害怕，使惊恐

诵读 The terror ended when armed police swooped on the car. 武警突袭了这辆车从而制止了这起恐怖活动。

textbook ['tekstbʊk] *n.* 课本，教科书

僻义 *n.* 典范

诵读 France Telecom is a textbook model of what can be achieved by a state-owned company. 法国电信是国有公司成功的典范。

throughout [θru:ˈaʊt] *prep.* 遍及，贯穿 *ad.* 到处，全部，始终

搭配 throughout the country/world 遍及全国/世界

诵读 The exhibition will gather more than 400 artifacts in evidence of the thriving cultures and arts along the Silk Road throughout centuries. 这次展览将汇集 400 多件文物，以见证几个世纪以来丝绸之路沿线繁荣的文化和艺术。

theater [ˈθɪətə] *n.* 剧院；戏剧

诵读 Excuse me, where is the entrance to the theater? 请问剧院的入口在哪里？

theme [θi:m] *n.* 题目，主题

巧记 同义词 issue，topic，subject

诵读 The need to strengthen the family has been a recurrent theme for the Prime Minister. 巩固家庭关系是首相屡次谈到的话题。

theory [ˈθɪəri] *n.* 理论，原理；学说

拓展 theoretical *a.* 理论（上）的

搭配 in theory 理论上（应该），照道理

诵读 There are some holes in that theory, some unanswered questions. 那个理论中有一些漏洞，一些问题没有解答。

therapy [ˈθerəpi] *n.* 治疗，物理疗法

拓展 therapist *n.* 治疗专家，治疗师

诵读 Family therapy showed us how to communicate with each other. 家庭疗法指导我们彼此之间的沟通交流。

thereafter [ðeərˈɑ:ftə] *ad.* 此后，在那之后

诵读 Thereafter she wrote articles for papers and magazines in Paris. 此后她给巴黎的报纸和杂志撰稿。

thereby [ˈðeəbaɪ] *ad.* 因此，从而

诵读 He became a British citizen, thereby gaining the right to vote. 他成了英国公民，因而得到了投票权。

thesis [ˈθi:sɪs] *n.* 论文；论题；论点

辨析 composition 多指学校里老师给学生布置的作文练习；article 多指在报刊、杂志上发表的新闻报道、学术论文等；essay 指任何一种非小说性的、篇幅不长、结构简练的文章；paper 多指在学术刊物上发表或在学术会议上宣读的专题论文；prose 专指散文；thesis 既可指毕业论文、学位论文，又可指一般的为阐述学术观点而写的论文。

诵读 To be specific, the argument in your graduation

thesis is logical. 具体地说，你的毕业论文符合逻辑。

thirst [θɜ:st] *n.* 渴，口渴 *vi.* 渴望

僻义 thirst for 渴望

拓展 thirsty *a.* 口渴的；渴望的

诵读 Children show a real thirst for learning. 孩子们对于学习表现出真诚的渴望。

thorough [ˈθʌrə] *a.* 彻底的，完全的

拓展 thoroughly *ad.* 彻底地；认真仔细地；完全地；非常

诵读 A thorough brushing helps to freshen up your mouth. 彻底刷牙有助于口气清新。

thoughtful [ˈθɔ:tfʊl] *a.* 认真思考的；体贴的

诵读 She had a thoughtful expression on her face. 她一脸若有所思的表情。

threat [θret] *n.* 恐吓，威胁

拓展 threaten *v.* 威胁，恐吓

诵读 A third of Africa is under threat of desertification. 非洲有三分之一的土地面临荒漠化的威胁。

throat [θrəʊt] *n.* 咽喉，嗓子

诵读 She took a sip of water to moisten her dry throat. 她抿了一口水，润一下发干的喉咙。

thumb [θʌm] *n.* 拇指

搭配 thumb through 快速阅览

诵读 He took the pen between his thumb and forefinger. 他用拇指和食指捏着笔。

ticket [ˈtɪkɪt] *n.* 票；（交通违章）罚款传票

诵读 The price of a single ticket is thirty-nine pounds. 单程票的价格是 39 英镑。

tie [taɪ] *n.* 领带；关系；束缚，约束

诵读 He was a big man, smartly dressed in a suit and tie. 他身材高大，穿着西服打着领带，非常帅气。

tip [tɪp] *n.* 末端，尖端，小费

僻义 *n.* 小建议，忠告

搭配 on the tip of one's tongue 差一点就能想起的

诵读 Here's an inside tip: The faster you rise, the harder you fall. 给你一个小忠告：爬得越快，摔得越疼。

tire [ˈtaɪə] *vt.* （使）疲倦，（使）厌倦

搭配 tire out 使极其劳累

拓展 tiresome *a.* 讨厌的，无聊的

诵读 His objective was to tire out the climbers. 他的目标是使登山者筋疲力尽。

tide [taɪd] *n.* 潮, 潮汐; 潮流, 趋势

搭配 tide over 克服, 渡过难关

诵读 Some stretches of beach are completely underwater at high tide. 海滩上有些地方在涨潮时完全淹没在水中。

tidy [ˈtaɪdi] *a.* 整洁的, 整齐的 *vt.* 整理, 收拾

诵读 How do you manage to keep the place so tidy? 你是怎样把这里保持得如此整洁的?

tiny [ˈtaɪni] *a.* 极小的, 微小的

诵读 The goldfish swam round and round in their tiny bowls. 金鱼在小小的鱼缸里一圈圈地游来游去。

together [təˈɡeðə] *ad.* 共同, 一起; 合起来

搭配 together with 同……一起, 和; 连同; 加之

诵读 They're trying their best to bring together those separated families. 他们正尽最大努力让离散的家人重聚。

tongue [tʌŋ] *n.* 舌, 语言

搭配 mother tongue 母语

诵读 She made a grime face and stuck out her tongue at him. 她做了个鬼脸, 向他吐了吐舌头。

total [ˈtəʊtəl] *n.&a.&vt.* 总数, 总计

搭配 in total 总计, 合计

诵读 The total cost of the project would be more than $240 million. 该项目的总成本会超过 2.4 亿美元。

tour [tʊə] *n.&vt.* 旅行, 游历

拓展 tourist *a.* 游客, 旅行者

诵读 The band are currently on a two-month tour of Europe. 乐队目前正在欧洲进行为期两个月的巡回演出。

tower [ˈtaʊə] *n.* 塔, 塔楼

僻义 *vi.* 高耸, 超越

诵读 They occupied the first two floors of the tower. 他们占用了塔楼的头两层。

track [træk] *n.* 小路; 轨迹 *vt.* 跟踪, 追踪

搭配 keep track of 通晓事态, 注意动向; lose track 失去联系

诵读 She had spent years trying to track down her parents. 她已经花了好多年时间试图追寻父母的下落。

toe [təʊ] *n.* 脚趾, 足尖

搭配 on one's toes 警觉的, 准备行动的

诵读 I kicked a dustbin very hard and broke my toe. 我狠狠地踢了一脚垃圾箱, 结果脚趾骨折了。

tolerate [ˈtɒləreɪt] *vt.* 容忍, 忍受

拓展 tolerant *a.* 容忍的, 宽容的; tolerance *n.* 宽容; 容忍

诵读 She can no longer tolerate the position that she's in. 她再也受不了自己的处境了。

tomb [tuːm] *n.* 坟

tone [təʊn] *n.* 音调, 语气

诵读 tone up 增强, 强化

诵读 The spokesman said the tone of the letter was very friendly. 发言人说信函的语气非常友好。

torch [tɔːtʃ] *n.* 手电筒; 火炬

诵读 I was perished. No jacket, no torch, wet through, exhausted. 我快冻僵了, 没有外衣, 没有火把, 浑身湿透了, 筋疲力尽。

tough [tʌf] *a.* 棘手的; 吃苦耐劳的; 粗暴的

诵读 She is tough, unwilling to take no for an answer. 她很强硬, 不达目的誓不罢休。

tow [təʊ] *vt.&n.* 拖, 牵引

诵读 She had a reporter and a photographer in tow. 她带着一名记者和一名摄影师。

train [treɪn] *n.* 列车, 火车 *vt.* 训练, 培养

僻义 *n.* 系列, 一串

拓展 training 训练, 培养

诵读 You can train people to be more expressive. 你可以训练人们变得更有表现力。

treasure [ˈtreʒə] *n.* 财富, 珍品 *vt.* 珍爱, 珍惜

诵读 We shall take the treasure away to a safe place. 我们应该把这些宝物带到一个安全的地方。

treat [triːt] *vt.* 对待; 治疗; 款待 *n.* 款待, 请客

拓展 treatment *n.* 疗法; 对待

诵读 No one knew how to treat this dreaded disease. 没人知道如何治疗这种可怕的疾病。

trick [trɪk] *n.* 诡计, 骗局

搭配 play tricks on 捉弄, 戏耍

诵读 It's an old trick but it just might work. 这是个老掉牙的把戏了, 不过也许会有用。

trip [trɪp] *n.* 旅行, 远足

搭配 have a nice trip 旅途愉快; 一路顺风

诵读 It would take three to six hours for a round trip. 往返行程需要 3 ～ 6 小时。

trace [treɪs] *n.* 痕迹，踪迹 *vt.* 跟踪，追踪

搭配 trace back to 追溯到

诵读 There was a trace of exasperation in his voice. 他的声音听上去有些愤怒。

trade [treɪd] *n.* 贸易，商业

拓展 trademark *n.* 商标

诵读 He traded his watch for Ade's basketball. 他用手表换艾德的篮球。

tradition [trəˈdɪʃən] *n.* 传统；惯例

拓展 traditional *a.* 传统的

诵读 Generally, the lower classes are considered to be the bearers of tradition. 总的来说，下层民众被认为是传统的保持者。

traffic [ˈtræfɪk] *n.* 交通，交通量

搭配 traffic jam 交通堵塞

诵读 Little traffic was to be seen on the streets. 街上车辆很少。

tragedy [ˈtrædʒɪdi] *n.* 悲剧；惨事，灾难

拓展 tragic *a.* 悲剧的

诵读 She was too exhausted and distressed to talk about the tragedy. 她太累了，而且无比悲伤，没法谈论那场悲剧。

trail [treɪl] *n.* 踪迹，痕迹；小路 *vt.* 追踪，跟踪

搭配 trail after 追随

诵读 I vote that you try to pick out the trail for us. 我提议由你来选我们该走哪条小路。

trait [treɪt] *n.* 特征，特点，特性

诵读 Creativity is a human trait. 创造力是人类的一种特性。

transaction [trænˈzækʃən] *n.* 交易

巧记 前缀 trans-从一者到另一者+词根action行动=交换行动→交易

诵读 He was always in the middle of a business transaction. 他总是忙着做生意。

transform [trænsˈfɔːm] *vt.* 变换；变形；改造

诵读 She actually wanted to reconstruct the state and transform society. 她实际上想要重建国家，改造社会。

translate [trænsˈleɪt] *v.* 翻译，解释；转化

搭配 translate... into... 把……转化为……

诵读 We must make efforts to translate our ideal into reality. 我们必须努力把理想变为现实。

transport [trænsˈpɔːt] *vt.&n.* 运输，运送

巧记 前缀 trans-从一者到另一者+词根 port 港口=从一个港口运到另一个→运输

拓展 transportation *n.* 运输系统，交通工具

诵读 The extra money could be spent on improving public transport. 多余的资金可以用于改善公共交通系统。

tremble [ˈtrembl] *n.&vi.* 发抖，颤抖

诵读 The leaves tremble in the breeze. 树叶在微风中抖动。

tremendous [trɪˈmendəs] *a.* 巨大的，极大的

诵读 He brought a tremendous infusion of hope to the people. 他给人们带来巨大希望。

trend [trend] *n.* 倾向，趋势

诵读 The latest lifestyle trend is downshifting. 最新的生活方式趋于放慢生活节奏。

trial [ˈtraɪəl] *a.* 试验的；审讯的 *n.* 试验；尝试

搭配 trial and error 反复试验

诵读 Many drugs were found by trial and error. 很多药物都是通过反复试验才发现的。

triangle [ˈtraɪæŋgl] *n.* 三角（形）

巧记 前缀 tri- 三+词根 angle角=三角（形）

诵读 The sum of all the angles of a triangle is 180 degrees. 三角形内角总和为180°。

triple [ˈtrɪpl] *n.&a.* 三倍

巧记 前缀 tri- 三+词根ple 表示堆积

诵读 The merger puts the firm in a position to triple its earnings. 合并可使公司利润增长两倍。

triumph [ˈtraɪəmf] *n.* 胜利，成功 *vi.* 得胜，战胜

巧记 triumph over 战胜

诵读 It's a triumph for the American people. 这是美国人民的胜利。

troublesome [ˈtrʌblsəm] *a.* 令人烦恼的，讨厌的

巧记 词根 trouble 麻烦+后缀-some=令人烦恼的

诵读 Teaching seems troublesome to him. 教书对于他来说好像是烦恼的事。

tuition [tjʊˈɪʃən] *n.* 学费

诵读 I'll have to cough up $10,000 a year for tuition. 我每年将不得不付 10 000 美元的学费。

tune [tjuːn] *n.* 调子，曲调

搭配 in tune with 与……协调，与……一致；out of

tune 跑调

诵读 Today, his change of direction seems more in tune with the times. 今天，他转变方向似乎更与时代合拍。

tunnel [ˈtʌnəl] *n.* 隧道，山洞

诵读 The Channel Tunnel is due to open towards the end of 2018. 海峡隧道预计 2018 年年底前开通。

tutor [ˈtjuːtə] *n.* 导师；家庭教师 *vt.* 辅导

诵读 He was my personal tutor at university. 他是我大学时的个人指导教师。

turbulent [ˈtɜːbjʊlənt] *a.* 狂暴的，骚乱的，混乱的

拓展 turbulence *n.* 骚乱

诵读 The present international situation remains tense and turbulent. 当前的国际局势依然紧张动荡。

turnover [ˈtɜːnˌəʊvə] *n.* 翻倒；人员调整；营业额

巧记 合成词：turn 翻转+over→翻倒

诵读 My turnover increased spectacularly. 我的营业额大幅上升。

twinkle [ˈtwɪŋkəl] *vi.*（星等）闪烁，（眼睛）发亮 *n.* 闪烁，闪光

巧记 twinkle twinkle little star 一闪一闪亮晶晶

诵读 The twinkle in his eyes was dimmed by tears. 他眼中闪烁的光芒被泪水模糊了。

twist [twɪst] *vt.* 拧；扭曲 *n.* 歪曲

搭配 twists and turns 蜿蜒曲折

诵读 The bag is resealed with a simple twist of the valve. 只需拧一下阀门，气囊就能重新密封。

typical [ˈtɪpɪkəl] *a.* 典型的，有代表性的

诵读 I am merely citing his reaction as typical of British industry. 我仅以他为例来说明英国工业界的典型反应。

type [taɪp] *n.* 类型 *vt.* 打字

诵读 She was certainly not the type to murder her husband. 她绝不是那种会谋杀亲夫的人。

translation [trænsˈleɪʃən] *n.* 翻译；译文

拓展 translate *v.* 翻译，转换

诵读 It can translate data from maps or remote sensing instruments into images. 它可以把从地图或遥感设备中得到的数据转换成图像。

transmit [trænzˈmɪt] *vt.* 传输；转送

诵读 This is currently the most efficient way to transmit certain types of data like electronic mail. 这是目前传输某些数据类型（如电子邮件）最有效的方法。

travel [ˈtrævəl] *n.&vi.* 旅行

诵读 The drop in travel is bad news for the airline industry. 旅游热降温对航空业来说是个坏消息。

tangible [ˈtændʒəbl] *a.* 明确的，确凿的，实际的

诵读 The policy has not yet brought any tangible benefits. 这项政策还没有带来任何实质性的好处。

toil [tɔɪl] *vi.* 长时间或辛苦地工作

诵读 The workers toiled all through the night. 工人们通宵达旦地辛勤劳动着。

tag [tæg] *n.* 标签 *vi.* 紧随

搭配 tag along with 紧随

诵读 She seems quite happy to tag along with them. 她好像很乐意跟着他们。

tame [teɪm] *a.* 温顺的；沉闷的，平淡的 *vt.* 驯服

拓展 tameness *n.* 温顺

诵读 The party was tame because all the people were sleepy. 聚会很沉闷，大家昏昏欲睡。

tangle [ˈtæŋgl] *n.&vi.* 缠绕；变乱

诵读 I was thinking what a tangle we had got ourselves into. 我在想，我们卷入了怎样的纷争之中。

tease [tiːz] *vt.&n.* 戏弄，取笑；挑逗

诵读 The best way to deal with a tease is to ignore him. 对付爱捉弄人的人，最佳方法就是不搭理他。

tedious [ˈtiːdɪəs] *a.* 乏味的，单调的，冗长的

拓展 tediously 沉闷地，冗长地

诵读 The band's approach tends to be crushingly tedious. 该乐队的演奏方式往往过于单调乏味。

temper [ˈtempə] *n.* 脾气

搭配 keep one's temper 捺住性子；out of temper 生气，发脾气；lose one's temper 发怒

诵读 I've never seen him get cross or lose his temper. 我从未见过他生气或者发火。

temperament [ˈtemprəmənt] *n.* 性格，性情；资质

诵读 Her mental capacity and temperament are as remarkable as his. 她的才智和气质和他一样出众。

tenant ['tenənt] *n.* 占有者；承租人；房客 *vt.* 租借，承租

巧记 联想：十只 ten 蚂蚁 ant 聚在一块，占据一个地方

诵读 The tenant was dispossessed for not paying his rent. 那名房客因未付房租而被赶走。

tender ['tendə] *a.* 脆弱的；温柔的 *n.*（正式）提出；投标

搭配 put sth. out to tender 招标

拓展 tenderly *ad.* 温和地，柔和地，体贴地

诵读 It is a beautiful meat, very lean and tender. 这块肉很好，又瘦又嫩。

tense [tens] *n.* 时态 *a.* 绷紧的，紧张的

拓展 tension *n.* 紧张状态，拉力；tensely *ad.* 紧张地

诵读 When we are under stress our bodies tend to tense up. 人一紧张，身体就会变僵硬。

tentative ['tentətɪv] *a.* 试探性的；犹豫不决的 *n.* 假设；尝试

诵读 She did not return his tentative smile. 她并没有对他怯生生的微笑作出回应。

terminal ['tɜːmɪnəl] *a.* 终点的；期末的 *n.* 终点（站）；终端

拓展 terminate *vi.*（使）停止；termination *n.* 结束

诵读 He was eventually diagnosed as suffering from terminal cancer. 他最终被诊断为癌症晚期。

terrific [təˈrɪfɪk] *a.* 极好的，非常的，极度的

诵读 He had a terrific sense of humour and could be very amusing. 他极具幽默感，很会逗人发笑。

territory ['terɪtəri] *n.* 领土；版图；领域，范围

拓展 territorial *a.* 领土的，区域的；土地的；地方的

搭配 come with the territory 天经地义，理应如此

诵读 The best thing to do when entering unknown territory is smile. 踏入未知地带最好的对策就是微笑。

testify ['testɪfaɪ] *vt.* 证明；表明，说明

巧记 词根 test 测试+后缀-ify

拓展 testimony *n.* 证据，证词；表明，说明

诵读 The government decided that their testimony would be irrelevant to the case. 政府认定他们的证词与案件不相关。

texture ['tekstʃə] *n.* 质地；构造；结构

巧记 词根 text 编织+后缀-ure=编织的状态→质地

诵读 Both the texture and condition of your hair should improve. 你头发的发质与健康状况都应改善。

theft [θeft] *n.* 偷窃行为

诵读 Her assistant was accused of theft and fraud by the police. 她的助手被警方指控犯有盗窃和欺诈罪。

thrift [θrɪft] *n.* 节约，节俭

拓展 thrifty *a.* 节俭的，节约的

诵读 He has the virtues of thrift and hard work. 他具有节俭和勤奋的美德。

thrill [θrɪl] *n.* 一阵激动(恐惧) *vt.* 使激动；(使)毛骨悚然

拓展 thrilling *a.* 令人兴奋的

诵读 It gave me a big thrill to meet my favourite author in person. 能见到我最喜欢的作者，使我兴奋不已。

thrive [θraɪv] *v.* 兴旺，茁壮成长，繁荣

诵读 New businesses thrive in this area. 新商家在这一地区蓬勃兴起。

tilt [tɪlt] *vi.&vt.*（使）倾侧，（使）倾斜

搭配 at full tilt 全速地，全力地

诵读 She wore her hat at a tilt over her left eye. 她歪戴着帽子遮住左眼。

timber ['tɪmbə] *n.* 木材，木料

诵读 They have been bartering wheat for cotton and timber. 他们一直用小麦交换棉花和木材。

timely ['taɪmli] *a.* 及时的，适时的

诵读 We are particularly grateful to him for his timely help. 我们特别感谢他及时帮助。

timid ['tɪmɪd] *a.* 胆怯的，怯懦的

诵读 He is too timid to venture upon an undertaking. 他太胆小，不敢从事任何事业。

toll [təʊl] *n.*（道路、桥等的）通行费；死伤人数

搭配 take a heavy toll on 造成重大损失

诵读 Winter takes its toll on your health. 冬天对健康不利。

torture ['tɔːtʃə] *n.&vt.* 拷问；折磨

巧记 词根 tort 扭+后缀-ure=扭打→折磨

诵读 I believed that in civilized countries, torture had ended long ago. 我原以为在文明国家严刑拷打早已销声匿迹。

torment [ˈtɔːment] *n.&vt.* 折磨；纠缠

诵读 Love is a sweet tyranny, because the lover endures his torment willingly. 爱情是甜蜜的暴政，情人甘心忍受它的折磨。

torrent [ˈtɒrənt] *n.* 激流，洪流；爆发

诵读 The stream had become a raging torrent. 小溪变成了一条汹涌的急流。

toss [tɒs] *vt.&n.* 投、扔；摇动

诵读 Do not toss the salad until you're ready to serve. 到快上菜时再轻轻搅拌色拉。

transcend [trænˈsend] *vt.* 超出，超越（经验、知识、能力的范围等）

巧记 前缀 trans-从一者到另一者+词根 scend爬=越爬越高→超越

诵读 We can't transcend the limitations of the ego. 我们无法超越自我的局限性。

transfer [trænsˈfɜː] *vt.&n.* 转移；转换；转让；过户

巧记 前缀 trans-从一者到另一者+词根 fer拿→拿着给另一个人→转移

诵读 He wants to transfer some money to the account of his daughter. 他想把一些钱转到女儿的账户上。

transient [ˈtrænziənt] *a.* 短暂的，转瞬即逝的；临时的

巧记 前缀 trans-从一者到另一者+ i 无意义+后缀-ent =转移速度很快→短暂的

诵读 In most cases, pain is transient. 大多数情况下，疼痛是短暂的。

transition [trænˈzɪʃən] *n.* 转变，变迁，过渡(时期)

巧记 前缀 trans-从一者到另一者+ i 无意义+后缀-tion→转变

诵读 In the past this process of transition has often proven difficult. 过去这一过渡过程常常很艰难。

transmission [trænzˈmɪʃən] *n.* 播送，发射；传送

拓展 transmit *vt.* 传输，传送；发射

诵读 The letter was delayed in transmission. 这封信在传递中被耽误了。

transparent [trænsˈpeərənt] *a.* 透明的，清澈的

僻义 *a.* 易理解的；明显的

诵读 The insect's wings are almost transparent. 这昆虫的翅膀几乎是透明的。

transplant [trænsˈplɑːnt] *n.&vt.* 移植（植物；组织，器官等）；迁移

巧记 前缀 trans-从一者到另一者+词根 plant 种植=移植

诵读 The arteries are diseased and a transplant is the only hope. 动脉已经发生病变，移植是唯一的希望。

trap [træp] *n.* 陷阱，圈套 *vt.* 诱捕；使中圈套

搭配 trap in 用……捕捉；使困于

诵读 I would hate him to think I'm trying to trap him. 我不希望他以为我在给他设圈套。

trash [træʃ] *n.* 垃圾；败类 *vt.* 废弃；贬低

诵读 Don't read that awful trash. 不要读那本拙劣的垃圾之作。

treaty [ˈtriːti] *n.* 条约，协议，协商

诵读 The treaty binds them to respect their neighbour's independence. 条约规定他们必须尊重邻国的独立。

trigger [ˈtrɪgə] *n.* 扳机 *vt.* 触发，引起

搭配 trigger action 触发作用；pull the trigger 开枪

诵读 Stress may act as a trigger for these illnesses. 压力可能会成为引发这些疾病的原因。

trim [trɪm] *a.* 整齐的；苗条的 *vt.&n.* 整理，修剪

诵读 The driver was a trim young woman of perhaps thirty. 司机是个大约 30 岁的身材苗条的年轻女子。

trivial [ˈtrɪvɪəl] *a.* 琐碎的；无足轻重的，不重要的

拓展 trifle *n.* 少量；小事

诵读 I know it sounds trivial, but I'm worried about it. 我知道这事听起来微不足道，但我还是放心不下。

tuck [tʌk] *vt.* 塞进

僻义 *n.* 零食或小吃（尤指儿童在学校吃的蛋糕或糖果等）

诵读 He stole a Mars bar from the school tuck shop. 他从学校小吃店偷了一条玛氏巧克力棒。

tug [tʌg] *vi.&vt.* 用力拖（或拉）；牵动

诵读 She knows exactly how to tug at readers' heartstrings. 她对如何牵动读者的心弦了如指掌。

tumble [ˈtʌmbl] *vi.* 摔倒；弄乱 *n.* 摔跤，跌倒

诵读 Many mothers and children tumble into poverty after divorce. 很多母亲和孩子在离婚后陷入贫困。

ugly ['ʌgli] *a.* 丑陋的

ultimate ['ʌltɪmɪt] *a.* 最后的，最终的

拓展 ultimately *ad.* 最后地

诵读 As an ultimate sanction, they can sell their shares. 作为最高处罚，他们可以出售他们的股份。

understand [,ʌndə'stænd] *vt.* 理解

拓展 understanding *n.* 理解 *a.* 能谅解的；宽容的

诵读 We had this understanding that courses were roughly the same weight. 我们已经了解到各门功课差不多一样重要。

uniform ['juːnɪfɔːm] *n.* 制服，军服

辨义 *a.* 相同的

诵读 He was identified only by his uniform and personal belongings. 他仅通过制服和个人物品被识别出来。

underestimate [,ʌndər'estɪmeɪt] *vt.* 低估

巧记 前缀 under-表示"不足，不够"+词根 estimate 估计→低估

诵读 The worst thing you can do is underestimate an opponent. 最严重的错误就是低估对手。

undergo [,ʌndə'gəʊ] *vt.* 遭受，经历

巧记 合成词：under 之下+go 走→从其下经过→遭受

诵读 The explorers had to undergo much suffering. 探险者不得不忍受很多困苦。

undergraduate [,ʌndə'grædjʊɪt] *n.* 大学生

巧记 前缀 under-之下+ graduate 毕业→还没毕业的学生→大学生

诵读 Aren't I a bit long in the tooth to start being an undergraduate? 我现在才去读大学本科不是有点太老了吗？

underground ['ʌndəgraʊnd] *a.* 地下的 *n.* 地铁

诵读 They are accused of organizing and financing an underground youth movement. 他们被指控组织并资助地下青年运动。

underlie [,ʌndə'laɪ] *vt.* 位于……之下，成为……的基础

巧记 前缀 under-之下+词根 lie 位于= 位于下面的→构成……的基础

诵读 These ideas underlie much of his work. 他的作品大部分都是以这些主题思想为基础。

underline [,ʌndə'laɪn] *vt.* 在……下画线；强调

巧记 前缀 under-之下+词根 line 线= 在下面画线→强调

诵读 His failures underline the difference between theatre and film direction. 他的失败说明了导演戏剧和导演电影是不同的。

underneath [,ʌndə'niːθ] *prep.* 在……下面 *ad.* 在下面，在底下

诵读 The space underneath could be used as a storage area. 底下的空间可用作储藏区。

undertake [,ʌndə'teɪk] *vt.* 承担，担任；从事

诵读 I can undertake that you will enjoy the play. 我保证你会喜欢这个剧。

undo [,ʌn'dʊ] *vt.* 取消；松开

巧记 前缀 un- 表示否定+词根 do=做的反向动作→取消

诵读 A heavy-handed approach from the police could undo that good impression. 警方的高压手段可能会毁掉这种良好印象。

undoubtedly [ʌn'daʊtɪdli] *ad.* 无疑，必定

诵读 Undoubtedly, political and economic factors have played their part. 毫无疑问，政治和经济因素在其中起了作用。

uneasy [ʌn'iːzi] *a.* 不安的，焦虑的

诵读 He sniffed, fidgeting in discomfort, uneasy at the suggestion. 他吸了吸鼻子，对这项提议感到窘迫不安，心烦意乱。

unemployment [,ʌnɪm'plɔɪmənt] *n.* 失业，失业人数

诵读 Unemployment is now a whisker away from three million. 现在的失业人数已接近 300 万。

unexpected [,ʌnɪk'spektɪd] *a.* 意外的；突然的

诵读 They were horrified at this unexpected turn of

events. 这种出乎意料的形势变化让他们无比震惊。

unfold [ʌnˈfəʊld] *vt.&vi.* 打开；显露

巧记 前缀 un- 表否定+词根 fold 折叠=折叠的反向动作→打开

诵读 Buds unfold in the sunshine. 花蕾在阳光下开放。

unfortunately [ʌnˈfɔːtʃənɪtli] *ad.* 不幸地，遗憾地

诵读 Unfortunately, this happy story finishes on a more sombre note. 遗憾的是，这个快乐的故事结局却比较伤感。

unique [juːˈniːk] *a.* 唯一的，独一无二的

诵读 With its unique heating element it makes perfect coffee. 其独特的电热元件使它能够煮出非常美味的咖啡。

universe [ˈjuːnɪvɜːs] *n.* 宇宙，万物

拓展 universal *a.* 普遍的，通用的；世界的

诵读 Behind his eyes was a whole universe of pain. 他眼神中隐藏着无尽的痛楚。

unlike [ˌʌnˈlaɪk] *prep.* 不像，和……不同

辨析 unlikely 是 likely 的反义词，表示"未必的，靠不住的"。

诵读 Unlike this way, it was highly unlikely that their paths would cross again. 不像这一次，他们再次偶遇的可能性非常小。

unload [ˌʌnˈləʊd] *vt.* 卸货

巧记 前缀 un- 表否定+词根 load 装载=装载的反向动作→卸载

诵读 Everyone helped to unload the luggage from the car. 大家都帮着从汽车上卸行李。

unusual [ˌʌnˈjuːʒʊəl] *a.* 不平常的，与众不同的

诵读 It is not unusual for women to work a 40-hour week. 女性普遍一周工作 40 小时。

update [ʌpˈdeɪt] *vt.* 更新，使现代化

诵读 We'll update you on the day's top news stories. 我们将为您提供当天的重要新闻。

upgrade [ˌʌpˈgreɪd] *vt.* 提升；升级

诵读 We need to upgrade the status of teachers. 我们需要提升老师的地位。

uphold [ʌpˈhəʊld] *vt.* 支持；维持；赞成；支撑

诵读 We have a duty to uphold the law. 维护法律是我们的责任。

upset [ʌpˈset] *a.* 难过的；失望的

僻义 *vt.* 打翻，弄翻

诵读 It is a deal that would upset the balance of power in the world's gold markets. 这笔交易将打破全球黄金市场的权力平衡。

up-to-date [ˌʌptəˈdeɪt] *a.* 现代化的，最新的

诵读 He was fired from his job after roughing up a colleague. 他因为对一位同事动粗而被开除了。

urban [ˈɜːbən] *a.* 城市的，市内的

诵读 There are problems of urban decay and gang violence. 存在城市衰败和帮派暴力的问题。

urge [ɜːdʒ] *vt.* 催促；怂恿 *n.* 强烈的欲望

诵读 He had an urge to open a shop of his own. 他很想自己开一家店。

urgent [ˈɜːdʒənt] *a.* 急迫的，紧要的，紧急的

诵读 It would be an exaggeration to call the danger urgent. 称那种危险为紧急事件有点夸张。

utilize [ˈjuːtɪlaɪz] *vt.* 利用

诵读 How can we utilize his knowledge and skill to our advantage? 我们如何利用他的知识和技巧来为我们谋利呢？

unanimous [juːˈnænɪməs] *a.* 一致同意的；无异议的

巧记 前缀un-单一+词根 anim 生命+后缀-ous=同一个生命→一致的

诵读 Their decision was unanimous. 他们的决定是全体通过的。

uncover [ˌʌnˈkʌvə] *vt.* 揭开；揭露

巧记 前缀 un- 表示否定+词根 cover 覆盖=覆盖的反向动作→揭开

诵读 Auditors said they had uncovered evidence of fraud. 审计人员说他们已经发现了欺诈的证据。

undermine [ˌʌndəˈmaɪn] *vt.* 削弱

巧记 前缀 under-表示在下面+词根mine挖=在下面挖→挖墙脚，削弱

诵读 This may help to undermine the brittle truce that currently exists. 这也许会火上浇油，破坏当前脆弱不稳的休战局面。

union [ˈjuːnjən] *n.* 联合；联盟；协会

unify [ˈjuːnɪfaɪ] *vt.* 使联合；使相同

巧记 词根 uni（来自 union 联合）+尾缀-fy

拓展 unity *n.* 团结；统一

诵读 To unify the country, our army has done its best. 为了统一国家，我们这支军队已经尽了全力。

upper [ˈʌpə] *a.* 上面的；上部的，较高的

诵读 He curled his upper lip in a show of scepticism. 他撇嘴表示怀疑。

upright [ˈʌpraɪt] *a.* 垂直的

僻义 *a.* 正直的，诚实的

诵读 He was handsome, upright and chivalrous. 他长相英俊，为人正直，风度翩翩。

uproar [ˈʌpˌrɔː] *n.* 骚动，喧嚣，鼎沸

诵读 The courtroom was in an uproar. 法庭上一片

哗然。

utter [ˈʌtə] *vt.* 说，发出（声音）

僻义 *a.* 彻底的，完全的

诵读 These reports are total and utter rubbish. 这些报告废话连篇。

ultraviolet [ˌʌltrəˈvaɪəlɪt] *a.&n.* 紫外线（的）

诵读 The sun's ultraviolet rays are responsible for both tanning and burning. 太阳的紫外线是皮肤晒黑和晒伤的原因。

umbrella [ʌmˈbrelə] *n.* 伞

utmost [ˈʌtməʊst] *a.* 极度的 *n.* 最大可能

诵读 It is a matter of the utmost urgency to find out what has happened to these people. 当务之急是弄清楚这些人出了什么事。

超高频词汇

value [ˈvæljuː] *n.* 价格；价值；重要性

僻义 *vt.* 评价；重视

搭配 place a high value on… 对……给予很高的评价

拓展 valuable *a.* 贵重的，有价值的

诵读 Over a given period, the value of shares will rise and fall. 股票的价值在某一特定时期内会有涨跌。

variety [vəˈraɪəti] *n.* 种种，多种多样；种类

搭配 a variety of 种种，各种

拓展 various *a.* 各种各样的；不同的

诵读 The most amazing thing about nature is its infinite variety. 大自然最让人惊叹的是它的无限多样性。

vast [vɑːst] *a.* 巨大的，辽阔的

诵读 The pollution has already turned vast areas into a wasteland. 污染已经使大片地区沦为不毛之地。

vain [veɪn] *a.* 徒劳的；自负的，爱虚荣的

搭配 in vain 徒劳

拓展 vanity *n.* 虚荣心，浮华

诵读 It became obvious that all her complaints were in vain. 很明显她所有的抱怨都是白费口舌。

valid [ˈvælɪd] *a.* 有效的；有根据的；正当的

拓展 反义词 invalid *a.* 无效的

诵读 For foreign holidays you will need a valid passport. 出国度假需持有效护照。

vary [ˈveəri] *vt.* 改变，变化，使多样化

拓展 variation *n.* 变化

辨析 variable *a.* 易变的，可变的；various *a.* 多种多样的

诵读 Prices may vary so it's well worth shopping around before you buy. 价格可能会有高有低，所以在买之前很有必要货比三家。

venture [ˈventʃə] *vi.* 冒险

巧记 词根 vent 走+后缀-ure＝走出去闯闯→冒险

僻义 *n.* 冒险事业（joint venture 合资企业）

诵读 When you venture outside, you are in for a surprise. 你外出探险时，定会遇上意想不到之事。

version [ˈvɜːʃən] *n.* 版本；译文；说法

诵读 A special remastered version of *Casablanca* is being released.《卡萨布兰卡》的特别修复版正在发行。

versus [ˈvɜːsəs] *prep.* 与……相对

巧记 直播赛事时，通常会在两个队伍名称之间用 versus 的缩写 vs. 表示对抗

诵读 It is France versus Brazil in the final. 决赛是法国队对巴西队。

via [ˈvaɪə] *prep.* 经；通过；凭借

诵读 The drug can be transferred to the baby via the placenta. 毒品会通过胎盘传给胎儿。

vice [vaɪs] *n.* 邪恶 *a.* 副的；代替的

拓展 vicious *a.* 恶毒的，凶残的

搭配 vicious circle 恶性循环

诵读 I think that the vice president was in the loop. 我认为副总统是局内人。

victim [ˈvɪktɪm] *n.* 牺牲品，受害者

辨析 同形词 vitamin *n.* 维生素

搭配 fall victim to... 成为……的牺牲品

诵读 The victim suffered a dreadful injury and lost a lot of blood. 受害者受了重伤，大量失血。

video [ˈvɪdɪəʊ] *n.* 电视；录像 *a.* 视频的；录像的

诵读 All of the four house wives like to watch video. 这四个家庭主妇都喜欢看录像。

view [vjuː] *n.* 风景；见解 *vt.* 观察；认为

拓展 viewpoint *n.* 观点

诵读 Fortunately, we don't have different viewpoints on the problem. 幸运的是，我们在这个问题上没有不同意见。

vigorous [ˈvɪɡərəs] *a.* 朝气蓬勃的，精力旺盛的

巧记 词根vigor活力+形容词后缀-ous =有活力的→朝气蓬勃的

诵读 As a football player, he is more vigorous than skillful. 作为一个足球运动员，他精力充沛，但球艺并不好。

violent [ˈvaɪələnt] *a.* 激烈的；暴力的

拓展 violence *n.* 猛烈，暴力

诵读 The mad man was crazy; he gave the man beside a violent kick. 那个疯子发疯了，他猛地踢了旁边的男子一脚。

virtual [ˈvɜːtjʊəl] *a.* 实际上的，事实上的

僻义 *a.* 网络虚拟的

诵读 This device helps make virtual reality a more usable and accessible technology. 这一装置有助于使虚拟现实成为更可用、更便利的技术。

virtue [ˈvɜːtjuː] *n.* 美德；功效，效力

搭配 in/by virtue of 凭借，由于

诵读 Among her many virtues are loyalty, courage and truthfulness. 她有很多美德，如忠贞、勇敢和诚实。

vision [ˈvɪʒən] *n.* 视力；洞察力；想象力

辨析 同义词 visible 表示"看得见，明显的"；visual 强调"视觉上的"，如 visual arts 视觉艺术。

诵读 We need a man of vision as president. 我们需要一个有远见的人当总统。

vital [ˈvaɪtəl] *a.* 生死攸关的，重大的

诵读 China has played a vital role in the international arena and the two countries share consensus on a wide range of international issues. 中国在国际舞台上发挥了至关重要的作用，两国就国际问题有着广泛的共识。

vivid [ˈvɪvɪd] *a.* 鲜艳的；生动的，栩栩如生的

巧记 词根viv(=life 生命)+后缀-id=有如生命→生动的，栩栩如生的

搭配 a vivid dream 生动的梦境

诵读 I have a vivid picture of my grandfather smiling down at me when I was very small. 我清楚地记得很小的时候祖父向我低头微笑。

vocation [vəʊˈkeɪʃən] *n.* 职业；天职；才能

辨析 同形词 vacation *n.* 休假，假期

诵读 Nursing is not just a job—it's a vocation. 护理不仅仅是一项工作，还是一种职业。

void [vɔɪd] *a.* 空虚的；无效的；空缺的

巧记 我们所熟悉的 avoid 反推回来 a+void→空出来→回避，void 空虚的

诵读 A spokeswoman said the agreement had been declared null and void. 女发言人称该协议已宣布无效。

volunteer [ˌvɒlənˈtɪə] *n.&vt.&vi.* 自愿（者，兵）

拓展 voluntary *a.* 自愿的，志愿的

诵读 She often does volunteer labour during holidays. 放假时她常去参加义务劳动。

vacant [ˈveɪkənt] *a.* 空闲的；空缺的；茫然的

巧记 词根 vac 空+后缀-ant

诵读 Half way down the coach is a vacant seat. 车厢中部有一个空座。

vanish [ˈvænɪʃ] *vi.* 突然不见；消失

诵读 All your troubles will vanish away when he

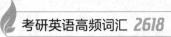

returns safely. 他平安回来后,你就无忧无虑了。

vehicle ['viːəkl] *n.* 车辆;媒介,载体

诵读 The driver managed to escape from the vehicle and shout a warning. 那名司机设法从车里逃了出来,并大声警告别人。

verge [vɜːdʒ] *n.* 边缘 *vi.* 濒临

搭配 on the verge of 濒于,濒临

诵读 I'm sad that Julie's marriage is on the verge of splitting up. 朱莉的婚姻濒临破裂,我为此感到难过。

verify ['verɪfaɪ] *vt.* 证实,查证;证明

诵读 I can verify that it takes about thirty seconds. 我能证明,这大约要用 30 秒的时间。

versatile ['vɜːsətaɪl] *a.* 通用的;多才多艺的

巧记 词根 vers 转+-at(e)构成动词+后缀-ile = 方方面面都能转通→通用的

诵读 Never before has computing been so versatile. 计算机的用途从没像现在这么广泛过。

violate ['vaɪəleɪt] *vt.* 违背;冒犯;侵犯

诵读 A country isn't respected if it violates an international agreement. 违背国际公约的国家是不被尊重的。

voyage ['vɔɪɪdʒ] *n.&vi.* 航海,航行

诵读 When he was only 24, he voyaged from American to China alone. 只有 24 岁的时候,他独自一人从美国坐船到中国。

vibrate [vaɪˈbreɪt] *vt.&vi.*(使)振动,(使)摇摆

诵读 The rough road made the car vibrate. 坑坑洼洼的道路使车颠得厉害。

vicinity [vɪˈsɪnɪti] *n.* 邻近,附近

搭配 in the vicinity of… 在……附近

诵读 Crowds gathered in the vicinity of the city square. 成群结队的人聚集在城市广场周围。

virgin ['vɜːdʒɪn] *n.* 处女 *a.* 纯洁的;原始的;未使用的

诵读 The mind of a child is virgin soil; it is not full of firmly held ideas and opinions that prevent it receiving new ones. 小孩的心灵是纯洁的,不排斥任何新观点与看法。

vote [vəʊt] *n.&vi.* 投票;选票

诵读 If he demands too much, the union will vote him down. 如果他要求太多,工会就会投票撤换他。

vulgar ['vʌlgə] *a.* 粗俗的,庸俗的

诵读 The film is tasteless, vulgar and even badly shot. 这部电影毫无品位、庸俗不堪,甚至可以说拍得很烂。

vulnerable ['vʌlnərəbl] *a.* 易受攻击的

搭配 be vulnerable to… 容易受到……的影响

诵读 Plants that are growing vigorously are less likely to be vulnerable to disease. 生命力强的植物不容易得病。

warn [wɔːn] *vt.&vi.* 警告,告诫

搭配 warn (sb.) against 告诫(某人)

诵读 I must warn you against raising your hopes. 我必须警告你不要期望过高。

wave [weɪv] *n.* 波浪 *n.&vt.&vi.* 挥手

搭配 wave goodbye to sb. 向某人挥手告别

诵读 She waved off the idea of more talk. 她挥挥手,表示不愿再谈了。

wage [weɪdʒ] *n.* 工资

巧记 不给发工资(wage),就发动战争(to wage a war)

诵读 In addition to my weekly wage, I got a lot of tips. 除了每周的薪水外,我还能得到不少小费。

waken ['weɪkən] *v.* 唤醒,弄醒;振奋;激发

巧记 词根 wake清醒的+后缀-en→弄醒,唤醒

搭配 waken up 醒来

诵读 Drink this coffee and it will waken you up. 把这杯咖啡喝了,它会让你清醒过来。

wallet ['wɒlɪt] *n.* 皮夹子,钱包

巧记 同义词 purse, burse, notecase

诵读 He took out his fat wallet and peeled off some notes. 他掏出鼓鼓的钱包,抽出几张钞票。

wander ['wɒndə] *vi.* 漫游，闲逛；胡思乱想

搭配 wander around/about 徘徊，转来转去

诵读 Grace allowed her mind to wander to other things. 格雷丝任由自己的思绪游走。

warmth [wɔ:mθ] *n.* 温暖，暖和；热情，热心

诵读 The warmth and strength of their relationship carried them through difficult times. 他们互相关心，关系牢固，这才熬过了艰难岁月。

waste [weɪst] *n.&vt.* 浪费，损耗 *a.* 废弃的，无用的，荒芜的

搭配 waste away 变得衰弱，逐渐消瘦

诵读 Overcrowding has taxed the city's ability to deal with waste. 人口过多使得城市的垃圾处理能力达到了极限。

weak [wi:k] *a.* 柔弱的，虚弱的

诵读 Strong winds can turn boats when the tide is weak. 潮水小的时候强风可以让船只改变航向。

wealth [welθ] *n.* 财产，财富

拓展 wealthy *a.* 富有的

诵读 Economic reform has brought relative wealth to peasant farmers. 经济改革给农民带来了一定的财富。

wear [weə] *vt.* 穿着，戴着 *vi.* 耐用

搭配 wear off 逐渐消逝；wear out 用破；耗尽，使筋疲力尽

诵读 In warm weather, you should wear clothing that is cool and comfortable. 热天时，应该穿凉快舒适的衣服。

weigh [weɪ] *vt.* 称重；权衡，考虑

僻义 *vi.* 具有重要性

拓展 weight *n.* 重量，体重；重要

诵读 You must weigh up the pros and cons. 你必须权衡利弊。

weapon ['wepən] *n.* 武器 *vi.* 武装，提供武器

诵读 The report outlined possible uses for the new weapon. 该报告概述了这种新式武器的可能用途。

weary ['wɪəri] *a.* 疲倦的；困乏的

搭配 weary traveler 疲倦的旅行者；be weary of 厌烦，疲倦

诵读 She was weary of being alone. 她厌倦了独处。

weave [wi:v] *vt.* 编织

诵读 People weave threads into cloth. 人们把线织成布。

web [web] *n.* 蜘蛛网，网状物；万维网

拓展 website *n.* 网站；webpage *n.* 网页

诵读 Yahoo is the oldest and best-known web directory service. 雅虎是最早且最知名的因特网目录服务网站。

weekday ['wi:kdeɪ] *n.* 平常日，工作日

weekly ['wi:kli] *a.* 每星期的，一周的

weep [wi:p] *vi.* 哭泣；流泪

诵读 There are times when I sit down and have a good weep. 有时候我会坐下来痛痛快快地哭一场。

weird [wɪəd] *a.* 古怪的，离奇的

诵读 He is different. He is weird. 他与众不同，有点怪。

welfare ['welfeə] *n.* 福利；幸福

巧记 词根 wel 福祉+后缀-fare→福利

诵读 The local welfare office is where government dispenses many of its services. 地方福利部门就是政府贯彻实施众多服务的窗口。

wheat [wi:t] *n.* 小麦

诵读 It would pay farmers to plough up the scrub and plant wheat. 它会出钱雇农民开垦这块低矮丛林来种植麦子。

wheel [wi:l] *n.* 车轮 *vt.* 转动，旋转

诵读 The wheel had long since rusted from years of disuse. 多年不用的车轮早已锈迹斑斑。

whisper ['wɪspə] *vi.&n.* 耳语，轻声说

诵读 I've heard a whisper that the Bishop intends to leave. 我听到有谣言说主教打算离开。

whatsoever [ˌwɒtsəʊ'evə] *pron.* 无论什么

诵读 I don't think they'll have any idea how I'm feeling. None whatsoever. 我认为他们并不了解我的感受，一点儿都不了解。

whereas [weər'æz] *conj.* 鉴于；然而；反之

诵读 Some of the studies show positive results, whereas others do not. 有一些研究结果令人满意，然而其他的则不然。

whip [wɪp] *vt.* 鞭打，抽打；严厉地折磨、责打或责备

诵读 Few people doubt his ability to whip the economy into shape. 几乎无人怀疑他整顿经济的能力。

whirl [wɜ:l] *n.&vi.* 旋转, 回旋

诵读 Your life is such a social whirl. 你总是在不停地参加社交活动。

whistle [ˈwɪsl] *vi.* 吹口哨; 鸣汽笛

搭配 whistle in the wind 徒劳无功

诵读 Hugh listened to the whistle of a train. 休听着火车呼啸而过。

wholly [ˈhəʊlli] *ad.* 完全地

巧记 同义词 all, entirely, altogether; 反义词 partly

诵读 Her advice has frequently been less than wholly helpful. 她的建议常常不是完全有帮助的。

wicked [ˈwɪkɪd] *a.* 邪恶的; 不道德的

诵读 She described the shooting as a wicked attack. 她称那次枪击为恶意袭击。

widespread [ˈwaɪdspred] *a.* 分布广泛的, 普遍的

巧记 合成词: wide 宽泛的+spread 传播→分布广泛的

诵读 There was widespread support for him among the rank and file. 那些普通职员都普遍支持他。

width [wɪdθ] *n.* 宽度; 宽阔

巧记 词根 wid (来自 wide 宽的)+后缀-th→宽度

诵读 The road was reduced to 18 feet in width by adding parking bays. 增加了停车区后, 这条路的宽度缩减到了 18 英尺。

wink [wɪŋk] *vi.* 眨眼 *n.* 眨眼; 小睡, 打盹

搭配 as easy as winking (非正式) 很容易, 易如反掌

诵读 I gave her a wink. 我朝她使了个眼色。

wisdom [ˈwɪzdəm] *n.* 智慧

巧记 词根 wis (来自 wise 明智)+名词后缀-dom→智慧

诵读 With knowledge and wisdom, evil could be vanquished on this earth. 拥有了知识和智慧就能够把恶势力从这个世界上铲除。

wit [wɪt] *n.* 风趣, 机智

诵读 The essays could do with a flash of wit or humor. 这些散文需要加入一丝机智或幽默。

withdraw [wɪðˈdrɔ:] *vt.* 收回, 撤销; 退出; 提取

巧记 合成词: with 拿着+draw 拉=拿着往外拉→撤退

诵读 She'd half expected him to withdraw from the course. 她多少已经预料到他会中途退出这门课程。

withhold [ˈwɪðhəʊd] *vt.* 使停止; 保留; 抑制

巧记 合成词: with 拿着+hold 拿住→拿住不让向前→阻止

诵读 It's never wise to withhold evidence. 藏匿证据绝非明智之举。

withstand [wɪðˈstænd] *vt.* 经受, 承受, 禁得起

巧记 合成词: with 拿着+stand 站立→拿着站着不动→经受

诵读 Their arguments do not withstand the most superficial scrutiny. 他们的论据经不起一点推敲。

witness [ˈwɪtnɪs] *n.* 目击者, 证人; 证据, 证明 *vt.* 做证人; 见证

诵读 The convictions rest solely on disputed witness and confessional statements. 仅仅根据有争议的目击者证言和供词就定了罪。

wind [wɪnd] *n.* 风

僻义 [waɪnd] *v.* 蜿蜒; 缠绕

搭配 like the wind 飞快地; in the wind 有可能发生的, 即将发生的

诵读 His long, uncovered hair flew back in the wind. 他那露在外面的长发随风向后飞舞。

wipe [waɪp] *vt.* 擦, 抹, 消除, 涂上, 刷卡

搭配 wipe out/off/away 擦去, 除去; 消灭, 毁灭

诵读 Why not wipe the slate clean and start all over again? 为什么不洗心革面、从头来过呢?

wonder [ˈwʌndə] *n.* 惊奇, 惊异 *vt.* 奇怪; 纳闷

搭配 no wonder 难怪, 怪不得

诵读 Under such circumstances, it is little wonder that they experience difficulties. 在这种情形下, 他们遇到困难就不足为怪了。

worth [wɜ:θ] *a.* 值得的 *n.* 财富, 财产; 价值

搭配 be worth doing 值得做某事

辨析 worthy 也表示有价值, 但通常用于 be worthy of 结构; worthwhile 也具有此意, 通常用于 it is worthwhile to do sth.

诵读 It's worth noting that the new round of technological revolution and industrial transformation is burgeoning and digital transformation in economy and society is accelerating, providing important opportunities for the high-quality development of all countries. 值得注意的是，新一轮科技革命和产业转型方兴未艾，经济社会数字化转型加速推进，为各国实现高质量发展提供了重要机遇。

wound [wuːnd] *n.&vt.* 伤，伤害

诵读 He is being treated for a self-inflicted gunshot wound. 他因开枪自残受伤正在接受治疗。

worldwide [ˈwɜːldwaɪd] *a.* 全世界的 *ad.* 遍及全世界

诵读 There is worldwide concern about the destruction of the rainforests. 全世界都在关注热带雨林遭到破坏的问题。

worship [ˈwɜːʃɪp] *n.&vt.* 崇拜

巧记 词根 wor（来自 worth 值得）+ship 状态→认为值得（信任）→尊敬

诵读 I enjoy going to church and worshipping God. 我喜欢去教堂做礼拜。

wrap [ræp] *vt.* 包裹

诵读 Wrap your baby snugly in a shawl or blanket. 拿一条披巾或毯子把宝宝舒舒服服地裹起来。

ward [wɔːd] *n.* 病房 *n.&vi.* 监视；守护

搭配 ward off 避开，挡住

诵读 Have a drop. It will ward off the cold of the night. 喝一口，挡一挡夜里的寒气。

warfare [ˈwɔːfeə] *n.* 战争，斗争，冲突

巧记 词根 war 战争+后缀-fare→战争

诵读 These clashes could develop into open warfare. 这些冲突可能会发展成为公开的战争。

warrant [ˈwɒrənt] *n.* 许可证 *vt.* 担保；授权

拓展 warranty *n.* 保证，担保；授权，批准

僻义 warranty card 保修卡

诵读 Officers armed with a search warrant entered the flat. 警察们持搜查证进入了那所公寓。

waterfall [ˈwɔːtəˌfɔːl] *n.* 瀑布

巧记 合成词：water 水+fall 掉落→瀑布

诵读 A waterfall cascades down the cliff from the hills behind. 一处瀑布从身后山崖上飞流直下。

waterproof [ˈwɔːtəpruːf] *a.* 防水的

巧记 词根 water 水+形容词后缀-proof 防……的→防水的

诵读 It is completely waterproof, yet light and comfortable. 它完全防水，而且轻巧舒适。

weed [wiːd] *n.* 杂草，野草 *vt.* 除草；消除

诵读 Two and a half years ago I gave up the evil weed. 两年半以前，我改邪归正，不抽大麻了。

weld [weld] *n.&vt.&vi.* 焊接

僻义 *vt.* 使紧密结合

诵读 She has both the authority and the personality to weld the party together. 团结全党所需的权威和个人魅力她两者兼具。

wholesome [ˈhəʊlsəm] *a.* 健全的；有益健康的，完全的，合乎卫生的

巧记 同义词 healthy，beneficial；反义词 harmful

拓展 wholesomely *ad.* 卫生地，有益健康地

诵读 They're trying to show clean, wholesome, decent movies. 他们尽量播放文明、健康、正派的电影。

workshop [ˈwɜːkʃɒp] *n.* 车间，工场；研讨会

诵读 This workshop helps young unemployed people in Grimsby. 该研习班会帮助格里姆斯比的失业青年。

wreath [riːθ] *n.* 花环，花圈 *vt.* 环绕

诵读 The Queen laid a wreath at the war memorial. 女王向阵亡将士纪念碑献了花圈。

wreck [rek] *n.* 失事船（或飞机）*vt.*（船等）失事，遇难；破坏

诵读 What would he tell his parents if he had a wreck? 如果他出了事故，该怎么向他的父母交代？

wrench [rentʃ] *v.* 猛拧；使扭伤 *n.* 扳手；痛苦

拓展 wretched *a.* 可怜的；悲惨的

诵读 He gave a wrench to his ankle when he jumped down. 他跳下去的时候扭伤了脚踝。

wrinkle [ˈrɪŋkl] *n.* 皱纹

诵读 The skin on her cheeks and around her eyes was beginning to wrinkle. 她两颊和双眼周围开始起皱纹了。

wrist [rɪst] *n.* 腕，腕关节

诵读 His fingers curled gently round her wrist. 他轻轻地用手指绕着她腕关节。

X-ray [ˈeksˌreɪ] *n.* X 光照片 *vt.* 照 X 光

诵读 X-rays have confirmed that he has not broken any bones. X 光片显示他没有骨折。

超 高 频 词 汇

yawn [jɔːn] *vi.* 打呵欠

诵读 She stretched her arms out and gave a great yawn. 她伸了个懒腰，打了个大哈欠。

yearly [ˈjɪəli] *a.* 每年的，一年一度的

巧记 year 年+形容词后缀-ly→每年的

诵读 In Holland, the government sets a yearly budget for health care. 在荷兰，政府会制定医疗保健部门的年度预算。

youngster [ˈjʌŋstə] *n.* 年轻人；少年，儿童

诵读 This plot revolves around a youngster who is shown various stages of his life. 这个故事情节围绕着一个年轻人展开，描述了他人生的各个阶段。

youth [juːθ] *n.* 青年；青春

诵读 In my youth my ambition had been to be an inventor. 我年轻时的抱负是成为一个发明家。

yield [jiːld] *vt.* 产出 *n.* 产量

僻义 yield to 屈服

诵读 The President is now under pressure to yield power to the republics. 总统现在面临着让权给共和党人的压力。

高 频 词 汇

zeal [ziːl] *n.* 热心，热忱，热情

拓展 zealous *a.* 热心的

诵读 They worked with great zeal to finish the project. 他们热情高涨地工作，以期完成这个项目。

zero [ˈzɪərəu] *n.* 零 *a.* 全无的

诵读 They have a policy of zero tolerance for sexual harassment. 他们对性骚扰采取零容忍的政策。

zigzag [ˈzɪgzæg] *a.* 锯齿形的，Z 字形的 *vi.* 弯弯曲曲地走路，曲折地前进

诵读 We had to proceed at high speed and by zigzag. 我们必须高速行驶，而且要曲折前进。

zone [zəun] *n.* 地区，区域

巧记 动感地带 M-Zone

诵读 The area could be turned into a demilitarized zone. 该地区可能会成为非军事区。

zoom [zuːm] *n.* 变焦镜头 *vi.* 快速移动，嗡嗡作响

僻义 *vi.* 急速增长

诵读 Your camcorder should have these basic features: autofocus, playback facility, zoom lens. 你的便携式摄像机应该具备以下基本功能：自动聚焦、回放功能、变焦镜头。

Unit 2

词根词缀

英语词汇是利用各种构词法，通过对词根或词干在词性、词义上的转换，构成不同的单词。因此，记住常用的前缀、后缀和词根及其含义是掌握派生词的关键。前缀、后缀就类似于中文的偏旁部首，掌握之后就能举一反三，所以词根词缀是加强记忆的有效方法！

【词缀一】a +双写辅音字母+核心词缀，用于加强语气

accelerate [ækˈseləreɪt] *vt.* 加快，促进（ac-加强语气，celer 速度 + 动词后缀-ate →加速度→加快，促进）

屠屠解词 celer-速度

celeron 即赛扬处理器。英特尔早期推出的性能较好、价格便宜的处理器产品。

accent [ˈæksənt] *n.* 口音；重音（ac-加强语气 + cent 唱→着重唱→重音）

屠屠解词 cent- 百；唱

cent-作为词根有两个含义，一个含义是"百，百分之……"，如 century（世纪，一百年），percentage（百分率）。另一个是"唱"的含义。

access [ˈækses] *n.* 进入；入口（ac-加强语气+cess 走→走进去→进入）

屠屠解词 cess-走

- accessible *a.* 能接近的；可进去的（access 接近+-ible 能……的→能接近的；可进去的）
- accessory *a.* 附属的（access 接近+形容词后缀-ory→接近的物→附加物，附属的）
- successive *a.* 连续的，继承的（suc-随后+cess 行走，前进+-ive……的→随后跟上→连续的）
- concession *n.* 迁就，让步（con-共同的+cess 走→共同退让）〈派生〉concede *v.* 让步，迁就
- recession *n.* 撤退；交还（re-往回+cess 走+名词后缀-ion→往回走→撤退）
- excess *n.* 过量，过剩（ex-向外+cess 走→向外走→越出→过量）〈派生〉excessive *a.* 过多的，过分的

accident [ˈæksɪdənt] *n.* 意外事件，事故（ac-加强语气+ cid 降临+名词后缀-ent→突然降临的事情）

屠屠解词 cid-降落

- incident *n.* 事变，事件（in-加强意义+cid 降+名词后缀-ent→突然降临的事）〈派生〉incidental *a.* 偶然碰到的
- coincide *vi.* 同时发生；重合，一致（co-共同+in-加强意义+ cid 降→同时降临）
- coincidence *n.* 巧合（co-共同+in-加强意义，cid 降+名词后缀-ence）

acclaim [əˈkleɪm] *vt.* 欢呼；称赞（ac-加强语气+claim 喊叫→用劲喊叫→欢呼）

accomplish [əˈkɒmplɪʃ] *vt.* 完成（ac-加强语气+compl 完成+动词后缀-ish→完成）

accompany [əˈkʌmpəni] *vt.* 陪同，伴随；为……伴奏（ac-加强+company 伙伴→陪伴）

accord [əˈkɔːd] *n.&vt.* 一致，符合（ac-加强语气+cord 绳子→绳子捆在一起→一致，符合）〈派生〉accordance *n.* 一致，和谐

accumulate [əˈkjuːmjuleɪt] *vt.* 积累，积蓄，堆积（ac-加强语气+cumulate 积累）

accuse [əˈkjuːz] *vt.* 指责、控告（ac-加强语气+cuse 同 curse 诅咒→指责别人）

accuracy [ˈækjərəsi] *n.* 准确，准确度（ac-加强语气+cur 治好+名词后缀-acy→彻底治好→方法准确）〈派生〉accurate *a.* 精确的，准确的

affirm [əˈfɜːm] *vt.* 断言，肯定（af-加强语气+firm 坚定→非常坚定→肯定）〈派生〉affirm-ative *a.* 肯定的

affiliate [əˈfɪlɪeɪt] *vt.* 加入，使……成为会员（af-加强语气+fil 填入+i 无意义+动词后缀-ate →填充进去→加入）

accustom [əˈkʌstəm] *vt.* (to) 使习惯（ac-加强语气+custom 习惯→使习惯）

addict [ˈædɪkt] *vt.* 沉溺于（ad-加强语气+dict-说→反复说→沉溺于）

屠屠解词 dict-说

- dictionary *n.* 词典，字典（dict-说话，断言，写+ion 状态+名词后缀-ary→措辞的书→字典）
- dictate *vt.* 听写；命令（dict 说话，断言，写+ate 表动词→说话→口授，命令）
- contradictory *a.* 对立的（contra-对立的+dict-说+ory……的→说话矛盾）
- indicate *vt.* 暗示；表明（in-在里面+dic同dict-说→不说出来→暗示）〈派生〉indication *n.* 指出，指示；表明，暗示；indicative *a.* (of)指示的，暗示的
- predict *vt.* 预言，预测（pre-前面，预先+dict 说→预先说出）

aggravate [ˈægrəveɪt] *vt.* 恶化，加重，加剧（ag-加强语气+grave 严重的+动词后缀-ate→进一步严重）

allege [əˈledʒ] *vt.* 宣称，断言（al-加强语气+leg 说→一再说→宣称）〈派生〉allegiance *n.* 忠贞，效忠

屠屠解词 leg-法律，说

leg-作为词根有两个含义，一是"法律"；如 legal（合法的），legislation（立法），legiti-mate（合法的）。二是表示"讲，读，说"，这个用法更为常见，如：

- legible *a.* 可辨认的，易读的（leg-讲，读，说+ible 能……的→能够读的）
- illegible *a.* 难读的，难认的（il-不+legible 可读的→难读的，难认的）
- legend *n.* 传说，传奇；图例（leg-讲，读，说+end→讲出的东西→传奇的故事；引申为地图的图例）
- delegate *vt.* 代表；委托（de-加强语气+leg 说+ate 表示身份→具有发言权的人→代表）

allocate [ˈæləkeɪt] *vt.* 分配，分派（al-加强语气+locate 位置→分配到位）

announce [əˈnaʊns] *vt.* 宣布（an-加强语气+nounce出声→宣布）〈派生〉announcer *n.* 播音员，报幕员

annoy [əˈnɔɪ] *vt.* 使苦恼，骚扰（an-加强语气+noy 同 noise→嘈杂声让人心情烦躁→使苦恼）

ally [əˈlaɪ] *n.* 同盟国 *v.* 使结盟（al-加强语气+ly 同 li 联合→同盟）〈派生〉alliance *n.* 结盟，联盟

apparent [əˈpærənt] *a.* 明显的（ap-加强语气+par 出现+形容词后缀 -ent→显而易见的）

alleviate [əˈliːvieɪt] *vt.* 减轻，缓解（al-加强语气+lev-变轻→进一步减轻）

例句扩展 The drug can temporarily alleviate patients' pains but cannot cure this disease radically. 这种药能暂时缓减病人的疼痛，但不能从根本上医治这种疾病。

appendix [əˈpendɪks] *n.* 附录，附属物（ap-加强语气+pend 悬挂，挂靠→附属）

屠屠解词 pend 悬挂

depend 与 appendix 为同根词，记住 depend 的构成，de-加强语气，pend 悬挂，挂靠，depend(on)依赖于。

appetite [ˈæpɪtaɪt] *n.* 欲望；胃口（ap-加强语气+pet 追求，寻求+名词后缀-ite→有欲望去追求）

applaud [əˈplɔːd] *vi.* 喝彩，欢呼，鼓掌（ap-加强语气+plaud 鼓励，赞扬→欢呼、喝彩）〈派生〉applause *n.* 鼓掌欢迎，欢呼

apply [əˈplaɪ] *vi.* 申请；应用（ap-加强语气+ply 填满→表格填满→申请）〈派生〉applicable *a.* 适当的

词汇扩展

apply 的名词有两种形式：application（申请）和 appliance（器具，装置）。例如：the practical application of the theory 理论的实际运用；electronic appliance 家用电器。

appoint [ə'pɔɪnt] *vt.* 委任（ap-加强语气+point 点→安置在某个点上→委任）〈派生〉appointment *n.* 任命
appraisal [ə'preɪzəl] *n.* 估量；评价（ap-加强语气+praise 赞扬→高度评价）
appropriate [ə'prəʊprɪət] *a.* （to）适当的，恰如其分的（ap-加强语气+proper 正确的→恰当）
approve [ə'pruːv] *vi.* （of）赞成，同意；批准（ap-加强语气+prove 证明→同意）〈派生〉approval *n.* 赞成，同意；认可，批准
approximate [ə'prɒksɪmət] *a.* 大概的；*vi.* 接近于（ap-加强语气+proxim 接近，靠近+动词后缀-ate→接近）
arrange [ə'reɪndʒ] *vt.&n.* 整理，排列（ar-加强语气+range 行列→排列）
array [ə'reɪ] *v.* 排列（ar-加强语气+ray 线→线并列射出→排列）
assemble [ə'sembl] *vi.* 集合，组合（as-加强语气+sembl 相似+动词后缀-e→相似一起）〈派生〉assembly *n.* 集合，集会

屠屠解词 sembl-相似

- semblance *n.* 类似（sembl-相似+名词后缀-ance→相同之处）
- dissemble *v.* 假装，掩饰（dis-否定+sembl相似→假装相似→掩饰）
- resemble *v.* 类似，像……一样（re-再+sembl 相似→再一样→类似）

arrogant ['ærəgənt] *a.* 傲慢的，自大的（ar-加强语气+rog 叫→+形容词后缀-ant 一再叫嚷→傲慢的，自大的）
assault [ə'sɔːlt] *vt.&n.* 袭击，攻击（as-加强语气+sault 跳→跃起袭击）
assert [ə'sɜːt] *vt.* 断言，宣称（as-加强语气+sert 插入→"断"言）

屠屠解词 sert插入

- insert *v.* 插入，嵌入（in-里面的+sert 插入）
- desert *v.* 抛弃，遗弃；沙漠（de-表示否定+sert 加入，插入→不再加入→抛弃/沙漠）

assign [ə'saɪn] *vt.* 分配，委派（as-加强语气+sign 信号→给出指示→分配）〈派生〉assignment *n.* 分配；任务，（课外）作业
assimilate [ə'sɪmɪleɪt] *vt.* 同化（as-加强语气+simil 相似的+动词后缀-ate 使……相似→同化）
assess [ə'ses] *vt.* 估价，评价（as-加强语气+sess 坐→（评委）坐着给出评价）

屠屠解词 sess 坐

汉语中"拥有"有个表达方式是"坐拥"，possess 拥有（pos-放+sess 坐→摆放出来你可以坐拥）。

- estimate 通常指由个人做出的主观估价。
- appraise 指以专家身份作了最终精确的估价。
- assess 通过估价以便更好利用。
- value 侧重指一般人对某物的价值或价格所做的估计。
- rate 专指评定价值等级的高低。

asset ['æset] *n.* 资产，有用的东西（as-加强语气+set 装置，设备→有用的东西）
assist [ə'sɪst] *vt.* 帮助，援助，协助（as-加强语气+sist 站着→站在旁边→协助）〈派生〉assistance *n.* 帮助，援助；assistant *n.* 助手，助教；*a.* 辅助的，助理的

屠屠解词 sist站着

- consist *vi.* 由……组成（con-共同+sist→站到一起→组成）
- insist *vi.* 坚持；硬要（in-加强语气+sist→一直站着→坚持）
- persist *vi.* 坚持到底（per-一直，始终+sist→始终站着→坚持到底）
- resist *vt.* 反抗，对抗（re-反+sist→站出来反对→反抗）
- irresistible *a.* 不可抗拒的（ir-不+resist 反抗+形容词后缀-ible→不可反抗的）

associate [ə'səʊʃɪeɪt] *vt.* 使联系；交往（as-加强语气+soci 同 social 社会→各种关系构成联系）〈派生〉association *n.* 协会；联合，联系

assure [ə'ʃʊə] *vt.* 使确信；保证，担保（as-加强语气+sure 确定→确保）〈派生〉assurance *n.* 确保；保证

assume [ə'sjuːm] *vt.* 承担，担当，假定（as-加强语气+sume 抓住→"抓住"责任就是承担责任）

屠屠解词 sume 拿，抓

- resume *v.* 重新开始（re-再一次+sume 拿→再一次拿起→重新开始）
- consume *vt.* 消耗；吃完；喝光（con-共同+sume 拿→全部拿完→消耗）
- presume *vt.* 假定，假设（pre-预先+sume 拿→提前拿出方案→假定）

attach [ə'tætʃ] *vt.*（to）系上；使依附（at-加强+tach词根"钉子"→钉住）

屠屠解词 tach 钉子

attach 的反义词是 detach（de-去掉+tach 钉子，接角→把钉上的分开→拆开），阅读理解中通常出现形容词形式 detached "超然的"，该词在态度题中出现，通常为错误答案。

attain [ə'tein] *vt.* 达到，获得（at-加强语气+tain 拿住+握住→获得）

屠屠解词 tain 拿住，握住

- obtain *vt.* 获得，得到（ob-加强动作+tain 拿住，握住→获得）
- sustain *vt.* 支撑；承受（sus-下面+tain 握住→在下面握住→支撑）
- retain *vt.* 保持，保留（re-反复+tain 拿住，握住→反复拿着）
- maintain *vt.* 坚持；主张（main 同 man-手+tain 拿住，握住→用手拿住→坚持）
- detain *vt.* 留住；拘留（de-加强语气+tain 拿住→留住，不让离开→引申为拘留）

attempt [ə'tempt] *n.&v.* 尝试，试图（at-加强语气+tempt 诱惑→在诱惑下→尝试）

attract [ə'trækt] *v.* 吸引，引诱（at-加强语气+tract 拉→吸引）〈派生〉attractive *a.* 有吸引力的，引起兴趣的，动人的

acknowledge [ək'nɒlidʒ] *vt.* 承认，公认；答谢（ac- 同 ak- 加强+knowledge 知晓→所有人都知晓→公认）

acquaint [ə'kweint] *vt.* 使熟知（ac-发音同 ak-加强语气+quaint认知→相互认知→熟悉）〈派生〉acquaintance *n.* 相识，熟人

ascertain [ˌæsə'tein] *vt.* 确定（as-加强语气+certain 开头发音为"s"，确定→确定）

acquire [ə'kwaiə] *vt.* 获得，学到（ac-发音同 ak-加强语气+quire 同 quest 寻求→获得）〈派生〉acquisition *n.* 获得，获得物

屠屠解词

acquire, obtain, gain, get 辨析

acquire, obtain, gain 都强调通过持续努力获得，但 obtain 侧重得到期盼已久的东西，gain 侧重获得某种利益或好处。get 使用广泛，可指以任何方式得到某物，也不一定要经过努力。

【词缀二】a-加强语气

abide [ə'baid] *vi.* 坚持，遵守（a-加强语气+bide 同 bite 咬住→咬住不放→坚持）

abound [ə'baund] *vi.* 充满，大量存在，富于（a-加强语气+bound 范围→整个范围都充满→富于）

amid [ə'mid] *prep.* 在……中间（a-加强语气+mid 中间）

avoid [ə'vɔid] *vt.* 防止，避免；逃避，避开（a-加强语气+void 空的→使……空出→避免）

await [ə'weit] *vt.* 等候（a-加强语气+wait 等待→等待）

awake [ə'weik] *a.* 醒着的 *vt.* 唤醒，使觉醒（a-加强语气+wake 醒→苏醒）

aware [ə'weə] *a.* 知道的，明白的，意识到的（a-加强语气+ware 意识到→明白）

award [əˈwɔːd] *n.* 奖励；*vt.* 授予（a-加强语气+ward 守卫，防卫→防卫受到嘉奖）

avail [əˈveɪl] *vi.* 有益于，有帮助（a-加强语气+vail 同 value 价值→有价值的）〈派生〉available *a.* 可用的，有效的

ashore [əˈʃɔː] *ad.* 向岸边（a-加强语气+shore 海岸→向岸边）

aside [əˈsaɪd] *ad.* 在旁边，到旁边（a-加强语气+side 旁边→在旁边）

arise [əˈraɪz] *v.* 出现，发生；（from）由……引起（a-加强语气+rise 上升→升起来→出现）

amount [əˈmaʊnt] *v.* 接近（to）；共计；*n.* 总数，数量（a-加强语气+mount 增长，山顶→靠近山顶→接近）

amend [əˈmend] *v.* 修正，改进，改正（a-加强语气+mend 修补→修正）

【词缀三】ad-加强语气

adopt [əˈdɒpt] *vt.* 采取；收养（ad-加强语气+ opt 选择→做出选择→采取）

adapt [əˈdæpt] *vt.* 使适应；改编（ad-加强语气+apt 恰当的，易于→使……恰当→适应）

adequate [ˈædɪkwɪt] *a.* 适当的，足够的（ad-加强语气+equ-对等+形容词后缀-ate→与之对等，适当、恰好→适当的）

adhere [ədˈhɪə] *v.* 黏附，胶着，坚持（ad-加强语气+her-黏着）

真题例句 For years executives and head-hunters have adhered to the rule that the most attractive CEO candidates are the ones who must be poached. 多年来，经理人和猎头们都遵循这样的规则：最具有吸引力的首席执行官人选是那些需要去挖的人。

adjacent [əˈdʒeɪsənt] *a.* 邻近的，接近的（ad- 加强语气+jac-连接+形容词后缀-ent→连接在一起→靠近）

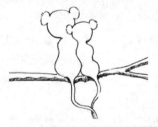

adjoin [əˈdʒɔɪn] *v.* 邻接，毗连（ad-加强语气+ join 加入→加入其中→连接一起）

adjust [əˈdʒʌst] *vt.* 调整，调节，使适合（ad-加强语气+just 正确的→不断寻求正确→调整）

adore [əˈdɔː] *v.* 崇拜，爱慕（ad-加强+or-说→反复说，常挂在嘴边→非常喜欢）

advent [ˈædvənt] *n.* 出现，到来，降临（ad-加强语气+vent 走→走来）〈派生〉adventure *n.* 冒险

屠屠解词 vent-走

- convention *n.* 集会；惯例（con 大家+vent-走+名词后缀-ion→大家来到一起→集会）

- event *n.* 事件（e-出+vent 走→出来的事→事件）

- invent *vt.* 发明，创造（in-加强语气+vent走→来到世上→发明）

- prevent *vt.* 防止，阻止（pre-预先+vent 走→预先来到→抢先一步，防止别人）

adverse [ˈædvɜːs] *a.* 不利的，敌对的，相反的（ad-加强语气+vers-转→转到对面→敌对的）

屠屠解词 vers-转

- versus *perp.* 对抗（vers-转+后缀-us→转过去构成对抗）

- diversity *n.* 多样性（di-两+vers- 转+名词后缀-ity→转向两个方向→不同）

- anniversary *n.* 周年纪念（anni-一+vers- 转+名词后缀-ary→转一周为一年）

- reverse *a.* 反转的，颠倒的（re-反+vers- 转+ e→反转的）

- versatile *a.* 多才多艺的，多方面的（vers-转+atile→玩得转，有才能的）

- conversely *ad.* 相反地（con-加强语气+vers 转→转到另一方向→相反）

- convert *vt.* 变换，转化（con-加强语气+vert 同 vers 转）〈派生〉conversion *n.* 变换，转化

- inverse *a.* 倒转的，反转的 *n.* 反面（in-在里面+vers 转→向里转→反转）

advocate [ˈædvəkeɪt] *n.* 提倡者 *v.* 提倡（ad-加强语气+voc-声音+动词后缀-ate→提高声音→提倡）

【词缀四】be-表示"是、成为、看成"

behalf [bɪˈhɑːf] *n.* 代表（be-成为+half 半→成为……另一半→不可分割的方面，可以代表对方）

behave [bɪˈheɪv] *vi.* 举动，举止，运转（be-成为+have 具有→具有的行为特征）〈派生〉behavior / behaviour *n.* 行为

below [bɪˈləʊ] *prep.* 在……下面（be-成为+ low 低→在……下方）

belittle [bɪˈlɪtl] *vt.* 轻视，使渺小（be-看成+ little 小→轻视）

beloved [bɪˈlʌvɪd] *a.* 心爱的（be-成为+loved 爱→内心充满爱）

beneath [bɪˈniːθ] *ad.* 在……之下（be-成为+ neath 在……下方）

benefit [ˈbenɪfɪt] *vt.* 有益于，有助于 *n.* 利益，好处（be-是+ne-无意义+fit-适合→合适的才能有帮助）〈派生〉beneficial *a.* 有好处的

betray [bɪˈtreɪ] *vt.* 出卖，背叛，泄露（be-是+ tray 盘子→和盘托出→背叛，泄露）

beware [bɪˈweə] *v.* 小心，谨防（be-是+ware 意识到→小心）

bewilder [bɪˈwɪldə] *vt.* 使迷惑，使不知所措，使昏乱（be-是+wild 狂乱、迷惑→使不知所措）

befriend [bɪˈfrend] *vt.* 待人如友，帮助（be-看成+ friend 朋友→把别人看作朋友）

【词缀五】co-、col-、com-、con-、cor-表示"一起、共同"或加强语气

coalition [ˌkəʊəˈlɪʃən] *n.* 合并，接合，联合（co-一起 +al 同 ally 结盟 +i- 无意义 + 名词后缀 -tion →联合）

coherent [kəʊˈhɪərənt] *a.* 一致的，协调的（co-一起+her 黏+形容词后缀-ent→黏在一起→步伐一致）

cohesive [kəʊˈhiːsɪv] *a.* 黏着的，有结合力的（co-一起+he 同 her 黏+形容词后缀-sive→黏在一起）

coincide [ˌkəʊɪnˈsaɪd] *v.* 同时发生；重合，一致（co-共同的+in-加强语气+cid 降→共同降落）〈派生〉coincidence *n.* 巧合；一致，符合

collaborate [kəˈlæbəˌreɪt] *v.* 协作，合作（col-共同的+labor 劳动+动词后缀-ate→一起劳动→协作）

collapse [kəˈlæps] *v.&n.* 倒坍，崩溃，垮台（col-全部+laps 流逝，逝去）

屠屠解词 laps-滑落

- lapse *n.* 流逝；下降；偏离（laps-滑走+e→[机会]滑走→失去[机会]→出了差错）
- elapse（时间）溜走；（光阴）逝去（e 出+laps-滑落→时光流去）

colleague [ˈkɒliːg] *n.* 同事，同僚（col-共同的+league 联盟，同盟）

collide [kəˈlaɪd] *vi.* 碰撞，抵触（col-共同的+ lid 盖子+动词后缀-e→两个都去盖→形成矛盾→抵触、碰撞）〈派生〉collision *n.* 冲突、碰撞

collocation [kɒləˈkeɪʃən] *n.* 排列，搭配（col-一起+location 位置→位置摆在一起→排列、搭配）

combat [ˈkɒmbæt] *v.&n.* 战斗，搏斗（com-共同的+bat 球拍，打→对打→战斗）

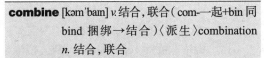

combine [kəmˈbaɪn] v. 结合，联合（com-一起+bin 同 bind 捆绑→结合）〈派生〉combination n. 结合，联合

command [kəˈmɑːnd] n.&v. 命令，指挥（com-加强语气+mand 命令）

屠屠解词 command / commend 辨析

command 表示"命令、指挥"的意思，常用的词组有 take command of...统领。commend 原意是"推荐"（com-共同的+mend修补→共同提出修补的方案→推荐），推荐过程中需要大力赞扬，因此引申为"称赞"。

commemorate [kəˈmeməreɪt] v. 纪念，庆祝（com-加强语气+memory 记忆，存储→加深记忆→纪念）

compact [ˈkɒmpækt] n. 合同，契约 [kəmˈpækt] a. 紧密的，简明的（com-加强语气+pact 合同，协定）

compassion [kəmˈpæʃən] n. 同情，怜悯（com-共同+passion 情感→感同身受→同情）

compel [kəmˈpel] v. 强迫，迫使（com-一起+ pel 推→一起推→迫使）

屠屠解词 pel 推

● impel vt. 驱动（im-进入+pel 推→推进，驱动）
● propel vt. 推进（pro-向前+pel 推→向前推）
● repel vt. 驱除，击退（re-回+pel 推→击退）
● dispel vt. 驱除，消除（dis-分开+pel 推→推开→驱除）
● expel vt. 开除，驱逐（ex-向外+pel 推→排出，驱逐）

compile [kəmˈpaɪl] v. 编辑，汇编（com-一起+ pile 堆起，积累→材料堆在一起→汇编）

compress [kəmˈpres] v. 压缩，浓缩（com-加强语气+press 压）

compromise [ˈkɒmprəmaɪz] n. 妥协，折中（com-一起+promise 承诺，一起做出承诺，相互妥协）

commerce [ˈkɒmɜːs] n. 商业（com-加强语气，merc-商业）〈派生〉commercial a. 商业的

commit [kəˈmɪt] vt. 把……交给；犯（错误），干（坏事）（com-全部+mit 放出，送→全部放出给别人→把……交给→引申为放纵自己犯错）〈派生〉commision n. 委托，授权

屠屠解词 mit 放出，送

● emit vt. 发出，放射，散发（e-出+mit 送，放出→释放）
● omit vt. 省略，删除（o-出+mit 送出→省略）
● permit vt. 允许，容许（per-始终+mit 送，放出，派，错过→始终放出→许可）
● submit vt. 提交；屈服，服从（sub-在下面+mit 送，放出→从下面送上去→提交）
● transmit vt. 传输，传达（trans-从一处到另一处+mit 送，放出→传输）
● intermittent a. 间歇的，断断续续的（inter-中间+mit 送，放出→把中间部分扔掉→不连贯→间断）

compensate [ˈkɒmpenseɪt] v. 偿还，补偿（com-加强语气+pens 费用→补偿）

comply [kəmˈplaɪ] vi. 遵从；依从（com-共同+ply 重叠，重复→观点重叠在一起→顺从，同意）

component [kəmˈpəʊnənt] n. 成分；a. 组成的，构成的（com-一起+pon- 放置+名词后缀-ent→摆放在一起→组成）

屠屠解词 pon-放置

● opponent 对手，反对者，敌手（op-反+pon- 放置+名词后缀-ent 人→敌对的人）
● postpone 推迟（post-后面+pon- 放+e→放到后面→推迟）

compose [kəmˈpəʊz] v. 组成（com-一起+pose 摆放→放在一起→组成）〈派生〉composite a.&n. 合成，复合；composition n. 合成，复合

compound [ˈkɒmpaʊnd] n.&a.&v. 调和，混合（com-一起+pound 重量单位→组成）

compete [kəmˈpiːt] v. 竞赛（com-一起+pet-追赶，追求→为一个目标一起追赶→竞争）〈派生〉competent a. 有能力的；competition n. 竞争；competitive a. 竞争的

conceal [kən'si:l] v. 隐藏，隐蔽，隐瞒（con-加强+ceal 源自 seal "密封"→隐藏起来）

concentrate ['kɒnsəntreɪt] v. 集中，专心；浓缩；n. 浓缩物（con-共同的+centr- 中心+动词后缀-ate→共同聚往中心）

concentric [kən'sentrɪk] a. 同中心的（con-共同的+ centr-中心+形容词后缀-ic→共同中心）

concise [kən'saɪs] a. 简明的，简洁的（con-全部的+cis-切开→全部切开→简单明了）

屠屠解词 cis-切开

precise a. 精确的；明确的（pre-提前+cis-切开→提前切开→明确）〈派生〉precision n. 精确性

condemn [kən'dem] v. 谴责，指责（con-加强语气+demn 音变自 damn→诅咒）

condense [kən'dens] v.（使）压缩，（使）凝结，精简，压缩（con-加强+dense 密集的）

confer [kən'fɜ:] v. 协商，交换意见（con-共同的+fer 拿→拿到一块探讨→交换意见）〈派生〉conference n. 会议

confess [kən'fes] v. 承认，坦白，忏悔（con-全部+fess 说→全都说出→坦白）

confidential [ˌkɒnfɪ'denʃəl] a. 机密的；亲信的，亲密的（con-全部+fid-信任→完全信任→亲信）

屠屠解词 confident / confidential 辨析

- confident 是"自信"的含义。
- confidential 既可以表示"亲密的、亲信的"，同义词有 intimate, familiar，也可以表示"机密"。

confirm [kən'fɜ:m] v. 使更坚定；确认（con-加强语气+firm 坚实的）〈区分〉conform v.（to）遵守，依照

conflict ['kɒnflɪkt] n.&v. 战斗；冲突（con-一起+flict 打击→一起打斗→冲突）

屠屠解词 flict 打击

- afflict vt. 受到痛苦，折磨（af-加强语气+flict 打击→折磨）
- inflict vt. 使遭受［损伤，苦痛等］，使承受（in-进入+flict 打击→进入打斗→导致痛苦）

confront [kən'frʌnt] v. 使面临；面对（con-一起+front 前方→一起面对）

confuse [kən'fju:z] v. 使混乱，混淆（con-一起+fuse 保险丝→全部熔合在一起→混乱，混淆）〈派生〉confusion n. 混乱，混淆

confine [kən'faɪn] v. 限制，局限（con-加强语气+fin 限制，范围）

屠屠解词 fine 范围，限制

- fine 罚款（fine 范围，限制→［罚款］以约束，限制）
- confine 限制；禁闭（con-全部+fine 限制→全部限制）
- define 下定义；阐述；阐释；限定，规定（de-加强+ fine 限制→加强限制）〈派生〉definite 确切的；确定的

conjunction [kən'dʒʌŋkʃən] n. 连接，联结；连接词（con-加强语气+junct 同 join 连接）

consensus [kən'sensəs] n. 一致，一致同意（con-共同的+sens- 感觉+名词后缀-us→感觉一样）

conserve [kən'sɜ:v] v. 保存，保藏（con-加强语气+ serve 保留→保存）〈派生〉conserva-tion n. 保存；conservatism n. 保守主义；con-servative a. 保守的，守旧的

consist [kən'sɪst] vi. 由……组成，一致（con-一起+sist 站→站在一起→组成）〈派生〉consistent a. 一致的，调和的

屠屠解词 consist 和 comprise 辨析

consist 和 comprise 是同义词，但是用法上有区别，consist of... 不能用于被动语态，而 comprise 是及物动词，词组为 be comprised of...

console [kən'səul] vt. 安慰（con-一起+ sole 独自→不再一个人，两个人在一起→获得安慰）

conspiracy [kən'spɪrəsi] n. 共谋，阴谋（con-共同+spir-呼气→一个鼻孔出气→共谋）

屠屠解词 spir-呼吸

- aspiring a. 热心的，积极的，有抱负的（a-加强语气+spir-呼吸+形容词后缀-ing→渴望的→积极

的，有抱负的）

- spirit *n.* 精神（spir-呼吸+动词后缀-it→深呼吸具有精神）

- inspire *vt.* 鼓舞，激励（in-往里+spir-呼吸→往里吹气→鼓舞，激励）

- respire *vi.* 呼吸（re-再次+spir- 呼吸，精神+e→*v.* 呼吸）

consolidate [kənˈsɒlɪdeɪt] *v.* 巩固，加强（con-加强语气+solid- 固体+动词后缀-ate）

conspicuous [kənˈspɪkjuəs] *a.* 显眼的，明显的（con-共同+spic- 看+形容词后缀-ous→大家都能看到→显眼）

consecutive [kənˈsekjutɪv] *a.* 连续的，连贯的（con-共同+sec-跟着+ut 同动词后缀-ate+形容词后缀-ive→大家都跟着→连贯的）

屠屠解词 sec 跟随

词根 sec 源自 second 的熟词僻义"支持"，支持就会一直追随。

- prosecute *vt.* 告发，起诉（pro-向前+sec 跟随+ute 同动词后缀-ate→追随到法院前面→告发，起诉）

- persecute 迫害（per-一直+ sec 跟随+ ute 同动词后缀-ate→一直跟踪→迫害）

constrain [kənˈstreɪn] *vt.* 强迫，抑制，拘束（con-加强语气+strain 拉紧→使劲拉→强迫）

conscience [ˈkɒnʃəns] *n.* 良心，道德心 conscience con-共同的+sci-拉丁词根知晓，知道+名词后缀-ence，共同知道的→公知良俗→公共道德→公德心〈派生〉conscientious *a.* 尽职尽责的

例句扩展 I have battled with my conscience over whether I should give a hand to the man lying on the street unconsciously. 我备受良心的煎熬，不知是否应该伸手帮助那个躺在地上昏迷不醒的人。（注意：conscience 译为"良知"，conscious 译为"有意识的"。）

contaminate [kənˈtæmɪneɪt] *v.* 污染（con-加强语气+tamin 接触+动词后缀-ate→被碰到→弄脏）

contemplate [ˈkɒntempleɪt] *v.* 凝视，沉思（con-加强语气+temple 熟词僻义"太阳穴"→紧摁太阳穴→沉思）

contempt [kənˈtempt] *n.* 轻视，轻蔑，耻辱，招人唾弃（con-一起+tempt 诱惑→诱惑所有人的行为→招人唾弃）

contend [kənˈtend] *v.* 斗争，竞争（con-一起+tend 延伸，看作to+end→一起冲向终点→竞争）

contest [ˈkɒntest] *n.* 竞争 [kənˈtest] *v.* 争夺（con-一起+test 测试→竞争）

context [ˈkɒntekst] *n.* 上下文，文章前后关系（con-一起+text 文章→与文章联系在一起）

contract [kənˈtrækt] *v.* 缩小，缩短；*n.* 契约，合同（con-一起+tract 拉→拉到一起，缩短距离）

converge [kənˈvɜːdʒ] *v.* 聚合，集中于一点（con-一起+verge 边缘→从边缘一起往里→集中于一点）

correlate [ˈkɒrɪleɪt] *v.* 使互相关联（cor-一起+relate 联系→相互联系）

correspond [ˌkɒrɪsˈpɒnd] *v.* 符合；通信（cor-共同的+respond 回应→保持一致）〈派生〉correspondence *n.* 通信；correspondent *n.* 记者；corresponding *a.* 符合的，相应的

coauthor [kəʊˈɔːθə] *n.* 合著者（co-共同+author 作者→共同创作的人→合著者）

coexist [ˌkəʊɪɡˈzɪst] *v.* 共存（co-共同+exist 存在→共存）

cooperate [kəʊˈɒpəreɪt] *v.* 合作（co-共同+operate 操作→一起操作→合作）〈派生〉cooperative *a.* 合作的

coordinate [kəʊˈɔːdɪneɪt] *a.* 同等的，并列的（co-共同的+ord 同 order 顺序+in 在里面+动词后缀-ate→处于顺序一样的状态中→协调）

【词缀六】contr-前缀构成的单词通常表示"矛盾、冲突"

contradict [ˌkɒntrəˈdɪkt] *v.* 矛盾

contradiction [ˌkɒntrəˈdɪkʃən] *n.* 矛盾，冲突

contrary [ˈkɒntrəri] *a.* 相反的

contrast [ˈkɒntræst] *v.&n.* 对比，对照

contranatural [kɒntrəˈnætʃərəl] *a.* 违背自然

controversial [ˈkɒntrəvɜːʃəl] *a.* 争论的，有争议的

controversy [ˈkɒntrəvɜːsi] *n.* 争论

【词缀七】de-系列

① de-前缀表示"向下"或否定含义

decay [dɪˈkeɪ] *vi.&n.* 衰减，腐朽，腐烂（de-向下+cay 珊瑚礁→越来越少）

deceive [dɪˈsiːv] *v.* 欺骗，蒙蔽（de-否定+ceive 拿→没有通过正当方式获得→欺骗，蒙蔽）〈派生〉deceit *n.* 欺骗，欺骗行为

屠屠解词 ceive 拿，抓，握住

- receive *v.* 接受；收到（re-往回+ceive 拿→拿回来→收到）

- conceive *vt.* 构思 *vi.* 怀孕（con-一起+ceive 拿→把相法拿到一起→构思）

- perceive *v.* 察觉，理解（per-全部+ceive 拿→全部握住→理解）

decrease [ˈdiːkriːs] *n.* 减少 [diːˈkriːs] *v.* 减少（de-向下+increase 增加）

decode [ˌdiːˈkəʊd] *vt.* 解码（de-否定+code 加密→解码）

deduce [dɪˈdjuːs] *vt.* 推论，演绎出（de-向下+duce 引导→向下引导→演绎得出）

屠屠解词 infer/deduce/deduct

- infer 指从已提供的论据或从已接受的前提出发而推断出的结论。

- deduce 指有充分根据的推论，也指逻辑学上的演绎。

- deduct 虽然也有推导演绎的含义，但是主要含义为"扣除"。

defy [dɪˈfaɪ] *v.* 反抗，违抗（de-否定+动词后缀-fy）

degenerate [dɪˈdʒenəreɪt] *v.* 衰退，堕落（de-否定，generate 产生）

destruction [dɪsˈtrʌkʃən] *n.* 破坏，消灭（de-否定+struct 结构+名词后缀-tion）〈派生〉destructive *a.* 破坏性

defect [ˈdiːfekt] *n.* 缺点 [dɪˈfekt] *vi.* 背叛；投敌（de-否定+fect 做→做得不够→缺陷）

屠屠解词 fect 做

- effect *n.* 影响（ef-出+fect 做→做出来→产生影响）

- perfect *a.* 使完美（per-全部+fect 做→全部做完→完善的）

- infect *vt.* 传染，感染（in-进入+fect 做→做进去→传染进去）

descend [dɪˈsend] *v.* 下来，下降（de-否定+ascend 增加）〈派生〉descendant *n.* 子孙后代；descent *n.* 下降；斜坡；血统

deficiency [dɪˈfɪʃənsi] *n.* 缺乏，不足；缺陷（de-否定+efficiency 效率→效率低下）

defer [dɪˈfɜː] *vi.* 推迟，延期（de-否定+fer 拿→往后拿→延期）

屠屠解词 fer 拿

- deferment *n.* 推迟；延迟（defer推迟+ment表名词→推迟；延迟）

- infer *vt.* 推论（in- 在里面 +fer 拿→拿到里面→将上一个命题带入下一个命题→推论）

- fertile *a.* 肥沃的，富饶的；能繁殖的（fert 同 fer 带来，拿来+ile 能……的→能带来粮食→肥沃的）

- transfer *vt.* 转移；转换；转让；过户；迁移；改乘（trans-变换，交换+fer 带→转移过去→转学，转移）

- confer *vi.* 协商，交换意见（con-共同+fer 带来，拿来→共同带来观点）

defeat [dɪˈfiːt] *v.* 战胜，挫败 *n.* 失败（de-否定+feat 丰功伟绩→失败）

delay [dɪˈleɪ] *v.* 耽搁，延迟，延期（de-否定+lay 放置→往后方置→延期）

deliberate [dɪˈlɪbərɪt] *a.* 慎重的，深思熟虑的；故意的（de-否定+liber 自由，随意+动词后缀-ate→不再自由随意→慎重，需要深思熟虑）

depress [dɪˈpres] *v.* 压下；压抑；使沮丧（de-向下+press 压→压下→引申为使人感到沮丧）

deprive [dɪˈpraɪv] *vt.* 剥夺，使丧失（de-除去+priv 私人的→不再是私人的→剥夺权利）

② de-表示加强语气，不影响原来核心词缀的意义

decent [ˈdiːsənt] *a.* 正派的，端庄的，有分寸的（de-加强语气+cent 分→有"分"寸的）

declare [dɪˈkleə] *v.* 声明；宣称（de-加强语气+clare 同 clear→说清楚）〈派生〉declaration *n.* 宣言，宣布，声明

default [dɪˈfɔːlt] *n.&v.* 犯错；不履行责任（de-加强语气+fault 错误→犯错）

defend [dɪˈfend] *v.* 防守；为……辩护（de-加强语气+fend 保护）〈派生〉defense *n.* 防御；defendant *a.* 辩护的 *n.* 被告

define [dɪˈfaɪn] *v.* 给……下定义；限定，（de-加强语气+fin-限定）

delight [dɪˈlaɪt] *n.* 快乐，高兴 *v.*（使）高兴，（使）欣喜（de-加强语气+light 光亮→见到光明很高兴）

derive [dɪˈraɪv] *v.* 源自，导出，引申（de-修饰+riv 河流→流动）

denote [dɪˈnəʊt] *v.* 指示（de-加强语气+note 通知→下发通知→指示）

depict [dɪˈpɪkt] *vt.* 描述，描写（de-加强语气+pict 图画→描绘）

真题例句 Today's double-income families are at greater financial risk in that they are deprived of unemployment or disability insurance. 如今的双收入家庭面临更大的经济风险，因为他们不能再享受失业和伤残保险。

despise [dɪsˈpaɪz] *v.* 蔑视（de- 向下 +spis 看，同 spic，spec，spect →看不起）

devalue [diːˈvæljuː] *v.* 贬值（de-否定+value 价值→价值贬低）

deteriorate [dɪˈtɪərɪəreɪt] *v.* 恶化（de-否定+ terior 同 terriority 领土→逐步恶化）

deviate [ˈdiːvɪeɪt] *v.* 背离（de-否定+via 通过→路线不对→偏离）

deposit [dɪˈpɒzɪt] *v.* 存放，储蓄，使沉淀；*n.* 存款，沉积物（de-加强语气+pos 放→放进去→存储）〈派生〉deposition *n.* 沉积作用，沉积物

denounce [dɪˈnaʊns] *v.* 公开指责（de-加强语气+nounce 出声→表达自己的声音→指责）

deplore [dɪˈplɔː] *v.* 表示悲痛（de-加强语气+plore 发出声音→悲痛）

屠屠解词 plore 哭，喊

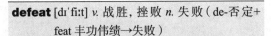

- **implore** *v.* 乞求，哀求（im-进入+plore 哭喊→进入喊哭状态→乞求）
- **explore** *vt.* 探测；探究，探索（ex-出+plore 喊→喊出来→探索奥秘）

designate [ˈdezɪgneɪt] *vt.* 指明，指出，任命，指派（de-加强语气+sign 签名→任命，委派）

desolate [ˈdesəlɪt] *a.* 荒凉的；孤独的；*v.* 使荒芜（de-加强语气+sol 同 sole 孤单+形容词后缀-ate）

devil [ˈdevl] *n.* 魔鬼，恶棍（de-加强语气+evil 恶魔）

diminish [dɪˈmɪnɪʃ] *v.*（使）减少,（使）变小（di 同 de-加强语气+mini-小+动词后缀-ish→减少）

【词缀八】dis-表示否定概念或"向四处分散"

① dis-表示否定含义

disable [dɪsˈeɪbl] *v.* 使残废（dis-否定+able 能够）

disappear [ˌdɪsəˈpɪə] *v.* 不见，消失（dis-否定+appear 出现）

disappoint [ˌdɪsəˈpɒɪnt] *v.* 使失望，使扫兴（dis-否定+appoint 委派→没有委派→失望）

disaster [dɪˈzɑːstə] *n.* 灾难，天灾（dis-否定+aster 星星→星象不吉→灾难）〈派生〉disastrous *a.* 灾难性的

屠屠解词 表示"灾难"词汇

catastrophe *n.* 灾难；tsunami *n.* 海啸；drought *n.* 干旱；hurricane *n.* 飓风；earthquake *n.* 地震；flood *n.* 洪水；typhoon *n.* 台风；snowstorm *n.* 暴风雪；hail *n.* 冰雹

disclose [dɪsˈkləʊz] *v.* 揭示，泄露（dis-否定+close 关闭→不关闭→揭露）

discount [ˈdɪskaʊnt] *n.* 折扣 [dɪsˈkaunt] *vi.* 折扣（dis-否定+count 计算→不计算的部分→打折）

discourage [dɪsˈkʌrɪdʒ] *v.* 使泄气，使失去信心（dis-否定+courage 勇气）

discover [dɪsˈkʌvə] *v.* 发现，显示（dis-否定+cover 覆盖）〈派生〉discovery *n.* 发现

disgrace [dɪsˈgreɪs] *n.* 耻辱；*v.* 玷辱，使蒙羞（dis-否定+grace 脸面）

② dis-表示"向四处分散"

discard [dɪsˈkɑːd] *v.* 丢弃，抛弃（dis-四处分开+card 卡片→到处扔卡片→丢弃）

discern [dɪˈsɜːn] *v.* 辨别，区分，识别（dis-分开+cern 搞清，区别→分开搞清→区别）

discourse [ˈdɪskɔːs] *n.* 演讲，论述，论文（dis-四处分开+course 课程→到处讲课→演讲）

discrepancy [dɪsˈkrepənsi] *n.* 差异（dis-四处分开+crep 同 creep 爬→向不同方向爬→差异）

dispose [dɪsˈpəʊz] *v.* 部署，处理，处置（dis-四处分开+pose 放置→各地放置→部署）〈派生〉disposal *n.* 处理，处置，布置；disposition *n.* 部署

display [dɪsˈpleɪ] *v.&n.* 展览，显示（dis-四处分开+play 演示→到处演示→展览）

dispatch [dɪsˈpætʃ] *v.* 发送，派遣，调遣；*n.*（公文）急件，书信（dis-四处分开+patch 碎片→纸片四处飘散→发送）

disguise [dɪsˈgaɪz] *n.&v.* 假装，伪装（dis-否定+guise 装束）

disgust [dɪsˈgʌst] *n.* 厌恶，恶心 *v.* 使厌恶（dis-否定+gust 口味，味道→不好闻的味道→恶心）

dismay [dɪsˈmei] *n.&v.* 沮丧（dis-否定+may 可能→事情不可能→沮丧）

disorder [dɪsˈɔːdə] *n.* 混乱，骚乱（dis-否定+order 顺序）

displace [dɪsˈpleɪs] *v.* 转移，取代（dis-否定+place 放置→没有放置原位→转移）〈派生〉displacement *n.* 移置，取代

dissolve [dɪˈzɒlv] *v.* 取消，溶解（dis-否定+solve 找到解决办法→取消）

dispute [dɪsˈpjuːt] *n.* 争论（dis-否定+put 放→放不下→与……争论）

distort [dɪsˈtɔːt] *vt.* 歪曲（dis-否定+tort 扭转→负面的扭转→歪曲）

disperse [dɪsˈpɜːs] *v.* 分散，驱散，解散（dis-四处分开+perse 分开→四处分散）

dissipate [ˈdɪsɪpeɪt] *v.* 驱散（dis-四处分开+sip 吸气+动词后缀-ate→向四处吹气→吹散，驱散）

distress [dɪsˈtres] *n.* 苦恼；不幸 *v.* 使苦恼（dis-四处分开+stress 压力→到处压力重重→苦恼）

能穿越吗？

distribute [dɪsˈtrɪbjuːt] *v.* 分配；分布；散布（dis-四处分开+tribut 给+动词后缀-e→四处分给→分配）

屠屠解词 tribut-给

- attribute *vt.* 归因于，归属于（at-加强动作+tribut-给予+动词后缀-e→[把原因]给出→归因于 ）
- contribute *vt.* 贡献；捐款（con-全部+tribut- 给予+动词后缀-e→全部给出→捐钱 ）

disturb [dɪsˈtɜːb] *v.* 扰乱，妨碍，使不安（dis-四处分开+turb 搅动→到处搅动→扰乱 ）〈派生〉disturbance *n.* 动乱，骚乱，干扰

diffuse [dɪˈfjuːs] *a.* 散开的 *v.* 散播，传播（dif 同 dis-四处分开+fuse 流淌→四处流淌→散播，传播 ）

【词缀九】em-、en-表示"进入"或加强语气

embarrass [ɪmˈbærəs] *v.* 使窘迫，使为难（em-进入+bar 障碍→拦在障碍里→尴尬、为难 ）

embed [ɪmˈbed] *vt.* 使插入，使嵌入（em-进入+bed 床→进入床这样的柔软物体→插入 ）

embody [ɪmˈbɒdi] *v.* 体现，使具体化（em- 进入 + body 主体→文章主体→体现重心，内容具体 ）

例句扩展 Achievement happens because you as a person embody the external achievement. 成就之所以出现，是因为作为一个人，你体现着外在成就。

embrace [ɪmˈbreɪs] *v.* 拥抱；包含（em-进入+brace 怀抱→进入怀抱→拥抱 ）

empower [ɪmˈpaʊə] *v.* 授予权利（em-进入+power 权力→给予权力 ）

enable [ɪˈneɪbl] *v.* 使能够，使成为可能（en-进入+able 能力→赋予能力 ）

enclose [ɪnˈkləʊz] *v.* 围住，圈起（en-进入+close 关闭→关在内→围起 ）〈派生〉enclosure *n.* 围住，圈起；附件

encounter [ɪnˈkaʊntə] *n.&v.* 遇到，遭遇（en-进入+counter 相对→进入相对状态→遭遇 ）

encourage [ɪnˈkʌrɪdʒ] *v.* 鼓励，怂恿（en-进入+courage 勇气→赋予勇气 ）〈派生〉encouragement *n.* 鼓励，激励

endanger [ɪnˈdeɪndʒə] *v.* 濒临灭绝（en-加强语气+danger 危险→处于危险境地 ）

endure [ɪnˈdjʊə] *v.* 忍受，持久，持续（en-加强语气+dur 持续→持久 ）〈派生〉endurance *n.* 忍耐力

enforce [ɪnˈfɔːs] *v.* 实施，执行；强制（en-加强语气+force 强迫→强制实施 ）

enhance [ɪnˈhɑːns] *vt.* 提高，增强（en-加强语气+hance 高→提高 ）

enlarge [ɪnˈlɑːdʒ] *v.* 扩大，放大，增大（en-加强语气+large 大→扩大 ）

enlighten [ɪnˈlaɪtən] *v.* 启发，启蒙，教导（en-进入+light 光亮→带来启蒙之光 ）

enrich [ɪnˈrɪtʃ] *v.* 富足，肥沃，丰富（en-加强语气+rich 富有→富足，丰富 ）

ensure [ɪnˈʃʊə] *v.* 确保，保证（en-加强语气+sure 确认的→确保 ）

endeavor [enˈdevə] *n.&v.* 努力，尽力（en-进入+deav 同 deaf 听力不好+名词后缀-or→努力听才能听到 ）

entail [ɪnˈteɪl] *vt.* 涉及，包括，需要（en-加强语气+tail 剪，割→切断后给别人 ）

屠屠解词 tail 剪，割

- detail *n.* 细节，详情 [de-分开+tail 剪，割→剪开→（取得）细节，详情]
- retail *n.* 零售（re-再+tail 剪，割→再分割→零售 ）

真题例句 Deliberate practice entails more than simply repeating a task. 刻意练习需要的不仅仅是简单地重复一项任务。

endow [enˈdaʊ] *v.* 捐赠，赋予（en-进入+dow- 同 down 下去→发放下去→捐赠 ）

enquire/inquire [inˈkwaɪə] *v.* 询问（en-加强语气+ quire 同 quest 需求→询问 ）

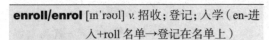

考研英语高频词汇 **2618**

enroll/enrol [ɪnˈrəʊl] v. 招收；登记；入学（en-进入+roll 名单→登记在名单上）

entitle [ɪnˈtaɪtl] v. 给……题名，给以权利（en-进入+title 标题→给予标题）

envisage [ɪnˈvɪzɪdʒ] v. 正视，面对；观察；想象（en-加强语气+vis 看+名词后缀-age 表状态→面对→看到后会有联想）

屠屠解词 vis-看

● vision n. 视力；远见；洞察力（vis-看+ion 名词）

● visit n.&v. 游览，参观（vis-看+it 走→边走边看→游览）

● previse vt. 预知，预先警告（pre-预先+vis 看+动词后缀-e→预先看到）

● visualize 想象（visual-看得见的，视觉的+动词后缀-ize→想象）

● revise 修订，校订（re-反复+vis 看+动词后缀-e→反复看→修正）

【词缀十】e-、ex-表示"出来，向外"

eject [ɪˈdʒekt] v. 喷射，排出；驱逐（e-向外+ject 喷射）

elaborate [ɪˈlæbəreɪt] a. 精心的，详尽的 n. 精心制作（e-出来+labor 劳动→通过劳动得出→精心制作）

elastic [ɪˈlæstɪk] a. 弹性的（e- 向外 +last 持续→可以持续向外拉伸→有弹性的）

elevate [ˈelɪveɪt] vt. 举起，提拔（e-出来+lev 同 raise 举起→从中举出来→提拔）〈派生〉elevator n. 电梯

eliminate [ɪˈlɪmɪneɪt] vt. 排除，消除（e-向外+limin 界限+动词后缀-ate→拉到界限以外→排除）

emigrate [ˈemɪgreɪt] v. 自本国移居他国（e-向外+migrate 迁徙）

enormous [ɪˈnɔːməs] a. 巨大的，庞大的（e-出来+norm 正常+形容词后缀-ous→正常范围之外→庞大的）

erupt [ɪˈrʌpt] v.（尤指火山）爆发（e-出来+rupt 破裂→破裂冲出→爆发）

emerge [ɪˈmɜːdʒ] v. 浮现，出现（e-出来+ merg 下沉→从下沉过程中出来→浮现）〈派生〉emergency n. 紧急情况

eligible [ˈelɪdʒəbl] a. 符合条件的，合格的（e-向外+lig 同 choose 选择→把符合条件的挑出来）

屠屠解词 lig-选择

● diligent a. 勤勉的，勤奋的（di- 分开 +lig- 选择 +ent……的→通过选择才能分开，这个过程需要付出努力→勤勉的，勤奋的）

● intelligent a. 聪明的（intel- 同 inter 在……中间 +lig- 选择 +形容词后缀 -ent……的→从中做出选择需要智慧）〈派生〉intelligence n. 智力

● negligence n. 疏忽，粗心（neg-没有+lig 选择+名词后缀-ence→没有选出→疏忽）

erase [ɪˈreɪz] vt. 抹去，擦掉（e-出来+ras 刮擦→擦掉）

erect [ɪˈrekt] a.&v. 直立的，竖立的（e-出来+ rect 直→直着出来）

屠屠解词 rect-正，直

● rectify vt. 纠正，整顿（rect-正，直+动词后缀-ify 使……→使……正→改正）

● rectangle n. 矩形，长方形（rect-正，直+angle 角→[四个角]都是直角→矩形）

● correct vt. 改正，纠正（cor-全部+rect 正→全部改正→纠正）

● direct a. 直接的 v. 指导；指向（di-离开+rect 正，直→直接离开→径直的→指向→指导）

escalate [ˈeskəleɪt] vi. 逐步升高，逐步增强（e-向外+scal 规模+动词后缀-ate→规模不断向外→逐步增强）

evaporate [ɪˈvæpəreɪt] v.（使）蒸发（e-向外+vapor 水蒸气+动词后缀-ate→蒸发）

156

evacuate [ɪˈvækjueɪt] *v.* 疏散, 撤出；排泄（e-出来+vac 空→空出来→疏散）〈派生〉evade *v.* 躲避

屠屠解词 vac 空

vac 作为词根, 通过 vacation（假期）就可以记住, vacation=vac 空+动词后缀-at+名词后缀-ion→空出时间去（度假）。

eminent [ˈemɪnənt] *a.* 显赫的, 杰出的（e-出来+min-凸出→从中凸显出来→杰出的）

屠屠解词 min-小, 凸出

词根 min-有两个意思, 一个是"小", 如 minute 原义是"分钟", 熟词僻义是"微小的, 细微的"。另一个是"凸出", 如 prominent *a.* 突出的；杰出的（pro-向前+min 凸起→向前突起→突出的）。

evaluate [ɪˈvæljueɪt] *vt.* 评价, 估计（e-出来+valu 价值+动词后缀-ate→把价值算出来→评估）

evoke [ɪˈvəʊk] *vt.* 唤起, 引起（e-出来+vok 同 voc-喊叫→喊出来→唤起）

例句扩展 A sense of period was evoked by complementing pictures with appropriate furniture. 给照片配上一些合适的家具, 唤起了一种年代感。

exaggerate [ɪɡˈzædʒəreɪt] *v.* 夸大, 夸张（ex-出来+ag 加强语气+ger 带来, 表达+动词后缀-ate→表达太过分）

exceed [ɪkˈsiːd] *v.* 越出；超过（ex-向外+ceed 同 cess 走→向外走→越出）〈派生〉exceedingly *ad.* 极端地, 非常

exclaim [ɪksˈkleɪm] *v.* 呼喊, 惊叫, 大声说（ex-向外+claim 宣称→向外宣称→呼喊）

exclude [ɪksˈkluːd] *v.* 拒绝, 把……排除在外, 排斥（ex-向外+clud 关闭→关在外面→排斥）〈派生〉exclusive *a.* 专有的, 独占的；排他的

exempt [ɪɡˈzempt] *v.* 免除（ex-向外+empt 拿→拿出→免除）

屠屠解词 empt 空的

empt 作为词根, 通过 empty（空的）就可以记住, empty 同 empt 拿+y 表示状态→拿走就空了。

exile [ˈeksaɪl] *n.* 放逐, 流放（ex-向外+il 同 soil 土壤→扔到国土以外→流放）

exotic [ɪɡˈzɒtɪk] *a.* 异国情调的, 外来的（ex-出来+ot 来自 boat+形容词后缀-ic→从外面坐船而来→舶来的）

XO 是外来的

expand [ɪksˈpænd] *v.* 膨胀, 扩张（ex-向外+ pand 扩展）〈派生〉expansion *n.* 扩张, 膨胀；张开, 伸展

expense [ɪksˈpens] *n.* 花费, 消费, 消耗（ex-向外+pens 钱→向外花钱→消费）〈派生〉expensive *a.* 昂贵的；expend *v.* 消费, 花费；expenditure *n.* 花费；（时间, 金钱等的）支出, 消耗

expedition [ˌekspəˈdɪʃn] *n.* 考察, 远航, 短途旅行（ex-出+ped 足, 脚+i+名词后缀-tion→走出去→远航）

屠屠解词 ped-足, 脚
● pedal *n.* 脚踏板（ped-足, 脚+名词后缀-al→踏板）
● pedestrian *n.* 步行者（ped-足, 脚+estrian……的人→用脚走路的人）

explicit [ɪksˈplɪsɪt] *a.* 详细说明的, 清楚的, 直率的（ex-向外+pli 满→所有都往外说→详细说明→清楚的）

explode [ɪksˈpləʊd] *v.*（使）爆炸,（使）爆发（ex-向外+plod 大声响→向外发出大声响→爆发）〈派生〉explosion *n.* 爆炸, 爆发；explosive *a.* 爆炸（性）的, 爆发（性）的 *n.* 爆炸物, 炸药

exploit [ɪksˈplɔɪt] *v.* 开拓, 开发（ex-向外+plo 同 plod 声响+it 去→向外去发出声响→探测新的能源→开发）

export [ɪkˈspɔːt] *v.&n.* 输出, 出口；*n.* 出口商品（ex-向外+port 港口）

expose [ɪks'pəʊz] v.（to）使暴露，受到；使曝光（ex-向外+pose 放置→放置出去→曝光、暴露）〈派生〉exposure n. 暴露，揭露；（to）受到

例句扩展 I think that the kinds of things that women are exposed to tend to be in more of a chronic or repeated nature. 我认为女性接触的事情往往更具有长期性和重复性。

express [ɪks'pres] a. 急速的；n. 快车，快递；vt. 表达，表示〈派生〉expression n. 表达

extend [iks'tend] v. 延长，延伸（ex-向外+tend 可看作 to+end→向外延伸到终点）〈派生〉extension n. 延长，伸展 extensive a. 广大的，广阔的

exterior [eks'tɪərɪə] a. 外部的，外面的 n. 外部（exter 同 ex-向外+形容词后缀 -ior）

external [eks'tɜːnl] a. 外部的，外面的（exter- 同 ex-向外+形容词后缀-nal）

extinguish [ɪks'tɪŋgwɪʃ] vt. 熄灭，消灭（ex-出来+ting 刺激→刺激出来没了→引申为火焰熄灭）

屠屠解词 sting 刺，刺激

- **distinguish** vt. 区别；辨认出（di-分开+sting 刺，刺激+uish 同 ish 表动词→把刺分开→辨别）
- **sting** v. 刺，刺痛，叮（sting 刺，刺激→刺，刺痛；刺）
- **stingy** a. 吝啬的，小气的 [sting 刺，刺激+y……的→像刺一样（小的心胸）→小气的]

extract [ɪks'trækt] v.&n. 拔出，抽出；摘录（ex-向外+tract 拉→向外拉→抽出）〈派生〉extraction n. 抽出，拔出

extravagant [ɪks'trævəgənt] a. 浪费的，奢侈的，过分的（extra- 同 ex- 向外，额外 + vag 走 + 形容词后缀 -ant→超越正常范围→浪费的）

【词缀十一】fore-/for-表示"前面的，提前"

forearm ['fɔːɑːm] n. 前臂 v. 准备战斗（fore-前面的+arm 手臂，武器→手臂的前面部分，提前准备好武器）

forecast ['fɔːkɑːst] v.&n. 预测，预报（fore-提前+cast 抛出→提前抛出信息）

foregoing ['fɔːgəʊɪŋ] a. 在前的，前述的（fore-前面的+go 走→走在前面的）

forehead ['fɔːhed] n. 额头（fore-前面的+head 头→额头）

foresee [fɔː'siː] vt. 预见，预知（fore-前面的+see 看见→提前看到→预测）

forthcoming [fɔːθ'kʌmɪŋ] a. 即将到来的（for-前面的+come 来临→即将到来）

forewarn [fɔː'wɔːn] v. 警示 for-提前+warn 警告→提前警告

【词缀十二】il-、im-、in-、ir-表示否定概念或"进入，在里面"

① 表示否定含义

illegal [ɪ'liːgəl] a. 不合法的，非法的（il-否定+legal 合法的→违法的）

illiterate [ɪ'lɪtərɪt] a. 文盲的，未受教育的（il-否定+literate 有读写能力的→没有文化的）

illusion [ɪ'luːʒən] n. 幻觉，幻想（il-否定+ lus 光亮+名词后缀-ion→没有光亮→黑暗中只有幻觉）

immense [ɪ'mens] a. 极广大的，无边的（im- 否定 +mens 计量，测量→不能测量→无限的）

immoral [ɪ'mɔːrəl] a. 不道德的（im-否定+ moral 道德的）

immune [ɪ'mjuːn] a. 互不影响的，免疫的（im-否定+mun 交流→不交流→互不影响的）

屠屠解词 mun-交流

要记住词根 mun-，只要记住 communication "交流"，com-一起+mun 交流→交流

impact [ˈɪmpækt] *n.&v.* 冲击，碰撞；影响（im-否定+pact 合同→与合同不符→冲击）

impair [ɪmˈpɛə] *v.* 损害；削弱，减少（im-否定+pair 一对→成不了一对→力量削弱）

impatient [ɪmˈpeɪʃənt] *a.* 不耐烦的，急躁的（im-否定+patient 耐心的）

indignant [ɪnˈdɪɡnənt] *a.* 愤怒的，愤慨的（in-否定+dign-身份→因身份受损而愤怒）〈派生〉indignation *n.* 愤怒，气愤

屠屠解词 dign 高贵

要记住词根 dign，只要记住 dignity "尊严、高尚"，dign 高贵+名词后缀-ity→高贵

indispensable [ˌɪndɪsˈpensəbl] *n.&a.* 不可缺少之物；不可或缺的（in-否定+dis-否定+ pens 钱+形容词后缀-able→不能没有钱→不可或缺）

innocent [ˈɪnəsnt] *a.* 清白的，无罪的（in-否定+noc 毒害+形容词后缀-ent→无毒的）

innumerable [ɪˈnjuːmərəbl] *a.* 无数的，数不清的（in-否定+numer 同 number 数字+形容词后缀-able→数不清）

incredible [ɪnˈkredəbl] *a.* 惊人的，不可思议的（in-否定+cred 信用+形容词后缀-ible→不可信任的）

inevitable [ɪnˈevɪtəbl] *a.* 不可避免的，必然发生的（in-否定+evit 逃跑+形容词后缀-able→逃脱不了→必然发生）

infinite [ˈɪnfɪnɪt] *a.* 无限的，无穷的（in-否定+fin

② 表示 "进入，在里面"

inhale [ɪnˈheɪl] *v.* 吸入（in-进入+hal 气→吸气）

illuminate [ɪˈljuːmɪneɪt] *vt.* 照明，照亮，阐明（il-进入+lum 同 lus 光+in+动词后缀-ate→光照进来→照亮）

illustrate [ˈɪləstreɪt] *vt.* 说明，图解（il-进入+lust 同 lus 光→光照进来→清晰明白）〈派生〉illustration *n.* 说明，插图

屠屠解词 explain/interpret/illustrate/clarify 辨析

- explain 指把某事向原来不了解、不清楚的人解释明白、说清楚等。

界限+形容词后缀-ite→无限的）〈派生〉infinity *n.* 无限，无穷

irregular [ɪˈreɡjʊlə] *a.* 不规则的，无规律的，不齐的（ir-否定+regular 规则）

irrespective [ˌɪrɪˈspektɪv] *a.* 不顾及的，不考虑的（ir-否定+respect 尊敬→不尊敬→不顾及）

instant [ˈɪnstənt] *a.* 立即的；速溶的，方便的；*n.* 瞬间，时刻（in- 否定 +stant 同 stand 站立不动，不着急→着急的→立刻，紧迫）〈派生〉instantaneous *a.* 瞬间的，即刻的；instantly *ad.* 立即，即刻

instinct [ˈɪnstɪŋkt] *n.* 本能，直觉，天性（in-否定+stinc 同 sting 刺→不需要刺激→本能）

intact [ɪnˈtækt] *a.* 完整无缺的，未经触动的，未受损伤的（in-否定+tact 触碰的→未经触碰的）

屠屠解词 tact-接触

要记住词根 tact-，只要记住 contact "接触、联系"，con-一起+tact 接触→相互接触→联系。

intuition [ˌɪntjuˈɪʃən] *n.* 直觉（in-否定+ tuition 学费，教导→不用教导→直觉）

invalid [ɪnˈvælɪd] *a.* 无效的；作废的；伤残的 *n.* 病人（in-否定+valid 有效的）

invaluable [ɪnˈvæljuəbl] *a.* 非常宝贵的，无价的（in-否定+valuable 有价值的→无法估价的）

invisible [ɪnˈvɪzəbl] *a.* 看不见的，无形的（in-否定+vis-看→看不到的）

invariable [ɪnˈvɛərɪəbl] *n.* 不变的，永恒的（in-否定+variable 可变化的→不变的）

- interpret 着重以特殊的知识、经验来解释难理解的事情。
- illustrate 多指用实例或插图、图表加以说明。
- clarify 指把已发生的事件、情况和现状说清楚。

immerse [ɪˈmɜːs] *vt.* 沉浸，使陷入（im-进入+mers 沉，没→沉进去→沉浸）

immigrant [ˈɪmɪɡrənt] *a.*（从国外）移来的，移民的 *n.* 移民（im-进入+migr 迁徙+名词后缀-ant→迁徙进来→外来移民）

implicit [ɪmˈplɪsɪt] *a.* 不言明的, 含蓄的;（in）固有的（im-进入+plic 重叠→进入重叠状态→不明说→含蓄, 没有言明）〈派生〉imply *v.* 意指, 暗示; implication *n.* 含意, 暗示

例句扩展 Branagh says that it was his intention to make explicit in the film what was only implicit in the play. 布莱纳说他的用意是将剧本中的隐晦含意在电影中清晰明白地表现出来。（注意: explicit "清晰明白" 与 implicit "隐晦含蓄" 互为反义。）

import [ɪmˈpɔːt] *v.* 进口, 输入 *n.* 进口, 输入（im-进入+port 港口→从港口运进来→进口）

impetus [ˈɪmpɪtəs] *n.* 推动力, 促进（im-进入+pet 追赶+名词后缀-us→推进, 促进）

impose [ɪmˈpəʊz] *vt.* 强加, 征税（im-进入+ pose 放→放进去→强加）

impress [ɪmˈpres] *v.*（on）印, 盖印; 留下印象, 引人注目 *n.* 印记（im-往里+press 挤压→往里挤压→留下印象）〈派生〉impression *n.* 印象, 感想; impressive *a.* 给人深刻印象的, 感人的

impulse [ˈɪmpʌls] *v.* 推动 *n.* 推动; 冲动, 刺激（im-进入+pulse 脉搏→注入脉搏→推动力）

incentive [ɪnˈsentɪv] *n.* 动机; *a.* 激励的（in-进入+cent 美分→受到钱的刺激）

include [ɪnˈkluːd] *v.* 包括, 包含（in-在里面+clud 关闭→关闭在内）〈派生〉inclusive *a.* 包括的; 范围广的

incorporate [ɪnˈkɔːpəreɪt] *v.* 合并, 包含 *a.* 合并的（in-在里面+corporate 公司→融入公司→合并）

infer [ɪnˈfɜː] *v.* 推断（in-在里面+fer 拿→拿到里面→将上一个命题带入下一个命题→推论）〈派生〉inference *n.* 推论

inferior [ɪnˈfɪəriə] *a.* 下等的, 下级的（in- 在里面 + fer 拿 + 形容词后缀 -ior →主命题带出次命题→次命题是 "下级"）

inherit [ɪnˈherɪt] *v.* 继承（in-里面的+her 黏着→黏在里面→继承而来）〈派生〉inherent *a.* 天生的, 固有的, 内在的

例句扩展 We inherit from our parents many of our

physical characteristics so they are deemed to be "inherent". 我们的许多身体特征都是从父母那里遗传而来的, 因此他们被认为是与生俱来的。

ingredient [ɪnˈɡriːdiənt] *n.* 成分, 因素（in-里面的+gred 生长+名词后缀-ient→在里面生长→成分）

inject [ɪnˈdʒekt] *v.* 注射（in-往里+ject 喷射→注射）

inland [ˈɪnlənd] *a.&ad.* 国内, 内地, 内陆（in-里面的+land 陆地→里面的陆地→内陆）

inlet [ˈɪnlet] *n.* 进口, 入口; 水湾（in-里面的+let 让→让……进入→进口）

inner [ˈɪnə] *a.* 内部的, 里面的; 内心的（in-里面的+ner 无实际含义）

install [ɪnˈstɔːl] *vt.* 安装, 安置（in-里面+stall 放→放里面→安装）〈派生〉installation *n.* 安装; installment *n.* 部分

instruct [ɪnˈstrʌkt] *v.* 教授; 命令, 指示（in-在里面+struct 结构→把 [知识] 加入进去→教授）〈派生〉instruction *n.* 教授; 指导;（pl.）用法说明（书）; instructor *n.* 指导者, 教员

insulate [ˈɪnsjʊleɪt] *v.* 隔离; 使绝缘（in-进入+sul 同 sol 独自+动词后缀-ate→进入独自状态→孤立）〈派生〉insulator *n.* 绝缘体

insure [ɪnˈʃʊə] *v.* 保险; 保证（in-在里面+sure 确认）〈派生〉insurance *n.* 保险, 保险费

intend [ɪnˈtend] *vt.* 想要, 打算（in-进入+ tend 延伸→心思延伸到里面→打算）〈派生〉intention *n.* 意图, 目的

intense [ɪnˈtens] *a.* 强烈的, 剧烈的（in-进入+ tense 紧张的→进入紧张状态→强烈的）〈派生〉intensity *n.* 强度

interior [ɪnˈtɪəriə] *a.* 内部的, 里面的; *n.* 内部, 内地（inter- 同 in-在里面+形容词后缀-ior）

internal [ɪnˈtɜːnəl] *a.* 内部的, 内的; 国内的, 内政的（inter- 同 in- 在里面 + 形容词后缀 -nal）

invade [ɪnˈveɪd] *v.* 入侵, 侵略, 侵害（in- 里面 + vad 走→往里走→入侵）〈派生〉invasion *n.* 侵入, 侵略

屠屠解词 vad 走

- pervade *vt.* 弥漫，普及（per-全部+vade 走→走遍，遍及）

- evade *vt.* 逃出，逃避（e-出+vade 走→走出去→逃避）

insight ['ɪnsaɪt] *n.* 洞察力，见识（in-里面+ sight 视野→看到里面→洞察力）

inspect [ɪn'spekt] *v.* 检查，调查，视察（in-里面+spect 看→往里看→检查）〈派生〉inspector *n.* 检查员，监察员，视察员

incline [ɪn'klaɪn] *v.* 倾斜，倾向于；偏向 *n.* 斜坡，斜面（in-进入+clin 倾斜，斜坡+动词后缀-e→倾斜，偏向）

屠屠解词 clin 倾斜

要记住词根 clin，只要记住 decline "下降"，de-加强语气+clin-倾斜→下降。

induce [ɪn'djuːs] *v.* 引诱；引起，导致（in-在里面+duce 同 duct 引导→往里引导→引诱）〈派生〉induction *n.* 感应，感应现象

inflation [ɪn'fleɪʃən] *n.* 通货膨胀（in-在里面+ flat 吹+名词后缀-ion→往里吹气→膨胀）

ingenious [ɪn'dʒiːniəs] *a.* 机灵的；有独创性的（in-进入+genious 同 genius 天才→进入天才状态→有独创性的）

intimidate [ɪn'tɪmɪdeɪt] *v.* 胁迫，威胁（in-在里面+timid 胆小→使……进入胆小状态→胁迫，威胁）

intricate ['ɪntrɪkɪt] *a.* 复杂的，错综的（in-在里面+tric 同 trick 诡计→在里面捣鬼→错综复杂的）

intrigue [ɪn'triːg] *n.* 阴谋，诡计；*vi.* 密谋（in-在里面+trig 同 tric 诡计→在里面捣鬼→诡计）

innovation [ˌɪnəʊ'veɪʃən] *n.* 改革，创新（in-在里面+nov-新颖的→带入新的东西→改革）

屠屠解词 nov-新的

要记住词根 nov-，只要记住 novel 除了"小说"，熟词僻义为"新的"。

【词缀十三】inter-、inti-、intr-表示"中间，相互"

interact [ˌɪntər'ækt] *v.* 互相作用，互相影响（inter-相互+act 作用→相互作用）

intercourse ['ɪntəkɔːs] *n.* 交际，往来（inter-相互的+course 路线→相互走对方的路线→交流，往来）

interview ['ɪntəvjuː] *v.&n.* 会见；采访；面试（inter-相互+view 看→相互观察→会面）

家人是做什么的？
面试
某公司招聘

interim ['ɪntərɪm] *a.* 中间的，临时的（inter-中间+im 同 in 里面→在里面）

interface ['ɪntəfeɪs] *n.* 分界线（inter-中间+ face 面→在中间划分→分界线）

interfere [ˌɪntə'fɪə] *v.* 妨碍；干涉（inter-中间+fer 拿→拿到中间→阻碍，妨碍）〈派生〉interference *n.* 干涉；妨碍

intermediate [ˌɪntə'miːdiət] *a.* 中间的；中级的 *n.* 中间体，媒介物（inter-中间+media 媒体→中间人）

interrupt [ˌɪntə'rʌpt] *v.* 中断，阻碍；打断话（inter-中间+rupt 破裂→中间破裂→中断）

屠屠解词 rupt-破裂

- abrupt *a.* 突然的，出其不意的；（行为等）粗鲁无礼的（ab-离开+rupt 断裂→突然的[断开，离开]）

- bankrupt *a.* 破产的（bank 银行+rupt 断裂→*a.* 破产的；彻底缺乏的 *v.* 使破产 *n.* 破产者）

- corrupt *a.* 腐败的；变坏的（cor-全部+rupt 断→全部断→变坏的，腐败的）

- disrupt *v.* 使混乱，使崩溃，使分裂（dis-分开+rupt 断裂→分开断→使崩溃，瓦解）

- erupt *v.* [尤指火山]爆发（e-出+rupt 断裂→断裂而喷出）

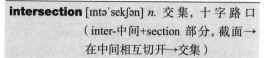

intersection [ˌɪntəˈsekʃən] *n.* 交集，十字路口（inter-中间+section 部分，截面→在中间相互切开→交集）

interval [ˈɪntəvəl] *n.* 间隔，间歇；幕间休息（inter-中间的+val无实际意义→断开的→间歇，休息）

intervene [ˌɪntəˈviːn] *v.*（in）干涉，干预；插入，介入（inter-中间+ven 同 vent 走→走到中间→干预）

intimate [ˈɪntɪmɪt] *n.* 密友 *a.* 亲密的 *vt.* 宣布（inti 同 inter-中间+mate 伙伴，伴侣→内部的伙伴→密友）

intrude [ɪnˈtruːd] *vi.* 闯入，侵入（intr 同 inter- 中间+rude 粗鲁→粗鲁地进入→闯入）

intrinsic [ɪnˈtrɪnsɪk] *a.* 固有的，内在的，本质的（intr- 同 inter-中间+in 里面→在里面的→内在的，本质的）

【词缀十四】pre-、pro-表示"提前，预先，前面"

precaution [prɪˈkɔːʃən] *n.* 预防，谨慎，警惕（pre-提前+caution 警惕→提前预测→预防）

preclude [prɪˈkluːd] *vt.* 妨碍；阻止（pre-提前+clud 关闭→提前关闭→阻止）

predecessor [ˈpriːdɪsesə] *n.* 前辈，前任（pre-前面的+de-向下+cess 走+名词后缀-or 人→后代之前的人→前辈）

predominant [prɪˈdɒmɪnənt] *a.* 占主导地位的；突出的（pre-前面+dominant 统治→在前面统治→占主导地位）

preface [ˈprefɪs] *n.* 序言，前言（pre-提前+ face 封面→序言）

prefer [prɪˈfɜː] *v.*（to）更喜欢，宁愿（pre-提前+fer 拿→提前拿到→特别喜欢）〈派生〉preferable *a.* 更可取的；preference *n.* 偏爱

prejudice [ˈpredʒʊdɪs] *n.* 偏见；损害（pre-提前+jud 评判+名词后缀-ice→提前做出评判→偏见）

preliminary [prɪˈlɪmɪnəri] *a.* 预备的，初步的（pre- 前面 +limin 界限 + 形容词后缀 -ary →在界限之前→预备）

premise [prɪˈmaɪz] *n.* 前提（pre-预先+mise 送，放出→预先送出→前提）

屠屠解词 mise 送，放出

利用同根词 promise "承诺" 进行记忆，promise= pro-前面+mise 送，放出→在做事前送出的话→允诺

premium [ˈpriːmɪəm] *n.* 保险费；额外费用，奖金（pre-前面的+mi 同 money 钱+名词后缀-um→先给钱→保险）

preside [prɪˈzaɪd] *v.* 主持，指挥（pre-前面的+sid 坐→坐在前面→主持）〈派生〉president *n.* 总统，校长，主席

屠屠解词 sid 坐

● reside *v.* 居住，驻扎（re-反复+sid 坐→居住）

● resident *n.* 居民（re-反复+sid 坐+名词后缀-ent 人）〈派生〉residence *n.* 住处；居住

● subsidy *n.* 补助金，津贴（sub-在下面+sid 同 sit 坐→坐在旁边→辅助，不是主要的→引申为"补助"）

prestige [presˈtiːʒ] *n.* 声望，威望，威信（pre- 前面+stige 同 string 拉紧→在前面拉紧→声望，威望）

presume [prɪˈzjuːm] *v.* 假定，假设（pre- 提前 + sume 拿→提前拿出方案→假定）〈派生〉presumably *ad.* 推测起来，大概

preserve [prɪˈzɜːv] *vt.* 保护，保持（pre-提前+serve 保留→提前保留→保护）〈派生〉preservation *n.* 保存，保藏；preserver *n.* 保护者，保存者

prevent [prɪˈvent] *v.*（from）预防，防止（pre-提前+vent 走→提前采取行动→预防）

previous ['priːvɪəs] *a.* 以前的；在……之前（pre-先前 +vi 路，引申为"走" + 形容词后缀 -ous →先走的，先前的）

precede [,priˈsiːd] *v.* 领先于；优先，先于（pre-提前 +ced 走→走在前面→领先）〈派生〉procedure *n.* 程序，手续；unprecedented *a.* 史无前例的

proceed [prəˈsiːd] *v.* 进行，继续下去；发生（pro-向前 +ceed 同 ced 走→向前走→进行）

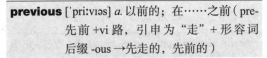 precede / proceed 辨析

两个单词前缀与词根保持一致，但是在引申过程中发生差异。

- precede 强调领先，形容词是 preceding，名词 precedent 表示"先例"。
- proceed 强调继续向前、前进，名词 proceeding 表示"行动"，procedure 表示"程序"。

probe [prəʊb] *v.* 探查，查明（pro-向前 +be 是→向前弄明白是什么→查明）

process ['prəʊses] *n.* 进程 *v.* 加工，处理（pro-提前 +cess 走→向前走→进程）〈派生〉procession *n.* 队伍，行列

proclaim [prəˈkleɪm] *vt.* 宣布，声明（pro-向前 +claim 宣称→宣布）

professor [prəˈfesə] *n.* 教授（pro-前面 +fess 说→在大家面前说知识→教授）〈派生〉profession *n.* 职业；professional *a.* 专业的

profile ['prəʊfaɪl] *n.* 剖面，外形，轮廓（pro-提前 +file 画，勾勒→提前勾勒→轮廓）

proficiency [prəˈfɪʃənsi] *n.* 熟练，精通（pro-提前 +fic 做 +名词后缀 -iency →提前做好→说明精通）

prohibit [prəˈhɪbɪt] *vt.* 禁止，阻止（pro-前面 +hibit 拿住→在前面拿住→不让前进→禁止）

屠屠解词 hibit 拿住

- exhibit *v.* 展出，陈列（ex-出 +hibit 拿住→拿出 ［展览］）
- inhibit *v.* 抑制，约束（in-里面 +hibit 拿住→抓住里面→抑制）

屠屠解词 inhabit/inhibit 辨析

- inhabit 表示"居住，栖息"，名词是 inhabitant（居民，住户）。

- inhibit 表示"抑制，制约"，同义词有 restrain，refrain，curb，suppress 等。

project [prəˈdʒekt] *n.* 计划，方案（pro-前面 +ject 扔出→在众人面前扔出方案）〈派生〉projector *n.* 放映机

prolong [prəˈlɒŋ] *vt.* 延长，拖延（pro-前面 + long 长→不断向前拉长→延长）

propel [prəˈpel] *vt.* 推进，驱使（pro-向前 + pel 推→向前推→推进）

propaganda [,prɒpəˈgændə] *n.* 宣传（pro- 提前 +pag 合同，商定 +anda 源自 "agenda 日常安排"→提前商定如何安排宣传）

propose [prəˈpəʊz] *vt.* 计划，建议（pro-前面 +pose 放→把自己的想法放在大家面前）〈派生〉proposal *n.* 建议

progress [prəʊˈgres] *n.&v.* 前进，进步（pro- 向前 +gress 走→向前走→前进）〈派生〉progressive *a.* 进步的

屠屠解词 表示"走"的词根

- cess: access, success
- ced: precede
- ceed: proceed, exceed, succeed
- vad: invade, evade
- vent: prevent, adventure
- gress: aggressive, progress

prospect ['prɒspekt] *n.* 前景，景色（pro-前面 +spect 看→前景）〈派生〉prospective *a.* 预期的

prosper ['prɒspə] *v.* 繁荣，昌盛（源于 prospect，前景一片大好→繁荣）〈派生〉prosperity *n.* 繁荣；prosperous *a.* 繁荣的

provoke [prəˈvəʊk] *v.* 挑动；激发；招惹（pro-向前，vok 同 voc 声音→向对方叫喊→招惹）

protest ['prəʊtest] *n.&v.* 主张，断言，抗议（pro-在前面 +test 测试→提出要测试→抗议，反对）

prototype ['prəʊtətaɪp] *n.* 原型（pro-在前面 +to 朝向 +type 类型→朝向前面的类型→原型）

【词缀十五】per-表示"一直，全部"

perceive [pə'siːv] v. 理解，领悟，感悟（per-全部+ceive 握住→全部握住→理解）

perform [pə'fɔːm] v. 履行；表演；完成（per-全部+ form 形式→全部形式都展现→完成，履行指责）

periodical [ˌpɪərɪ'ɒdɪkəl] a. 周期的，定期的；n. 期刊，杂志（period 期间+形容词后缀-ical→定期的）

perish ['perɪʃ] vi. 毁灭，死亡，腐烂（per-全部+动词后缀-ish=finish→全部都没了→毁灭）

例句扩展 Death is normal; we are genetically programmed to disintegrate and perish, even under ideal conditions. 死亡属于正常现象，因为基因决定了，即使在最理想的状态下，我们也注定要衰老和死亡。

permanent ['pɜːmənənt] a. 永久的，持久的（per-一直+man 手→停留→持久的）

permeate ['pɜːmɪeɪt] vt. 弥漫，渗透，透过，充满（per-一直+me 同 move 移动→一直往里去→渗透）

perpetual [pə'petʃuəl] a. 永久的（per-一直+ pet 追寻+形容词后缀-ual→一直追求不放弃→永久的）

persevere [ˌpɜːsɪ'vɪə] v. 坚持（per-一直+ severe 严格的，严厉的→一直严格不放松→坚持）

perplex [pə'pleks] v. 困惑（per-全部+plex 同 pile 重叠→全部都叠在一起→不清楚，让人困惑）

persist [pə'sɪst] v. (in) 坚持，持续（per-一直+sist 站→一直都站着→坚持）

perspective [pə'spektɪv] n. 远景；观点，看法（per-全部+spect 看→全部都看在眼里→才能发表观点看法）

【词缀十六】mis-表示否定概念

mischief ['mɪstʃɪf] n. 损害，伤害；胡闹（mis-否定+ chief 首领→没有首领→危害极大）

misery ['mɪzəri] n. 痛苦，悲惨，不幸（mis-否定+ ery 无实际意义）〈派生〉miserable a. 痛苦的，悲惨的

misfortune [mɪs'fɔːtʃən] n. 不幸，灾祸，灾难（mis-否定+fortune 财富，运气→不幸）

mislead [ˌmɪs'liːd] v. 把……带错路，误导（mis-否定+lead 引导→误导）

missing ['mɪsɪŋ] a. 漏掉的，失去的，失踪的（mis-否定）

mistake [mɪs'teɪk] n.&v. 弄错，错误（mis-否定+ take 拿→拿错）

misunderstand [ˌmɪsʌndə'stænd] v. 误解（mis-否定+ understand 理解→误解）

【词缀十七】para-表示"反，旁边的"

parachute ['pærəʃuːt] n. 降落伞；v. 跳伞（para-旁边+ chute 落下，音似"shu~"→从飞机侧面落下→跳伞）

parade [pə'reɪd] n. 游行，检阅 v. (使)列队行进，游行（para-旁边+de 无实际意义→从主席台旁边走过→检阅）

parallel ['pærəlel] a.&n. 平行线；类似，相似物（para-旁边+ll 平行线→两条线在彼此旁边，没有交集→平行）

paralyze ['pærə,laɪz] v. 瘫痪；丧失作用（para-旁边+ lyze 同 loose 松开→身体某一侧松开→瘫倒）

parameter [pə'ræmɪtə] n. 参数（para-旁边+meter 计量→在旁边做计量→参考数）

paradise ['pærədaɪs] n. 天堂（para-反+dise同 death 死→不死的地方→天堂）

paradox ['pærədɒks] n. 似非而是的话；反论（para-反+dox 说话→正话反说）

例句扩展 The paradox of exercise is that while using a lot of energy it seems to generate more. 锻炼的矛盾之处在于消耗很多能量却似乎又产生更多的能量。

【词缀十八】mal-表示否定概念

malfunction [ˌmælˈfʌŋkʃn] *n.&v.* 失灵；功能失常（mal-否定+function 功能→功能失常）

maltreat [ˌmælˈtriːt] *v.* 虐待（mal-否定+treat 对待→虐待）

malformation [ˌmælfɔːˈmeiʃən] *n.* 难看，畸形（mal-否定+form 形式→形式变形→畸形）

malnutrition [ˌmælnjuːˈtriʃn] *n.* 营养不良（mal-否定+nutrition 营养）

【词缀十九】op-表示"对立的"

opponent [əˈpəʊnənt] *a.* 对立的，对抗的 *n.* 对手，反对者（op-对立的+ pon-同pose，放+形容词后缀-ent→放在对立位置→对抗）

oppose [əˈpəʊz] *vt.* 反对，抗争（op-对立的+pose 放→放在对立位置→反对）〈派生〉opposite *a.* 相对的，对立的

oppress [əˈpres] *vt.* 压迫，压抑（op-对立的，press 挤压→人们反抗，逆向挤压→压迫）

optimistic [ˌɒptiˈmistik] *a.* 乐观的（op-对立的+tim 胆小的+名词后缀-ist+形容词后缀-ic→与胆小相对的→勇敢乐观）

optimum [ˈɒptiməm] *n.&a.* 最适宜（源自optimistic）

【词缀二十】over-表示"超过，超越；在……的上面"

overcome [ˌəʊvəˈkʌm] *v.* 战胜，克服（over-超越+come 来→过来超越→战胜）

overflow [ˌəʊvəˈfləʊ] *v.* （使）外溢，（使）溢出；溢出（over-超过+flow 流动→过多的流→溢出）

overhead [ˌəʊvəˈhed] *a.* 在头上方（over-在……的上面+head 头部→在头上方）

overhaul [ˌəʊvəˈhɔːl] *v.&n.* 大修，仔细检查（over-在……的上面+haul 拉出→拉到上面来检查→仔细检查）

overhear [ˌəʊvəˈhiə] *v.* 无意中听到，偷听（over-在……上面+hear 听→趴上面偷听）

overlook [ˌəʊvəˈluk] *v.* 俯瞰；疏忽（over-从……上面+look 看→从高处看→俯瞰）

overlap [ˌəʊvəˈlæp] *v.* 重叠，与……交叠；*n.* 重叠（over-在……上面+lap 重叠）

overnight [ˌəʊvəˈnait] *a.&ad.* 一夜间，一下子；突然（over-超过+night 夜晚→过了一夜）

overpass [ˈəʊvəpɑːs] *n.* 过街天桥（over-在……上面+pass 通过→从上面通过→过街天桥）

overseas [ˌəʊvəˈsiːz] *a.* 外国的，海外的 *ad.* 在海外（over-越过+sea 海洋→越过海洋→海外）

overtake [ˌəʊvəˈteik] *v.* 追上，赶上；袭击，压倒（over-超过+take 拿→拿过来超越→压倒）

overthrow [ˌəʊvəˈθrəʊ] *v.&n.* 推翻，颠覆（over-在……上面+throw 扔→往上扔东西→颠覆）

overtime [ˈəʊvəˌtaim] *a.* 超时的，加班的 *ad.* 加班（over-超过+time 时间→超时的）

overturn [ˌəʊvəˈtɜːn] *n.&v.* 推翻（over-超过+turn 翻转→翻过去→推翻）

165

overwhelm [,əʊvə'hwelm] *v.* 压倒，制服（over-在……上面+whelm 车轮=wheel→车轮压过→压倒）〈派生〉overwhelming *a.* 势不可挡的，压倒的

例句扩展 It is not easy to talk about the role of the mass media in this overwhelmingly significant phase in European history. 在欧洲历史上这个具有非凡意义的阶段，讨论大众媒体所发挥的作用绝非易事。

【词缀二十一】hypo-/pseudo-表示"非真实的，假的"

hypocrisy [hɪ'pɒkrəsi] *n.* 伪善，虚伪（hypo-假的+cris 判别→假惺惺地做出判断→虚伪）

屠屠解词 cris 判断

要记住词根 cris，只需要记住 crisis "危机"。cris判断，分辨，评判+is→需要做出判断的时刻→危机时刻。

hypothesis [haɪ'pɒθɪsɪs] *n.* 假设（hypo-假的+thesis 论题→虚假论题→假设）

pseudonym ['su:dənɪm] *n.* 假名，笔名（pseudo-假的+nym 同 nom 名字→假名）

pseudoscience ['su:dəsaɪns] *n.* 假科学，伪科学（pseudo-假的+science 科学→伪科学）

【词缀二十二】re-表示"再次，反复，返回，往回"

① re-表示"再次，反复"

reassure [,ri:ə'ʃʊə] *vt.* 使……安心，再保证（re-再次+assure 确认→再次确认）

recall [rɪ'kɔ:l] *vt.* 回忆，回想（re-再次+call 呼唤→再次唤起→回想）

recite [rɪ'saɪt] *v.* 背诵，朗读（re-再次+cite 引用，唤起→再[把记的东西]引出）

recollect [,rekə'lekt] *v.* 回忆，想起（re-再次+ col 全部+lect 说→想到全部说过的话语）

recover [rɪ'kʌvə] *vt.* 重新获得，恢复（re-再次+cover 覆盖→再次覆盖占有→重新获得）〈派生〉recovery *n.* 恢复

recreation [,rekrɪ'eɪʃn] *n.* 消遣，娱乐（re-重新+create 生长→恢复精力→娱乐，消遣）

recycle [,ri:'saɪkl] *v.* 再循环，反复应用（re-再次+cycle 循环→再次循环）

recur [rɪ'kɜ:] *vi.* 复发，重现（re-再次+cur 跑→再次跑出来→复发）

屠屠解词 cur 跑

- incur *v.* 招惹（in-往里+cur 跑→跑进去招惹）
- occur *v.* 出现（oc-加强+cur 跑→跑出来→出现）

reckon ['rekən] *vt.* 计算，总计，估计，猜想（re-反复+ckon 计算，源自 count→反复计算→总计）

reciprocal [rɪ'sɪprəkəl] *a.* 互惠的，相互的（re-反复+ cip-拿+roc 同 rich 富余的→反复拿来好的东西→互惠的）

recommend [,rekə'mend] *vt.* 推荐（re-反复+commend 赞扬→一再赞扬）

redeem [rɪ'di:m] *vt.* 赎回，挽回，恢复（re-再次+deem 考虑→重新考虑→挽回）

redundant [rɪ'dʌndənt] *a.* 多余的（red-同re-再+und 溢出，波动+形容词后缀-ant→多余的）

reconcile ['rekənsaɪl] *vt.* 使和解，使和谐（re- 再次+ con 共同+cil 召集→[双方]再次召到一起→和解）

屠屠解词 cil 召集

要记住词根 cil，需要回忆单词 council "理事会，委员会"，coun=con- 一起+cil 召集→召集在一起构成委员会。

release [rɪ'lɪs] *n.&v.* 释放（re- 重新+lease 同 lax 松→释放）

reinforce [ˌriːɪnˈfɔːs] vt. 加强,增援(re-再次+in 往里+force 力量→再次注入力量→加强)

reproduce [ˌriːprəˈdjuːs] v. 繁殖,再生,复制(re-再次+produce 生产→再次生产→再生)

replace [rɪˈpleɪs] vt. 取代,替换(re-再次+place 位置→再次安放一个位置→替换)

remedy [ˈremɪdi] n. 药物,治疗法 v. 治疗;纠正(re- 一再+med 医治→治疗)

remind [rɪˈmaɪnd] vt. 提醒,使想起(re-再次+mind 思维→再次出现在思维中→使想到)

remove [rɪˈmuːv] vt. 移动(re-再次+move 移动→再次移动→移除)〈派生〉removal n. 移动,免职

renew [rɪˈnjuː] vt. 使更新,使恢复(re-再次+new 新的→使更新)

renovate [ˈrenəveɪt] vt. 革新,刷新,修复(re-再次+nov 新+动词后缀-ate→再次赋予新的内容→革新,刷新)

repair [rɪˈpeə] n. 修理,修补(re-再次+pair 对→重新配成对→修好)

repression [rɪˈpreʃən] n. 镇压,抑制,压抑(re-反复+press 压+名词后缀-ion→反复压制→抑制)

rehearse [rɪˈhɜːs] vt. 彩排,排演(re-反复+hear 听→反复听→彩排)

refine [rɪˈfaɪn] vt. 精炼,精制(re-反复+fine 好→反复弄变得更好→精炼)

② re-表示"往回,回来"

recede [rɪˈsiːd] v. 后退(re-往回+cede 走→往回走→后退)

reclaim [rɪˈkleɪm] vt. 要求归还;收回(re-往回+claim 呼喊,叫喊→喊回来→收回来)

reference [ˈrefrəns] n. 提及,涉及,参考,参考书目(re-往回+fer 拿→往回拿→借用,参考)〈派生〉refer v. 提到,涉及,查阅,咨询

refrain [rɪˈfreɪn] n. 重复,叠句 vi. 节制,避免,制止(re-往回+frain 同 strain 拉紧→节制,避免,制止)

reform [rɪˈfɔːm] n. 改革(re-再次+form 形式→再次更换形式→改革)

remark [rɪˈmɑːk] n. 注意,观察;话语;评论(re-再次+mark 标记→再次做出标记→引起注意)〈派生〉remarkable a. 显著的,引人注意的

resemble [rɪˈzembl] vt. 象,类似(re-再次+sembl 相类似,一样→像,类似)〈派生〉resemblance n. 相似处,类似

resign [rɪˈzaɪn] n. 辞去(职务)v. 辞去,辞职(re-再次+sign 签字,标记→第一次签字是入职→再次签字辞职)

resolve [rɪˈzɒlv] v. 决心;决心要;溶解;解决(re-反复+solve 解决→充满决心)〈派生〉resolute a. 有决心的,不动摇的;resolution n. 决心

resume [rɪˈzjuːm] vt. 重新开始 n. 摘要,概略,履历(re-再次+sume 拿,取→重新拿起→再用;恢复)

restore [rɪˈstɔː] v. 恢复,使回复,归还,交还,修复,重建(re-再次+store 储存→再次储存→使……恢复原样)

retrieve [rɪˈtriːv] v. 重新得到;n. 找回(re-再次+tri 同 try 尝试→再次尝试→重新找回)

revise [rɪˈvaɪz] v. 修订,校订(re-反复+vis-看→反复看→找出问题进行修订)

revive [rɪˈvaɪv] v. 苏醒,复兴,复活(re-再次+viv 生命→再次获得生命→复活,苏醒)

refund [riːˈfʌnd] v.&n. 退还,偿还(re-往回+fund 资金→资金返回→退还)

reflect [rɪˈflekt] v. 反射,反映,表现(re-返回+flect 弯曲→弯曲返回→反射)〈派生〉reflection n. 反射

真题例句 McGee says leaving without a position lined up gave him time to reflect on what kind of company he wanted to run. 麦吉说在没有找到新的工作之前就辞职,给了他时间思考想经营什么样的公司。

reign [reɪn] *n.&v.* 统治，支配（简写为rein）（foreign 对外+fo-敌对→reign对内→统治，支配）

reject [rɪˈdʒekt] *vt.* 拒绝，抵制（re- 向后 +ject 抛掷→向后抛掷→抵制）

屠屠解词

- subject *a.* 隶属的；易遭受……的（sub-在下面+ject 投掷，扔→扔下去→服从的，扔下去大家讨论的主题）
- inject *v.* 注射；注入（in-进入+ject 投掷，扔→扔进去→注射）
- object *v.* (to) 反对（ob-逆，反+ject 投掷，扔→反着扔→反对→引申为扔向目标）
- eject *v.* 喷出，排出（e-向外+ject 投出，掷出→向外射出）

repay [riːˈpeɪ] *v.* 偿还，报答（re-往回+pay 支付→往回支付→偿还）

repel [rɪˈpel] *vt.* 击退，抵制（re-往回+pel 推动→击退）

relay [rɪˈlei] *n.* 接替（re-向后+lay 拖延→留给后面）

reproach [rɪˈprəʊtʃ] *v.* 责备（re-往回+proach 接近→不准接近→指责）

reserve [rɪˈzɜːv] *vt.* 保留，储备（re-往回+ serve 保留→保留下来）〈派生〉reservation *n.* 保留，预定；reservoir *n.* 水库

resist [rɪˈzɪst] *v.* 抵抗，反抗（re-往回+sist 站）〈派生〉resistance *n.* 抵制，resistant *a.* 有抵抗力的

respond [rɪˈspɒnd] *v.* 回答，响应（re-往回+ spond 同 promise 承诺→承诺回去→回答）〈派生〉response *n.* 回答，响应

restrain [rɪsˈtreɪn] *vt.* 抑制，制止（re-往回+ strain 拉紧→拉回去→抑制）〈派生〉restraint *n.* 抑制，限制

restrict [rɪsˈtrɪkt] *vt.* 限制，约束，限定（re-往回+strict 同 strain 拉紧→往回拉紧→限制）

retort [rɪˈtɔːt] *v.* 反驳，反击（re-往回+tort 扭曲→反过来扭→报复）

retreat [rɪˈtriːt] *vi.* 撤退，退却（re-往回+ treat→后退，撤退）

retrospect [ˈretrəspekt] *n.* 回顾（retro-同 re-往回+spect 看→向后看）

revenge [rɪˈvendʒ] *n.&vt.* 替……报仇，复仇（re-往回+venge 惩罚→惩罚回去→报仇）

reverse [rɪˈvɜːs] *n.* 相反，反面 *a.* 相反的（re-反+vers 转→转到反面）

review [rɪˈvjuː] *v.&n.* 回顾，复习（re-往回+ view 看，查→回顾，复习）

【词缀二十三】sub-表示"在……下面"

submarine [ˈsʌbməriːn] *n.* 潜水艇，潜艇 *a.* 水下的，海底的（sub-在下面+marine 海的→水下的）

submerge [səbˈmɜːdʒ] *v.* 浸没，淹没（sub-在下面+ merg 沉没→沉到水下→淹没）

屠屠解词 merg 沉没

- emerge *v.* 浮现（e-出+merg 沉没+e→沉没的东西出现→浮现）
- emergent *a.* 紧急的，浮现的，突然出现的，自然发生的（emerge- 浮现+形容词后缀-ent→突然出现的→紧急的）
- emergence *n.* 出现（emerge-浮现+名词后缀-ence→出现）

- emergency *n.* 紧急情况，突然事件，非常时刻（emerge- 浮现+名词后缀-ency→突然出现的事情）
- immerge 浸入，浸没，隐没，埋头（im-进入+merg 沉没+e→沉进去→沉入）

subordinate [səˈbɔːdɪnət] *a.* 次要的，从属的，下级的 *n.* 下属（sub-在下面+ord 同 order 顺序+in 处于……状态+形容词后缀-ate→顺序在下面→次要的）

subsequent [ˈsʌbsɪkwənt] *a.* 后来的，并发的（sub-在下面+sequ 同 sec 跟随→随后的）

substantial [səbˈstænʃəl] *a.* 坚固的，实质的，大量的（sub-在下面+stant 同 stand 站立→站在下面→坚固的东西才能支撑）

substitute [ˈsʌbstɪtjuːt] *n.* 代用品，代替者，替代品 *v.* 代替（sub-在下面+stit 站→站在次要位置→替代品）

subtle [ˈsʌtl] *a.* 不易被察觉，微妙的，精细的（sub-在下面+形容词后缀-tle→下面不易被察觉的，细微的事物）

suburb [ˈsʌbɜːb] *n.* 市郊，郊区（sub-在下面+ urb 城市→城市下面的→郊区）

subway [ˈsʌbweɪ] *n.* 地道，[美] 地铁（sub-在下面+ way 路→下面的路→地道）

【词缀二十四】sur-表示"超过，在……上面"（在同辅音词根前表示"在下面"）

surface [ˈsɜːfɪs] *n.* 表面；外表 *a.* 表面的，肤浅的（sur-在上面+face 脸→脸上面→表面）

surge [sɜːdʒ] *vi.* 汹涌，彭湃（sur-在上面+ge 无意义→到上面来→汹涌）

surname [ˈsɜːneɪm] *n.* 姓（sur-在上面+name 名字→名字获得之前→姓）

surpass [səˈpɑːs] *vt.* 超过，胜过（sur-在上面+pass 通过→超越）

surplus [ˈsɜːpləs] *n.* 过剩，剩余（sur-在上面+plus 加→在上面再增加）

汽车产能

survey [səˈveɪ] *v.&n.* 俯瞰；全面审视，调查（sur-在上面+vey 同 vise 看→从上面观察→俯瞰）

survive [səˈvaɪv] *v.* 幸免于，幸存；比……长命（sur-超过+viv 生命→活下来了→幸免于）〈派生〉survival *n.* 幸存，生存；幸存者

屠屠解词 viv-、vi-生命

- vivid *a.* 鲜艳的；生动的，栩栩如生的（viv-生命+id……的→鲜艳的；生动的，栩栩如生的）
- viable *a.* 可行的，能活下去的（vi- 同 viv-生命+able 能……的→可行的，能活下去的）
- survival *n.* 幸存，生存（survive 幸免于+形容词后缀-al 表状态→经过事故活着→幸存）
- revive *v.* 恢复；（使）复苏（re-再+viv 生命+e→再活→复活）

surround [səˈraʊnd] *vt.* 包围，环绕（sur-在下面+round 围着→从下面围着上去→包围）〈派生〉surroundings *n.* 周围的事物，环境

surrender [səˈrendə] *n.&vi.* 投降，屈服 *vt.* 放弃，交出（sur-在下面+render 给予→把[枪]交给别人→投降）

【词缀二十五】sym-（ syn- ）表示"相同的，共同的，一起的"

symmetry [ˈsɪmɪtri] *n.* 对称（性）；匀称，整齐（sym-相同的+metr 同 meter 测量、距离→两边测量距离相同→对称）

sympathy [ˈsɪmpəθi] *n.* 同情，同情心；同感（sym-相同的+path 感情→相同的感情→同情）〈派生〉sympathetic *a.* 有同情心的 *n.* 交感神经；sympathize *v.* 同情；共鸣，同感（with）

symphony [ˈsɪmfəni] *n.* 交响乐，交响曲（sym-共同的+phon 声音→各个声音一起演奏→交响乐）

symposium [sɪmˈpəʊzɪəm] *n.* 讨论会，专题报告会（sym-一起的+pos 放+名词后缀-ium→放在一起[共同讨论]→专题讨论）

symptom [ˈsɪmptəm] *n.* 症状；征兆（sym-相同的+p 无意义+tom 切→切入寻找相同症状）

system [ˈsɪstəm] *n.* 系统（sy- 同 sym- 一起 +stem 茎→茎缠绕在一处→构成系统，体系）〈派生〉systematic *a.* 系统的，有组织的

【词根二十六】super- 表示"超过，在……上面"

superb [ˌsuːˈpɜːb] *a.* 极好的，杰出的；华丽的（super- 在……上面，超过 +b 无意义→在……之上，超过→杰出的）

superficial [ˌsuːpəˈfɪʃəl] *a.* 表面的；肤浅的（super-在……上面+fic 做+形容词后缀-ial→在表面上做）

superfluous [suːˈpɜːfluəs] *a.* 多余的，过剩的（super-超过+flu 流+形容词后缀-ous→超过了流出来）

superior [suːˈpɪərɪə] *a.* 优良的，卓越的；上级的 *n.* 上级（super-超级+形容词后缀-ior→超级的，上级的）〈派生〉superiority *n.* 优越，优势

supermarket [ˈsuːpəˌmɑːkɪt] *n.* 超级市场（super-超级+market 市场→超级市场）

supervise [ˈsuːpəvaɪz] *v.* 管理，监督（super- 在……上面+vis 看→从上面看→监督）

supreme [suːˈpriːm] *a.* 极度的，最重要的；至高的，最高的（supre-=super 在……上面）

superstition [ˌsuːpəˈstɪʃən] *n.* 迷信（super-在……上面+stit-站→建立在人[理智]之上的东西→迷信）

屠屠解词 stit 站

- constitute *v.* 组成，构成（con-一起+sti 同 stit 站+动词后缀-ute→站在一起→组成）
- constituent *a.* 组成的，构成的（constitute 组成+形容词后缀-ent→组成的，构成）
- constitution *n.* 组成，构成（constitute 组成+名词后缀-ion→组成，构成）
- institute *v.&n.* 设立，制定；研究所（in-进入+stit 站→站在土地里→设立）
- substitute *v.* 代替（sub-在下面+stit 站→站在次要位置→替代品）

【词缀二十七】trans-表示"从……转移至……，穿过"

transaction [trænˈzækʃən] *n.* 处理；交易；事务（trans-从……转移至……+action 动作，行动→从一者到另一者的动作→交易）

transcend [trænˈsend] *v.* 超过，胜过（trans-从……转移至……+scend 上升→从低处升到高处→越过、超过）

transfer [trænsˈfɜː] *v.* 移动，传递（trans-从……转移至……+fer 拿→从一处拿到另一处→移动）

transform [trænsˈfɔːm] *v.* 转换，变形（trans-从……转移至……+form 形式→从一种形式转换成另一种形式变形）

transient [ˈtrænzɪənt] *a.* 短暂的，瞬间的（trans-穿过+ ient 无实际意义→穿过→迅速的，短暂的）

transistor [trænˈsɪstə] *n.* 晶体管（trans-从……转移至……+sist 站→电流传输中，中间站个东西阻碍→晶体管）

transit [træn'zɪt] *v.* 运输，转变（trans-从……转移至……+动词后缀-it→把物体从一处转移到另一处→运输）

transmission [trænz'mɪʃən] *n.* 发射，传输（trans-从……转移至……+mission 使命→任务是从一处传输到另一处

transparent [træns'peərənt] *a.* 透明的（trans-穿过+ parent 明显的→从一边穿透到另一边→透明的）

transplant [træns'plɑːnt] *v.* 移植（trans-从……转移至……+plant 种植→从一者转移到另一者种植→移植）

【词缀二十八】uni-表示"一"

uniform ['juːnɪfɔːm] *a.* 相同的，一律的 *n.* 制服（uni-统一的+form 形式→形式一样→引申为"制服"）

unify ['juːnɪfaɪ] *v.* 使统一；使相同，使一致（uni-统一的+动词后缀-fy）

union ['juːnjən] *n.* 联合；联盟；协会，社团；和谐（uni-统一的+名词后缀-on→一个整体）

unique [juː'niːk] *a.* 唯一的，独一无二的（uni-统一的+形容词后缀-que）

unit ['juːnɪt] *n.* 单位，单元；部件；机组，装置（uni-统一的）

unite ['juːnaɪt] *vi.* 联合，团结；统一，合并 *vt.* 使联合（uni-统一的）〈派生〉unity *n.* 团结；统一，一致，整体

universe ['juːnɪvɜːs] *n.* 宇宙，万物（uni- 统一的+vers 转→宇宙独自转动）〈派生〉universal *a.* 普遍的，全体的，通用的；宇宙的

unanimous [juː'nænɪməs] *a.* 意见一致的，无异议的（un- 同 uni-统一的+anim 生命+形容词后缀-ous→一个生命→同呼吸共命运）

【词缀二十九】un-通常表示否定概念

注意： 词根为动词或名词时，表示词根的反向概念。

uncover [ˌʌn'kʌvə] *v.* 揭开，揭露（un-表示反向概念+动词 cover 覆盖→揭开）

unload [ˌʌn'ləʊd] *v.* 卸货（un-表示反向概念+load 装载→卸载）

undo [ˌʌn'duː] *v.* 取消，解开，松开（un-表示反向概念+ do 做→取消）

unfold [ʌn'fəʊld] *v.* 打开，显露（un-表示反向概念+ fold 叠起→揭开）

undress [ʌn'dres] *v.* 脱衣服，暴露，卸去装饰（un-表示反向概念+ dress 穿上→脱下）

unveil [ˌʌn'veɪl] *v.* 揭开面纱，揭露（un-表示反向概念+ veil 面纱→脱下）

【词缀三十】表示数字概念的前缀

anniversary [ˌænɪ'vɜːsəri] *n.* 周年纪念日

annual ['ænjʊəl] *a.* 每年的

monopoly [mə'nɒpəli] *n.* 垄断（mono-一）

monotonous [mə'nɒtənəs] *a.* 单调的，无变化的（mono-一+ton 声音+形容词后缀-ous→单调的）〈派生〉monotone *a.& n.* 单调的

bilingual [baɪ'lɪŋgwəl] *a.* 双语的（bi-二+ lingu 语言+形容词后缀-al→双语的）

bicycle ['baɪsɪkl] *n.* 自行车（bi-二+cycle 循环）

triangle ['traɪæŋgl] *n.* 三角形（tri-三+angle 角度→三角形）〈派生〉triangular *a.* 三角形的

tricycle [ˈtraɪsɪkl] n. 三轮车（tri-三+cycle 循环→三轮车）

triple [ˈtrɪpl] n.&a. 三倍（tri-三）

quarter [ˈkwɔːtə] n. 四分之一（quar-四）

【词缀三十一】表示计量单位的前缀

semiconductor [ˌsemɪkənˈdʌktə] n. 半导体（semi-半+duct 引导+名词后缀-or→半导体）

semicircle [ˌsemɪˈsəkl] n. 半圆形（semi-半+circle 圈→半圆）

semifinal [ˌsemɪˈfaɪnəl] n. 半决赛（semi-半+final 决赛→半决赛）

polycentric [ˌpɒlɪˈsentrɪk] a. 多中心的（poly-多+centric中心的→多中心的）

multipurpose [ˈmʌltiˈpəpɜːs] a. 多种用途的（multi-多+purpose 目的，用途→多用途的）

multinational [ˈmʌltiˈnæʃənəl] a. 跨国的（multi-多+national 国家的→跨国的）

multimedia [ˈmʌltiˈmiːdiə] n. 多媒体（multi-多+media 媒体→多媒体）

multiple [ˈmʌltɪpl] a. 多重的（multi-多+ple 重→多重的）

multiply [ˈmʌltɪplaɪ] v. 乘；增加；繁殖（multi-多+ply 同 ple 重→重叠多次→乘）

multitude [ˈmʌltɪtjuːd] n. 大量；多数；群众（multi-多+tude 状态→多的状态→多数）

centigrade [ˈsentɪɡreɪd] n.&a. 摄氏度（的）（centi-百分之一+grade 等级→百分度的，摄氏度）

centimeter [ˈsentimiːtə] n. 厘米（centi-百分之一+meter 米→厘米）

kilogram [ˈkɪləʊɡræm] n. 公斤（kilo-千+gram 克→千克）

kilometer [ˈkɪləˌmiːtə] n. 千米（kilo-千+meter 米→千米）

microscope [ˈmaɪkrəskəʊp] n. 显微镜（micro-微小+scope 看→看小东西→显微镜）

microphone [ˈmaɪkrəfəʊn] n. 扩音器（micro-微小+phon 声音→声音小需要扩大用扩音器）

miniature [ˈmɪnɪətʃə] n. 缩小的模型，缩图 a. 微型的（mini-小+ture 源自 picture 画→微型画）

minimize [ˈmɪnɪmaɪz] v.（minimise）使减少到最少（mini-小+mize 动词后缀→减少）

minimum [ˈmɪnɪməm] n. 最小值，最低限度 a. 最小的（mini-小+mum 源自 number 数字→最小值）

minor [ˈmaɪnə] a. 较小的，较次要的（min-= mini-小+-or 形容词比较级后缀→较小的）〈派生〉minority n. 少数，少数民族

minus [ˈmaɪnəs] a. 负的，减的 prep. 减去 n. 负号，减号（min-同 mini-小→使之变小→减去）

【词缀三十二】动词后缀-fy

amplify [ˈæmplɪfaɪ] vt. 放大，增强（ample 充足的+动词后缀-ify→使之更充足→增强）〈派生〉amplifier n. 扩音器，放大器

clarify [ˈklærɪfaɪ] v. 澄清，阐明（clar-同 clear 清楚的+动词后缀-ify→将事情弄清楚）〈派生〉clarity n. 清楚，透明

exemplify [ɪɡˈzemplɪfaɪ] vt. 例证，例示（exempl-同 example 例子+动词后缀-ify→例证）

simplify [ˈsɪmplɪfaɪ] v. 简化，使单纯（simpl-同 simple 简单+动词后缀-ify→简化）

terrify ['terɪfaɪ] v. 使害怕，使惊恐（terr-同 terror 恐惧+动词后缀-ify→感到害怕）

signify ['sɪgnɪfaɪ] v. 表示，意味（sign 标志+动词后缀-ify→通过标志表明，意味着）

purify ['pjʊərɪfaɪ] vt. 使纯净 v. 净化（pur 纯净的+动词后缀-ify→净化）

testify ['testɪfaɪ] v. 作证，证明；（to）表明，说明（test 测试+动词后缀-ify→作证）

verify ['verɪfaɪ] vt. 证实，查证；证明（ver-同 very 真正的+动词后缀-ify→查证）

identify [aɪ'dentɪfaɪ] v. 识别，鉴别（ident 同 identity 身份+动词后缀-ify→使身份得以确认→辨认）〈派生〉identification n. 识别；证件

例句扩展 As soon as you awaken, identify what is upsetting about the dream. 你一醒过来，就立刻分辨梦里哪些部分是不愉快的。

qualify ['kwɒlɪfaɪ] v.（使）具有资格，证明合格；vt. 限制，限定（qual-同 quality 品质+动词后缀-ify→具有某种品质才具有资格）〈派生〉qualification n. 资格

quantify ['kwɒntɪfaɪ] vt. 量化（quant-同 quantity 数量+动词后缀-ify→量化）

modify ['mɒdɪfaɪ] vt. 更改，修改（mod-同 mode 模式+动词后缀-ify→模式矫正过来）

【词缀三十三】动词后缀-ate

articulate [ɑː'tɪkjʊleɪt] v.&a. 发音清晰；善于表达（artic-关节+动词后缀-ulate→关节咬住，引申为说话清楚）

dedicate ['dedɪkeɪt] vt. 奉献，献身（de-加强+dic 源自拉丁动词 dicaus 说，奉献+动词后缀-ate→努力献身）

differentiate [ˌdɪfə'renʃɪeɪt] v. 区分，区别，辨别（different 不同的+动词后缀-ate→区分）

donate [dəʊ'neɪt] v. 捐赠，捐献（don-给予+动词后缀-ate→捐赠）

discriminate [dɪ'skrɪmɪneɪt] v. 歧视；区别；辨出（dis-分开+希腊语词根 crit 判断，区分，决定+动词后缀-ate→把不同罪行区分开来→辨别→辨别中带有歧视）

irritate ['ɪrɪteɪt] v. 刺激，使兴奋；激怒（ir-使……+rit 擦+动词后缀-ate→使进入摩擦→激怒）

irrigate ['ɪrɪgeɪt] v. 灌溉；冲洗（ir-使……+rig 水+动词后缀-ate→进水→灌溉）

humiliate [hjʊ'mɪlɪeɪt] vt. 羞辱；使……丢脸；耻辱（humili 源自拉丁语词根 humilis 卑微的+动词后缀-ate→接近地面，使低下）

屠屠解词 hum-泥土，卑微的

- human n. 人（hum-泥土+an 一个→泥捏出的一个人）
- humility n. 谦逊，谦恭（humili 源自拉丁语词根 humilis 卑微的+名词后缀-ty→谦恭）
- exhume v. 掘出，挖出（ex-出+hum 泥土→出土→挖出）
- inhume v. 埋葬（in-进入+hum 泥土→进入土中）

locate [ləʊ'keɪt] vt. 定位，位于（local 当地的+动词后缀-ate→定位，位于）

lubricate ['luːbrɪkeɪt] v. 润滑（lubric 滑+动词后缀-ate→润滑）

mediate ['miːdɪeɪt] vt. 考虑；企图 vi. 冥想；沉思〈派生〉meditation n. 冥想；沉思

motivate ['məʊtɪveɪt] vt. 促动，激发，诱导；刺激（motive 动机+动词后缀-ate→激发，诱导）

necessitate [nə'sesɪteɪt] vt. 使……成为必要（necessary 必要的+动词后缀-ate→使……成为必要）

ventilate ['ventɪleɪt] vt. 使通风；公开（vent-风+il 同 soil 土壤+动词后缀-ate→松动土壤有利于空气进入）

vibrate [vaɪ'breɪt] v.（使）振动（vibr 摇摆+动词后缀-ate→振动）

旧词新说

备考过程中最容易忽略却又最致命的词汇问题就是"熟词僻义"。这些单词在阅读翻译过程中会直接影响句子的理解。在开始学习核心词汇之前,将"熟词僻义"一网打尽是备考初期的重要战役!

allowance [əˈlaʊəns] *n.* 允许

高频考点

① *n.* 津贴;补助

真题再现 Even the very phrase "jobseeker's allowance" — invented in 1996 — is about redefining the unemployed as a "jobseeker". [2014 年阅读Text 1] 甚至 1996 年发明的词汇"求职者的补贴"也是关于将失业者重新定义为"求职者"。

② *n.* (make ~ for sb.)宽容;体谅;考虑

例句 She failed one of the exam papers, but we ought to make allowance for the fact that she was ill. 她有一门考试不及格,但我们必须考虑到她当时生病了。

average [ˈævərɪdʒ] *a.* 平均的

高频考点 *a.* 普通的

真题再现 Being average just won't earn you what it used to. [2013 年英语(二)Text 1]表现平平可以挣钱的日子一去不复返了。

argue [ˈɑːgjuː] *vi.* 辩论

高频考点 *vt.* 认为,主张;说服

真题再现 It is hard, the state argues, for judges to assess the implications of new and rapidly changing technologies. [2015 年阅读 Text 2] 该州认为,法官很难评估新颖、日新月异的新技术带来的影响。

afford [əˈfɔːd] *v.* 供应得起

高频考点 *v.* 提供;给予

真题再现 The Internet affords anonymity to its users, a blessing to privacy and freedom of speech. [2011年英语(二)完形填空] 互联网允许网络用户匿名,这对隐私保护和言论自由来说是件好事。

approach [əˈprəʊtʃ] *vi.* 接近

高频考点

① *vt.* 着手处理;解决

真题再现 While his accomplishments may contribute to the solution of moral problems, he has not been charged with the task of approaching any but the factual aspects of those problems. [2006 年翻译] 尽管他的成果可能有助于解决道德问题,但他承担的任务只不过是处理这些问题的事实方面。

② *n.* (科学的)方法,途径

真题再现 In physics, one approach takes this impulse for unification to its extreme. [2012 年翻译] 物理学中,有一种方法将这种对统一性的紧迫需求发挥到了极致。

account [əˈkaʊnt] *n.* 账户,重要性 *v.* 认为

高频考点

① of no account 毫不重要,无足轻重

真题再现 Is it true that the American intellectual is rejected and considered of no account in his society? [2006 年翻译] 在美国社会,美国的知识分子被排斥,被认为没有地位,这是真的吗?

② take sth. into account=take account of sth. 把……考虑在内

真题再现 They argue that their work gives a correct baseline, which future management efforts must take into account. [2006年阅读Text 3] 他们认为他们的工作提供了一个准确的捕捞数量基线,是未来管理层必须要考虑的事情。

③ account for 解释,说明;占……比例

真题再现 What might account for this strange phenomenon? [2007 年阅读 Text 1] 导致这一奇怪现象的原因可能是什么?

As recently as 1995, the top four railroads accounted for under 70 percent of the total ton-miles moved by rails. [2003 年阅读 Text 3] 就在 1995 年,四大铁路公司占整个铁路运量的近 70%。

④ by all accounts 根据各种说法

真题再现 By all accounts he was a freethinking person, and a courageous one, and I find courage an essential quality for the understanding, let alone the performance, of his works. [2014 年翻译] 人们认为,他是个思想自由、充满勇气的人,我发现勇气这一品质,是理解他作品的关键,更不必说是演出其作品。

appeal [əˈpiːl] n. 请求,上诉 v. 要求,起诉

高频考点

① n. 吸引力,魅力

真题再现 Besides generating income, the presence of other marketers makes the site seem objective, gives companies opportunities to learn valuable information about the appeal of other companies' marketing. [2011 年阅读 Text 3]除了可以带来收入,其他营销者的投放也能使该网站看起来客观公正,使企业有机会了解其他公司市场营销的魅力所在。

② n.&vi. 呼吁,请求

真题再现 NBAC members also indicated that they will appeal to privately funded researchers and clinics not to try to clone humans by body cell nuclear transfer. [1999 年阅读 Text 4] NBAC 的成员表示,他们将呼吁受私人资金资助的研究人员和诊所不要尝试通过人体细胞核移植来克隆人。

③ vi. (~to sb. for sth.) 起诉

真题再现 Shippers who feel they are being overcharged have the right to appeal to the federal government's Surface Transportation Board for rate relief. [2003 年阅读Text 3] 如果托运商觉得被索要高价,他们有权上诉到联邦政府的陆上交通运输委员会,要求降低费率。

aggressive [əˈɡresɪv] a. 侵略的,好斗的

高频考点

① a. 强有力的

真题再现 Now it is a social policy: the most impor-

tant and aggressive promoter of gambling in America is the government. [2006 年新题型] 现在这是一种社会政策,即美国赌博业最重要的和最强有力的支持者是政府。

② a. 大胆的

真题再现 It identifies the undertreatment of pain and the aggressive use of "ineffectual and forced medical procedures that may prolong and even dishonor the period of dying" as the twin problems of end-of-life care. [2002 年阅读 Text 4] 报告指出了医院临终关怀护理中存在的两个问题:对病痛处理不力和大胆使用"无效而强制性的医疗程序——这些程序可能会延长死亡期,甚至会让死亡期难堪"。

attach [əˈtætʃ] vi. (~to) 贴上,使依附,系上

高频考点

① vi. (~to) 附加,附带;隶属于

真题再现 They just want Ottawa to fork over additional billions with few, if any, strings attached. [2005 年新题型] 他们只希望政府当局额外支付几十亿加元,如有可能,还会附带条件。

② vt. (~ importance to) 重视

真题再现 Government attached great importance to the Internet. [2001 年阅读 Text 2] 政府非常重视互联网。

academic [ækəˈdemɪk] a. 学术的

高频考点 n. 学者,大学教师

真题再现 Leonard Schlesinger, a Harvard academic and former chief executive of Au Bong Pain, a rapidly growing chain of bakery cafes, says that much "reengineering" has been crude. [1998 年阅读 Text 2] 哈佛学者伦纳德·施莱辛格是一家迅速扩张的烘焙咖啡店的前总裁,他说许多"企业重组"都不成熟。

address [əˈdres] n. 地址,住址

高频考点

① vt. 致函,给……写信

真题再现 Prior to his departure, he addressed a letter to his daughter. [1986 年词汇题] 他在离开之前给女儿写了一封信。

② vt. 向……讲话

真题再现 I was addressing a small gathering in a suburban Virginia living room — a women's group that had invited men to join them. [2010 年英语(二)阅读 Text 2] 我正在弗吉尼亚郊区的一间会客室的

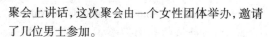

聚会上讲话,这次聚会由一个女性团体举办,邀请了几位男士参加。

③ *vt.* 处理,解决问题

真题再现 This rule is meant to address the difficulty that students from impoverished or chaotic homes might have in completing their homework. [2012 年英语(二)阅读 Text 1] 这个规定旨在解决来自贫穷家庭或混乱家庭的学生在完成家庭作业方面的困难。

air [eə] *n.* 空气

高频考点 *n.* 气氛;神态

真题再现 Even Tommasini calls him "an unpretentious musician with no air of the formidable conductor about him". [2011 年阅读 Text 1] 甚至托马西尼都认为他是"一位谦逊的音乐家,在他身上没有指挥家那种令人望而生畏的神态"。

act [ækt] *vi.* 表演

高频考点

① *n.* 行为;行动

真题再现 Anyway, the act of laughing probably does produce other types of physical feedback. [2011 年完形填空] 无论如何,笑这一行为的确有可能会引起其他的身体反应。

② *vi.* 起作用;(~as)扮演……的角色

真题再现 Paid and owned media are controlled by marketers promoting their own products. For media, such marketers act as the initiator for users' responses. [2011 年阅读 Text 3] 营销人员通过付费和自媒体推销其产品,而在"有偿"媒介方面,这种营销人员的作用就像是触发用户响应的初始催化剂。

③ *n.* 法案

例句 Congress passed an act to regulate the U.S. railroad industry. 美国国会通过了一项监管铁路行业的法案。

atmosphere ['ætməsfiə] *n.* 大气,空气

高频考点 *n.* 气氛,氛围

真题再现 These men wrote and published extensively, reaching both New World and Old World audiences, and giving New England an atmosphere of intellectual earnestness. [2009 年阅读 Text 4] 这些人写作并出

版了大量的著作,影响了新旧世界的读者,这也为新英格兰营造了一种求知的氛围。

absence ['æbsəns] *n.* 缺席

高频考点 *n.* 缺乏,缺少 → absent *a.* 缺席的

真题再现 There is "the democratizing uniformity of dress and discourse, and the casualness and absence of deference" characteristic of popular culture. [2006 年阅读 Text 1] 流行文化的特点就是"着装和话语的民主化统一,以及随意和缺乏尊重"。

absorb [əb'sɔːb] *v.* 吸收

高频考点

① *vt.* 承受;承担

真题再现 During the same period, families have been asked to absorb much more risk in their retirement income. [2007 年阅读 Text 3] 与此同时,家庭成员的退休收入也要承担更多的风险。

② *vt.* 吸引

真题再现 People are absorbed into "a culture of consumption" launched by the 19th-century department stores that offered vast arrays of goods in an elegant atmosphere. [2006 年阅读 Text 1] 人们沉迷于一种由19世纪的百货商店掀起的"消费文化"中。这些商店有着优雅的购物环境和琳琅满目的商品。

alien ['eɪliən] *a.* 外国的,外来的

高频考点 *a.* 陌生的;格格不入的→alienate *v.* 离间、挑拨

真题再现 There exists a social and cultural disconnection between journalists and their readers, which helps explain why the "standard templates" of the newsroom seem alien to many readers. [2001 年阅读 Text 3] 新闻记者和读者之间存在着一种社会和文化的脱节,这就是为什么新闻编辑室的"标准模式"与众多读者的意趣格格不入的原因。

advance [əd'vɑːns] *vi.* 前进

高频考点

① *n.* 进步→advanced *a.* 先进的

真题再现 Scientists need to respond forcefully to animal rights advocates, whose arguments are confusing the public and thereby threatening advances in health knowledge and care. [2003 年阅读 Text 2] 科学家应该对动物权利鼓吹者做出强有力的回应,因为他们的言论混淆了公众的视听,从而对卫生知

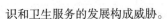

识和卫生服务的发展构成威胁。

② *vt.* 提出(建议、看法、理论等)

例句 The theory was advanced by an American professor. 该理论由一位美国教授提出。

acute [ə'kjuːt] *a.* 急性的；强烈的

高频考点 *a.* 精明的；有洞察力的

真题再现 Acute foreign observers related American adaptiveness and inventiveness to this educational advantage. [1996 年阅读 Text 1] 敏锐的外国观察家把美国人的适应能力和创新能力与这种教育优势联系起来。

agent ['eɪdʒənt] *n.* 代理

高频考点

① *n.* 原动力，动因

真题再现 Since much of the variation is due to genes, one more agent of evolution has gone. [2000 年阅读 Text 2] 因为大部分差异是由基因引起的，又一个进化的因素消失了。

② by the agency of sb./sth. 由于……帮助；由于……影响

例句 He obtained his position by the agency of friends. 由于朋友的帮助，他获得了一个职位。

assumption [ə'sʌmpʃn] *n.* 假定，假想

高频考点

① *n.* 信念

真题再现 As is true of any developed society, in America a complex set of cultural signals, assumptions, and conventions underlies all social interrelationships. [1996 年阅读 Text 2] 同任何发达国家一样，一系列复杂的文化特征、信念和习俗构成了美国所有社会交往的基础。

② *n.* 想法

真题再现 Such behaviour is regarded as "all too human", with the underlying assumption that other animals would not be capable of this finely developed sense of grievance. [2005 年阅读 Text 1] 这种行为被看作"人之常情"，其潜在的想法是其他动物不可能具有如此高度发达的埋怨意识。

③ *n.* 担任；承担

例句 His assumption of power was welcomed by everyone. 他掌权受到大家的欢迎。

attend [ə'tend] *vt.* 参加

高频考点 *vi.*(~ to)注意，关注

真题再现 38. In bringing up the concept of GASP, the author is making the point that _____. [A] shareholders' interests should be properly attended to [2007 年阅读Text 4] 38. 作者提出 GASP 的概念是想说明_____。[A] 应适当关注股东的利益

attendant [ə'tendənt] *n.* 服务员

高频考点 *a.* 伴随而来的

真题再现 Even demographics are working against the middle class family, as the odds of having a weak elderly parent—and all the attendant need for physical and financial assistance—have jumped eightfold in just one generation. [2007 年阅读 Text 3] 就连人口统计数据也对中产阶级不利，因为家庭成员中有一个年老体弱的父母——以及随之而来的体力和经济援助上的需求——的概率在一代人的时间里就猛增了八倍。

arm [ɑːm] *n.* 手臂

高频考点 *vt.* (~ sb. with) 武装

真题再现 Similarly, some Wall Street investment firms armed themselves with patents for financial products, even as they took positions in court cases opposing the practice. [2010 年阅读 Text 2] 无独有偶，一些华尔街投资公司通过为多项金融产品申请专利来武装自己，即使他们在法庭上对专利授予持反对态度。

appreciate [ə'priːʃieɪt] *vt.* 欣赏

高频考点

① *vt.* 意识到

真题再现 39. According to Paragraph 4, what puzzles the author is that some bosses fail to _____. [D] appreciate the economic value of trust [2007 年阅读 Text 4] 39. 根据文章第四段，作者感到困惑的是一些老板没有_____。[D]意识到信任的经济价值

② *vt.* 感激

例句 I really appreciate your taking time to read my letter. 我非常感谢您抽空读我的信。

accommodate [ə'kɒmədeɪt] *vt.* 提供住宿

高频考点 *vt.* 适应，调节

真题再现 Teachers need to be aware of the emotional, intellectual, and physical changes that young adults experience. And they also need to give serious thought

177

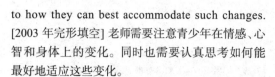
to how they can best accommodate such changes. [2003 年完形填空] 老师需要注意青少年在情感、心智和身体上的变化。同时也需要认真思考如何能最好地适应这些变化。

apple [ˈæpl] *n.* 苹果

高频考点 *n.* 掌上明珠

例句 Penny's only son was the apple of her eye. 彭妮的独子是她的心肝宝贝。

acid [ˈæsɪd] *a.* 酸的

高频考点 *a.* 尖酸刻薄的

例句 Nobody likes to hear the acid remarks. 没有人喜欢听尖酸刻薄的话。

administer [ədˈmɪnɪstə] *vt.* 管理

高频考点

① *vt.* 给予，实施（惩罚）

例句 Retribution was administered to those found guilty. 对有罪者予以惩罚。

② *vi.* 有助于

例句 Physical exercise administers to the circulation of the blood. 体育锻炼有助于血液循环。

agreeable [əˈɡriːəbl] *a.* 欣然同意的

高频考点

① *a.* 容易相处的

例句 I find her a very agreeable woman. 我发现她是个和蔼可亲的女人。

② *a.* 宜人的

例句 You should choose a city with agreeable weather to have a holiday. 你应该选一个天气宜人的城市去度假。

agitate [ˈædʒɪteɪt] *vt.* 搅动，摇动

高频考点 *vt.* 激起

例句 His fiery speech agitated the crowd. 他热情洋溢的讲话让群众感到很激动。

appropriate [əˈprəʊprɪət] *a.* 正确合适的

高频考点 *vt.* 占用，挪用

例句 The minister was found to have appropriated government money. 部长被查出挪用了公款。

army [ˈɑːmi] *n.* 军队

高频考点 *n.* 大批，大群

例句 The increasing army of the unemployed has attracted the attention of the economist. 不断增长的失业大军引起了这名经济学家的关注。

arrest [əˈrest] *vt.* 逮捕

高频考点

① *vt.* 终止，抑制

例句 The treatment arrested the growth of the disease. 治疗抑制了病情的发展。

② *vt.* 吸引

例句 An unusual painting arrested his attention. 一幅不寻常的画吸引了他的注意。

assassinate [əˈsæsɪneɪt] *vt.* 暗杀，行刺

高频考点 *vt.* 中伤，破坏（名誉等）

例句 Telling lies seems to be trivial but to assassinate a person's reputation. 撒谎看似无足轻重但会损害一个人的名誉。

automatic [ɔːtəˈmætɪk] *a.* 自动的

高频考点 *a.* 不假思索的

例句 A boy who has good manners stands up in an automatic movement when a lady enters the room. 一个有礼貌的孩子，在一个女士进入房间时，便会不假思索地站起来。

attribute [æˈtrɪbuːt] *n.* (~to) 归结于

高频考点 *n.* 特性，特质

例句 Kindness is one of her attributes. 仁慈是她的特性之一。

avenue [ˈævənjuː] *n.* 林荫道

高频考点 *n.* 方法；途径

例句 We have explored every avenue in order to stop the epidemic. 我们探讨了各种方法，试图制止这次流行病。

bargain [ˈbɑːɡən] *v.* 讨价还价

高频考点 *n.* 廉价品

真题再现 Priestly explains how the deep blue color of the assistant's sweater descended over the years from fashion shows to department stores and to the bargain bin in which the poor girl doubtless found her garment. [2013 年阅读Text 1] 普里斯特利解释说，助理身上穿的深蓝色的外套，就是一步一步从时装秀台上沦落到百货商店再沦落到折扣摊。很明显，这位可怜的女孩就是在折扣摊上买的这件衣服。

bull [bʊl] *n.* 公牛

高频考点 *n.* 价格上涨；股市上涨，牛市

真题再现 The longest bull run in a century of art-market history ended on a dramatic note with a sale

178

of 56 works by Damien Hirst. [2010 英语（二）阅读 Text 1] 随着达米恩·赫斯特 56 件作品的出售，艺术市场一个世纪以来最长的牛市戏剧性地落幕了。

bird [bɜːd] *n.* 鸟

高频考点 *n.* 人

真题再现 He is that rare bird, a scientist who works independently of any institution.[2008 年完形填空] 他是个特立独行的人，身为科学家，却非任何机构成员。

brain [breɪn] *n.* 大脑

高频考点 *n.*（*pl.*）智力

真题再现 Few authors have brains enough or literary gift enough to keep their own end up in journalism. [2010 年阅读 Text 1] 极少数作家有足够的聪明才智和文学天赋来精神饱满地应对新闻工作。

breath [breθ] *n.* 呼吸

高频考点 *n.* 气息

真题再现 It's a message even more bitter than a clove cigarette, yet, somehow, a breath of fresh air. [2006 年阅读 Text 4] 这一启示甚至比丁香烟草还要苦，但却不知为何带来了一股清新的气息。

business ['bɪznɪs] *n.* 商业，交易，生意

高频考点

① *n.* 企业

真题再现 The future of this company is at stake: many of its talented employees are flowing into more profitable net-based businesses. [2001 年词汇] 这家公司的未来生死未卜：许多优秀人才正流向利润更高的网络企业。

② *n.* 行业

真题再现 With $3.5 billion being lost on Internet wagers this year, gambling has passed pornography as the Web's most profitable business. [2006 年新题型] 今年网络赌博造成了 35 亿美元的损失，超过色情，成为网上最有利可图的行业。

buy [baɪ] *vt.* 购买

高频考点 *vt.* 听信，认同

真题再现 Lots of Americans bought that nonsense, and over three decades, some 10 million smokers went to early graves. [2005 年阅读 Text 2] 许多美国人相信了这些胡言乱语，在三十多年中，差不多有 1 000 万烟民早早地进了坟墓。

block [blɒk] *n.* 木块，街区

高频考点 *vt.* 阻碍，限制

真题再现 A lateral move that hurt my pride and blocked my professional progress promoted me to abandon my relatively high profile career. [2001 年阅读 Text 5] 一次平级的人事调动伤了我的自尊心，并阻断了我的事业发展，这促使我放弃自己地位较高的职业。

bitterly ['bɪtəli] *ad.* 痛苦地

高频考点 *ad.* 猛烈地

真题再现 Some have breathed sighs of relief, others, including churches, right-to-life groups and the Australian Medical Association, bitterly attacked the bill and the haste of its passage. [1997 年阅读 Text 1] 一些人如释重负，另一些人，包括教会，生命权利组织以及澳大利亚医学会成员都对这一决议及其仓促的通过进行了猛烈的抨击。

bill [bɪl] *n.* 账单

高频考点 *n.* 法案，议案

真题再现 A bill by Democratic Senator Robert Byrd of West Virginia, which would offer financial incentives for private industry, is a promising start. [2005 年阅读 Text 2] 西弗吉尼亚州的民主党参议员罗伯特·伯德提出一项议案，从经济上激励私企，就是一个良好的开端。

bound [baʊnd] *v.* 弹跳

高频考点

① *n.* 界限 → boundary *n.* 分界线，边界

真题再现 Unlike most of the world's volcanoes, they are not always found at the boundaries of the great drifting plates that make up the earth's surface. [1998 年阅读 Text 5] 和世界上大多数火山不同的是，它们并不总是在构成地球表面的巨大漂流板块之间的边界上出现。

② be bound for 前往

例句 He got up late so that he missed the plane bound for Britain. 他起晚了，没有赶上飞往英国的飞机。

③ be bound to 注定

真题再现 64.The author is strongly opposed to the practice of examinations at schools because _____.
[B] some students are bound to fail [1995 年阅读 Text 4] 64. 作者强烈反对学校的考试方式，因

为_____。有些学生注定会失败

backward [ˈbækwəd] *ad.* 向后

高频考点 *a.* 迟钝的

例句 Backward children need a special kind of schooling. 天赋差的孩子需要特殊的教育。

bridge [brɪdʒ] *n.* 桥

高频考点 *vt.* 弥合（分歧），消除（隔阂）

例句 It is unlikely that the two sides will be able to bridge their differences. 双方不太可能消除彼此之间的分歧。

bearing [ˈbeərɪŋ] *n.* 忍受

高频考点

① *n.* 举止，风度

例句 Her dignified bearing throughout the trial made everyone believe she was innocent. 在整个审讯的过程中，她那端庄的举止使得每个人都相信她是无辜的。

② *n.* 方面

例句 We must consider this question in all its bearings. 我们应该考虑到问题的方方面面。

beam [biːm] *n.* 梁

高频考点

① *n.*（灯光、日光等的）束，道，柱

例句 I had promised to focus on the economy like a laser beam. 我曾许诺将"像一束激光那样"专注于经济。

② *vi.* 堆满笑容

例句 He always beams with satisfaction every time we see him. 我们每次看到他，他的脸上都洋溢着满意的微笑。

breed [briːd] *vt.* 孕育

高频考点 *vt.* 导致

例句 War breeds misery and ruin. 战争带来苦难和破坏。

blossom [ˈblɒsəm] *vi.* 开花

高频考点 *vi.* 发展，长成

例句 New industries can blossom overnight if we find an outlet for their products. 如果我们为新兴产业的产品找到销路，它们短期内就会成长起来。

blue [bluː] *a.* 蓝色的

高频考点 *a.* 沮丧的，失落的

例句 He was blue over his dismissal. 他因被解雇而

情绪低落。

blast [blɑːst] *n.* 爆炸

高频考点 *vt.* 损害

例句 His fame was blasted by his rude behaviors. 他的名誉因他的粗鲁行为而受到损害。

blaze [bleɪz] *n.* 火焰，火灾

高频考点 *vt.* 开拓

例句 It is what led generations of pioneers to blaze a westward trail. 正是这种精神指引了一代又一代先驱者开拓西进之路。

blunt [blʌnt] *a.* 钝的

高频考点

① *a.* 了解或感觉能力迟钝的

例句 His isolation has made him blunt about the feelings of others. 他的孤立使他对别人的感情木然无知。

② to be blunt（with you）（用作插入语）老实说（= to tell the truth）

brake [breɪk] *n.* 刹车

高频考点

① *n.* 阻碍

例句 Arrogant acts as a brake to progress. 骄傲使人落后。

② *n.*（put a ~ on）削减

例句 The government determined to put a brake on the public spending. 政府决定削减公共事业开支。

breach [briːtʃ] *n.* 裂口

高频考点

① *n.*（关系）破裂，不和

例句 A trivial misunderstanding caused a breach between them. 小小的误会引起了他们之间的不和。

② *n.&vt.* 破坏，违背

例句 These flaws breach one of the three principles of sound taxation. 这些缺点违反了良好税收政策的三条原则之一。

breast [brest] *n.* 胸部

高频考点 *n.* 内心，心情

例句 His guilty conscience forced him to make a clean breast of everything. 他感到十分内疚，坦白了一切。

brilliant [brɪliənt] *a.* 灿烂的，成功的，辉煌的

高频考点 *a.* 聪明的，才华横溢的

例句 He is really a brilliant scientist. 他真的是一位才华横溢的科学家。

brittle ['brɪtl] *a.* 脆的；易碎的

高频考点

① *a.* 易怒的

例句 She has a brittle temper. 她动辄发脾气。

② *ad.* 脆弱的

例句 For all its outward confidence, America has a brittle alter ego. 尽管美国对外信心十足，但也有其脆弱的一面。

critical ['krɪtɪkəl] *a.* 批评的

高频考点 *a.* 关键的，重要的

真题再现 It was not until the mid-1980s that pink fully came into its own, when it began to seem inherently attractive to girls, part of what defined them as female, at least for the first few critical years. [2012 年英语（二）阅读 Text 2] 直到20世纪80年代中期，粉红色才迎来其全盛时期，开始看起来对女孩有了致命的吸引力，至少在最初的那几年，粉红色甚至成了女性的特征之一。

cloak [kləʊk] *n.* 斗篷，披风

高频考点 *vt.* 掩饰，掩盖

真题再现 Rather than cloaking his exit in the usual vague excuses, he came right out and said he was leaving "to pursue my goal of running a company". [2011 年阅读 Text 2] 他没有用一些常见的模棱两可的借口掩饰自己的离开，反而坦言离职是为了"追求自己经营一家公司的目标"。

credit ['kredɪt] *n.* 信用，学分

高频考点 *n.* 荣誉，赞扬

真题再现 Once a discovery claim becomes public, the discoverer receives intellectual credit. [2012 年阅读 Text 3] 一旦科学发现声明被公开，发现者将获得学术界的赞誉。

conduct [kən'dʌkt] *vt.* 传导

高频考点

① *vt.* 进行，开展

真题再现 Ericsson grew up in Sweden, and studied nuclear engineering until he realized he would have more opportunity to conduct his own research if he switched to psychology. [2007 年阅读 Text 1] 艾瑞森在瑞典长大，刚开始他研究核工程，后来他意识

到如果转学心理学，会获得更多机会来开展自己的研究。

② *n.* 行为

真题再现 Nevertheless, Williams's suit charges that the casino, knowing he was "helplessly addicted to gambling", intentionally worked to "lure" him to "engage in conduct against his will". [2006 年新题型] 然而，威廉姆斯控告赌场，明知道他已经"无药可救地沉溺于赌博"，还故意"引诱"他"作出违背自己意愿的行为"。

cultivate ['kʌltɪveɪt] *v.* 耕种，种植

高频考点 *v.* 培养

真题再现 31. According to Dr. Curtis, habits like hand washing with soap_____. [A] should be further cultivated [2010 年英语（二）阅读 Text 3] 31. 在科蒂斯教授看来，用肥皂洗手的习惯_____。[A]应当进一步培养

counsel ['kaʊnsl] *n.* 法律顾问

高频考点 *vt.* 咨询；建议

真题再现 Every entrance ticket lists a tollfree number for counseling from the Indiana Department of Mental Health. [2006 年新题型] 每张门票上都列有来自印第安纳州心理健康部门的免费咨询电话号码。

concrete ['kɒnkriːt] *n.* 混凝土

高频考点 *a.* 具体的

真题例句 Many Americans regard the jury system as a concrete expression of crucial democratic values. [2010 年英语（二）阅读 Text 4] 很多美国人把陪审团制度看作是其民主价值观的具体体现。

code [kəʊd] *n.* 代码，代号；密码

高频考点 *n.* 法规；规范

真题再现 But his primary task is not to think about the moral code, which governs his activity. [2006 年翻译] 但是，他的主要任务并非思考控制其行为的道德规范。

casualty ['kæʒʊəlti] *n.* 伤亡人数

高频考点 *n.* 受害者；牺牲品

真题再现 For a while it looked as though the making of semiconductors, which America had invented and which sat at the heart of the new computer age, was going to be the next casualty. [2000 年阅读 Text 1] 半导体是由美国人发明的，在新计算机时代处于核心

地位。曾有一段时间，美国半导体产业似乎将成为下一个牺牲品。

chair [tʃɛə] *n.* 椅子

高频考点 *vt.* 主持，担任主持，使就任要职

真题再现 Supreme Court Justice Sandra is in her 70s, and former surgeon general Koop chairs an Internet start-up in his 80s. [2003 年阅读Text 4] 桑德拉任最高法院法官时 70 多岁，前外科医生协会总裁库普在 80 多岁时还担任一家互联网初创公司的领导。

cover [ˈkʌvə] *vt.* 覆盖

高频考点

① *vt.* 掩饰，掩盖

真题再现 I covered my exit by claiming "I wanted to spend more time with my family". [2001 年阅读 Text 5] 我用"我想多陪陪家人"为借口，掩饰辞职的原因。

② *vt.* 支付（费用）

真题再现 The railroad industry as a whole, despite its brightening fortunes, still does not earn enough to cover the cost of the capital it must invest to keep up with its surging traffic.[2003 年阅读 Text 3] 从整体来说，虽然铁路行业有耀眼的资产，但收入仍然不足以支付为满足不断增长的运输需要而进行的固定资产投资。

③ *vt.* 走完（一段路程）

例句 We covered about 30 miles a day. 我们一天走了大约 30 英里。

④ *vt.* 报道

例句 The best reporters were sent to cover the war. 最优秀的记者被派去前线进行战地报道。

climate [ˈklaɪmɪt] *n.* 气候

高频考点 *n.* 风气，社会思潮

真题再现 When the work is well done, a climate of accident-free operations is established where time lost due to injuries is kept at a minimum. [1999 年完形填空] 如果此项工作能做得好，就会形成无事故作业的好风气，因此那儿因工伤事故造成的时间损失就会被控制在最低限度。

celebrate [ˈselɪbreɪt] *vt.* 庆祝，祝贺

高频考点 *vt.* 表扬，赞美→celebrity *n.* 名人

真题再现 In a society that so persistently celebrates procreation, is it any wonder that admitting you regret having children is equivalent to admitting you support kittenkilling? [2011 年阅读 Text 4] 在一个一贯赞美生育的社会中，承认后悔生育孩子就相当于承认自己支持残杀幼猫，这还有什么奇怪的吗？

真题再现 Practically every week features at least one celebrity mom, or mom-to-be, smiling on the newsstands. [2011 年阅读 Text 4] 实际上，每周都有至少一位名人母亲或者准母亲在杂志上笑迎读者。

cement [sɪˈment] *n.* 水泥

高频考点 *vt.* 巩固，加强

真题再现 Egypt's leadership in the Arab world was cemented by the Aswan High Dam. [1998 年阅读 Text 1] 埃及由于建造了阿斯旺大坝而巩固了其在阿拉伯世界的领导地位。

channel [ˈtʃænl] *n.* 海峡，频道

高频考点 *n.* 方法，方式

真题再现 30.Which of the following best summarizes the main idea of the text? [C] Authors welcome the new channel for publication. [2008 年阅读 Text 2] 30. 下面哪个选项最能概括文章的主旨？[C] 作者欢迎新的出版方式。

charge [tʃɑːdʒ] *n.* 电荷，指控，掌管

高频考点

① *v.* 收费

真题再现 Railroads typically charge such "captive" shippers 20 to 30 percent more than they do when another railroad is competing for the business. [2003 年阅读 Text 3] 通常，铁路公司对这些"被控"客户的收费要比有另一铁路公司竞争业务时多 20% ～ 30%。

② *v.* 充电

例句 There was nothing in the brochure about having to drive the car every day to charge up the battery. 手册里只字没提必须每天开车给电池充电。

③ *n.&v.* 批评，指责

真题再现 On the other hand, he did not accept as well founded the charge made by some of his critics that, while he was a good observer, he had no power of reasoning. [2008 年翻译] 另一方面，某些人批评他虽然善于观察，却不具备推理能力，而他认为此种说法缺乏根据。

④ *v.* 指控

例句 Police have charged Mr Bell with murder. 警方

以"谋杀罪"起诉了贝尔先生。

cloud [klaʊd] *n.* 云团

高频考点 *vt.* 威胁，损害

真题再现 A turbulent business environment also has senior managers cautious of letting vague pronouncements cloud their reputations. [2011 年阅读 Text 2] 动荡的商业环境也使得高级经理们格外小心，避免让模糊不清的表态损害他们的名誉。

conventional [kənˈvenʃənl] *a.* 例会的，常规的

高频考点 *a.* 传统的→convention *n.* 会议；惯例；习俗

真题再现 The conventional view that education should be one of the very highest priorities for promoting rapid economic development in poor countries is wrong. [2009 年阅读 Text 3] 那种认为"教育应该是促进贫穷国家经济快速发展的重要因素之一"的传统观点是错误的。

chronic [ˈkrɒnɪk] *a.* (疾病)慢性的

高频考点 *a.* 长期的，长时间的

真题再现 I think that the kinds of things that women are exposed to tend to be in more of a chronic or repeated nature. [2008 年阅读 Text 1] 我认为女性接触到的事情往往更具有长期性和重复性。

cling [klɪŋ] *vi.* 粘着

高频考点 *vi.* (~ to) 坚持，依附于，依靠

经典例句 29. It can be inferred from the last paragraph that_____. [A] top performers used to cling to their posts [2011 年阅读 Text 2] 29. 从文章最后一段话中可以得出_____。[A] 优秀员工过去总是坚守自己的岗位

command [kəˈmɑːnd] *v.* 命令

高频考点

① *vt.* 掌握

真题再现 Americans no longer expect public figures, whether in speech or in writing, to command the English language with skill and gift. [2005 年阅读 Text 4] 美国人已不再期待公众人物在演讲或写作中运用技巧和文采来驾驭英语。

② *vt.* 俯瞰

例句 The hill commands a fine view. 从这座山上可以俯瞰到一片美景。

③ *vt.* 博得，赢得

例句 This great man is able to command everyone's respect. 这位伟人能博得大家的尊敬。

curb [kɜːb] *n.* 路边

高频考点 *n.& vt.* 控制，约束

真题再现 Several fast-fashion companies have made efforts to curb their impact on labor and the environment. [2013 年阅读 Text 1] 几家快时尚公司已经努力减少对劳动力和环境的影响。

counter [ˈkaʊntə] *n.* 柜台

高频考点 *a.* 相反的 *v.* 反击

真题再现 John McWhorter sees the triumph of 1960s counter-culture as responsible for the decline of formal English. [2005 年阅读 Text 4] 约翰·麦克沃特认为，20世纪60年代反主流文化的胜利是正式英语衰落的原因。

count [kaʊnt] *v.* 数数

高频考点

① *vi.* (~ on) 依赖于

真题再现 During the past generation, the American middle-class family that once could count on hard work and fair play to keep itself financially secure had been transformed by economic risk and new realties. [2007 年阅读 Text 3] 在过去的一代人中，美国中产阶级家庭已经被经济危机和新的现实所改变。过去他们曾还能指望依靠艰苦工作和公平竞争来使自己在经济生活中获得安全保障。

② *vi.* 有价值

Every minute counts. 每一分钟都是有价值的。

carrot [ˈkærət] *n.* 胡萝卜

高频考点 *n.* (用以引诱的)报酬；好处；许诺

例句 He is expert in the policy of stick and carrot. 他善于使用软硬兼施的政策。

challenge [ˈtʃælɪndʒ] *n.* 挑战

高频考点

① *vt.* 质疑

例句 All the people in the meeting challenged the wisdom of a procedure. 所有与会者对程序的合理性提出了质疑。

② *n.& vt.* 要求

例句 The challenge today is not merely to improve the material standards of living. 今天的要求不仅在于改进物质生活的标准。

champion [ˈtʃæmpiən] *n.* 冠军

高频考点 *n.&vt.* 拥护，支持

例句 Republicans could champion the things they believe will enhance productivity and mobility. 共和党人可能会支持他们认为可以提高生产效率和灵活性的计划。

clash [klæʃ] *n.* 碰撞

高频考点 *n.&v.* 争论；不协调

例句 Mary and her husband clash over the question where they should live. 对于在何处定居的问题，玛丽和丈夫意见不一。

climax [ˈklaimæks] *n.* 顶点

高频考点 *n.* 高潮

例句 This passage foreshadows the climax of the story. 这一段为故事的高潮做了铺垫。

coarse [kɔːs] *a.* 粗糙的

高频考点 *a.* 粗鲁的

例句 Don't use coarse words before a lady. 在女士面前不要讲粗鲁的话。

compass [ˈkʌmpəs] *n.* 指南针

高频考点 *n.* 范围，界限

例句 Finance is not within the compass of this department. 财政不在这个部门的管辖范围之内。

concert [ˈkɒnsət] *n.* 音乐会

高频考点 *vt.* 达成一致 *n.* 一致，和谐

例句 We will get together to concert our differences. 我们将聚集一起协调分歧。

corner [ˈkɔːnə] *n.* 角落

高频考点 *vt.* 逼入困境

例句 The police finally cornered the thief. 警察终于把那个小偷逼入一个角落。

cripple [ˈkripl] *n.* 跛子，瘸子

高频考点 *vt.* 削弱，破坏

例句 A total cut-off of supplies would cripple the country's economy. 全面切断商品供应会使该国经济陷入瘫痪。

conviction [kənˈvikʃn] *n.* 判罪

高频考点 *n.* 说服，信服

例句 His argument has brought conviction to many waverers. 他的论点使许多犹豫不决的人信服。

craft [krɑːft] *n.* 工艺，手艺

高频考点 *n.* 诡计，手腕

例句 He used a certain amount of craft to make the sale. 他为这次买卖使了手腕。

cradle [ˈkreidl] *n.* 摇篮

高频考点 *n.* 发源地

例句 Mali is the cradle of some of Africa's richest civilizations. 马里是非洲一些最悠久文明的发源地。

cream [kriːm] *n.* 奶酪，奶油

高频考点 *n.* 精华；佼佼者

例句 Therefore, the best Chinese schools then had the cream of the crop among Hong Kong's secondary school students. 因此，当时最好的几所中文学校拥有香港最好的中学生。

cross [krɒs] *n.* 十字路口 *vt.* 穿过

高频考点

① *n.* 磨难，苦难

例句 Everyone has a cross to bear. 每一个人都有自己的苦难。

② *a.* 发怒的

例句 Don't get cross with me, for it wasn't my fault. 不要对我生气，那不是我的错。

crystal [ˈkristl] *n.* 水晶

高频考点 *a.* 清楚的，明显的

例句 It is crystal clear what we must do. 我们该做什么是很明显的。

culture [ˈkʌltʃə] *n.* 文化

高频考点 *n.* 教养，修养

例句 The highest possible stage in moral culture is when we recognize that we ought to control thoughts. 道德修养有可能达到的最高境界是认识到我们应该控制自己的思想。

cunning [ˈkʌniŋ] *a.* 狡猾的，阴险的

高频考点 *a.* 巧妙的；熟练的

例句 The cunning bit is to turn the maths into an effective card trick. 巧妙之处在于如何让数学变成奏效的纸牌戏法。

due [djuː] *a.* (to) 由于

高频考点 *a.* 预计的

真题再现 Google said that Internet Explorer 10, the version due to appear in Windows 8, would have DNT as a default. [2013 年阅读 Text 2] 谷歌说，Internet

Explorer 10 浏览器——预计将于 Windows 8 上市时启用——将 DNT 作为默认设置。

dictate [dɪkˈteɪt] *v.* 口述；听写

高频考点 *v.* 支配，控制

真题例句 I had not realized how profoundly marketing trends dictated our perception of what is natural to kids, including our core beliefs about their psychological development. [2012 年英语（二）阅读 Text 2] 我原来没有意识到市场营销趋势竟如此深刻地影响着我们对孩子天性的看法，包括他们心理发展的核心信念。

deny [dɪˈnaɪ] *v.* 否认→denial *n.* 否认

高频考点 *v.* 避免

真题再现 Markets have lost faith that the euro zone's economies, weaker or stronger, will one day converge thanks to the discipline of sharing a single currency, which denies uncompetitive members the quick fix of devaluation. [2011 年英语（二）阅读 Text 4] 市场已经失去信心，不再相信：欧元区的经济体，无论强弱，终有一天都会因遵循使用统一货币——这可以阻止缺乏竞争力的成员国利用货币贬值快速解决经济问题——而走向融合。

discipline [ˈdɪsɪplɪn] *n.* 纪律

高频考点 *n.* 学科

真题再现 No disciplines have seized on professionalism with as much enthusiasm as the humanities. [2011 年新题型] 没有哪个学科像人文学科那样看重专业水平。

distinction [dɪˈstɪŋkʃn] *n.* 区别

高频考点 *n.* 荣誉，光荣

真题再现 If ambition is to be well regarded, the rewards of ambition — wealth, distinction, control over one's destiny — must be deemed worthy of the sacrifices made on ambition's behalf. [2000 年阅读 Text 5] 个人的雄心如果能被正确看待的话，那么它的回报——财富、声誉、对命运的掌握——则应该被认为值得为之付出牺牲。

domestic [dəˈmestɪk] *a.* 国内的

高频考点 *a.* 家庭的

真题再现 The kinds of interpersonal violence that women are exposed to tend to be in domestic situations, by, unfortunately, parents or other family members, and they tend not to be one-shot deals. [2008 年阅读 Text 1] 女性面对的人际暴力通常发生在家庭环境中，不幸的是，这往往是父母或其他的家庭成员实施的，而且这种暴力行为发生不止一次。

diversion [daɪˈvɜːʃn] *n.* 转移，分散注意力

高频考点 *n.* 娱乐，消遣

真题再现 Strangers and travelers were welcome sources of diversion, and brought news of the outside world. [1997 年阅读 Text 2] 陌生人和旅行者很受欢迎，他们带来了娱乐消遣，还带来了外面世界的消息。

dawn [dɔːn] *n.* 黎明

高频考点

① *n.&vi.*（时代，局面等）开始出现

真题再现 Since the dawn of human ingenuity, people have devised ever more cunning tools to cope with work that is dangerous, boring, burdensome, or just plain nasty. [2002 年阅读 Text 2] 当开始发现自身创造力后人类已设计出更加巧妙的工具来应对那些危险、乏味、繁重甚至是有点脏的工作。

② *vi.*（~ on sb.）顿悟；明白

例句 Then a more disconcerting discovery began to dawn on him: he was smarter than his parents. 随后他渐渐发现一件让他困惑不安的事实：他比他的父母更聪明。

dramatically [drəˈmætɪkli] *ad.* 戏剧性地

高频考点 *ad.* 引人注目地；急剧地

真题再现 The bodies playing major professional sports have changed dramatically over the years. [2008 年阅读 Text 3] 这些年来，参加各大职业赛事的球员的身高发生了很大改变。

deliver [dɪˈlɪvə] *vt.* 传递

高频考点

① deliver *vt.* 发言

真题再现 Include a few casual and apparently off-the-cuff remarks which you can deliver in a relaxed and unforced manner.[2002 年阅读 Text 2]（练习幽默）内容包括一些很随意看上去是即兴的话，你可以用轻松、不做作的方式说出来。

② delivery *n.* 演讲（或唱歌）的姿态

真题再现 Often it's the delivery which causes the audience to smile, so speak slowly. [2002 年阅读 Text 2] 往往是你说话的风格让听众发笑，因此建议说慢

一些。

dampen ['dæmpən] *vt.* 使潮湿

高频考点 *vt.* 减弱，抑制

真题再现 Even though the day-to-day experience of raising kids can be soul-crushingly hard, Senior writes that "the very things that in the moment dampen our moods can later be sources of intense gratification and delight." [2011 年阅读 Text 4] 即使抚养孩子的日子漫长难熬，令人筋疲力尽，但是森尼尔撰文写道：正是那些一时让我们沮丧的事情带来了日后由衷的欣喜。

decline [dɪ'klaɪn] *vi.* 下倾，下降

高频考点 *vt.* 拒绝

真题再现 Depending on the comments received, the editor would accept the paper for publication or decline it. [2008 年阅读 Text 2] 根据评论意见，编辑将决定是否发表。

doom [duːm] *n.* 厄运

高频考点 *n.* 毁灭，死亡

真题再现 26. The author begins his article with Edmund Burke's words to _____. [C] warn of the doom of biomedical research [2003 年阅读 Text 2] 26. 作者用埃德蒙·伯克的话作为文章的开头是为了_____。[C] 警告生物医学末日即将到来

delicate ['delɪkɪt] *a.* 精巧的，精致的

高频考点 *a.* 微妙的

真题再现 37. We may infer from the second paragraph that_____。[B] in its early days the U.S. was confronted with delicate situations [2008 年阅读 Text 4] 37. 我们可以从第二段中推断出_____。[B] 美国早期面临着非常微妙的局面

drain [dreɪn] *n.* 排水沟

高频考点

① *n.* (财富、人才等的) 不断外流

真题再现 This "brain drain" has long bothered policy-makers in poor countries. [2012 年英语 (二) 翻译] 这种 "人才流失" 现象长期困扰贫困国家的决策者。

② *vt.* 耗尽

例句 The civil war drained the country of its manpower and wealth. 内战耗尽国家的人力和财富。

desert ['dezət] *n.* 沙漠

高频考点

① *a.* 荒凉的

例句 We can see civilizations adapt and flourish in the rugged desert southwestern North America. 我们可以看见文明在荒凉的北美洲西南部适应下来并繁荣发展。

② [dɪ'zət] *vt.* 放弃；遗弃

例句 At the edge of the desert, he came across a deserted church. 在沙漠的边缘地带，他碰巧发现了一个被遗弃的教堂。

departure [dɪ'paːtʃə] *n.* 离开

高频考点

① *n.* 背离，违背

例句 The new policy represents a complete departure from their previous position. 新政策说明他们完全背离了之前的立场。

② *n.* 事业；冒险

例句 Working on a farm is a new departure for him. 在农场工作对他来说是一项新事业。

desperate ['despərət] *a.* 令人绝望的

高频考点 *a.* 极度渴望的

例句 He's desperate for a job. [2011年英语 (二) 翻译] 他极渴望得到工作。

device [dɪ'vaɪs] *n.* 装置

高频考点 *n.* 手段，策略

例句 Her illness is merely a device to avoid seeing him. 她所谓生病只是避免见他的花招。

domain [dəʊ'meɪn] *n.* 领土，领地

高频考点 *n.* (活动、学问等) 范围，领域

例句 She enjoys years of reputation in the domain of medicine. 她在医学领域多年以来享有盛名。

drastical ['dræstɪkəli] *ad.* 猛烈地

高频考点 *ad.* 彻底地

例句 This new style of printing has drastically transformed the market. 这种新的印刷方式彻底地改变了整个市场。

drift [drɪft] *n.&vi.* 冲洗，漂流

高频考点 *n.* 趋势，动向，倾向

例句 There is a slow drift into crisis. 有一种渐入危机的趋势。

dynamic [daɪ'næmɪk] *a.* 动力的

高频考点 *a.* 性格活跃，精力充沛的

例句 We should be trained to be a man of dynamic personality. 我们应该把自己培养成性格活跃的人。

effect [ɪˈfekt] *n.* 影响

高频考点

① *v.* 实现，产生

真题再现 Though several fast-fashion companies have made efforts to curb their impact on labor and the environment, Cline believes lasting change can only be effected by the customer. [2013 年阅读 Text 1] 虽然几家快时尚公司已经努力减少对劳动力和环境的影响，克莱恩认为持久的变化只能依赖于消费者才能实现。

② to the effect that 其大意是

真题再现 Scientists jumped to the rescue with some distinctly shaky evidence to the effect that insects would eat us up if birds failed to control them。[2010 年翻译] 科学家们急忙介入，但是他们提出的证据显然站不住脚，大意是：如果鸟类不能控制害虫的数量，害虫就会吞噬我们人类。

exercise [ˈeksəsaɪz] *n.* 练习

高频考点 *vt.* 运行，行使

真题再现 From the middle-class family perspective, much of this, understandably, looks far less like an opportunity to exercise more financial responsibility. [2007 年阅读 Text 3] 可以理解的是，从中产阶级家庭的角度来看，这根本不像是一个行使更多经济职责的机会。

ease [iːz] *n.* 轻松，舒适

高频考点 *v.* 缓解

真题再现 . 38. Benjamin Friedman believes that economic recessions may _____ . [D] ease conflicts between races and classes [2012年英语（二）Text 4] 38. 本杰明·弗里德曼认为经济萧条会_____。[D]缓解种族与阶级之间的冲突

employ [ɪmˈplɔɪ] *v.* 雇佣

高频考点 *v.* 使用

真题再现 Like other modern architects, he employed metal, glass and laminated wood. [2011 年英语（二）阅读Text 3] 和其他现代建筑师一样，他使用了金属、玻璃和胶合板。

even [ˈiːvn] *ad.* 甚至 *a.* 偶数的

高频考点 *a.* 相等的，均衡的

真题再现 English names are fairly evenly spread between the halves of the alphabet. [2004 年阅读 Text 2] 英语名字很均匀地分布在字母表的前后两部分。

engineer [ˌendʒɪˈnɪə] *n.* 工程师

高频考点 *vt.* 设计；策划

真题再现 And that's the problem with a social cure engineered from the outside: in the real world, as in school, we insist on choosing our own friends. [2012 年阅读 Text 1] 这就是外界设计出的社会治疗问题：在现实世界里，正如在学校，我们会坚持选择自己的朋友。

engage [ɪnˈɡeɪdʒ] *v.* 约定；婚约

高频考点

① *v.* 聘用

真题再现 Journals should also take a tougher line, "engaging reviewers who are statistically literate and editors who can verify the process". [2015 年阅读 Text 3] 杂志也应该采取更为强硬的态度，"聘请有良好统计学背景的评审员和能够评审该过程的编辑"。

② *v.* (～in) 从事；参与

真题再现 40. The text suggests that early settlers in New England_____. [A] were mostly engaged in political activities [2009 年阅读 Text 4] 40. 文章暗示，新英格兰的早期移民_____。[A] 几乎都参与了政治活动

③ *v.* (～with) 理会，处理

真题再现 Toyota Motor, for example, alleviated some of the damage from its recall crisis earlier this year with a relatively quick and well-orchestrated social-media response campaign, which included efforts to engage with consumers directly on sites such as Twitter and the social-news site Digg. [2012 年 Text 3] 比如，在今年较早前发生的召回危机中，丰田汽车公司通过较快且较有序的社交媒体回应行动，包括在推特和掘客等社会新闻网站上与客户进行直接交流，从而挽回了部分损失。

enterprise [ˈentəpraɪz] *n.* 企业

高频考点 *n.* 事业心，进取心

例句 He is a man of great enterprise. 他很有进取心。

escape [ɪˈskeɪp] *vi.&n.* 逃跑

高频考点

① *n.* 消遣，解闷

例句 She read detective stories as an escape. 她通过看侦探小说来解闷。

② a narrow escape 九死一生

例句 Did he have a narrow escape from the big fire? 他从那场大火中逃出来了吗?

excursion [ɪkˈskɜːʃn] *n.* 远足,游览

高频考点 *n.* 离题

例句 We often make the mistake of excursion when describing the connotation from the pictures. 我们在描述图画内涵时,经常会犯偏题的错误。

execute [ˈeksɪkjuːt] *vt.* 执行

高频考点 *vt.* 判处死刑,处决

例句 This boy's father had been executed for conspiring against the throne. 这个男孩的父亲因为密谋反对君主而被处死。

excite [ɪkˈsaɪt] *v.* 激动

高频考点 *vt.* 激发,引起

例句 The professor's lecture excited our interest. 教授的讲座引起了我们的兴趣。

exhaust [ɪgˈzɔːst] *v.* 筋疲力尽

高频考点 *vt.* 详细阐述

例句 Karl Marx's books about human nature exhausted this subject. 卡尔·马克思有关人性的书籍对此问题阐述极为详尽。

figure [ˈfɪgə] *n.* 数字

高频考点

① *n.* 人物

真题再现 37. Influential figures in the Congress required that the AAAS reports on how to _____. [C] keep a leading position in liberal education [2014 年阅读 Text 4] 37. 国会重要人物要求 AAAS 报告。[C] 如何在文科教育方面保持领先地位

② *v.* (~ out) 弄明白,搞懂

真题再现 It's not obvious how the capacity to visualize objects and to figure out numerical patterns suits one to answer questions that have eluded some of the best poets and philosophers. [2007 年阅读 Text 2] 人们还不清楚,想象物体、判断数字模式的能力如何使一个人能够回答出难倒一些最杰出诗人和哲学家的问题。

fade [feɪd] *vi.* 褪去,褪色

高频考点

① *vi.* 衰老

真题再现 As the brain fades, we refer to these

occurrences as "senior moments". [2014 年完形填空] 当大脑衰退时,我们把这种现象称为"老年时刻"。

② *a.* 乏味的,平淡的

例句 What we should see is the happiness fade as water. 我们要看到的是如水般平淡的幸福。

frame [freɪm] *n.* 框架

高频考点 *v.* 造成

真题再现 In many respects, the dearth of moral purpose frames not only the fact of such widespread phone hacking but the terms on which the trial took place. [2015 年阅读 Text 4] 在很多方面,道德目的的缺失不仅体现在如此普遍的电话窃听事实上,同时体现在审判发生所依据的法律条款上。

fund [fʌnd] *n.* 基金

高频考点 *vt.* 投资;资助

真题再现 Many, like the Fundamental Physics Prize, are funded from the telephone-number-sized bank accounts of Internet entrepreneurs. [2014 年阅读 Text 3] 类似于基础物理学奖的很多奖项都是由有着巨额账户的互联网企业家资助的。

fashion [ˈfæʃn] *n.* 时尚

高频考点 *v.* 形成,组成,构成

真题再现 Arizona had attempted to fashion state police that ran parallel to the existing federal ones. [2013 年阅读 Text 4] 亚利桑那州试图组建与现有的联邦警察系统平行的州级警察系统。

feature [ˈfiːtʃə] *n.* 特征

高频考点

① *vt.* 特写,设置特别的专栏

真题再现 Practically every week features at least one celebrity mom, or mom-to-be, smiling on the newsstands. [2011年阅读 Text 4] 实际上,每周都有至少一位名流母亲或者准母亲在杂志上笑迎读者。

真题再现 For the past several years, *the Sunday newspaper* supplement *Parade* has featured a column called "Ask Marilyn". [2007 年阅读 Text 2] 在过去的几年里,《星期日报》的增刊《漫步》开设了一个名为"询问玛丽琳"的专栏。

② *vi.* (~in) 起重要作用;作为主要角色

例句 Economic issues featured very largely in the Prime Minister's speech. 首相的讲话中有很大一部分涉及经济问题。

file [faɪl] *n.* 档案

高频考点

① *vt.* 用锉锉

真题再现 But the 47-year-old manicurist isn't cutting, filing or polishing as many nails as she'd like to, either. [2004 年阅读 Text 3] 但是这位 47 岁的美甲师修剪指甲、锉指甲或打磨指甲的次数也没有她想要的那么多了。

② *vi.* 提起（诉讼）

真题再现 As the auctioneer called out bids, in New York one of the oldest banks on Wall Street, Lehman Brothers, filed for bankruptcy. [2010 年英语（二）阅读 Text 1] 就在拍卖师大声喊出报价时，纽约华尔街最古老的银行之一雷曼兄弟申请破产。

foreign [ˈfɒrɪn] *a.* 外国的

高频考点 *a.* 不相干的；外来的；异质的

真题再现 21. When any non-human organ is transplanted into a person, the body immediately recognizes it as ＿＿＿＿. [D] foreign [2001 年词汇题] 21. 当任何非人体器官被植入人体时，身体会立即识别出它的＿＿＿＿。[D] 异质性

fuel [ˈfjʊəl] *n.* 燃料

高频考点 *vt.* 刺激

真题再现 On another level, many in the medical community acknowledge that the assisted-suicide debate has been fueled in part by the despair of patients for whom the modern medicine has prolonged the physical agony of dying. [2002 年阅读 Text 4] 从另一方面来讲，许多医学界的人承认，致使协助自杀的争论升温的部分原因是病人的绝望，对于他们来说，现代医学延长了死亡前的痛苦。

firm [fɜːm] *a.* 坚固的，稳固的

高频考点 *n.* 公司；商号

真题再现 Until California recently passed a law, American firms did not have to tell anyone, even the victim, when data went astray. [2007 年阅读 Text 4] 最近加利福尼亚州通过一项法律，在这之前美国公司在数据丢失时不需要通知任何人，甚至是受害者本人。

fetch [fetʃ] *vt.* 取来

高频考点 *vt.*（某货物）卖得（多少钱）

真题再现 These rules say they must value some assets at the price a third party would pay, not the price managers and regulators would like them to fetch. [2010 年阅读 Text 2] 这些规则规定，银行必须以第三方愿意支付的价格来估价一些资产，而不是以价格经理和管理者想要把这些资产卖出去的价格。

function [ˈfʌŋkʃn] *n.* 功能

高频考点 *n.* 职务，职责

真题再现 His function is analogous to that of a judge, who must accept the obligation of revealing in as obvious a manner as possible the course of reasoning which led him to his decision. [2006 年翻译] 他的职责与法官相似，他必须承担这样的责任：用尽可能明了的方式来展示自己做出决定的推理过程。

fat [fæt] *n.* 脂肪，肥肉 *a.* 肥大的

高频考点 *a.* 丰厚的

真题再现 Bankers' fat pay packets have attracted much criticism, but a public-sector system that does not reward high achievers may be a much bigger problem for America. [2012 年阅读 Text 4] 银行家高额的薪酬招致了众多批评，但公共部门系统不奖励优秀人才可能是美国面临的更大问题。

fabric [ˈfæbrɪk] *n.* 织品，织物

高频考点 *n.* 结构，建筑物，构造

真题再现 Creating a "European identity" that respects the different cultures and traditions which go to make up the connecting fabric of the Old Continent is no easy task and demands a strategic choice. [2005 年翻译] 不同文化和不同的传统把欧洲大陆编织在一起，要创造出一种尊重这些文化和传统的"欧洲身份"绝非易事，需要人们做出战略性选择。

faculty [ˈfækəlti] *n.*（大学的）系，科

高频考点

① *n.* 全体教职员工

真题再现 The growth in public money for academic research has speeded the process: federal research grants rose fourfold between 1960 and 1990, but faculty teaching hours fell by half as research took its toll. [2011年新题型] 用于学术研究的公用资金的增长加速了这一进程：联邦政府提供的研究经费在 1960—1990 年增长了四倍，但是由于忙于学术研究，教师的授课时间减少了一半。

② *n.*（~for/of）本领，能力

例句 He has a great faculty for mathematics. 他的数

学能力很强。

③ n.（~of）（身体、精神的）器官功能

例句 He has lost his faculty of memory. 他失去了记忆力。

fever ['fiːvə] n. 发烧

高频考点 n. 狂热→feverish a. 狂热的→feverishly ad. 积极地

真题再现 That group—the National Bioethics Advisory Commission (NBAC)—has been working feverishly to put its wisdom on paper, and at a meeting on 17 May, members agreed on a near-final draft of their recommendations. [1999 年阅读 Text 4] 国家生物伦理学顾问委员会（NBAC）一直致力于将其智慧诉诸笔端。在5月17日的一次会议上，委员们就接近定稿的建议书达成一致。

faciliate [fəˈsɪlɪteɪt] vt. 使便利

高频考点 vt. 推动, 促进

真题再现 28. According to the text, online publication is significant in that_____. [D] it facilitates public investment in scientific research [2008 年阅读 Text 2] 28. 根据本文, 在线出版非常重要, 因为_____。[D] 它促进了对科学研究的公共投资

foster [ˈfɒstə] vt. 养育, 收养

高频考点 vt. 培养, 培育

真题再现 That's a lie that we have perpetuated, and it fosters commonness. Knowing what you're good at and doing even more of it creates excellence. [2009 年阅读 Text 1] 这是一个我们已经使之永恒的谎言, 这造就了平庸。了解你擅长什么并且多去实践就会成就卓越。

fine [faɪn] a. 晴朗的, 美好的, 细致的

高频考点 v.&n. 罚金, 罚款

真题再现 In the literary world, where writers are protected from plagiarism by international copyright laws, the penalty may range from a small fine to imprisonment and a ruined career. [大纲样题] 在文学界, 作家受国际版权法的保护, 不受剽窃行为的侵害, 处罚小到罚款, 大到监禁和事业败落。

fair [feə] a. 公平的, 合理的

高频考点 n. 集市, 交易会

例句 I will participate in an antiques fair on the weekend. 周末我要去参加古玩交易会。

fault [fɔːlt] n. 错误

高频考点 n. 地质断层

例句 Variations in rock type and structure in the fault zone would entail variations in slippage rate along the trace. 断层区的岩石类型和构造的不同将会引起沿断痕滑动的速率的变化。

fibre [ˈfaɪbə] n. 纤维

高频考点 n. 品质, 品格

搭配 every ~ of one's being 全身心

例句 I wanted to be an actress with every fibre of my being. 我一心一意想当演员。

flat [flæt] a. 扁平的

高频考点 a. 单调的, 无聊的

例句 After the excitement was over, she felt flat. 兴奋过后, 她感到平淡无味。

flood [flʌd] n. 洪水

高频考点 n. 大量, 大批

例句 There followed a great flood of indignation in the newspapers. 随后, 报纸大批地刊载了表示义愤的文章。

fortune [ˈfɔːtʃn] n. 财富

高频考点 n. 转折点

例句 The party's fortune were at their lowest level after the election defect. 选举失利过后, 这个党的命运正处于最低潮。

formula [ˈfɔːmjʊlə] n. 公式

高频考点 n. 方法, 方案

例句 Clever exploitation of the latest technology would be a sure formula for success. 灵活利用最新技术必将带来成功。

fringe [frɪndʒ] n. 边缘

高频考点 n. 次要的事物; 初步知识

例句 I'm still limited in the fringes of philosophy. 我仅限于了解哲学的初步知识。

frontier [ˈfrʌntɪə] n. 边境

高频考点 n. 尚待开发的领域

例句 They are highly interested in the frontiers of science. 他们对科学的新领域有浓厚的兴趣。

fuse [fjuːz] n. 保险丝

高频考点 vt. 使融合

例句 He skillfully fuses these fragments into a cohesive whole. 他巧妙地把这些片段拼成一个整体。

fuss [fʌs] *n.* 忙乱

高频考点 *n.&vi.*（make a～）大惊小怪

例句 Stop fussing and do your work! 别大惊小怪，干你的工作吧！

ground [ɡraʊnd] *n.* 地面

高频考点

① *n.* 理由，根据

真题再现 But there are few places where clients have more grounds for complaint than America. [2014 年阅读 Text 2] 很少有地方能像美国一样，当事人有更多的理由去抱怨。

② *n.*（on the grounds that...）根据，依据

真题再现 Railroads justify rate discrimination against captive shippers on the grounds that in the long run it reduces everyone's cost. [2003 年阅读 Text 3] 铁路公司对"被控"客户收费进行区别对待的依据是，从长远来看，这样做会降低所有人的成本。

good [ɡʊd] *a.* 好的

高频考点 *n.* 永远，永久

真题再现 About a quarter of all Italian immigrants, for example, eventually returned to Italy for good. [2013 年英语（二）阅读 Text 2] 例如，大约四分之一的意大利移民最终永远回到了意大利。

guide [ɡaɪd] *n.* 导游

高频考点 *n.* 指南；向导

真题再现 The rough guide to marketing success used to be that you got what you paid for. No longer. [2011 年阅读 Text 3] 过去，市场营销成功的大致准则就是一分钱一分货。那种情景现在已不复存在了。

game [ɡeɪm] *n.* 游戏，比赛

高频考点 *n.* 猎物

真题再现 The large, slow-growing animals were easy game, and were quickly hunted to extinction. [2006 年阅读 Text 3] 这种体型大、生长缓慢的动物很容易被猎杀，并且将很快灭绝。

given [ˈɡɪvn] *v.* 被给予

高频考点 *prep.*（表示原因）考虑到；（表示假设）倘若；假定

真题再现 Given all this, they did not exactly need their art to be a bummer too. [2006 年阅读 Text 4] 由于这个，他们并不需要艺术再来表现这种失落感。

gasp [ɡɑ:sp] *vi.* 喘气

高频考点 *vi.*（～after/for）热望，切望

例句 I came out of the water and gasped for breath. 我钻出水面急切地喘了口气。

glamour [ˈɡlæmə] *n.* 魔力，魅力

高频考点 *n.&vt.* 迷惑

例句 I would feel ashamed if I just designed something for glamour or to show some kind of fake image. 他说："如果我只是设计了用于迷惑或者宣传假象的东西，我会感到羞耻。"

gloomy [ˈɡlu:mi] *a.* 阴沉沉的

高频考点 *a.* 令人沮丧的；令人失望的

例句 When I saw their gloomy faces, I knew something was wrong. 当我看到他们沮丧的脸时，我知道出事了。

gut [ɡʌt] *a.*[复]内脏

高频考点

① *n.* 勇气，胆量

例句 That employers believe in themselves is the headspring of employees to get gut. 老板的自信是员工产生胆量的源泉！

② *a.* 本质的

例句 This is what gut decisions are—this is why we say they "feel right". 这就是本能的决定——这就是为什么我们说他们"觉得对"。

③ 固定词组

gut feeling 直觉

grave [ɡreɪv] *n.* 墓穴，坟墓

高频考点

① *a.* 严肃的；严重的

例句 But the grave question was, ought she to do this? 但是有一个严重的问题就是她应不应该这样做？

② *a.* 颜色黯淡的，经济不景气的

例句 The grave forecasts by Toyota will likely have ripple effects throughout Japan's export-dependent economy. 丰田给出的严峻预测将对依赖出口的日本经济产生连锁反应。

graze [ɡreɪz] *n.&vt.* 放牧，吃草

高频考点 *n.&vt.* 擦伤

例句 He didn't have any injuries at all, not even a graze. 他根本没有受伤，甚至连擦伤都没有。

gulf [gʌlf] *n.* 海湾

高频考点 *n.* 分歧,鸿沟

例句 The gulf between the two generations cannot be bridged. 两代人之间的鸿沟难以跨越。

handsome [ˈhænsəm] *a.* 帅气的

高频考点 *a.* 数量多的

真题再现 The report makes heavy reading for publishers who have, so far, made handsome profits. [2008 年阅读 Text 2] 这篇报告的内容使目前收入丰厚的出版商们感到汗颜。

hawk [hɔːk] *n.* 鹰

高频考点 *vt.* 沿街叫卖,兜售

真题再现 "There is a kind of false precision being hawked by people claiming they are doing ancestry testing," says Trey Duster, a New York University sociologist. [2009 年阅读 Text 2] 纽约大学的社会学家特雷·达斯特说,"那些声称可以进行血统测试的人在散播一种虚假的精确信息。"

hit [hɪt] *vi.* 撞击

高频考点

① *n.* 成功而风行一时的事物

例句 The new play is the hit of the season. 这出新戏是本季度的热门剧目。

② *vt.* 达到;使遭受

真题再现 Many captive shippers also worry they will soon be hit with a round of huge rate increases. [2003 年阅读 Text 3] 许多受牵制的客户还担心他们会受到新一轮大幅涨价的冲击。

horizon [həˈraɪzn]

高频考点 *a.* (on the~)邻近的,即将发生的

真题再现 More and more of these credit cards can be read automatically, making it possible to withdraw or deposit money in scattered locations, whether or not the local branch bank is open. For many of us, the "cashless society" is not on the horizon — it's already here. [1994 年阅读 Text 4] 越来越多的信用卡可以自动读取,于是持卡人就可以在不同地方存取,不管本地支行是否营业。对于我们很多人来说,"无现钞的社会"不是即将来临,而是已经到来。

hinder [ˈhɪndə] *a.* 后面的

高频考点 *vt.* 阻碍,打扰

真题再现 What does the author mean by "paralysis by analysis"? [C] Prudent planning hinders progress. [2005 年阅读 Text 2] 作者所谓的 "paralysis by analysis" 意思是什么? [C] 谨慎的计划会阻碍进步。

hammer [ˈhæmə] *n.* 铁锤

高频考点

① *vi.* (~ away at)重申,一再强调

例句 The teacher hammered away at the multiplication tables. 老师不停地朗读乘法表。

② *vi.* (~ away/at)努力不懈于

例句 Why do you hammer at the subject day after day? 你为何日复一日地钻研那个科目?

③ *vt.* (~ home)反复讲透,精讲

例句 He hammered home the points he wanted to convey. 把他要传达的重点讲得非常透彻。

harbour [ˈhɑːbə] *n.* 海港

高频考点

① *vt.* 怀着,怀有

例句 Don't harbour unkind thoughts. 不要心怀不轨。

② *vt.* 庇护,藏匿

例句 It's an offence to harbour the criminals. 窝藏罪犯是犯罪行为。

hazard [ˈhæzəd] *n.* 危险

高频考点 *n.* 不利之处;缺点

例句 Spending too much time on the computer has several hazards as follows. 在计算机上花费太多时间有以下缺点。

humble [ˈhʌmbl] *a.* 卑微的;谦逊的

高频考点 *vt.* 贬低

例句 They tried to humble your importance in that achievement. 他们企图贬低你在那次成就中的重要性。

hatch [hætʃ] *v.* 孵化

高频考点 *vt.* 秘密策划

例句 They hatched a plot to murder the king. 他们谋划杀害国王。

hearty [ˈhɑːti] *a.* 衷心的

高频考点

① *a.* 健壮的;精神饱满的

例句 The children are all lively and hearty. 孩子们都很活泼健康。

② *a.*（饭菜）丰盛的

例句 He ate a hearty breakfast. 他享用了一顿丰盛的早餐。

herald [ˈherəld] *n.* 使者，通报者

高频考点

① *n.* 先驱，预兆

例句 Dawn is the herald of day. 曙光是白昼的先驱。

② *vt.* 预示，传达

例句 One falling leaf heralds the coming of autumn. 一片落叶预示着秋天的来临。

human [ˈhjuːmən] *n.* 人

高频考点 *a.* 有人性的，通人情的

例句 Kehr is a very human person. 凯尔是一个极富人情味的人。

humour [ˈhjuːmə] *n.* 幽默

高频考点

① *n.* 心境，情绪，脾气

例句 I'll do it when the humour takes me. 我心情好时就去做。

② *vt.* 迎合；迁就

例句 It's not always wise to humor a small child. 迁就小孩子并不总是明智的。

husband [ˈhʌzbənd] *n.* 丈夫

高频考点 *v.* 节约

例句 It is too late to husband when all is spent. 花光了再讲节约，为时已晚。

interpret [ɪnˈtəːprɪt] *vt.* 翻译，口译

高频考点 *vt.* 解释，说明→interpretation *n.* 解释，说明

真题再现 One could interpret much of the work of Beethoven by saying that suffering is inevitable, but the courage to fight it renders life worth living. [2014 年翻译] 我们可以这样解释贝多芬的大部分作品：苦难是不可避免的，但是与痛苦抗争的勇气使得生命值得继续。

ill [ɪl] *a.* 生病的

高频考点 *n.* 问题

真题再现 Science and technology would cure all the ills of humanity, leading to lives of fulfillment and opportunity for all. [2013 年阅读 Text 3] 科学技术能治愈人类所有的弊病，给所有人带来满足感和机会。

immune [ɪˈmjuːn] *a.* 免疫的

高频考点 *a.* 不受影响的

真题再现 Some Americans fear that immigrants living within the United States remain somehow immune to the nation's assimilative power. [2006 年阅读 Text 1] 一些美国人担心，住在美国的移民以某种方式对该国同化力免疫。

invite [ɪnˈvaɪt] *vt.* 邀请

高频考点 *vt.* 引起

真题再现 By giving in to critics now they are inviting pressure to make more concessions. [2010 年阅读 Text 4] 现在向批评者妥协是自寻压力，他们会进一步做出让步。

institution [ˌɪnstɪˈtuːʃn] *n.* 公共机构

高频考点

① *n.* 习俗；制度

例句 Fish and chips have become a British institution. 吃炸鱼和薯条已成为英国人的一种习俗。

② *n.* 制定；建立

例句 There was never an official institution of censorship in Albania. 在阿尔巴尼亚从未设立过官方审查制度。

intelligence [ɪnˈtelɪdʒəns] *n.* 智商

高频考点 *n.* 情报

真题再现 The spooks call it "open-source intelligence," and as the Net grows, it is becoming increasingly influential. [2003 年阅读 Text 1] 间谍们把它称为"开源情报"，随着互联网的发展，这样的情报变得越来越有影响力。

independent [ˌɪndɪˈpendənt] *adj.* 独立的

高频考点 *a.* 无私的；无偏见的

真题再现 Yet, in several instances, justices acted in ways that_____ the court's reputation for being independent and impartial. [B] weakened [2012 年完形填空] 然而，在几次事件中，法官的行为_____法院公正无私的美誉。[B] 削弱

introduce [ˌɪntrəˈdjuːs] *v.* 介绍

高频考点 *vt.* 引进，采用

真题再现 Last year Mitsuo Setoyama raised eyebrows when he argued that liberal reforms introduced by the American occupation authorities after World War II had weakened the "Japanese morality of respect for parents".[2000 年阅读 Text 4] 去年,濑户光夫争辩说,第二次世界大战后由美国占领当局引入的自由主义革新削弱了日本民族"尊敬父母的道德品质",舆论哗然。

immediate [ɪˈmiːdɪət] *a.* 立即的,即时的

高频考点 *a.* 直接的,最接近的

真题再现 But a decision among projects none of which has immediate utility is more difficult. [1996 年翻译] 但是在没有直接效用的项目中做抉择就难多了。

implication [ˌɪmplɪˈkeɪʃn] *n.* 暗示

高频考点 *n.* 影响

真题再现 Scholars, policymakers, and critics of all stripes have debated the social implications of these changes, but few have looked at the side effect: family risk has risen as well. [2007 年阅读 Text 3] 学者、决策者以及各类批评人士对这些变化的社会影响争论不休,但很少有人关注这些变化的副作用:家庭风险也增加了。

issue [ˈɪʃuː] *n.* 话题

高频考点 *vt.* 发行,发布

真题再现 The Organization for Economic Cooperation and Development (OECD) has just issued a report describing the far-reaching consequences of this. [2008 年阅读 Text 2] 经济合作及发展组织（OECD）近日发布一项调查,描述了这一现象所产生的深远影响。

ignite [ɪgˈnaɪt] *vt.* 引燃,点火

高频考点 *vt.* 使激动;引起

例句 His speech ignited the crowd greatly. 他的演讲使群众激动万分。

implement [ˈɪmplɪmənt] *n.* 工具,器具

高频考点 *vt.* 贯彻,实行,执行

例句 Identify when, where, and how you'll implement them. 确定时间、地点和怎样实行。

impossible [ɪmˈpɒsəbl] *a.* 不可能

高频考点 *a.* 难以忍受的,很难对付的

例句 She is an impossible woman to work with. 跟她一起工作真令人无法忍受。

initiate [ɪˈnɪʃɪeɪt] *vt.* 开始,创始

高频考点 *vt.* 发动;发起

例句 Mrs. Li initiated a program to monitor the health of the survivors. 李女士发起了一个监测幸存者健康的计划。

incident [ˈɪnsɪdənt] *n.* 事件

高频考点

① *n.* (两国间的) 摩擦,冲突

例句 The serious border incident along increased our fears of the war. 边境上紧张的军事行动加重了我们对战争的忧虑。

② *a.* 伴随而来的

例句 He is fully aware of the risks incident to the life of a racing driver. 他完全了解赛车生涯所伴随的风险。

industry [ˈɪndəstri] *n.* 工业

高频考点

① *n.* 勤劳,勤奋

例句 The industry of these little ants is wonderful to behold. 这些小蚂蚁辛勤劳动,真令人惊叹。

② *n.* 产业

例句 the people employed in the movie industry 电影业从业人员

interest [ˈɪntrɪst] *n.* 兴趣;趣味

高频考点 *n.* 利息

例句 Make sure you put out your savings at a high rate of interest. 确保你的储蓄得到高利息。

invest [ɪnˈvest] *vt.* 投资

高频考点

① *vt.* 授予

例句 The boy was invested with full power to be in charge of the meeting arrangement. 男孩被授予全权,负责会议的安排工作。

② *vt.* 赋予

例句 History books often seem to be invested with an air of unreality. 史书似乎常被赋予几分不真实的色彩。

imperative [ɪmˈperətɪv] *n.&.a.* 命令的

高频考点 *a.* 紧急的,必要的

例句 This is part of reform for a healthy future, and it is imperative. 这是为了健康未来实行的改革的一部分,也是当务之急。

jump [dʒʌmp] *vi.* 跳跃

高频考点

① *n.* 快速行动；迅速采取行动

真题再现 Scientists jumped to the rescue with some distinctly shaky evidence to the effect that insects would eat us up if birds failed to control them. [2010 年翻译] 科学家们急忙介入，但是他们提出的证据显然站不住脚，大意是：如果鸟类不能控制害虫的数量，害虫就会吞噬我们人类。

② *n.* 跳槽

真题再现 As the first signs of recovery begin to take hold, deputy chiefs may be more willing to make the jump without a net. [2011 年阅读 Text 2] 随着经济复苏的初步迹象开始出现，公司副总们更愿意在没有现成职务的情况下跳槽。

letter [ˈletə] *n.* 字母；书信

高频考点

① *n.* 法律字眼

真题再现 Verdicts should represent the conscience of the community and not just the letter of the law. [2010年英语（二）阅读 Text 4] 判决应该代表良知而不仅代表法律条文。

② 固定搭配 to the letter 分毫不差地

例句 She obeyed his instructions to the letter. 她完全遵照他的吩咐去做。

lean [li:n] *vi.* 倚靠，倾斜

高频考点 *a.* 瘦的，贫乏的，歉收的

真题再现 They all seem to look alike (though they come from all over)—lean, pointed, dedicated faces, wearing jeans and sandals, eating their buns and bedding down for the night on the flagstones outside the theatre. [2006 年阅读 Text 2] 他们虽然来自世界各地，但看起来似乎都一样——消瘦、率直、专注的脸庞，穿着牛仔裤和便鞋，吃着圆面包，在剧场外的石板上过夜。

loom [lu:m] *n.* 织布机，织机

高频考点 *v.* 隐现，（危险、忧虑等）迫近

真题再现 My wife and I lectured about this looming danger twenty years ago. [2001 年阅读 Text 2] 我和妻子 20 年前就曾谈及这个临近的危险。

late [leɪt] *a.* 晚的

高频考点

① *a.* 已故的

例句 Her late husband was an outstanding scientist. 她已故的丈夫曾是位杰出的科学家。

② *a.* 前任的

例句 The visitor is the late President, now a scholar. 这位来访者是前总统，现为学者。

③ *a.* 最新的

例句 This is the late development of science. 这是科学的新发展。

liable [ˈlaɪəbl] *a.* 有可能的

高频考点

① *a.*（~to）易……的，有……倾向的

例句 You're liable to get cold if you are not careful. 你若不当心，就有可能感冒。

② *a.*（~for）对……负责

例句 You will be liable for any damage caused. 你必须对造成的任何损失负赔偿责任。

loose [lu:s] *a.* 宽松的

高频考点

① *a.* 不精确的，不严密的

例句 He is a loose thinker. 他是个思维不慎密的人。

② *vt.* 释放；失去控制

例句 He loosed the ropes that bound the prisoner, thus allowing him to jump up and escape. 他解开了绑在囚犯身上的绳子，囚犯跳起来就跑了。

manner [ˈmænə] *n.* 举止，礼貌

高频考点 *n.* 方式；方法

真题再现 On the other, the law links these concepts to everyday realities in a manner which is parallel to the links journalists forge on a daily basis as they cover and comment on the news. [2007 年翻译] 另一方面，法律将这些概念和日常现实生活结合起来，就像新闻记者报道、评论新闻时结合日常生活一样。

mean [mi:n] *v.* 意思是

高频考点

① *a.* 中间的，平均的

真题再现 This group generally does well in IQ test, scoring 12-15 points above the mean value of 100. [2008 年完形填空] 这个群体通常在智商测试中得分高，比平均值 100 分高出 12 ～ 15 分。

② *a.* 卑鄙的，不善良的

例句 He took a mean advantage of me. 他利用卑鄙手段占我便宜。

③ *a.* 吝啬的；自私的

例句 We don't like to make friends with a mean man. 我们不愿意和自私的人做朋友。

④ *a.* 低微的

例句 He is a man of mean birth. 他出身低微。

mute [mju:t] *a.* 哑巴的

高频考点 *v.* 减轻，使柔和

真题再现 Our ability to mute our hard wired reactions by pausing is what differentiates us from animals. [2013 年英语（二）阅读 Text 3] 我们能够通过停顿减少本能反应，这使我们有别于动物。

mixed [mɪkst] *a.* 混合的

高频考点 *a.* 喜忧参半

真题再现 In many respects, the U.S. was more socially tolerant entering this recession than at any time in its history, and a variety of national polls on social conflict since then have shown mixed results. [2012年英语（二）Text 4] 在很多方面，美国这次进入萧条要比历史上任何时期都更有社会容忍度，各种关于社会冲突的全国民意调查显示出了不同的结果。

move [mu:v] *vt.* 移动，迁居

高频考点

① *n.* 行动、措施、行为

真题再现 Instead, the company has done precisely what it had long promised it would not. It's a stunning move. [2012 年阅读 Text 2] 相反，该公司做了它一直承诺不会做的事情。这个做法让人震惊。

② *n.* 提案、提议

真题再现 In a move that has intellectual-property lawyers abuzz the U.S. Court of Appeals for the Federal Circuit said it would use a particular case to conduct a broad review of business-method patents. [2010 年阅读 Text 2] 在一项被知识产权律师们议论纷纷的提议中，美国联邦巡回上诉法院声称它将利用某个具体案件来对商业方法专利进行广泛的复审。

mask [mɑ:sk] *n.* 面具

高频考点 *v.* 掩饰，掩盖

真题再现 Mies's sophisticated presentation masked the fact that the spaces he designed were small and efficient, rather than big and often empty. [2011年英语（二）阅读Text 3] 密斯的精巧展示让人们忘记了他所设计的空间小而精，而不是那种大而空。

might [maɪt] *aux.* 可能的

高频考点 *n.* 力量；威力；权力

真题再现 The process sweeps from hyperactive America to Europe and reaches the emerging countries with unsurpassed might. [2001 年阅读 Text 4] 这个浪潮从异常活跃的美国席卷到欧洲，并以不可比拟的威力影响到新兴国家。

modest ['mɒdɪst] *a.* 谦虚的

高频考点

① *a.* 适度的，有节制的

真题再现 Politicians have repeatedly "backloaded" public-sector pay deals, keeping the pay increases modest but adding to holidays and especially pensions that are already generous. [2012 年阅读 Text 4] 政治家不断调整公务员的薪水，保持工资上涨不快，但实际上增加了假期，尤其是本已优厚的养老金。

② *a.* 不太大的，一般的

真题再现 The Supreme Court knocked out much of Arizona's immigration law Monday—a modest policy victory for the Obama Administration. [2013 年阅读 Text 4] 周一，最高法院驳回了亚利桑那州移民法的大部分内容——对于奥巴马政府来说算是政策上的小小胜利。

matter ['mætə] *n.* 物质；事情

高频考点 *v.* 有关系，要紧

真题再现 That matters because theory suggests that the maximum sustainable yield that can be cropped from a fishery comes when the biomass of a target species is about 50% of its original levels. [2006 年阅读 Text 3] 这确实重要，因为理论告诉我们如果一个渔场的总储量连起初的最大可承受的捕鱼量的50%都不到，就应该降低捕鱼数量了。

mirror ['mɪrə] *n.* 镜子

高频考点 *n.&v.* 反映，反射

例句 The book inevitably mirrors my own interests and experiences. 这本书必然地反映出我个人的喜好与经历。

magnet ['mægnɪt] *n.* 磁铁

高频考点 *n.* 有吸引力的人或物

例句 The actress was the magnet that drew great

audiences. 那位女演员曾吸引过许多观众。

mushroom [ˈmʌʃruːm] *n.* 蘑菇

高频考点 *vt.* 迅速生长，迅速增加

例句 A sleepy capital of a few hundred thousand people has mushroomed to a crowded city of 2 million. 一座只有几十万人的沉寂首都迅速发展成为一座拥有两百万人口的拥挤都市。

marriage [ˈmærɪdʒ] *n.* 结婚

高频考点 *n.* 紧密结合

例句 The marriage of words and melody in that song was unusually effective. 那首歌里词与曲搭配相得益彰，产生了非同凡响的效果。

margin [ˈmɑːdʒɪn] *n.* 边缘部分；页边的空白

高频考点

① *n.* 边缘

例句 He is on the margin of death. 他已濒临死亡。

② *n.* 盈余；利润

例句 He would rather reject an order than sacrifice margin. 他宁愿拒绝订单，也不愿牺牲利润率。

merit [ˈmerɪt] *n.* 长处，优点

高频考点

① *n.* 价值

例句 That remedy comes from economics so the discipline is not without merit. 这个补救措施源自经济学研究，因此不是毫无价值的。

② *vt.* 值得

例句 History affords us lessons that merit attention. 历史给我们提供了值得注意的借鉴。

mock [mɒk] *vt.* 嘲笑

高频考点

① *v.* 模仿

例句 He made the other boys laugh by mocking the way the teacher spoke. 他模仿老师说话，把其他男生逗乐了。

② *a.* 伪造的；模仿的

例句 There were screenshots given to the press but it is highly possible that these were actually mock-ups. 媒体拿到了一些截屏，但是很可能都是伪造的。

minute [ˈmɪnɪt] *n.* 分钟

高频考点

① *n.* (the ~) ……就……

例句 He will write to you the minute he arrives in Shanghai. 他一到上海就会给你来信。

② [maɪˈnjuːt] *a.* 极小的；极少的

例句 There were minute differences between the two copies. 这两册之间存在着细微的差别。

③ *a.* 极详细的；准确的

例句 The doctor made a minute study of the illness. 医生详细研究了这种疾病。

name [neɪm] *n.* 名字，名称

高频考点 *vt.* 命名，提名

真题再现 Within two weeks, he was talking for the first time with the board of Hartford Financial Services Group, which named him CEO and chairman on September 29. [2011 年阅读 Text 2] 辞职不到两周，麦吉和美国哈特福德金融服务公司的董事会举行了第一次会谈。该公司于 9 月 29 日任命他为首席执行官兼董事长。

novel [ˈnɒvəl] *n.* 小说

高频考点 *a.* 新颖的→novelty *n.* 新颖

真题再现 One of the more novel ideas in the report is the creation of a "Culture Corps" in cities and town across America to "transmit humanistic and social scientific expertise from one generation to the next". [2014 年阅读 Text 4] 报告中较为新颖的想法之一是在美国的城镇创建一个"文化团"，"一代代传递人文社会科学知识"。

narrow [ˈnærəʊ] *a.* 狭窄的

高频考点

① *vt.* 使变窄；限制；缩小（范围等）

真题再现 The Federal Circuit's action comes in the wake of a series of recent decisions by the Supreme Court that has narrowed the scope of protections for patent holders. [2010 年阅读 Text 2] 联邦巡回法院的这一裁决效仿了最高法院。最高法院最近做出了一系列的判决，缩小了专利持有者的受保范围。

② *a.* 勉强的；微弱的

例句 He was elected chairman by a narrow margin. 他以微弱优势当选为主席。

nerve [nɜːv] *n.* 神经

高频考点

① *n.* 紧张不安

真题再现 We live in a society in which the medicinal

and social use of substances (drugs) is pervasive: an aspirin to quiet a headache, some wine to be sociable, coffee to get going in the morning, a cigarette for the nerves. [1997 年阅读 Text 3] 我们生活在一个物质（药物）在医疗和社交方面的使用都很广泛的社会里：用来缓解头痛的阿司匹林，用来应酬的酒，早晨用来提神的咖啡，还有定神用的香烟。

② *n.* 勇气，胆量

例句 He had the nerve to ask me to prove who I was. 他竟敢要求我证明身份。

nobody [ˈnəʊbɒdi] *pron.* 谁也不

高频考点 *n.* 小人物，无足轻重的人

例句 He is a mere nobody, and it is mere a matter of time for people to recognize him. 他只不过是个小人物，要大家认清这一点只是时间问题。

nothing [ˈnʌθɪŋ]

高频考点 *n.* 无关紧要的人或事

例句 She is an interesting person but her husband is a real nothing. 她是个十分有趣的人，但她的丈夫真就不及她了。

observation [ˌɒbzəˈveɪʃən] *n.* 观察

高频考点 *n.* 言论，评论，意见

真题再现 To be fair, this observation is also frequently made of Canadians, and should best be considered North American. [1997 年阅读 Text 2] 公正地说，人们对加拿大人也有这样的评论，应当认为这是北美的普遍现象。

obscure [əbˈskjʊə] *a.* 暗的，朦胧的

高频考点

① *vt.* 遮盖

真题再现 The trend in sports, though, may be obscuring an unrecognized reality: Americans have generally stopped growing. [2008 年阅读 Text 3] 但是，体育界的这种趋势可能掩盖了一个没有被承认的现实：美国人基本上停止生长了。

② *a.* 模糊不清，晦涩的

真题再现 The legal issues in the case are obscure: whereas the Supreme Court has ruled that states do have some regulatory authority over nuclear power, legal scholars say that Vermont case will offer a precedent-setting test of how far those powers extend. [2012 年 阅读 Text 2] 该案的法律问题尚不明确：虽然最高法院裁定各州的确有权管理核电站，但法学

家说佛蒙特州的案件将会对"州政府的权力究竟有多大"提供一个先例。

odd [ɒd] *a.* 奇数的，反常的，古怪的

高频考点

① *a.* 临时的，不固定的

真题再现 Left, until now, to odd, low-level IT staff to put right, and seen as a concern only of data-rich industries such as banking, telecoms and air travel, information protection is now high on the boss's agenda in businesses of every variety. [2007 年阅读 Text 4] 信息保护过去一直是临时的、低级的信息技术员的工作，并且只被诸如银行、电信、航空这类拥有大量数据的行业所关注，而现在各行业老板将信息保护放在重要议程上。

② odds *n.* 可能性，概率

真题再现 Even demographics are working against the middle class family, as the odds of having a weak elderly parent have jumped eightfold in just one generation. [2007年阅读 Text 3] 甚至人口统计状况也对中产阶层家庭不利，因为家有一个年迈体弱的父母的概率在仅仅一代人的时间里就增加了八倍。

owe [əʊ] *vt.* 欠

高频考点 *vt.* (...to...)将……归因于……

真题再现 22. According to the author, the department stores of the 19th century_____. [D] owed its emergence to the culture of consumption [2006 年阅读 Text 1] 22. 作者认为 19 世纪的百货商店_____。[D] 其出现要归功于消费文化

oblige [əˈblaɪdʒ] *vt.* 强制，强迫

高频考点 *v.* 使感激

例句 I would be obliged if you could read it to us. 您若能把它读给大家听，我将不胜感激。

objective [əbˈdʒektɪv] *a.* 客观的

高频考点 *n.* 目标

例句 Our main objective was the recovery of the child safe and well. 我们的主要目标是使孩子恢复健康。

provision [prəˈvɪʒn] *n.* 供应

高频考点

① *n.* 规定；条款

真题再现 In Arizona v. United States, the majority overturned three of the four contested provisions of Arizona's controversial plan. [2013 年阅读 Text 4] 在

亚利桑那州诉联邦政府一案中, 亚利桑那州这一富有争议的方案里受到质疑的四项条款中的三项被大多数 (法官) 投票否决了。

② *n.(pl.)* 食物; 粮食; 给养

例句 Provisions were kept in the storehouse. 食品放在仓库里。

---

picture [ˈpɪktʃə] *n.* 图画

高频考点

① *n.* 背景, 环境

真题再现 But Dr. Uri Simonson speculated that an inability to consider the big picture was leading decision-makers to be biased by the daily samples of information they were working with. [2013 年完形填空] 但乌里·西蒙逊博士认为, 不考虑大环境会导致决策者受到其日常接触的样本信息的影响而产生偏见。

② *vt.* 绘画; 描绘

例句 The speaker pictured the suffering of the poor vividly. 演讲者生动地描述了穷人的生活。

---

produce [prəˈdjuːs] *vt.* 生产

高频考点

① *vt.* 引起; 导致

真题再现 Laughter does produce short-term changes in the function of the heart and its blood vessels, boosting heart rate and oxygen consumption. [2011 年完形填空] 笑确实能引起心脏和血管功能的短期变化, 提高心率和增强氧气消耗。

② *vt.* 培养

真题再现 The commission ignores that for several decades America's colleges and universities have produced graduates who don't know the content and character of liberal education and are thus deprived of its benefits. [2014 年阅读 Text 4] 委员会忽视了一个事实: 几十年来, 美国大学和学院培养的毕业生不知道文科教育的内容和特点, 从而他们无法从中受益。

---

prime [praɪm] *a.* 首要的, 最初的

高频考点 *a.* 使准备好, 事先指导

真题再现 Psychologists found that viewing a fast-food logo for just a few milliseconds primes us to read 20 percent faster, even though reading has little to do with eating. [2013年英语 (二) 阅读 Text 3] 心理学家发现即使看东西与吃没多大关系, 但看快餐店标

志仅需要花几毫秒的时间就能使我们阅读速度提高 20%。

---

process [ˈprəʊses] *n.* 过程, 进程; 程序

高频考点 *vt.* 加工, 处理

真题再现 And hours of watching TV shows with canned laughter only teaches kids to process information in a passive way. [2007 年新题型] 连续看几小时的喜剧电视节目只能教会孩子被动地处理信息。

---

present [ˈpreznt] *a.* 现在的, 目前的

高频考点 *vt.* 提出; 呈现; 赠送

真题再现 The most glaring flaw of the social cure as it's presented here is that it doesn't work very well for very long. [2012 年 阅读Text 1] 这里说的社会治疗的最明显缺点是不能持久地发挥良好的作用。

---

practice [ˈpræktɪs] *n.* 练习

高频考点 *n.* 方式; 方法

真题再现 25. Ryan's comments suggest that the practice of standard testing _____. [A] prevents new habits form being formed [2009 年阅读 Text 1] 25. 莱恩的话暗示了, 标准化考试的方式 _____。[A]阻碍了新习惯的形成

---

parallel [ˈpærəlel] *a.* 平行的

高频考点

① *adj.* (~to) 与……类似

真题再现 On the other, the law links these concepts to everyday realities in a manner which is parallel to the links journalists forge on a daily basis as they cover and comment on the news. [2007 年翻译] 另一方面, 法律将这些概念和日常生活结合起来, 就像新闻记者们报道、评论新闻时结合日常生活一样。

② *n.* 类似, 相似物

真题再现 There are upsetting parallels today, as scientists in one wave after another try to awaken us to the growing threat of global warming. [2005 年阅读 Text 2] 现在出现了 (与吸烟) 类似的令人忧虑的景象。科学家们前仆后继, 试图使我们意识到全球气候变暖所带来的日益严重的威胁。

---

piece [piːs] *n.* 篇, 片

高频考点 *vt.* 凑合; 凑成

真题再现 Pearson has pieced together the work of hundreds of researchers around the world to produce a unique millennium technology calendar. [2001 年翻译] 皮尔森汇集世界各地数百位研究人员的成果,

编制了一个独特的技术千年历。

position [pəˈzɪʃən] *n.* 位置

高频考点 *n.* 立场；见解

真题再现 It's a theory to which many economists subscribe, but in practice it often leaves railroads in the position of determining which companies will flourish and which will fail. [2003 年阅读 Text 3] 这种理论得到了许多经济学家的认同，但实际上，它常使铁路公司处于决定哪家公司盈利哪家公司亏损的立场。

promise [ˈprɒmɪs] *vi.* 承诺

高频考点 *n.* 希望，前途

真题再现 Hofstadter says our country's educational system is in the grips of people who "joyfully and militantly proclaim their hostility to intellect and their eagerness to identify with children who show the least intellectual promise". [2004 年阅读 Text 4] 霍夫斯坦说我们国家的教育体制掌握在这样的一群人手中，"他们沾沾自喜、霸气十足地公然宣称他们对才智的敌意，也迫不及待地表现出对那些在才智上没有前途的孩子们的认同"。

perfect [ˈpɜːfɪkt] *a.* 完美的

高频考点 *v.* 完善

真题再现 Over the past decade, many companies had perfected the art of creating automatic behaviors—habits—among consumers. [2010 年英语（二）阅读 Text 3] 在过去的十年里，多家公司已经完善了引导消费者无意识行为（即习惯）的艺术。

particular [pəˈtɪkjʊlə] *a.* 特别的

高频考点

① *a.* 特定的

真题再现 Their methods do not attempt to estimate the actual biomass of fish species in particular parts of the ocean, but rather changes in that biomass over time.[2006年 阅读 Text 3] 他们的方法并非旨在估算特定海域中鱼类的确切生物量，而是研究这些生物量随时间推移而产生的变化。

② *a.* 过于讲究的，苛求的，挑剔的

例句 She is so particular about her housework that servants will not work for her. 她对家务活是如此的挑剔以至于仆人们都不愿意为她做家务。

③ *n. (pl.)* 详情；细目

例句 Your mother must be anxious to know the particulars. 你的母亲一定是急于了解详情。

program [ˈprəʊɡræm] *n.* 程序

高频考点 *vt.* 规划；拟……计划；编排

真题再现 One possible response is for classical performers to program attractive new music that is not yet available on record. [2011 年阅读Text 1] 对于古典音乐演奏家而言，可能的应对措施是编排出唱片上没有的、吸引人的新曲目。

party [ˈpɑːti] *n.* 党派、晚会

高频考点 *n.* 一方，当事人

真题再现 These rules say they must value some assets at the price a third party would pay, not the price managers and regulators would like them to fetch. [2010 年阅读 Text 4] 规则规定他们必须以第三方愿意收购的价格，而非按照管理者和监管者期望它们能够卖得的价格来评估部分资产的价值。

principal [ˈprɪnsəpl] *n.* 校长

高频考点 *a.* 重要的

真题再现 They found that the principal requirement for what is called "global cascades" is the presence not of a few influentials but, rather, of a critical mass of easily influenced people. [2010 年阅读 Text 3] 他们发现，要实现所谓的"全球传播"，最关键的条件不是需要少数有影响力的人，而是需要大量易受影响人群的广泛参与。

peer [pɪə] *n.* 同龄人

高频考点 *v.* 偷窥

真题再现 Several massive leakages of customer and employee data this year have left managers hurriedly peering into their intricate IT systems and business processes in search of potential vulnerabilities. [2007 年阅读 Text 4] 今年，几起客户和员工数据的重大泄密事件使得管理人员匆忙检查复杂的数据系统和商业流程，以便寻找潜在的弱点。

prudent [ˈpruːdnt] *a.* 节俭的

高频考点 *a.* 慎重的；智慧的

真题再现 With the risks obvious and growing, a prudent people would take out an insurance policy now. [2005 年阅读 Text 2] 随着风险越来越明显，并且不断增加，一个谨慎的民族现在应该准备一份保单了。

performance [pəˈfɔːməns] *n.* 表演

高频考点 *n.* 性能；发展

真题再现 We are fortunate that it is wrong, because constructing new educational systems there and putting enough people through them to improve economic performance would require two or three generations. [2009 年 Text 3] 我们庆幸这个传统观点的确是错误的，因为创建新的教育系统，让足够多的人接受教育以推动经济发展需要两代或三代人来完成。

press [pres] *n.&v.* 压

高频考点

① *n.* 报刊；新闻界；记者们

真题再现 These men believed in journalism as a calling, and were proud to be published in the daily press. [2010 年阅读 Text 1] 这些评论家们相信报刊评论是一项职业，并且他们的文章能够在报纸上发表，他们会感到很自豪。

② *v.* (~ for) 迫切要求

真题再现 Instead of a plan of action, they continue to press for more research — a classic case of "paralysis by analysis". [2005 年阅读 Text 2] 他们没有出台行动计划，相反只是继续迫切要求进行更多的研究 —— 这是一个经典的"分析导致麻痹案例"。

panel [ˈpænl] *n.* 面板；仪表盘

高频考点 *n.* 专门小组

真题再现 In late 1994 the panel of economists which *The Economist* polls each month said that America's inflation rate would average 3.5% in 1995. [1997 年阅读 Text 5] 1994年年底，每月接受《经济学人》意见调查的一组经济学家指出，美国在 1995 年的平均通货膨胀率将达到 3.5%。

pant [pænt] *vi.* 喘气

高频考点 *vi.* (~for/after) 渴望

例句 Can't you see she is panting for a part in the new play? 你难道看不出她渴望在新戏中扮演一个角色吗？

pattern [ˈpætən] *n.* 模式

高频考点 *vt.* 模仿

例句 She patterned herself after her mother. 她模仿她的母亲。

priority [praɪˈɒrɪti] *n.* 优先权

高频考点

① *n.* 最重要的事情

例句 The government's priority is to build more power plants. 政府的首要任务是新建更多的发电站。

② *v.* (take ~ over) 优先于；比……重要

例句 The fight against inflation took priority over measures to combat the deepening recession. 抵制通货膨胀比抑制日益加剧的经济衰退更为重要。

pioneer [ˌpaɪəˈnɪə] *n.* 先驱

高频考点 *vt.* 开拓，开发，创始

例句 This company pioneered the use of silicon chip. 这家公司率先使用硅芯片。

polish [ˈpɒlɪʃ] *v.* 磨光

高频考点 *n.* 优美，完善

例句 Four years of college gave her considerable polish. 四年的大学教育使她更加完美。

pool [puːl] *n.* 水池

高频考点 *v.* 聚集，聚拢

例句 We pooled ideas and information. 我们共享了信息。

prejudice [ˈpredʒʊdɪs] *n.* 偏见

高频考点 *vt.* 不利于，损害

例句 Your bad spelling may prejudice your chances of getting this job. 糟糕的拼写会妨碍你获得这个工作的机会。

prize [praiz] *n.* 奖赏

高频考点 *vt.* 珍视，珍惜

例句 One of the gallery's most prized pos-sessions is the portrait of *Ginevra de'Benci*. 这个美术馆最珍贵的藏品之一是《吉内薇拉·班琪》。

pupil [ˈpjuːpil] *n.* 学生

高频考点 *n.* 瞳孔

例句 Your eye pupil adjusts automatically. 你眼睛的瞳孔是自动调节的。

purpose [ˈpɜːpəs] *n.* 目的

高频考点 *n.* 意志；毅力；决心

例句 I know she is steady in her purpose. 我知道她意志坚定。

rigid [ˈrɪdʒɪd] *a.* 刚硬的

高频考点

① *a.* 严格的

真题再现 39. After the Jury Selection and Service Act was passed, _____.[B] educational requirements became less rigid in the selection of federal jurors [2010 年英语（二）阅读 Text 4] 39. "陪审团挑选与服务法案"通过之后，_____。[B]在联邦陪审员的选择上教育背景的要求没有那么严格了

② *a.* 固执的，死板的

真题再现 Hindrance to the reform of the legal system originates from the rigid bodies governing the profession. [2014 年阅读 Text 2] 法律系统改革的阻力主要来自掌管这个职业的部门过于僵化。

rule [ruːl] *n.* 规则

高频考点 *vt.* 规定，裁决

真题再现 Whereas the Supreme Court has ruled that states do have some regulatory authority over nuclear power, legal scholars say that Vermont case will offer a precedentsetting test of how far those powers extend. [2012 年阅读 Text 2] 虽然最高法院裁定，各州的确有权管理核电站，但法学家说佛蒙特州的案件将会对"州政府的权力究竟有多大"提供一个先例。

rosy [ˈrəʊzi] *a.* 玫瑰色的

高频考点 *a.* 愉悦的，美好的

真题再现 To be sure, the future is not all rosy. But we are now knowledgeable enough to reduce many of the risks that threatened the existence of earlier humans. [2013年阅读 Text 3] 当然，未来的一切并不都是美好的。但是我们有足够的知识去减少很多威胁早期人类生存的风险。

rocket [ˈrɒkɪt] *n.* 火箭

高频考点 *vi.* 飞速上涨

真题再现 The reason, of course, is that costs have rocketed and ticket prices have stayed low. [2006 年阅读 Text 2] 当然，原因是（演出）成本激增了，然而票价仍然很低。

reflection [rɪˈflekʃn] *n.* 反射

高频考点 *n.* (~on) 深思；回忆；考虑

真题再现 They may teach very well and more than earn their salaries, but most of them make little or no independent reflections on human problems which involve moral judgment. [2006 年翻译] 他们可以教得很好，而且不仅仅是为了挣薪水，但他们大多数人却很少或没有对涉及道德判断的人类问题进行独立思考。

rest [rest] *vi.* 休息

高频考点 *vi.* (~on/upon) 取决于

真题再现 Furthermore, it is obvious that the strength of a country's economy is directly bound up with the efficiency of its agriculture and industry, and that this in turn rests upon the efforts of scientists and technologists of all kinds. [2000 年翻译] 此外，很明显，一个国家的经济实力与其工农业生产效率密切相关，而生产效率的提高则又取决于各种科技人员的努力。

realize [ˈrɪəlaɪz] *vt.* 意识到

高频考点 *vt.* 实现，发挥

真题再现 Richard Lamm has been quoted as saying that the old and infirm "have a duty to die and get out of the way", so that younger, healthier people can realize their potential. [2003 年阅读 Text 4] 理查德·拉姆曾说，老年多病者"有责任死去和让位"，以让更年轻、更健康的人们去发挥他们的潜能。

rear [rɪə] *n.* 后面，后方 *a.* 后面的

高频考点 *vt.* 抚养；栽培；举起

真题再现 Nothing gets people talking like the suggestion that child rearing is anything less than a completely fulfilling, life-enriching experience. [2011 年阅读 Text 4] 养孩子绝不是一种能令人满足和丰富人生的体验。这样的说法最能引起人们的谈兴。

respect [rɪˈspekt] *vt.&n.* 尊敬

高频考点

① *n.* 细节，方面

真题再现 In limited respects, perhaps the recession will leave society better off. [2012 英语（二）阅读 Text 4] 在有限的方面，经济衰退可能会让社会得到好转。

②(in ~ of) 关于

真题再现 A parallel situation exists in respect of predatory mammals and fish-eating birds. [2010 年翻译] 肉食哺乳动物和捕食鱼的鸟类也存在类似的情形。

run [rʌn] *vi.* 跑

高频考点

① *n.* (the ~ of) 状态；趋势；动向

真题再现 He adds humbly that perhaps he was "superior to the common run of men in noticing things which easily escape attention, and in observing them carefully". [2008 年翻译] 他谦虚地补充道，或许他"和普通人相比，更能注意到他们容易忽略的细节，更能对这些细节进行仔细观察"。

② *vt.* 管理；经营

真题再现 McGee says leaving without a position lined up gave him time to reflect on what kind of company he wanted to ru*n*. [2011 年阅读 Text 2] 麦吉说没有找到下家就辞职给了他时间去思考他想去经营什么类型的公司。

rigorous ['rɪgərəs] *a.* 严格的

高频考点 *a.* 一丝不苟的；谨慎的

例句 We should have rigorous scholarship whatever we do. 无论我们做什么，都应该持有严谨的治学态度。

recognition [ˌrekəg'nɪʃn] *n.* 认出

高频考点 *n.* 赏识；表彰；公认

例句 The chemist has won worldwide recognition. 那位化学家赢得举世公认。

regard [rɪ'gɑːd] *vt.* 认为

高频考点

① *vt.* 致意；问候

例句 Please send my regards to your family. 请代我向你的家人问好。

② *n.* (with~to) 关于

例句 With regard to hardness, the diamond is in a class by itself. 讲硬度，金刚钻是独一无二的。

rate [reɪt] *n.* 比率

高频考点 *vt.* 对……估价；对……评价

例句 The film was rated excellent by 90 percent of children. 90%的孩子都表示这部电影很精彩。

resort [rɪ'zɔːt] *n.* 度假胜地

高频考点

① *n.* 采用的方法

例句 A repetition of practices is the resort of gaining genuine knowledge. 反复实践是取得真知的方法。

② *v.* (~to) 求助于，采用

例句 I'm sorry you have resorted to deception. 我很遗憾你竟用欺骗手段。

restless ['restlɪs] *a.* 不休息的

高频考点 *a.* 焦躁不安的；不耐烦的

例句 She was restless and needed a new impetus for her talent. 她感到厌倦了，需要新的动力来激发她的才能。

surface ['sɜːfɪs] *n.&a.* 表面

高频考点 *vi.* 出现

真题再现 The conflict has been surfacing since 2002, when the corporation bought Vermont's only nuclear power plant. [2012 年阅读 Text 2] 2002 年开始这个冲突逐渐显现出来，当时该公司购买了佛蒙特州唯一一家核电站。

subject ['sʌbdʒɪkt] *n.* 科目，课题，主题

高频考点

① *v.* 服从于，遭受，受到……的影响

真题再现 The computer programs a company uses to estimate relationships may be patented and not subject to peer review or outside evaluation. [2009 年阅读 Text 2] 公司用来评估血缘关系的计算机程序可能申请了专利，不能对其进行同行审查或外界评估。

② *n.* 研究对象

真题再现 The study is a genome-wide analysis conducted on 1,932 unique subjects. [2015 年完形填空] 该项研究对 1 932 名独特实验对象进行了全基因组分析。

sweep ['swiːp] *v.* 扫

高频考点 *a.* 彻底的，一概而论的，笼统的

真题再现 California has asked the justices to refrain from a sweeping ruling. [2015 年阅读 Text 2] 加利福尼亚州呼吁法官们不要做出太笼统的裁定。

swallow ['swɒləʊ] *n.* 燕子；*v.* 吞咽

高频考点

① *v.* 轻信

真题再现 But the justices should not swallow California's argument whole. [2015 年阅读 Text 2] 但是法官们也不应该完全相信加利福尼亚州的论点。

② *vt.* 忍受；抑制

例句 Gordon has swallowed the anger he felt. 戈登压抑住了内心的愤怒。

share [ʃeə] *vt.* 分享

高频考点 *n.* 股份；股价

真题再现 In fact, allowing non-lawyers to own shares in law firms would reduce costs and improve services to customers. [2014 年 阅读Text 2] 事实上，允许非律师拥有律所的股份能减少成本，提高客服水平。

secure [sɪˈkjʊə] *a.* 安全的，可靠的

高频考点 *vt.* 确保；保护

真题再现 The capital intended to broaden the export base and secure efficiency gains from international trade was channeled instead into uneconomic import substitution. [2000 年词汇题] 原本打算用来扩大出口基地和确保提高国际贸易效益的资金改用到了非经济的进口替代中。

stress [stres] *n.* 压力

高频考点 *vt.* 强调

真题再现 While often praised by foreigners for its emphasis on the basics, Japanese education tends to stress test taking and mechanical learning over creativity and self-expression. [2000 年 阅读 Text 4] 虽然日本的教育因强调基础知识而经常受到外国人的赞扬，但是日本教育倾向于强调考试和机械学习，而不是创造力和自我表达。

sensation [senˈseɪʃn] *n.* 感觉，知觉

高频考点 *n.* 轰动→sensational *a.* 耸人听闻的

真题再现 Their sometimes sensational findings were filled with warnings about the growing competition from overseas. [2000 年 阅读Text 1] 他们有时耸人听闻的结论充满着对日益激烈的海外竞争的警示。

save [seɪv] *vt.* 解救，保存

高频考点 *prep.* 除……之外

真题再现 Yet only one of his books is now in print, and his vast body of writings on music is unknown except to specialists. [2010 年阅读 Text 1] 但是，如今他的著作中仅有一本仍在出版，他的大量音乐评论除了专业人士鲜有人知。

sound [saʊnd] *n.* 声音，语音 *vi.* 听起来

高频考点 *a.* 合理的，有效彻底的，健康的（sound and safe 安然无恙）

真题再现 If we are ever going to protect the atmosphere, it is crucial that those new plants be environmentally sound. [2005年阅读 Text 2] 如果我们准备保护大气，关键要让这些新建发电厂对环境无害。

say [seɪ] *vt.* 说话

高频考点

① *vt.* 比方说；比如

真题再现 Rather than, say, Quebec, negotiating on behalf of seven million people, the national agency would negotiate on behalf of 31 million people. [2005 年新题型] 比方说，魁北克省只能代表700万公民去议价，而全国性代理机构可代表3 100万加拿大人进行谈判。

② *n.* 决定权，发言权

例句 He wasn't allowed much say in choosing his holiday. 在选择假期的问题上，他没有很多发言权。

scale [skeɪl] *n.* 比例，刻度 *vt.* 攀登

高频考点

① *n.* 规模

真题再现 In dealing with a challenge on such a scale, it is no exaggeration to say "United we stand, divided we fall". [2005 年翻译] 在应付如此大规模的挑战时，我们可以毫不夸张地说，"合则存，分则亡"。

② scale back 缩减；限制

真题再现 Now the nation's top patent court appears completely ready to scale back on business-method patents. [2010年阅读 Text 2] 现在（美国）国家最高级专利法院似乎完全准备限制经营方法专利的颁发。

spark [spɑːk] *n.* 火花

高频考点 *vt.* 导致 *n.* 直接原因；导火线

真题再现 23. The 215-page manuscript, circulated to publishers last October, _____ an outburst of interest. [C] sparked [2000 年词汇题] 23. 去年十月传到出版商的那 215 页手稿_____他们浓厚的兴趣。[C] 引起了

sphere [sfɪə] *n.* 球体

高频考点 *n.* 范围，领域

真题再现 While still catching up to men in some spheres of modern life, women appear to be way ahead in at least one undesirable category. [2008 年阅读 Text 1] 在现代生活的某些领域，女性仍在追赶男性，但至少在一个不受欢迎的领域，女性似乎遥遥领先。

shape [ʃeɪp] *n.* 形状

高频考点

① *vt.* 对……有重大影响；决定……的性质

真题再现 The harsh realities of the frontier also shaped this tradition of hospitality. [1997 年阅读 Text 2] 边境严酷的现实也促成了这种好客的传统。

② *n.* 情况；状态

例句 The market has been in poor shape lately. 近来市场情况不好。

span [spæn] *n.* 跨度

高频考点

① *n.* 范围

真题再现 With the first subject, after about 20 hours of training, his digit span had risen from 7 to 20. [2007 年阅读 Text 1] 在经过大约 20 小时的训练之后，第一个试验对象复述的数字范围从 7 个上升到 20 个。

② *n.* 一段时间 (a span of...)

例句 Over a short span of three years a surprising amount has been achieved. 在短短三年时间里，已经取得了惊人的成绩。

spare [speə] *n.* 备用品 *a.* 多余的，备用的

高频考点

① *vt.* 抽出

真题再现 Canada's premiers might spare a moment to do something, together, to reduce health-care costs. [2005 年新题型] 加拿大各省的总理们也许会抽出时间来共同做一些事情以降低医疗保健费用。

② *vt.* 饶恕，赦免

例句 The prisoner was spared. 那个因犯被赦免了。

settle ['setl] *vt.* 解决，安放，定居

高频考点 *vt.* 决定，安排

真题再现 Sexual confusion, economic frustrations, and religious hope—all came together in a decisive moment when he opened the *Bible*, told his father the first line he saw would settle his fate...[2009 年阅读 Text 4] 性的困惑、经济挫折和宗教期望都会在一个决定性的时刻汇集涌现出来。这个时刻就是当他打开《圣经》对父亲说，他看到的第一行字将会决定他的命运……

slim [slɪm] *a.* 苗条的

高频考点

① *a.* (书、钱包等) 薄的

真题再现 Readers are paying more for slimmer products. Some papers even had the nerve to refuse delivery to distant suburbs. [2011年英语（二）阅读 Text 2] 报纸变薄但售价上升。一些报纸甚至下决心取消了偏远乡村的配送业务。

② *a.* (希望，可能性) 渺茫的

例句 His chances for getting the scholarship were very slim. 他获奖学金的希望甚微。

shield [ʃiːld] *n.* 盾，盾状物

高频考点 *vt.* 保护，防护

真题再现 Shielded by third-party payers from the cost of our care, we demand everything that can possibly be done for us, even if it's useless. [2003 年阅读 Text 4] 由于医疗费用由第三方支付，我们常常要求用尽所有的医疗手段为我们治疗，哪怕这些治疗不起任何作用。

shrink [ʃrɪŋk] *v.* 缩水

高频考点 *vi.* 下降

真题再现 Income inequality usually falls during a recession, but it has not shrunk in this one. [2012年英语（二）阅读 Text 4] 收入不均的情况通常会在萧条期好转，但这次没有。

slack [slæk] *a.* 松弛的 *v.* 懈怠，使松弛

高频考点

① *a.* 懈怠的，懒散的

真题再现 Indeed, if he has a reputation for slacking, you might even be outraged. [2005 年阅读 Text 1] 事实上，如果他还有懒散的名声，你甚至可能会非常愤怒。

② *a.* 萧条的 *n.* 淡季

例句 The whole shopping center will be in a slack season as winter comes. 随着冬天的到来，整个商业中心将进入商业淡季。

spring [sprɪŋ] *a.* 春天，弹簧 *v.* 跳

高频考点

① *n.* 泉水

真题例句 Then beverage companies started bottling the production of far-off springs, and now office workers unthinkingly sip bottled water all day long. [2010年英语（二）阅读Text 3] 饮料企业开始生产取自遥远山泉的瓶装水，现在人们在办公室整天都会不假思索地喝着瓶装水。

② *vi.* 涌现；惊现

例句 A terrible storm sprang up. 一场可怕的暴风雨突然袭来。

③ *vt.* (使)开动;(使)运转

例句 He prepared to spring his trap. 他准备启动捕捉机。

stem [stem] *n.* 根,茎

高频考点 *v.* (~ from)起源于

例句 Much of the instability stems from the economic effects of the war. 不稳定局面多半是由战争对经济的影响造成的。

safe [seɪf] *a.* 安全的

高频考点

① *n.* 保险箱

例句 The files are now in a safe to which only he has the key. 文件目前放在一个只有他才能打开的保险柜里。

② *a.* 无害的;安全可靠的

例句 Most foods that we eat are safe for birds. 我们食用的大多数食物对鸟类都无害。

③ *a.* 安然无恙的

例句 A baby boy is safe after rescue workers pulled him from a 12-foot-deep construction hole. 营救人员将一名男婴从 12 英尺深的建筑深坑里拉出来时,安然无恙。

scheme [ski:m] *n.* 阴谋

高频考点 *v.* 策划;图谋

例句 They schemed out a new method of bridge building. 他们设计了一种新的造桥方法。

sane [seɪn] *a.* 神志清醒的;心智健全的

高频考点 *a.* 明智的

例句 No sane person wishes to see conflict or casualties. 理智的人都不愿意看到冲突或伤亡。

school [sku:l] *n.* 学校

高频考点

① *n.* 学派,流派

例句 A hundred schools of thought contend. 百家争鸣。

② *vt.* 训练;磨炼

例句 This politician has shown that he has been well schooled in foreign languages. 这位政治家表现出了受过良好的外语训练。

seal [si:l] *n.* 封条

高频考点

① *n.* 象征;标志

例句 Their handshake was a seal of friendship. 他们的握手是友谊的象征。

② *vt.* 决定

例句 The arrival of reinforcements sealed our victory. 增援部队的到来决定了我们的胜利。

skirt [skɜ:t] *n.* 裙子

高频考点 *n.* 边缘,外围

例句 He lives on the skirts of the city. 他住在市郊。

side [saɪd] *n.* 旁边,侧面

高频考点 *vi.* (~ with) 支持

例句 We should side with the people. 我们要站在人民这一边。

sparkle [ˈspɑ:kl] *n.* 火光

高频考点 *v.* 焕发活力

例句 She always sparkles at parties. 她在聚会上总是神采奕奕。

square [skweə] *n.* 广场,正方形,平方

高频考点 *a.* 公正的;正直的,诚实守信的

例句 She'd been as square with him as anybody could be. 她对他的公正一直不亚于其他任何人。

start [stɑ:t] *vi.* 开始

高频考点 *n.&vt.* 惊跳,惊起

例句 We started two birds as we walked in the wood. 我们在树林里散步时惊起了两只鸟。

stomach [ˈstʌmək] *n.* 胃

高频考点

① *n.* 欲望,倾向

例句 I don't have the stomach to find out. 说老实话,我没有兴趣去查明真相。

② *vt.* 忍受,忍耐

例句 I can't stomach the self-righteous attitude of some managers. 我无法忍受某些经理自以为是的态度。

substance [ˈsʌbstəns] *n.* 物质

高频考点 *n.* 主旨;要义

例句 The substance of his speech was that he was better than the other candidates. 他演讲主旨就是他比其他候选人更好。

suit [sjuːt] *n.* 一套衣服 *v.* 适合于

高频考点 *n.* 诉讼

例句 He will bring a suit against his boss. 他要对老板提出控告。

swarm [swɔːm] *n.* 一大群

高频考点 *vi.* 密集，云集，挤满

例句 The place swarmed with tourists. 那个地方游人云集。

schedule [ˈskedʒuːl] *n.* 时间表，进度表

高频考点 *v.* 安排，预定

例句 A presidential election was scheduled for last December. 总统选举原计划在去年 12 月举行。

scope [skəup] *n.* （活动）范围

高频考点 *n.* 机会

例句 He believed in giving his staff scope for initiative. 他认为应给员工提供发挥主动性的机会。

sentiment [ˈsentɪmənt] *n.* 感情

高频考点

① *n.* 情绪

例句 Public sentiment rapidly turned anti-American. 公众情绪迅速转变，开始反对美国。

② *n.* 看法，想法，意见

例句 I must agree with the sentiments expressed by John Prescott. 我不得不对约翰·普雷斯科特的见解表示赞同。

settlement [ˈsetlmənt] *n.* 解决，和解

高频考点 *n.* 居留区；定居点

例句 The village is a settlement of just fifty houses. 这个村子里只住了 50 户人。

shatter [ˈʃætə] *n.* 碎片；粉碎

高频考点

① *vt.* （梦想）破灭

例句 A failure would shatter the hopes of many people. 一次失败会使很多人希望破灭。

② *vt.* 受到重大打击

例句 He had been shattered by his son's death. 儿子的死让他深受打击。

shed [ʃed] *n.* 棚，小屋

高频考点

① *vt.* 摆脱，去除，抛弃

例句 He had maintained a rigid diet, shedding some twenty pounds. 他严格地坚持节食，减了差不多 20 磅。

② （~ light on sth.）为……提供线索；阐明……

例句 However, the report also shed light on some grim realities of begging. 然而，这项调查也揭示了一些乞讨行为的严酷现实。

sheer [ʃɪə] *a.* 陡峭的，险峻的

高频考点 *a.* （用于强调）纯粹的，完全的，十足的

例句 Sheer chance quite often plays an important part in sparking off an idea. 灵感的激发通常纯粹是靠运气。

shoulder [ˈʃəuldə] *n.* 肩，肩部

高频考点 *v.* 肩负，承担

例句 He has had to shoulder the responsi-bility of his father's mistakes. 他得为父亲的过错承担责任。

skeleton [ˈskelɪtn] *n.* 骨骼；骨架

高频考点 *n.* 梗概，提要

例句 Examples were used to flesh out the skeleton of the argument. 通过例证使议论文的框架充实起来。

sniff [snɪf] *v.* 嗅……味道

高频考点 *vt.* 对嗤之以鼻，蔑视

例句 Foreign Office sources sniffed at reports that British troops might be sent. 外交部消息人士对有可能派出英国军队的报道不屑一顾。

sophisticated [səˈfɪstɪkeɪtɪd] *a.* 老练的，久经世故的

高频考点

① *a.* 见多识广的

例句 Claude was a charming, sophisticated companion. 克劳德是一个很有魅力、见多识广的伙伴。

② *a.* （机器装置）精密的；（方法）复杂的

例句 Honeybees use one of the most sophisticated communication systems of any insect. 蜜蜂之间的交流方式是昆虫中最复杂的方式之一。

sponsor [ˈspɒnsə] *n.* 发起人 *v.* 发起

高频考点 *v.* 赞助

例句 Most DES students are sponsored by the National Department of Education. 多数环境科学系的学生是由国家教育部资助的。

spoil [spɔɪl] *v.* 溺爱

高频考点 *vt.* 损坏，糟蹋

例句 He is a man who will spoil rather than accomplish things. 他这个人成事不足，败事有余。

staple [steɪpl] *n.* 钉书钉

高频考点

① *a.* 主要的，基本的

例句 Rice is the staple food of more than half the world's population. 稻米是全世界一半以上人口的主食。

② *n.* 主要部分；主要成分

例句 Political reporting has become a staple of American journalism. 政治新闻已成为美国新闻报道的主要内容。

steep [stiːp] *a.* 陡峭的；险峻的

高频考点 *a.* 急剧的

例句 Consumers are rebelling at steep price increases. 消费者在抗议物价飞涨。

stern [stɜːn] *n.* 船尾

高频考点

① *a.* 严厉的

例句 He said stern measures would be taken against the killers. 他说将严惩凶手。

② *a.* 坚强的，坚定的

例句 She's made of sterner stuff than I am. 她比我坚强。

stroke [strəʊk] *n.* 中风

高频考点

① *n.* 泳姿

例句 She spent hours practising the breast stroke. 她花了数小时练习蛙泳。

② *n.* 突发事件

例句 It didn't rain, which turned out to be a stroke of luck. 天没下雨，结果成了件幸事。

③ *vt.* 抚摸

例句 She walked forward and embraced him and stroked his tousled white hair. 她走上前拥抱他，并轻抚他凌乱的白发。

stubborn [ˈstʌbən] *a.* 顽固的

高频考点 *a.* 棘手的

例句 The first and most stubborn problem was that of reductions in the number of aircraft. 最首要也是最棘手的问题是飞机数量的减少。

swift [swɪft] *n.* 雨燕

高频考点 *a.* 迅速的；敏捷的

例句 The White House was swift to deny the rumours.

白宫立刻对这些传言予以否认。

swell [swel] *n.&v.* 肿胀；膨胀

高频考点 *v.* 增大；增加

例句 By the end of this month the size of the mission is expected to swell to 280 people. 到这个月底，参加该任务的人员规模将有望增至 280 人。

track [træk] *n.* 跑道，小路

高频考点 *n.*（keep ~ of）轨迹 *vt.* 跟踪，追踪

真题再现 Your pages will be easier to keep track of that way, and, if you have to clip a paragraph to place it elsewhere, you will not lose any writing on the other side. [2008 年新题型] 这样做便于你整理文章每一页的内容，当你需要剪切某段，将其放在其他地方时，也不会丢失写在背面的内容。

train [treɪn] *n.* 火车

高频考点 *n.*（~of）一连串，系列

真题再现 He asserted, also, that his power to follow a long and purely abstract train of thought was very limited. [2008 年翻译] 他还认为，在深入理解冗长且完全抽象的一系列观点方面，自己的能力非常有限。

trace [treɪs] *n.* 痕迹 *vt.* 追踪

高频考点

① *vt.* 追溯；探索

真题再现 Razitch's latest book traces the roots of anti-intellectualism in our schools, concluding they are anything but a counterbalance to the American distaste for intellectual pursuits. [2004 年阅读 Text 4] 莱维西最新著作探索学校里反智主义倾向的根源，书中的结论是：美国学校绝没有抵制美国人对才学追求的厌恶。

② *n.*（a ~ of）丝毫，微量

例句 He always spoke with a trace of sarcasm. 他说话总带着一丝讽刺。

trap [træp] *n.* 陷阱

高频考点 *n.* 困境

真题再现 Thus poor countries might not be able to escape their poverty traps without political changes that may be possible only with broader formal education. [2009年阅读Text 3] 因此，政治改革才可以使贫穷国家摆脱贫困，而政治改革则只能靠更广泛的正规教育实现。

thumb [θʌm] *n.* 拇指

高频考点 *vi.* (~ through) 翻阅

真题再现 It has long been known that a taxi firm called AAAA cars has a big advantage over Zodiac cars when customers thumb through their phone directories. [2004 年阅读 Text 4] 人们早已知道在客户翻阅电话簿时，名叫 AAAA 的出租汽车公司要比 Zodiac 出租汽车公司有很大的优势。

translate [træns'leɪt] *vt.* 翻译

高频考点 *vt.* (~into) 使转化，使转变；转移，调动

真题再现 Annas says lawyers can play a key role in insisting that these well-meaning medical initiatives translate into better care. [2002 年阅读 Text 4] 安纳斯说，在要求把医疗界的这些善意行为转变成更好的护理行动方面，律师可发挥关键作用。

term [tɜːm] *n.* 学期，期间

高频考点 *vt.* 把……称为，把……叫作

真题再现 Downshifting — also known in America as "voluntary simplicity" — has, ironically, even bred a new area of what might be termed anti-consumerism. [2001 年阅读 Text 5] 放慢生活 —— 在美国也称"返璞归真" —— 甚至为所谓的"反消费主义"开辟了新阵地。

tap [tæp] *vt.* 轻拍 *n.* 水龙头

高频考点 *vt.* 开发

真题再现 In the first year or so of Web business, most of the action has revolved around efforts to tap the consumer market. [1999 年阅读 Text 2] 大约在网上交易的第一年，大部分业务活动围绕努力开发消费者市场展开。

taste [teɪst] *vt.* 品尝

高频考点 *n.* (~for/in) 爱好，兴趣；鉴赏力

真题再现 Journalistic tastes had changed long before his death, and postmodern readers have little use for the richly upholstered Vicwardian prose in which he specialized. [2010 年阅读 Text 1] 在他去世之前，新闻业的品位早已发生改变，而且他所擅长的措辞华丽的维多利亚爱德华时期的散文风格对后现代的读者没有什么用处。

trigger ['trɪɡə] *n.* 扳机；起动装置

高频考点 *n.&vt.* 引发，触发

真题再现 Studies of both animals and humans have shown that sex hormones somehow affect the stress response, causing females under stress to produce more of the trigger chemicals than do males under the same conditions. [2008 年阅读 Text 1] 对动物和人类的研究都表明，性激素会在某种程度上影响面对压力的反应，导致在同样的条件下，女性比男性产生更多的致病化学物质。

tackle ['tækl] *n.* 滑车；用具

高频考点 *vt.* 处理，解决

例句 The first reason to tackle these problems is to save children's lives. 果断处理这些问题的首要原因是为了挽救孩子们的生命。

trifle ['traɪfl] *n.* 少量；小事，琐事

高频考点 *vt.* 玩弄；忽视

例句 You should not trifle with your health. 你不要疏忽你的健康。

temple ['templ] *n.* 庙寺

高频考点 *n.* 太阳穴

例句 Threads of silver ran through his beard and the hair at his temples. 他的胡须和鬓发里夹杂着缕缕银丝。

territory ['terɪtəri] *n.* 领土

高频考点 *n.* 势力范围

例句 He seems to regard that end of the office as his territory. 他似乎把办公室那一端视为自己的势力范围。

tight [taɪt] *a.* 紧的

高频考点

① *a.* 密封的，透不过的

例句 This is a light-tight container. 这是一个不透光的容器。

② *a.* (钱) 拮据的

例句 Some banks tightened up on their credits. 一些银行收紧了信贷。

touch [tʌtʃ] *n.&vt.* 触摸

高频考点

① *vt.* 涉及，关系到

例句 The new law doesn't touch his case. 新法律与他的案子没关系。

② *n.* 少许，一点

例句 The young man recited his poems with a touch of pride. 那个青年带着一点骄傲朗诵他的诗作。

travel ['trævl] *vi.* 旅行

高频考点 *vi.* 传播

例句 Sound waves will not travel through a vacuum. 声波在真空里不能传播。

tune [tu:n] *n.* 曲调

高频考点 *n.&vi.* (in tune with / out of tune with) 协调，一致

例句 A person out of tune with his surroundings is unhappy. 一个与环境格格不入的人是不会快乐的。

threshold ['θreʃhəʊld] *n.* 门槛

高频考点 *n.* 开始

例句 We are on the threshold of a new era in astronomy. 我们很快就将迎来天文学的新纪元。

upset [ʌp'set] *a.* 焦虑不安的

高频考点 *v.* 推翻，打乱

真题再现 The decision was an 8-0 defeat for the Administration's effort to upset the balance of power between the federal government and the states. [2013年阅读 Text 4] 政府试图推翻联邦与各州之间的平衡，这一努力最终以 0 比 8 的结果失败告终。

uniform ['ju:nɪfɔ:m] *n.* 制服

高频考点 *a.* 一样的，始终如一的→uniformity *n.* 统一性，一致性

真题再现 There is "the democratizing uniformity of dress and discourse, and the casualness and absence of deference" characteristic of popular culture. [2006年阅读Text 1] 着装和话语的民主统一性，还有随意和对尊重的漠视，这些构成了通俗文化的特性。

upside ['ʌpsaɪd] *n.* 上面，上边

高频考点 *n.* 积极意义

真题再现 The upside is the possibilities contained in knowing that everything is up to us; where before we were experts in the array of limitations, now we become authorities of what is possible. [2011 年翻译] 积极的一面在于，既然我们知道一切取决于我们自己，那么我们就拥有无限的可能；我们曾经可以熟练应对各种局限，而如今我们则主宰各种可能。

voice [vɔɪs] *n.* 声音

高频考点 *vt.* 表达，吐露

真题再现 Passionate consumers will voice their opinions in quicker, more visible, and much more damaging ways. [2011年阅读 Text 3] 充满激情的消费者将会以更快捷、更明显和更具杀伤力的方式表达他们的意见。

view [vju:] *n.* 风景

高频考点 *vt.* 看待

真题再现 Traditionally, legal learning has been viewed in such institutions as the special preserve of lawyers. [2007 年翻译] 传统上，这些院校一直把学习法律看作是律师专有的特权。

vision ['vɪʒn] *n.* 视觉

高频考点 *n.* 洞察力；展望

真题再现 Up until a few decades ago, our visions of the future were largely — though by no means uniformly — glowingly positive. [2013 年阅读 Text 3] 直到几十年前，我们对未来的构想大部分还是（尽管这不是所有人的共识）阳光灿烂般美好。

virgin ['vɜ:dʒɪn] *n.* 处女

高频考点 *a.* 原始的；未使用的

例句 Within 40 years there will be no virgin forest left. 过不了 40 年，就将不会再有未开发的森林了。

weather ['weðə] *n.* 天气

高频考点 *vt.* 经受风雨；渡过难关

真题再现 This "added-worker effect" could support the safety net offered by unemployment insurance or disability insurance to help families weather bad times. [2007 年阅读 Text 3] 这种"附加工人效应"可以支持失业保险或残疾保险所提供的保障制度，帮助家庭渡过困难时期。

walk [wɔ:k] *v.* 走路

高频考点 *n.* 职业，活动领域，地位

例句 It's a good experience for a writer to know people from all walks of life. 能够了解社会各阶层人物对一个作家来说是极佳的体验。

well [wel] *ad.* 好地

高频考点

① *n.* 来源；源泉

例句 An encyclopedia is a well of knowledge. 百科全书是知识的源泉。

② *vi.* well up（情感）涌起

例句 All the old bitterness began to well up inside her again. 过去的苦难又一次在她心中涌起。

wooden ['wʊdn] *a.* 木制的

高频考点 *a.* 呆板的；笨拙的

例句 She is one of the most wooden actresses of all time. 她一直是个最呆板的女演员之一。

weigh [weɪ] *v.* 称重

高频考点

① *v.* 重要于

真题再现 67. The author wants to prove with the example of Isaac Newton that _____. [D] unpredictability weighs less than prediction in scientific research [1999 年阅读 Text 5] 67. 作者想通过艾萨克·牛顿的例子证明_____。[D]在科学研究中，不可预测性比预测的重要性要小

② *v.* 认真考虑，斟酌

例句 He is weighing the possibility of filing criminal charges against the doctor. 他正在仔细考虑对医生提起刑事诉讼的可能性。

yield [jiːld] *n.* 产量，收获

高频考点

① *vt.* 出产，生长

例句 Last year 400,000 acres of land yielded a crop worth $1.75 billion. 去年，40 万英亩的土地产值达 17.5 亿美元。

② *vt.* 带来（收益或效益）

例句 It yielded a profit of at least $36 million. 它带来了至少 3 600 万美元的收益。

③ *vi.*（~to）屈服

例句 Will she yield to growing pressure for her to retire? 要求其隐退的声浪越来越大，她会屈服吗？

④ *vi.*（~up）揭露

例句 The public asked law firms to yield up their deepest secrets. 公众要求律师事务所揭露其隐藏最深的秘密。

zigzag [ˈzɪgzæg] *n.* Z 字形，锯齿形

高频考点 *vi.* 曲折前进

例句 Expertly he zigzagged his way across the field, avoiding the deeper gullies. 他熟练地左一拐右一拐地绕过深沟，穿过了原野。

zoom [zuːm] *n.* 嗡嗡声

高频考点 *v.* 高速上升

例句 Profits zoomed from nil in 1981 to about $16 million last year. 利润从 1981 年的零收益飙升至去年的约 1 600 万美元。

Unit 4

必备词组

第一节 基础词组

in addition 另外，从另一方面来讲

in addition to sb./sth. 除……以外（还）

above all 首先

after all 最终还是，毕竟

all in all 总的来看

in all 总共，合计

along with... 和……一起

as if/though 好像

pay attention to 关注

on behalf of sb./on sb.'s behalf 代表某人

come into being 产生，形成

to begin with 开始；首先，第一

believe in 相信

do/try one's best 尽力

beyond belief 难以置信的

at best 至多

be better off 比以前有钱；比别人富裕

had better do sth. 最好，应该

in brief 简言之

a bit 一点儿，轻微地

bit by bit 一点一点地，逐渐地

turn a blind eye (to sth.) 装作没看见

on board 在船（飞机或火车）上

break out 爆发

break through 突破，扫除（障碍）

break up 弄破；散会

hold one's breath 屏着呼吸

out of breath 上气不接下气

burn down 烧毁

burst out laughing/crying/singing 突然大笑/大哭/唱歌

a piece of cake 容易的事，小菜一碟

take care 当心，小心

take care of 照顾，照料，照看

in case 以防，万一

call on/upon 号召，呼吁

call on/upon sb. 拜访，看望

be capable of (doing sth.) 有（做某事）的能力

in any case 无论如何，不管怎样

catch up with 追上，赶上

in charge of 管理，掌管

take charge of 管理，掌管

be characterized by... 以……为特征

take a chance 冒险，碰运气

check in（在旅馆、机场等）登记，报到

check out 调查，核实；结账离开（旅馆等）

clean up 收拾干净；清理，整顿

come out 出版，出现

come to 结果是，总计，达到

comment on 评论，发表意见

in common 共有

as far as... is concerned 就……而言

in control (of sth.) 控制，操纵

out of control 失去控制

under control 处于控制之下

on the contrary 与此相反，恰恰相反

cool down 变冷，冷却

cut down 削减

cut off 打断，中断

cut out 删掉

out of date 过时

day and night 夜以继日

deal with 处理，对付

be in debt 欠债，负债

go into detail(s) 详细叙述，逐一说明

in demand 被很多人需要，需求大

in detail 具体地，详细地

go/be on a diet 节食

out of doors 户外，在户外

in the end 最后，结果

enter for 报名参加

even if/though 即便是，纵然；尽管，虽然

to a certain/some/an extent 在……程度上

be fond of 喜爱

as a matter of fact 事实上

fall behind 落后，落在……的后面

fall in love with sb. 爱上某人

in favor (of sb./sth.) 支持，赞成，同意

for fear of/that 生怕，以免

quite a few 相当多，不少

focus on 集中精力

at fault 出错

as follows 如下

first and foremost 首要地，最重要地

and so forth/and so on 等等

set free 释放

from now on 从现在开始

from the bottom up 从头开始

make fun of 拿……开玩笑，愚弄

get along (with sb.) 相处融洽，与……相处融洽

give in 认输，投降

give up 停止，放弃，不再做

at a glance 一眼，一看就

go after 追逐，追求

go through 经过，完成；经历；检查

take... for granted 认为……理所当然

grow up 长大，成熟

hand sth. in 提交，呈上

lend sb. a hand 帮助……协助……

On the one hand, … On the other hand, … 一方面……另一方面……

can't/couldn't help 情不自禁，忍不住

help (sb.) out 帮助（某人）摆脱困境

here and there 到处，任何地方

make history 名垂千史，载入史册

catch/get/take hold of 握住，抓住

keep up with 与（某人）并驾齐驱；熟悉，了解

for lack of 因为缺乏

at least 至少，起码

not in the least 丝毫不，一点不

no less than 不少于；多达

let sb. down 让某人失望

in line with 与……排成一排

line up 排成一行；排队

log in 登录；注册；进入（计算机系统）

log out 退出；注销（计算机系统）

look back sth. 回首往事；回忆；回顾

look down on sb. 瞧不起，轻视，蔑视（某人）

look forward to (doing sth.) 热切地盼望，期待

look into sth. 调查

make it（尤指在困难情况下）准时到达，实现成功

make up 编造（故事或谎言）

make up for 补偿；弥补

meet with sb. 和某人碰面

in memory of sb. 对某人的纪念

bear/keep in mind 想起

in your mind's eye 想象

make up one's mind 做决定

by means of 借助……手段；依靠……方法

at the moment 此刻，目前

for the moment 目前，暂时

at most 至多

make the most of 最大限度利用（某物）；充分利用

be on the move 在活动，在行进，在前进

only if 只要

all at once 突然

once in a while 一起，同时

once more/again 再一次，再次

once upon a time 从前

in the open 在户外；（意见，秘密等）公开

open up 开门，营业

come/go/bring/put into operation 实施，使生效

in order that 目的在于，为了

on one's own 独自

be proud of/take pride in 为……而骄傲

play a part/role in 扮演角色，参与，起作用

take part (in) 参加，参与

in particular 特别，尤其

pass away 去世

pass by 经过，从……旁走过

in place 在合适的位置

in place of 代替，取代，交换

in the first place 第一，首先

out of place 不适当的，不相称

take place 发生，进行，举行

take the place of 代替，取代

pick out 挑出

pick up 拣起；开车接人

point out 指出

put sth. into practice 实施，实行

at present 目前，现在

plug in 给……接通电源，连接

in the presence of sb. /in sb.'s presence 在……面前，有……在场

prior to 在前，居先

on purpose 故意地，有意地

put off 推迟，推延

put up with 容忍，忍受

at the rate of 以……速率

be referred to 被提及，被提交

regardless of 不管，不顾

would rather (than) 宁愿……而不愿

rather than 而不是

be for real 认真的；真实的，真正的

in reality 实际上，事实上

refer to…as… 把……称作……

in response to 作为对……的反应

in return (for) 作为对……的报答（或回报，交换）

as a result 因此

get rid of 摆脱，除去，处理掉

ring off 挂断电话

ring up 打电话给

be at risk 处境危险，冒风险

at the risk of 冒着……的危险

as a rule 通常，一般来说

run out (of) 用完，耗尽；到期，期满

or so 大概，大约

be for sale 待售的，供出售的

be on sale 出售的，上市的；折价销售

scarcely…when… 一……就……

behind the scenes 在后台，在幕后

ahead of/behind schedule 提前/推迟

in a sense 从某种意义上说

on schedule 按时间表，及时，准时

at sea 困惑，茫然，不知所措

in search of sth. 寻找，搜寻

make sense 有道理，有意义，讲得通

set out 出发，动身，启程

set out to do sth. 开始工作

in short 简而言之，总之

shoulder to shoulder 并肩，齐心协力

show off 炫耀自己，卖弄自己

show up 出现，露面

catch sight of 发现，突然看见

in sight 看得见

lose sight of sth. 忽略，忘记

out of sight 看不见，在视野之外

slow down 放慢速度

as soon as 一……就，刚……便

no sooner…than… 一……就……

sooner or later 迟早，早晚有一天

sort out 整理，区分出来，辨别出来

speed up 使加快速度

in spite of 不管，尽管

stand for 是……的缩写，代表

stand out 清晰地显现；杰出

stick to 坚持，忠于，信守

stick with 持续，坚持；紧随，不离开（某人）

subject…to… 使……服从于……

for the sake of 因……的缘故，看在……的份上

sum up 总结，概括

in summary 总的来说，概括起来

for sure 确切地，肯定

make sure 确保，设法保证

switch sth. off 关掉

switch on 开启

take a page from 向……学习

take over 接替，接任，接手，接管

lose one's temper 发脾气，发怒

be tired of 厌倦，厌烦

all the time 一直，始终

at a time 每次，逐一，依次

at all times 随时，总是，永远

at the same time 同时，一起

at times 有时，间或

for the time being 眼下，暂时

from time to time 有时，不时

in total 总共

in terms of 根据；按照；在……方面

in no time 立即，马上

be in/out of touch 联系，接触/不联系，不接触

in trouble 陷入困境

come true 实现，成为事实

try on 试穿

try out 试验，测试

in turn/by turns 依次地，轮流地，逐个地

take turns 依次，轮流

turn around/round 好转，扭转，有起色；转身，翻转

turn back 返回做（某事），原路折回

turn up 翻上领子，调高；出现

turn down 翻下领子，调低；拒绝

turn out 结果是，证明是，原来是

turn to sb./sth. 向……求助

up to 取决于……的，须由……决定的

in vain 徒劳

in use 在用的

make use of 利用

out of use 没有人在用的，不再被用的

use up 用完，用光

in view of 鉴于，考虑到，由于

in the/sb.'s way 挡道，妨碍某人

under way 已经开始，在进行中

by the way 顺便提一下

once in a while 偶尔

when it comes to… 当谈到……

as a whole 作为一个整体，整个看来

no wonder 并不奇怪，难怪

in a word 简而言之

in other words 换而言之

work at/on 致力于，从事于

worn out 筋疲力尽

what is worse 更糟的是

go wrong 发生故障，出毛病

as yet 迄今为止

and yet 然而

第二节　核 心 词 组

arise from 由……产生的；由……带来的

同义 result from, root in, stem from

例句 The country's present difficulties arise from the reduced value of its money. 该国目前的困境是货币贬值导致的。

abide by 遵守，接受，遵循（决定、规则、协定等）

同义 comply with, adhere to, conform to

例句 You must abide by the results of your mistakes. 你必须承担犯错造成的后果。

be about to do 即将，正要（做某事）

例句 The moment of recessionary uplift may be about to pass. 经济衰退加剧的时刻可能就要过去。

keep abreast of sth. 与……齐头并进，跟上……的步伐

同义 stay abreast of, be in parallel with, keep pace with

例句 We can't keep abreast of the developing situation unless we study harder. 我们如果不加强学习，就会跟不上形势。

in abundance 大量，丰富，充裕，充足

例句 At the feast there was food and drink in abundance. 宴会上的饮食十分丰盛。

by accident 偶然，意外地

同义 by chance

区分 by accident of 因……的机会，由于……方面的运气

例句 Many a bright idea has been hit on by accident. 许多好主意都是偶然想到的。

be in accord with 与……相一致，与……相符合

同义 coincide with, be in accordance with, identify with, be in tune with, be consistent with

反义 out of tune with sb./sth. 与……（不）协调，与……（不）一致

例句 Most people are in accord with their desire for peace. 大多数人都渴望和平。

on account of 由于，因为

同义 owing to, thanks to, as a result of, due to, in/by virtue of, out of sth., by reason of, in conse-quence of

例句 The match was postponed on account of the weather. 由于天气原因，比赛延期举行。

on no account 绝不

同义 by no means, at no time, in no case, under/in no circumstances, on/under no condition, in no way

区分 in no time 立即，马上

例句 We must on no account view problems superficially and in isolation. 我们绝不能从表面上孤立地看问题。

take account of sth. 仔细考虑清楚

同义 take sth. into account, take sth. into consideration

例句 Practitioners ought to take account of the significance of subtle distinctions. 律师应考虑到细小差别的重大意义。

act on/upon sth. 对……起作用；根据（建议、命令、信息等）行事

例句 A patient will usually listen to the doctor's advice and act on it. 患者通常都会遵照医嘱行事。

be out of action 不再运转，失去效用

例句 Huge sections of the rail network are out of action. 铁路网的很多区段停运。

add up to 合计达，总共是

例句 Many small victories add up to a big one. 积小胜为大胜。

in advance (of sth.) 预先，事先；在……之前

同义 ahead of time, ahead of schedule

例句 There is no reason that you shouldn't tell them in advance when you are going. 你没理由不事先告诉他们你打算要走。

take advantage of 利用，占……的便宜

例句 In spring we usually set the clocks ahead one hour to take advantage of the summer daylight. 春季我们通常把钟拨快一小时以充分利用夏天的白昼。

to advantage 用某种方法使优点突出

例句 Hang the picture somewhere where it will show up to advantage. 把这幅画挂在便于它显示较好效果的地方。

be in the air 存在的，即将出现的

区分 be on/off (the) air 广播中/广播结束

例句 The boatmen want to hear everything on the air while on the waves. 船工们出海时希望通过广播听到各种各样的消息。

be up in the air 悬而未决

例句 Plans for the picnic are still up in the air since we can't decide where to go. 由于我们不能决定去哪儿，野餐计划还未定。

on the alert (for) 警戒着，随时准备着

例句 Drivers must be on the alert for traffic signals. 驾驶员必须密切注意交通信号。

allow for sb./sth. 考虑到，体谅

同义 make allowance(s) for

例句 When arranging our work, we should allow for unforeseen circumstances. 我们安排工作时应该考虑到不可预见的情况。

one after another 一个接一个；相继、依次

区分 one another 相互

例句 They went into the classroom one after another. 他们一个接一个地走进教室。

answer for 对……负有责任，因……而受到惩罚

例句 You will have to answer for your rush and carelessness. 你这样毛躁非吃苦头不可。

anything but 绝对不

区分 nothing but 只有，只不过

例句 The problem is anything but easy but the solution depends on nothing but reasonable plans. 这个问题绝不容易，但是要解决只有依靠合理的计划。

apart from 除了

同义 aside from, other than

例句 Apart from some spelling mistakes, the composition is fairly good. 除了一些拼写错误，这篇文章写得很不错。

as for 关于，至于

同义 as to, with regard to, with respect to, with reference to

例句 As for science, we should do our best to catch up with the world's highest level. 至于科学，我们应当努力赶上世界最高水平。

as it were 可以说，在一定程度上

例句 He became, as it were, a man without a country. 可以说，他成了一个无国籍的人。

be associated with 与……有关，与……有关系

同义 be involved with, link to, be related to, be bound up with, be involved with

例句 Research shows that involvement in arts is associated with gains in math, reading, cognitive ability, critical thinking and verbal skills. 研究表明，参与艺术活动可以提高数学、阅读、认知能力、批判性思维和语言技能。

ascribe...to... 把……归因于……

同义 attribute...to..., be put down to...

例句 He ascribes his low mark to the noisy study environment. 他把低分归因于嘈杂的学习环境。

on the average 平均；通常

例句 We figured that we were losing on the average an hour's working time each day. 我们估计平均每天损失一小时的工作时间。

be aware of 意识到

同义 be conscious of

例句 It is inconceivable that the professor was not aware of the problem. 令人难以置信的是，那位教授竟然没有意识到这个问题。

back and forth 来回地，反复地

同义 time and again, over and over

例句 The wind moved the trees gently back and forth. 风吹得树轻轻地来回摇晃。

bend one's mind to 专心于

同义 bury oneself in

例句 He couldn't bend his mind to his studies. 他未能专心致志地学习。

make a clean breast of 坦白，招供

例句 His guilty conscience forced him to make a clean breast of everything. 内疚使他坦白。

be born with 天生具有

例句 One had to be born with those qualities, they could not be created. 一个人必须先天就具备这些特性，而不可能后天创造。

give birth to 产生，引起

例句 Metaphors are not to be trifled with. A single metaphor can give birth to love. 不要轻易使用隐喻。仅仅一个隐喻即可萌生爱情。

bring about 导致

同义 lead to, result in, contribute to, be responsible for, account for

例句 Several circumstances concurred to bring about the result. 几种情况合在一起导致了这个结局。

do one's bit 尽职，做好分内之事

例句 One must do his bit for his country. 一个人必须为国家尽自己的一份力。

behind the scenes 私下，暗地里

例句 Beware of people stirring up trouble behind the scenes. 警惕有人在背后挑拨。

break in 打断，插嘴；开始工作

例句 Don't break in when he is telling the story. 他讲故事的时候别打断他。

take sb.'s breath away 使（某人）惊叹不已

同义 be startled by, be shocked by, be amazed by, be taken aback by

例句 The beautiful view from the top of the mountain took my breath away. 从山顶看到的美景，使我目瞪口呆。

bring forward 提出，提议

同义 come up with, put forward

例句 We'll bring forward the matter at the next conference. 我们将在下次会议上把这事提出来。

build up 增加，增强；增进

例句 The facts added together to build up a theory which was indisputable. 这些事实汇集在一起足以构成一条不容置疑的理论。

in bulk 大量，大批

例句 Buying in bulk is more economical than shopping for small quantities. 批量采购要比零买实惠很多。

get down to business 开始着手处理，言归正传

例句 Stop arguing about (questions of) procedure and let's get down to business. 别再为程序（问题）争辩了，咱们着手议正事吧。

but for 假如没有，要不是

例句 But for the rain we should have had a pleasant journey. 要不是下雨，我们会有一次愉快的旅行。

cannot but 不得不（做某事），禁不住（要做某事）

例句 The caves cannot but inspire wonder in the beholder. 这些洞穴让观者无不叹为观止。

by and large 大体上来看，总的来说

同义 in general, to sum up, in summary, on the whole, all in all

例句 By and large, women can bear pain better than men. 一般来说，女人比男人更能忍受痛苦。

cater to 迎合

例句 Exercise classes cater to all levels of fitness. 各种健身班会照顾到不同身体状况的人。

call off 转移视线；取消，停止进行

例句 Don't let anything call off your attention from your studies. 不要让别的事转移你学习的注意力。

区分 call for sth. 应有，需要

carry on (with) 继续进行

例句 We must try to carry on as if nothing had happened. 我们必须继续下去，当作什么都没有发生过。

carry out 实施，落实；完成

同义 carry through 实现，完成

区分 carry sb. through (sth.) 帮助（某人）渡过难关

例句 The educational department will carry out a series of measures to improve students' physical health and enhance education equality. 教育部门将采取一系列措施，提高学生的身体素质，促进教育平等。

a case in point 有关的事例，例证

例句 A case in point of this is the steady increase in crime in New York. 这方面典型的例子是纽约市的犯罪率在不断地上升。

in case of 如果发生，假如

同义 in the event of

例句 She had had the foresight to prepare herself financially in case of an accident. 她有先见之明，经济上作了准备，以防万一。

cast/shed light on 阐明某事

例句 Recent research has cast new light on the causes of the disease. 最新研究使人们进一步了解了这种疾病的起因。

center on 把……集中在，以……为中心

同义 focus on

例句 We're going to center on the relationship between freedom and necessity. 我们将集中讨论自由和必要性之间的关系。

check up on 监督；核实，核对

例句 The inspector glanced quickly around the room to check up on the others. 督察迅速地环视了教室，检查屋内的其他人。

cheer on 鼓气，向……喝彩

例句 But we really need something to help us cheer on the team! 但是我们真的需要一些东西来为球队加油！

chew over 仔细考虑，深思熟虑；详细讨论

例句 There is plenty of time for us to chew over our plan. 还有足够的时间让我们充分讨论这个计划。

choke up 装满；因激动而说不出话来，(喻)找不到方法

例句 When presented with more options, though, we choke up. 当有更多种选择时，我们就不知道该怎么办。

clear up （天气）转晴；解决

例句 Let's try to clear up our difficult and doubtful points. 让我们设法解决难处和疑点。

round the clock 日夜不停地

同义 day and night, day in and day out

例句 We are working all round the clock to finish this book! 我们在为完成这本书而昼夜不停地工作着！

come across 偶遇；偶然发现

同义 meet with, run across, run into , tumble upon

例句 We must hang in whenever we come across difficulties. 我们遇到困难时一定要坚持不懈。

be composed of 由……组成,由……构成

同义 consist of , be made up of

例句 All matter is found to be composed of atoms and molecules. (人们)发现所有物质都是由原子或分子构成的。

on condition that 若是,只要

例句 He has been granted his freedom on condition that he leaves the country. 他已获准恢复自由,条件是离开这个国家。

out of condition 健康不佳,身体不适

反义 in (good) shape, in good health, keep fit

例句 I've had no exercise for ages, and I'm really out of condition. 我已经很久没运动了,现在健康状况欠佳。

in confidence 私下地,秘密地

同义 under the counter, in secret, on the sly

例句 I should like to exchange a few words with you in confidence. 我想私下和你交谈。

be confined to 限制在,局限于

同义 be restricted to, be limited to

例句 The previously free distribution of text books will now be confined to students who are needy. 以前免费发放课本,现在只限贫困学生。

by/in comparison (with) 相比之下

区分 in contrast to/with 与……形成鲜明对比,与……明显不同

例句 In comparison with the disastrous damage made by the earthquake, my personal loss is negligible. 比起地震造成的灾难性破坏,我个人的这点损失实在算不了什么。

cook up 编造,捏造

同义 draw up, work out

例句 I had to cook up an excuse about my long delay. 我得编个理由解释自己为什么耽搁了这么久。

turn the corner 转危为安;扭转困境

同义 tide over the crisis

例句 Facing the earthquake, we should turn the corner together! 面对地震,我们应该团结在一起渡过难关!

at all cost (s) 不惜任何代价

同义 spare no expense, at any cost, at any expense, at any price

例句 The women's volleyball team put up a desperate fight to win the world championship at all costs. 女子排球队为赢得世界冠军不惜一切代价,殊死拼搏。

count on/upon 依靠,指望

同义 rest on, depend on, rely on

区分 count in 把算入,包括在内

例句 Don't count on other people to help you out of trouble. 别指望他人能帮你摆脱困境。

in the course of sth. 在……过程中

例句 I hope the problem could be settled in the course of nature. 我希望这个问题能够自然而然地解决。

区分 in due course 到时候,在适当的时候

例句 You will understand in due course. 到时候你自然明白。

commit oneself to 贡献

同义 devote oneself to

例句 She made a decision to commit herself to philanthropy. 她下定决心要献身于慈善事业。

by courtesy of 蒙……批准, 蒙……的好意, 由于

例句 This picture appears in the exhibition by courtesy of the local government. 这幅画蒙地方政府的允许在画展上展出。

give credit to 相信, 称赞

区分 be given credit for 由于……受到称赞

例句 Did the board ever give credit to the chairman for inventing the plan? 董事会认可董事长的计划吗?

cotton on 懂得, 逐渐认识到

例句 At last she's cottoned on to what they mea*n*. 她终于明白了他们的意思。

correlate with 符合于; 接近于; 把……联系起来

例句 The results of this experiment don't correlate with the results of earlier ones. 这次试验的结果与以往毫不相干。

dedicate...to... 把……献给……

同义 devote oneself to

例句 She vowed to herself that she would dedicate her life to scientific studies. 她默默地发誓, 要献身于科学研究。

be deprived of 被剥夺

例句 Countries in the sub-Sahara belt will eventually be deprived of their tropical agriculture production. 撒哈拉以南地区将最终无法生产热带农产品。

It dawns on sb. …被(某人)理解, 意识到

区分 sb. comes to know…

例句 It gradually dawned upon me that I still had talent and ought to run again. 我渐渐明白了自己还有才能, 应该再次参加竞选。

turn a deaf ear 置若罔闻, 装作没听见

例句 If you turn a deaf ear to the masses' criticism, sooner or later you will have to pay for it. 听不进群众意见, 早晚要吃苦头的。

take delight in 以……为乐

同义 be happy to, be willing to, take pleasure in, be ready to

例句 I fully agree to the arrangement and take delight in it (take it with delight). 我完全赞成并乐于接受这一安排。

in depth 深入地, 全面地

同义 in full

例句 This is a new subject and needs to be explored in depth. 这是个新课题, 需要深入研究。

die away (声音、风、光等)逐渐变弱

例句 No sooner did one crisis die away than another claimed the headlines. 一个危机还没有消逝, 另一个危机成为报上的头条新闻。

区分 die down (某事物的程度)逐渐地减弱; die out 逐渐消失, 灭绝

例句 He is the last of the family, after his death the name will die out. 他是家族活在这世上的最后一个成员, 他一死, 他们家族便不复存在。

in dispute 正处于争论中

同义 at issue, in issue

例句 The principal issues in dispute concern the duration of the future treaty. 争议主要涉及条约的期限。

doze off 打瞌睡，打盹儿

同义 have a cat nap

例句 Do not go doze off in the middle of the meeting. 不要在开会中打盹儿。

drop out (of sth.) 不再参与（某项活动），退出，离开

同义 withdraw from

例句 Why did you drop out in the middle of the marathon? 为什么你退出马拉松比赛?

dwell on/upon sth. 老是想着，详述（不愉快的事）

例句 Sometimes his mind would dwell on the horrors he had been through. 有时他老是想着曾经历的种种恐惧。

take effect 生效，起作用

同义 bring/carry/put sth. into effect, come into effect

例句 The traffic laws don't take effect until the end of the year. 交通法要到年底才生效。

in effect 实际上，事实上

同义 in essence, as a matter of fact, in fact, in practice, in reality

例句 His reply is in effect an apology, so I think you should accept his apology. 他的答复事实上是一种道歉，所以我觉得你应该接受他的道歉。

to the effect that 大概意思是，以便

例句 He made a declaration to the effect that he would soon resign. 他发表声明，大意是他将很快辞职。

or else 否则，要不然

例句 You must study harder (or) else you'll fail in the English examination. 你必须努力学习，否则英语考试会不及格。

end up 结束，告终

同义 come to an end

例句 Be careful! you could end up by getting hurt. 当心! 你可能最终会受伤。

be exposed to sth. 暴露于；接触到

同义 bring into contact with, come into contact with, have access to

例句 Will the children ever be exposed to a profound idea at home? 孩子们在家能接触到高深的思想吗?

be of the essence 绝对需要的，不可缺少的，极重要的

例句 Speed is of the essence in dealing with an emergency. 在处理紧急事件时，速度是非常重要的。

(be) in evidence 引人注目，显眼

例句 Poverty is much in evidence in the city slums. 城市贫民窟的穷困是显而易见的。

exercise control over 控制

例句 The editor should exercise some control over the language that is used. 编者应该掌握语言的应用。

in excess of sth. 超过（一定数量）

同义 go beyond

例句 He devoted in excess of seventy hours a week to the performance of his duties. 为了完成任务，他每周工作超70小时。

embark on 着手，开始做某事

例句 Although more than half of Harvard undergraduates end up in law, medicine or business, future doctors and lawyers must study a non-specialist liberal-arts degree before embarking on a professional qualification. 尽管一半以上的哈佛本科生最终主修法律、医学，或者商业，但是着手进行专业资格学习之前，这些未来的医生或者律师必须获取一个非专业的文科学位。

exert yourself to do 努力，尽力

同义 do all one can, do sth. to the best of one's ability, try one's best, do one's utmost, do one's endeavor, take pains, spare no efforts

例句 We must exert ourselves to catch up with them, or it would be too late. 我们要急起直追，否则就太晚了。

make an exhibition of oneself 出洋相，当众出丑

同义 make a spectacle of oneself, make a show of oneself, make an ass of oneself, make a fool of

例句 Stop making me cry in the street, I hate making an exhibition of myself. 别弄得我在街上哭，我讨厌当众出丑。

at the expense of 以……为代价

同义 at the cost of

例句 He finished the job at the expense of his health. 他完成了那项工作，但却损害了健康。

keep an eye on 照看；照管；留心；注意

同义 look out for, take notice of, take note of

例句 Will you please keep an eye on my luggage? 劳驾帮我看一下行李。

be equivalent to 等同于，相当于

同义 the same as, equate…with…

例句 Changing her job like that is equivalent to giving her the sack. 那样调换她的工作等于是解雇她。

fail to 未能做

例句 With such favourable conditions, we'll have no excuse if we fail to increase output. 条件这样好，再不增产，可说不过去。

in the fashion of 以……方式

例句 He was scorned by the teacher because he won in the fashion of cheating. 他受到老师的批评，因为他作弊才获胜。

face up to sth. 勇敢地接受（或对付）

例句 We must face up to our responsibilities and not try to get out of them. 我们必须勇敢地担起责任，而不应试图推卸责任。

far from 远非，不像期待的样子

例句 So far from admitting his own mistake, he falsely accused his critic. 他非但不认错，还倒打一耙。

figure out 想出，理解，明白

同义 be clear of, find out, work out

例句 I simply couldn't figure out his intention. 我不能理解他的用意。

be free from/of 免于

同义 be immune from

例句 The dictionary, despite the care exercised in compiling it, cannot in the nature of things be free from error. 本词典虽非草率之作，但错误仍在所难免。

区分 for free 免费

例句 You can get the ticket for free. 你可以免费获得这张票。

get around 四处转转，说服

例句 That child can always get around you and get what it wants. 那个孩子总是会哄人，要的东西都能得到。

区分 get around to do sth. 抽出时间来做（某事）

例句 I'll get around to doing my homework after the baseball game. 棒球赛结束之后，我会找时间做功课。

get away with 侥幸逃脱，逃脱处罚

例句 No one can flout the rules and get away with it. 谁也不能违反这些规则而不被处分。

get down to sth. 开始认真处理，着手做

同义 go about doing, set about doing, move on to

例句 Time ran out before we could get down to the real nitty-gritty. 我们还没来得及探讨真正的细节，时间就过去了。

give off 放出，释放

例句 If plastic and rubber are burnt, they'll give off poisonous gases. 要是塑料和橡胶被焚，就会放出有毒的气体。

区分 give out 分发，放出

例句 There were people at the entrance giving out leaflets. 有人在入口处散发传单。

give away 泄露；赠送

例句 Don't give away the end of the story. 别把故事结局说出来。

例句 We can also give away free shirts for more publicity. 我们也可以通过赠送运动衫来达到更多宣传效果。

be glued to sth. 盯住不放，沾上

同义 stick to

例句 All eyes will be glued to the television tonight. 今天晚上所有人都会看电视。

go astray 堕落；误入歧途

同义 go downhill, fall into a wrong path

例句 Many young people living alone in the city go astray for lack of parental control. 许多在城市里独居的年轻人，由于没有父母的管教而误入歧途。

in hand 在手头，可供使用

例句 Let us address ourselves to the matter in hand. 咱们处理手头这件事吧。

区分 in one's hands 受……照顾，被……控制；on hand 在手边，在附近

out of hand 无法控制；终于

同义 at last, in the end, in time

例句 Her wish to be a doctor has come true out of hand. 她想做一个医生的愿望终于实现了。

keep one's head 保持冷静

同义 keep a cool head, be calm, keep calm

反义 lose one's head 慌乱，失去理智、信心

例句 She managed to keep her head in a difficult situation. 她在困境中设法保持冷静的头脑。

hit on/upon sth. 忽然想到，偶然发现

同义 stumble across 偶然发现

例句 After some thought he hit on a plan to crack the nut. 经过一番思考，他想到一个解决问题的办法。

be/feel at home 感到舒适，无拘束

例句 Waitresses are very friendly, which makes us feel at home. 服务员们非常友好，让我们宾至如归。

区分 at home 在本国，在国内

例句 These things can all be manufactured at home. 这些东西国内都能制造。

区分 be at home with sth. 熟悉，精通

例句 He is quite at home with the Chinese language. 他精通汉语。

bring home to 使（某人）更清楚（某事）

例句 We should bring home to people the value of working hard. 我们应该让人们明白努力的价值。

on the horizon 即将发生的

例句 Business is good at the moment, but there are one or two problems on the horizon. 目前营业状况很好，但有一两个问题已露端倪。

a host of 大量

同义 a body of, a many, a multitude/multitudes of, a world of

反义 a pocket of, a touch of

例句 The Tang Dynasty produced a host of great poets, such as Li Bai, Du Fu and Bai Juyi. 唐朝有很多大诗人，像李白、杜甫、白居易等。

例句 A little discipline would do him a world of good. 略加惩处对他会大有好处。

例句 The ornamental ironwork lends a touch of elegance to the house. 铁艺饰件为房子略添雅致。

hand on 转交；转送；传下来；传给下一代

例句 The government is criticized for not handing on information about missing funds. 政府因未能就下落不明的资金提供相关信息而遭到批评。

区分 hand out 分发，散发

例句 Please hand out the reading materials to the students. 请把这些阅读材料分发给学生。

区分 hand over 交出，移交

例句 You must hand over your passport before you leave. 离境前必须交回护照。

have a bearing on 与……有关系；对……影响

同义 have an effect on, react on, act on

例句 Could online fantasy games actually have a bearing on the real world? 网络虚拟游戏真能影响现实世界吗？

hold back 控制；阻碍；踌躇

例句 She closed her eyes tightly in a vain attempt to hold back the tears. 她紧闭双眼，却无法忍住眼泪。

例句 Stagnation in home sales is holding back economic recovery. 国内销售停滞不前，正阻碍着经济复苏。

区分 hold down 限制，镇压；压住

例句 They tried every means to hold down the workers on strike. 他们采取一切手段镇压罢工工人。

hold on 继续，握住不放，坚持

同义 persist in

例句 They determined to hold on to the last. 他们决定坚持到最后。

identify with 同情；认同；与一致

例句 Reading this book, we can identify with the main character. 读这本书时，我们会与主人公产生共鸣。

例句 We cannot identify happiness with wealth. 我们不能把幸福与财富混为一谈。

in the interest of 为了……（的利益）

同义 for the benefit of, for the good of

例句 In the interest of protecting such resources, a great many state laws were passed. 为了保护这些资源，各州立了许多法律。

at intervals 每隔一段时间（或距离），不时

例句 She woke him for his medicines at intervals throughout the night. 她夜里每隔一段时间就叫他起来服药。

keep sb. from sth. 抑制，阻止

例句 Embarrassment has kept me from doing all sorts of things. 我总是害怕受窘，什么事都不敢去做。

keep a close watch on 密切关注

同义 watch out for, keep an eye on, pay close attention to

例句 We keep a close watch on the development of the financial market. 我们密切关注金融市场的发展。

kill off 彻底停止，完全根除

例句 These figures kill off any lingering hopes of an early economic recovery. 这些数字使人们对经济早日复苏所抱的一线希望彻底毁灭。

to one's knowledge 据……所知

例句 To my knowledge, the government has launched a variety of activities to develop the public consciousness. 据我所知，政府已经发起各种活动来提升公众意识。

for lack of 因为缺乏

同义 in default of

例句 The project was hung up for lack of funds. 由于缺少资金，这项工程被搁置下来。

at large 总地，一般地

例句 The country at large is hoping for great changes. 总的来说，这个国家希望能有巨大变化。

区分 be at large（危险的人和动物）未被抓住，在逃

例句 The escaped prisoner is still at large. 那个逃犯仍逍遥法外。

lay aside 放弃（某种习惯）；积蓄（金钱）；以备后用

例句 It is the time we lay aside old prejudices. 是撇开旧偏见的时候了。

例句 You ought to lay aside some money for future use. 你应该存点钱以备将来之需。

区分 lay down 以备后用；制定或宣布（条例和规则）

例句 Taxis must conform to the rigorous standards laid down by the police. 出租车必须遵守警方的严格规定。

lay off 停止使用，解雇

同义 call off 停止，give the sack 解雇

例句 The doctor advised me to lay off cigarettes. 医生建议我戒烟。

例句 They did not sell a single car for a month and had to lay off workers. 一个月来一辆汽车都卖不出去，他们只好裁员。

lay out 安排，设计

例句 She is always hard up because she doesn't lay out her money wisely. 她总是缺钱花，因为她胡乱花钱。

not in the least 丝毫不，一点不

例句 We feel quite free and easy with him, not in the least constrained. 跟他在一起很轻松，一点儿也不拘束。

let alone 更不用说

同义 not to mention

例句 We fear no death, let alone difficulties. 我们死都不怕，更别说困难。

区分 leave sb. alone 不打扰（某人），让……独自待

at leisure 闲散，悠闲

例句 He put the idea by until he was at leisure to consider it carefully. 他把这个念头放在一边，到空闲时再去认真考虑它。

at length 充分地；详尽地；最后；终于

例句 He talked at length about his work and his family. 他详细聊了一下工作和家庭。

例句 At length the young lady raised her head and looked steadily at his intelligent face. 那个年轻女士终于抬起头，目不转睛地盯着他心领神会的脸。

in (the) light of 按照，根据

同义 according to

例句 How can free will exist in light of the findings of science? 根据科学发现，自由意志怎么能够存在？

out of line with 立场上与……不一致；不成一直线

例句 Our prices are out of line with those of our competitors. 我们的价格和竞争者的价格相差悬殊。

live off 以……为生；依靠……生活

同义 live on, feed on

例句 If you live on a mountain, you live off the mountain, if you live by the water, you live off the water. 靠山吃山，靠水吃水。

live up to 达到；符合；不辜负

例句 Man is tempted to live up to woman's idealized conception of himself. 男人一般很想使自己成为女人心目中理想化的那个人。

look into 深入地检查；调查；观察

例句 The government will look into how to reduce unemployment. 政府将研究如何降低失业率。

at a loss 不知所措；困惑

同义 be bewildered (by)

例句 He found himself at a loss for words of consolation. 他简直想不出安慰人的话来。

make reflections on 对……进行思考

同义 reflect on

例句 We have to make reflections on the current economic situation before laying down the concerned regulations. 在制定相关规定前，我们不得不对目前的经济形势加以思考。

make-believe 虚构（或假想）的事物

例句 He is always longing for the glamorous make-believe world of show business. 他一直都向往娱乐界令人眼花缭乱的虚幻世界。

make for 促成；有助于

例句 The great disparity between the teams did not make for an entertaining game. 两队实力悬殊，所以比赛并不精彩。

make out 弄懂

同义 catch on

例句 The poem is so complicated that I cannot make out its meaning. 这首诗太复杂，我理解不了它的意思。

at the mercy of 在……的支配下；任凭……摆布

同义 under the control of

例句 A future lived at the mercy of terrible threats is no peace at all. 如果未来的生活听任可怕的威胁摆布，就毫无和平可言。

get a move on 赶快，加紧

例句 We'd better get a move on before it rains. 我们最好在下雨之前赶快完成。

more often than not 时常；常常；多半；通常

同义 off and on

例句 When it's foggy the trains are late more often than not. 雾大时火车往往会晚点。

get nowhere 一无所获，毫无进展

例句 At first he was most dictatorial and aggressive in what he said, but when he realized that he would get nowhere by that means, he began to sing another tune. 起初他的说法十分专横武断，但当他认识到这样做行不通时，他就开始改弦易辙了。

not necessarily 不一定

例句 Wealth is not necessarily synonymous with happiness. 财富未必等同于幸福。

be obliged to sb. 感激某人

区分 be obliged to do 被迫

例句 We may be obliged to give him a new identity. 我们可能使他成为另外一个人。

on occasion(s) 偶尔，偶然，有时

同义 once in a while, now and then

例句 Some of the players may, on occasion, break the rules and be penalized. 这些球员中有些可能偶尔会因违规而受罚。

against all (the) odds 尽管有极大的困难，尽管极为不利

例句 He was admitted to graduate school against all odds. 他克服困难进了研究所。

at odds with 有差异，相矛盾

例句 This action is greatly at odds with his previous attitude. 这一行动与他以往的态度大相径庭。

once (and) for all 一劳永逸地，一次了结的

例句 This is not a something that can be completed once for all. 这不是件可以一劳永逸的事情。

at/from the outset 开端，开始

同义 from the beginning

例句 The novel fascinates the reader from the outset. 这部小说一开始就把读者迷住了。

part with 放弃，离开，卖掉

例句 He parted with much of his collection to pay his gardening bills. 他卖掉了大部分藏品来付园艺费。

pay off 还清（债务）；使得益

例句 I need to pay off all my debts before I leave the country. 我得在离开该国前偿清所有债务。

例句 The investor believes that his investment will pay off handsomely soon. 这个投资者相信他的投资不久会有相当大的收益。

in person 亲自，本人

例句 It is highly regrettable that the minister cannot be here in person. 很遗憾，部长不能亲自出席。

phase in 逐步引入（或采用）

反义 phase out 逐步停止使用

例句 We should phase in the new working plans. 我们应逐步采用这个新的工作计划。

pin down 确定，证实

例句 It has proven difficult for authorities to pin down the exact death toll. 当局很难确定确切的死亡人数。

in place 在合适的位置

反义 out of place 不适当的，不相称

例句 The proposal is not quite in place. 那项提议并不是非常适合。

beside the point 离题的，不相关的

反义 keep to the point

例句 Your speech should not have been interlaced with these facts beside the point. 你的讲话不该涉及这些无关的事情。

make a point of 特别注意（做某事），重视

同义 attach importance to, pay attention to, think highly of, take sth. seriously, place a premium on

例句 You should make a point of civilization and manners. 你应该注意文明礼貌。

例句 They place a high premium on honesty largely because it is essential to their career. 他们非常重视诚信，主要是因为诚信对他们的事业至关重要。

be at a premium 稀缺的，难得的

例句 Fresh water was at a premium after the reservoir was contaminated. 在水库被污染后，淡水便因稀少而珍贵了。

without prejudice (to sth.) （对……）没有不利，无损于

例句 You should make a decision without prejudice to our rights. 你应该作出一项无损于我们权益的决定。

press for 敦促；迫切要求

例句 They agreed to press for the conference to deal with the problem. 他们同意敦促大会处理这个问题。

beyond question 确定无疑的，毫无疑问的

反义 in question 正在讨论中；被质疑的

例句 To my mind, Mark Twain was beyond question the large man of his time. 在我看来，马克·吐温无疑是他所处时代了不起的人物。

out of the question 毫无可能的；绝对不允许的

例句 Without peace, development and sexual equality are out of the question. 没有和平就谈不上发展，谈不上男女平等。

区分 without question 毫无疑问，毫无异议

例句 He was willing to do, without question, any favor we might ask him. 毫无疑问，他很乐意尽可能满足我们提出的要求。

at random 随便地，任意地

例句 The teacher might suddenly address individual students at random. 老师可能突然与个别学生随机谈话。

at any rate 无论如何

同义 in any case

例句 He doesn't understand me, or at any rate not fully. 他并不了解我，至少了解得不全面。

reckon with 处理，对付；估计到

例句 We must reckon with all possible difficulties when we are considering the cost of the contract. 我们考虑合同费用时必须考虑到所有潜在的困难。

in retrospect 回想起来，事后看来

例句 In retrospect, I wish that I had thought about alternative courses of action. 回想起来，我真希望自己当时考虑过其他做法。

take root 植根，深入人心，确立

例句 The apple trees know how to take root, sprout, bloom and fruit. 苹果树"知道"怎样生根、发芽、开花、结果。
The prejudices of parents usually take root in their children. 父母的偏见通常深植于子女的头脑中。

in ruins 成废墟，毁坏，毁灭

例句 The city lay in ruins after the earthquake. 地震之后，这座城市成为一片废墟。

rule out 宣布……不可能，排除……的可能性；消除；不考虑

例句 Rule out neatly any words which you don't wish the examiner to read. 把你不想让主考人看的词句整整齐齐地划掉。

例句 The Prime Minister is believed to have ruled out cuts in child benefit or pensions. 据信，首相已经排除了削减儿童救济金或养老金的可能性。

in the long run 从长远看

同义 in the long term

例句 In the long run, it is an economy to buy good quality goods. 从长远角度来看，购买优质物品还是合算的。

be superior to 优于

反义 be inferior to 劣于

例句 These methods, unfortunately, are not very sensitive and may not be superior to the soap-bubble test. 不过，这些方法不是很灵敏的，并且不可能比肥皂泡试验法好。

to say the least 至少可以说

例句 His conduct that evening was to say the least curious. 他那天晚上的举动至少可说是古怪的。

scale back 减少

同义 scale down

例句 Regulators are clamping down on these institutions, forcing them to raise capital and scale back lending. 监管部门也在向这些机构施压，要求他们筹资并削减贷款。

seal off 封闭，封锁

同义 block out

例句 The enemy made a desperate attempt to seal off the gap through which we had burst. 敌人拼命想堵住我们已经冲开的那个突破口。

fall short of 未达到，不符合（标准等）

例句 As such, he is foredoomed to fall short of our expectations. 既然如此，他注定不能达到我们的期望。

shrug off 对（某事）满不在乎，对（某事）不屑一顾

同义 make nothing of, be totally unconcerned

例句 I admire the way she is able to shrug off unfair criticism. 我很佩服她能对错误的批评意见不予理会。

sign up 签约雇用；报名

同义 enter for

例句 He was not the only one to sign up. 他不是唯一的报名者。

sink in（信息，事实等）被理解，被领会

例句 It took a long time for the bad news to sink in. 人们花了很长时间才弄明白这个坏消息。

a spell of 一段时间

例句 Jim went to work for a large insurance firm after a spell of working in the advertising business. 在从事广告行业一段时间之后，吉姆去了一家大型保险公司。

on the spot 立即，马上，当场

例句 He discussed business and concluded transactions with us on the spot. 他与我们谈判业务并当场成交。

at stake 在危急关头，在危险中

例句 We cannot afford to take risks when people's lives are at stake. 现在人命关天，不容我们有闪失。

in step 步伐一致；（观点，行动）协调一致

反义 out of step

例句 The decision has been accepted by everyone, so now we are all in step. 这个决定已被大家接受，所以我们现在步调一致。

stir up 搅起；激起（争执、事端等）

同义 set...on fire

例句 They argued that his presence in the village could only stir up trouble. 他们认为他在村里出现只会招惹麻烦。

out of stock 无现货的，无库存的

反义 in stock

例句 So many people have bought bikes that the store is now out of stock. 那么多人买自行车，商店现在已经没货了。

at a stretch 不停地，连续地

同义 in series, in succession

例句 He would stay for hours at a stretch in the laboratory. 他在实验室里一蹲就是好几个小时。

take in 收留；吸入；领会；蒙骗

例句 The kind old lady offered to take in the poor homeless stranger. 那位好心的老太太愿意收留这个贫困且无家可归的陌生人。

例句 Lesley explains possible treatments but you can tell she's not taking it in. 莱斯利解释了各种可行的疗法。不过，你可以看出来，她并没有领会。

例句 They will certainly need to take in plenty of liquid. 它们当然需要吸收大量液体。

例句 I married in my late teens and was taken in by his charm—which soon vanished. 我十八九岁时结了婚，那时被他的魅力所迷惑——可他的魅力很快就荡然无存。

take off 脱衣服；起飞；（产品、活动、事业等）腾飞，突然成功

例句 They need to expand the number of farmers who are involved if the scheme's going to really take off. 这个方案要想真正成功，他们就需要让更多的农场主参与进来。

tear down 拆掉，拆除，毁掉

同义 pull down

例句 The city will tear down these buildings to make room for the new highway. 市政当局要拆掉这些建筑物以腾出地方修筑新公路。

tell apart 区分,辨别

例句 In fact, experts say the two are almost impossible to tell apart. 事实上,专家说这两种病毒难以区分。

thumb through 快速浏览

例句 Thumb through any dictionary, and you will see pages of words followed by definitions. 只要(用拇指)翻遍任何一本词典,就可看到整页整页的词后面均有解释。

keep track of 了解;记录,跟踪

同义 track down 追踪

反义 lose track of

例句 The pilot was ordered to keep track of the strange object. 那位飞行员接到命令去跟踪这个奇特的物体。

例句 As a doctor, Brooks has to keep track of the latest developments in medicine. 作为一名医生,布鲁克斯必须了解医学的最新发展。

keep one's own end up 坚持到底,勉力而行

例句 So few authors have enough brains to keep their own end up in journalism. 很少有作者有足够的智力在新闻行业坚持到底。

a variety of 种种的,多种多样的

同义 a train of, a series of, an array of

例句 This passage is open to a variety of interpretations. 这篇文章可以有各种不同的解释。

be vulnerable to 容易受到……的影响

同义 be susceptible to, be apt to

例句 A system without anti-virus software will be vulnerable to a hacker attack. 没有防毒软件的系统很容易被黑客攻击。

in the wake of 随着……而来,作为……的结果,跟随在……之后

例句 Social problems cropped up in the wake of natural disasters. 自然灾害导致了许多社会问题。

give way to 被……代替;屈服,退让,让步

同义 make a concession

例句 A deadlock was reached in the discussions, as neither side would give way to the other. 讨论陷入僵局,因为双方各不相让。

wear out 穿破,磨损;厌倦,筋疲力尽

例句 The young people run around kicking a ball, wearing themselves out. 年轻人跑来跑去踢着球,把自己弄得精疲力竭。

carry weight 有影响力;举足轻重

例句 He spoke calmly, but every sentence carried weight. 他说话平静,但每句话都有分量。

write off 取消,注销

例句 We'll just have to write off the arrangement if we can't find the money for it. 如果筹不到钱,这项计划就得取消。